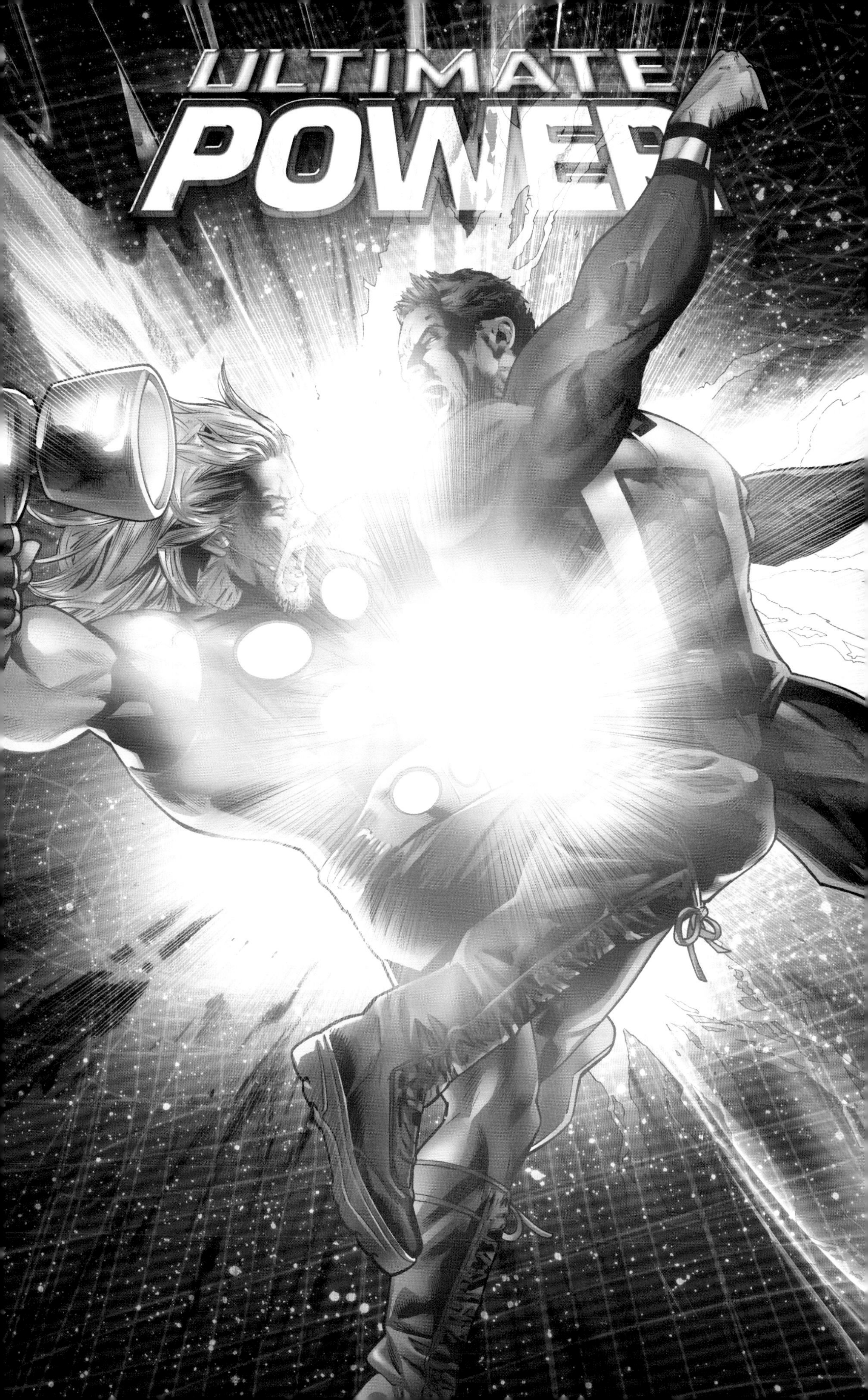
ULTIMATE

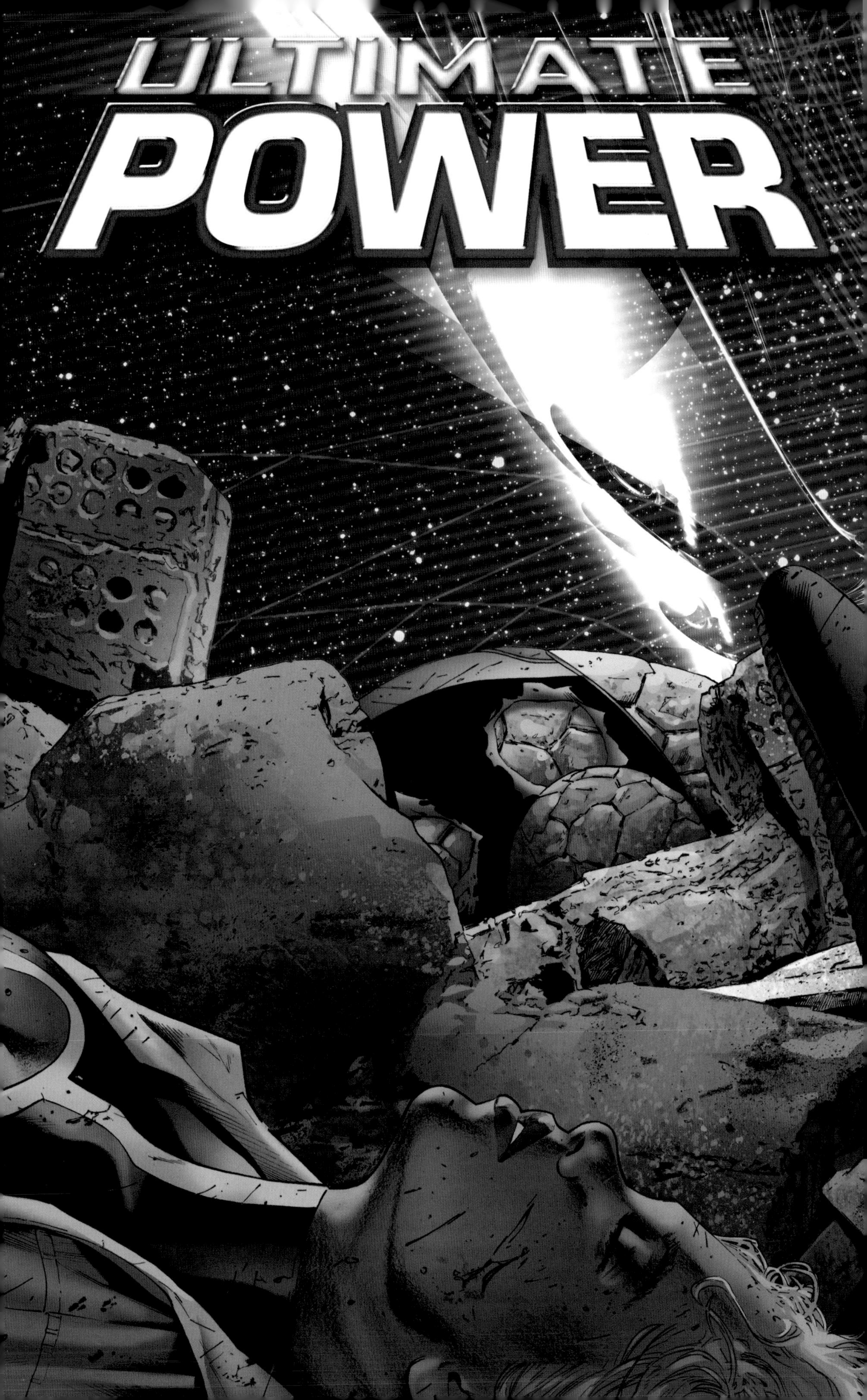
ULTIMATE
POWER

WRITERS: **Brian Michael Bendis** (Issues #1-3)
J. Michael Straczynski (Issues #4-6)
Jeph Loeb (Issues #7-9)
PENCILER: **Greg Land**
INKERS: **Jay Leisten** & **Matt Ryan**
COLORISTS: **Justin Ponsor** with **Sotocolor's A. Crossley**
LETTERERS: **Chris Eliopoulos, Virtual Calligraphy's Cory Petit**
& Comicraft's Albert Deschesne
ASSISTANT EDITOR: **Lauren Sankovitch**
EDITORS: **John Barber** & **Ralph Macchio**
with **Bill Rosemann**

SPECIAL THANKS TO **Axel Alonso**

COLLECTION EDITOR: **Mark D. Beazley**
ASSISTANT EDITORS: **John Denning** & **Cory Levine**
EDITOR, SPECIAL PROJECTS: **Jennifer Grünwald**
SENIOR EDITOR, SPECIAL PROJECTS: **Jeff Youngquist**
SENIOR VICE PRESIDENT OF SALES: **David Gabriel**
PRODUCTION: **Jerry Kalinowski**
BOOK DESIGNER: **Rodolfo Muraguchi**

EDITOR IN CHIEF: **Joe Quesada**
PUBLISHER: **Dan Buckley**

ULTIMATE POWER. Contains material originally published in magazine form as ULTIMATE POWER #1-9. First printing 2008. ISBN# 978-0-7851-2366-8. Published by MARVEL PUBLISHING, INC., a subsidiary of MARVEL ENTERTAINMENT, INC. OFFICE OF PUBLICATION: [...] Avenue, New York, NY 10016. Copyright © 2007 and 2008 Marvel Characters, Inc. All rights reserved. $34.99 per copy in the U.S. and $56.00 in Canada (GST #R127032852); Canadian Agreement #40668537. All characters featured in this issue and the distinctive [na]mes and likenesses thereof, and all related indicia are trademarks of Marvel Characters, Inc. No similarity between any of the names, characters, persons, and/or institutions in this magazine with those of any living or dead person or institution is intended, and any [simi]larity which may exist is purely coincidental. **Printed in the U.S.A.** ALAN FINE, CEO Marvel Toys & Publishing Divisions and CMO Marvel Entertainment, Inc.; DAVID GABRIEL, SVP of Publishing Sales & Circulation; DAVID BOGART, SVP of Business Affairs & [M]anagement; MICHAEL PASCIULLO, VP of Merchandising & Communications; JIM O'KEEFE, VP of Operations & Logistics; DAN CARR, Executive Director of Publishing Technology; JUSTIN F. GABRIE, Director of Editorial Operations; SUSAN CRESPI, Production [Ma]nager; STAN LEE, Chairman Emeritus. For information regarding advertising in Marvel Comics or on Marvel.com, please contact Mitch Dane, Advertising Director, at mdane@marvel.com. For Marvel subscription inquiries, please call 800-217-9158.

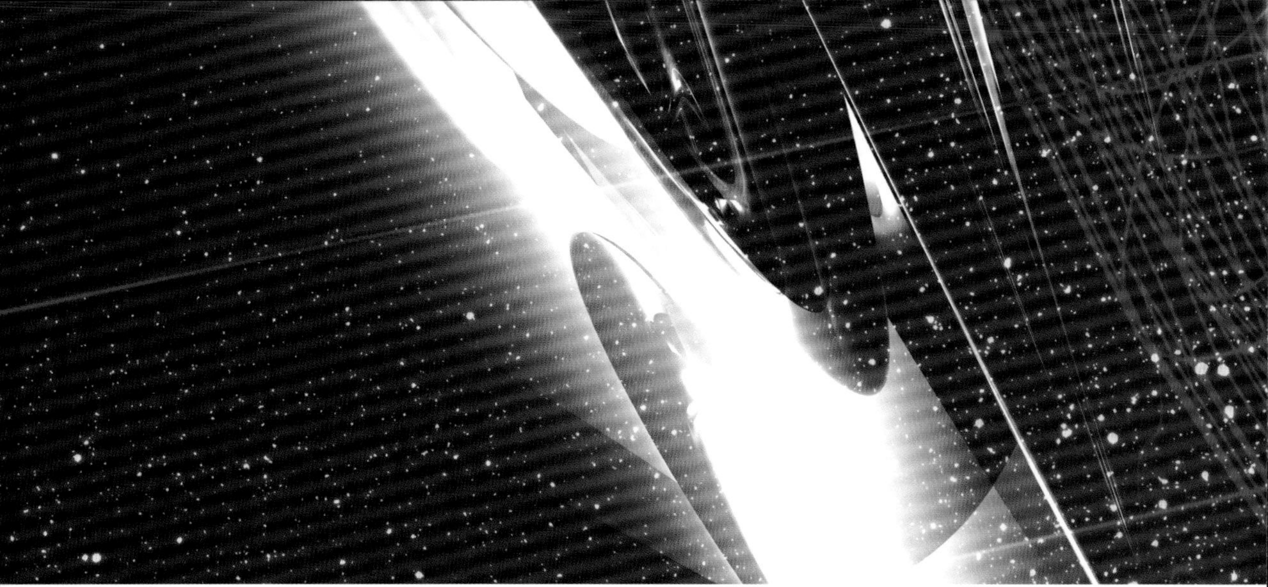

PREVIOUSLY IN THE **ULTIMATE UNIVERSE**

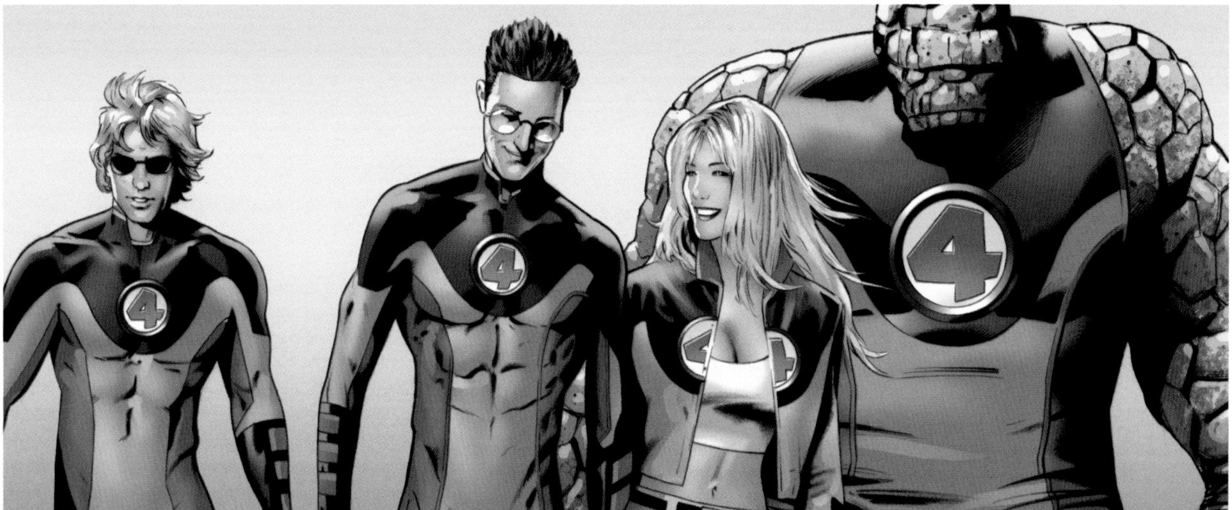

Young Reed Richards is handpicked to join the Baxter Building — a think tank of young geniuses right in the heart of New York City. It is there that Reed meets young scientist Sue Storm and her little brother Johnny.

Reed, his childhood friend Ben Grimm, Sue and Johnny are accidentally transformed into superhumans during a dimensional teleportation accident.

This is the birth of the now-world-famous Fantastic Four.

Though their adventures are already the stuff of legend, Ben Grimm lives in constant despair over the hand that's been dealt him. Reed has promised to do everything in his power to change him back to normal.

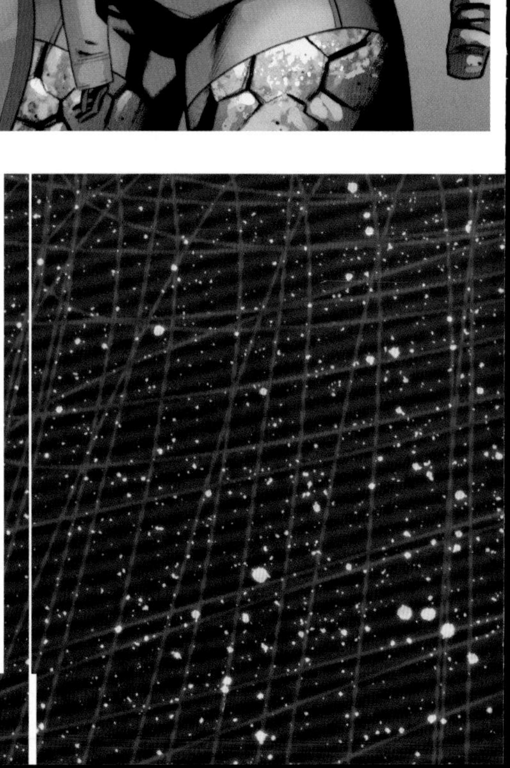

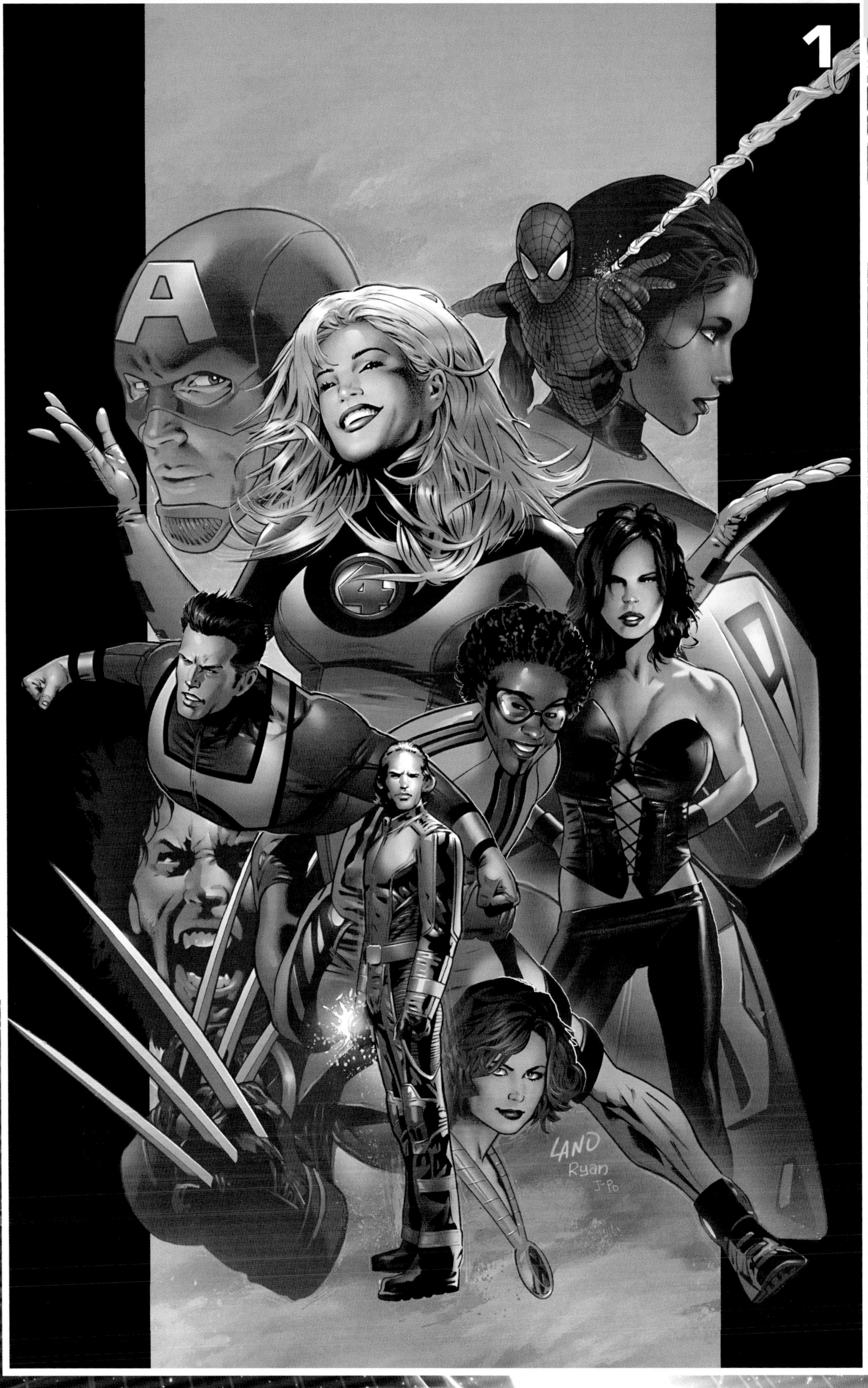
1
LAND
Ryan
J-Po

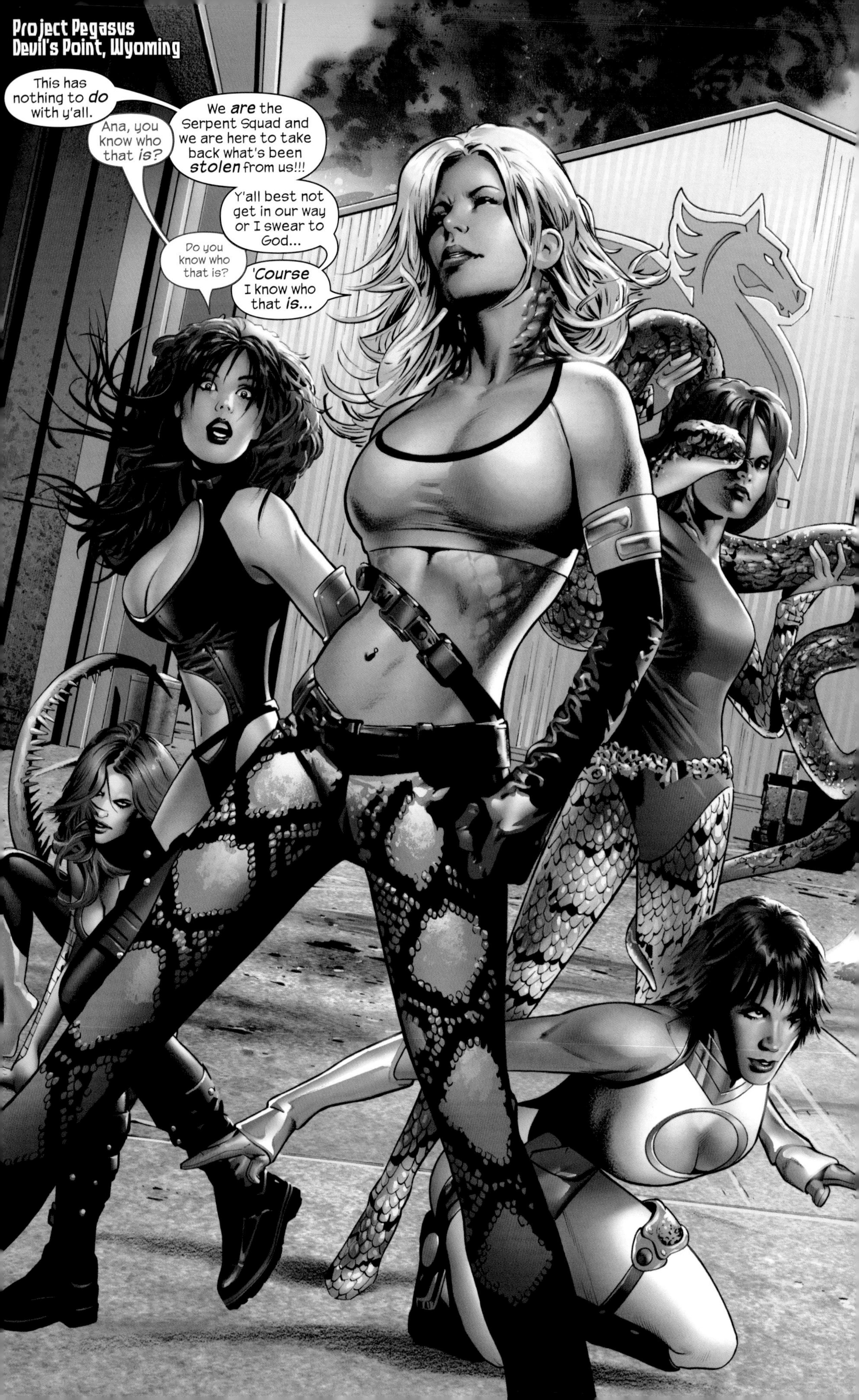
Project Pegasus
Devil's Point, Wyoming
This has nothing to *do* with y'all.
We *are* the Serpent Squad and we are here to take back what's been *stolen* from us!!!
Ana, you know who that *is*?
Y'all best not get in our way or I swear to God...
Do you know who that is?
'*Course* I know who that *is*...

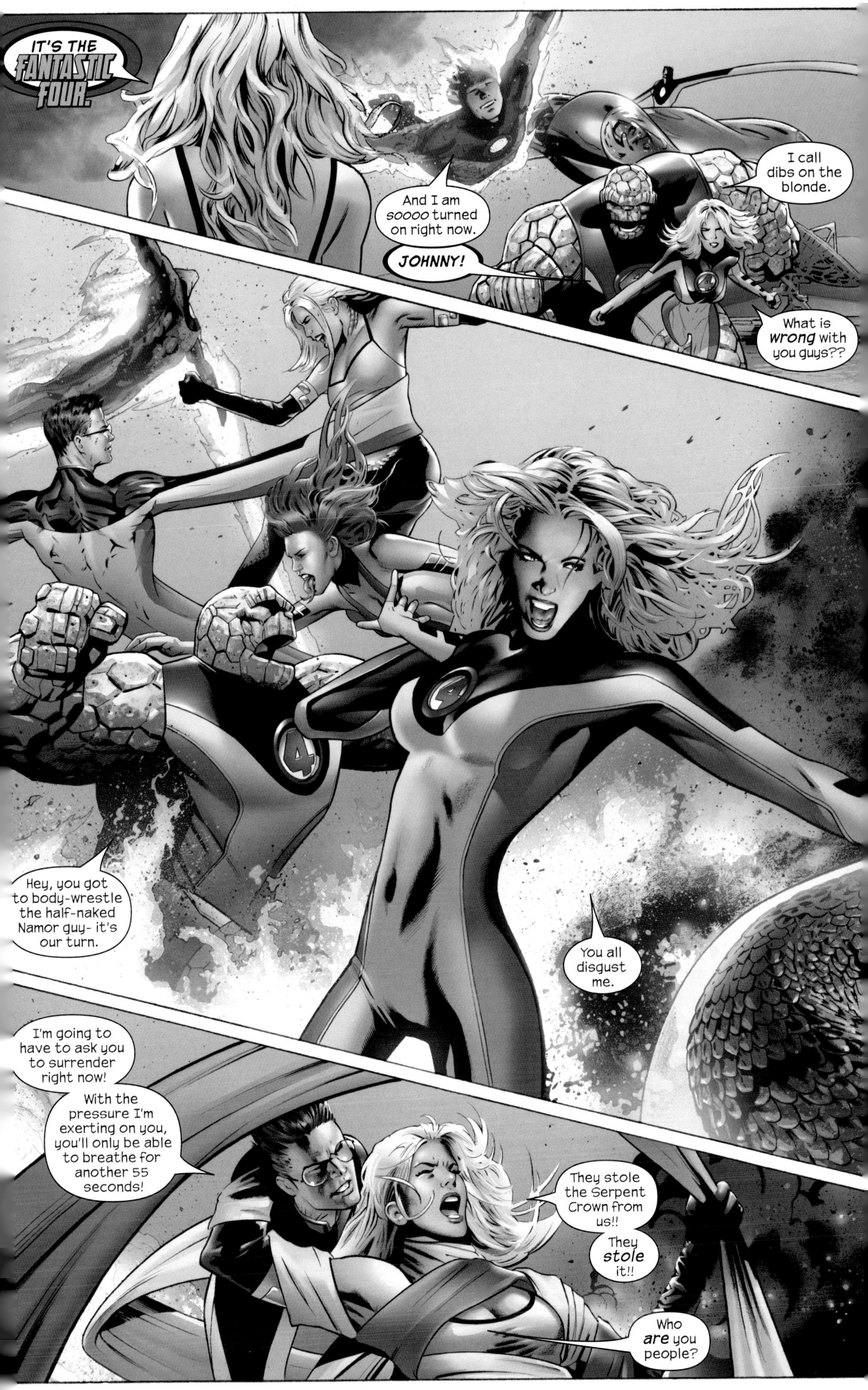
IT'S THE FANTASTIC FOUR.
And I am soooo turned on right now.
I call dibs on the blonde.
JOHNNY!
What is *wrong* with you guys??
Hey, you got to body-wrestle the half-naked Namor guy- it's our turn.
You all disgust me.
I'm going to have to ask you to surrender right now!
With the pressure I'm exerting on you, you'll only be able to breathe for another 55 seconds!
They stole the Serpent Crown from us!!
They *stole* it!!
Who *are* you people?

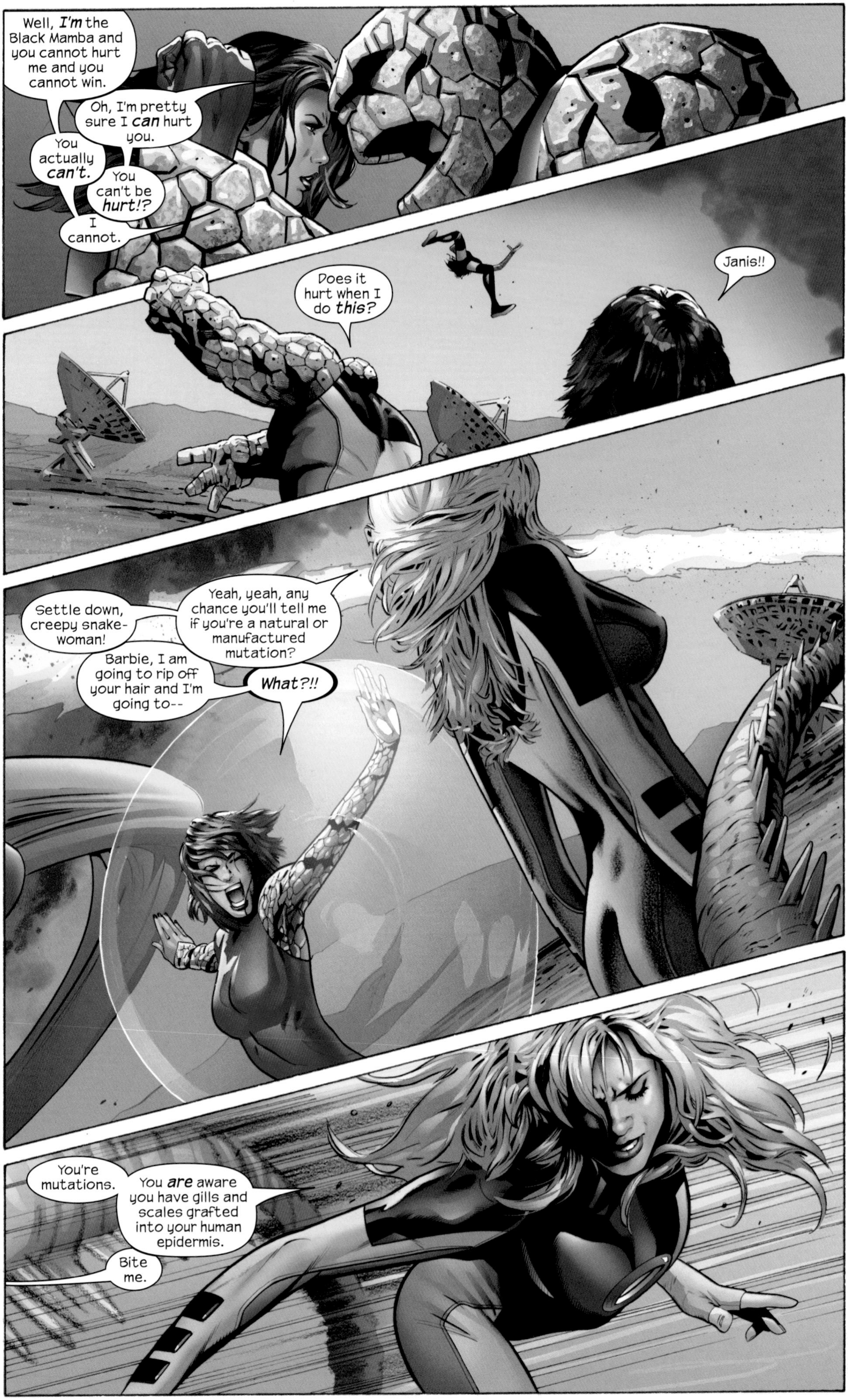
Well, *I'm* the Black Mamba and you cannot hurt me and you cannot win.
Oh, I'm pretty sure I *can* hurt you.
You actually *can't.*
You can't be *hurt!?*
I cannot.
Does it hurt when I do *this?*
Janis!!
Settle down, creepy snake-woman!
Yeah, yeah, any chance you'll tell me if you're a natural or manufactured mutation?
Barbie, I am going to rip off your hair and I'm going to--
What?!!
You're mutations.
You *are* aware you have gills and scales grafted into your human epidermis.
Bite me.

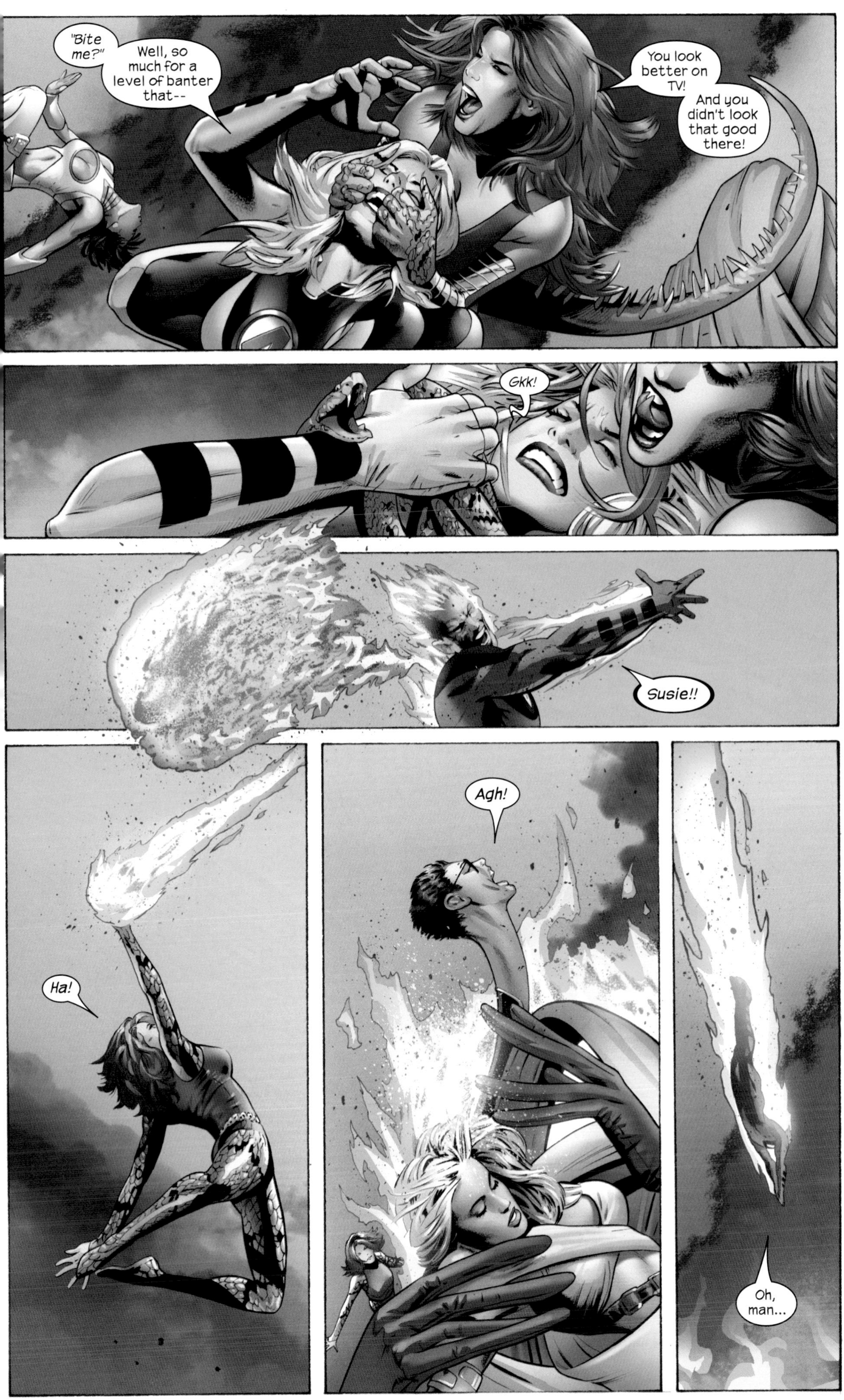
"Bite me?"
Well, so much for a level of banter that--
You look better on TV!
And you didn't look that good there!
Gkk!
Susie!!
Ha!
Agh!
Oh, man...

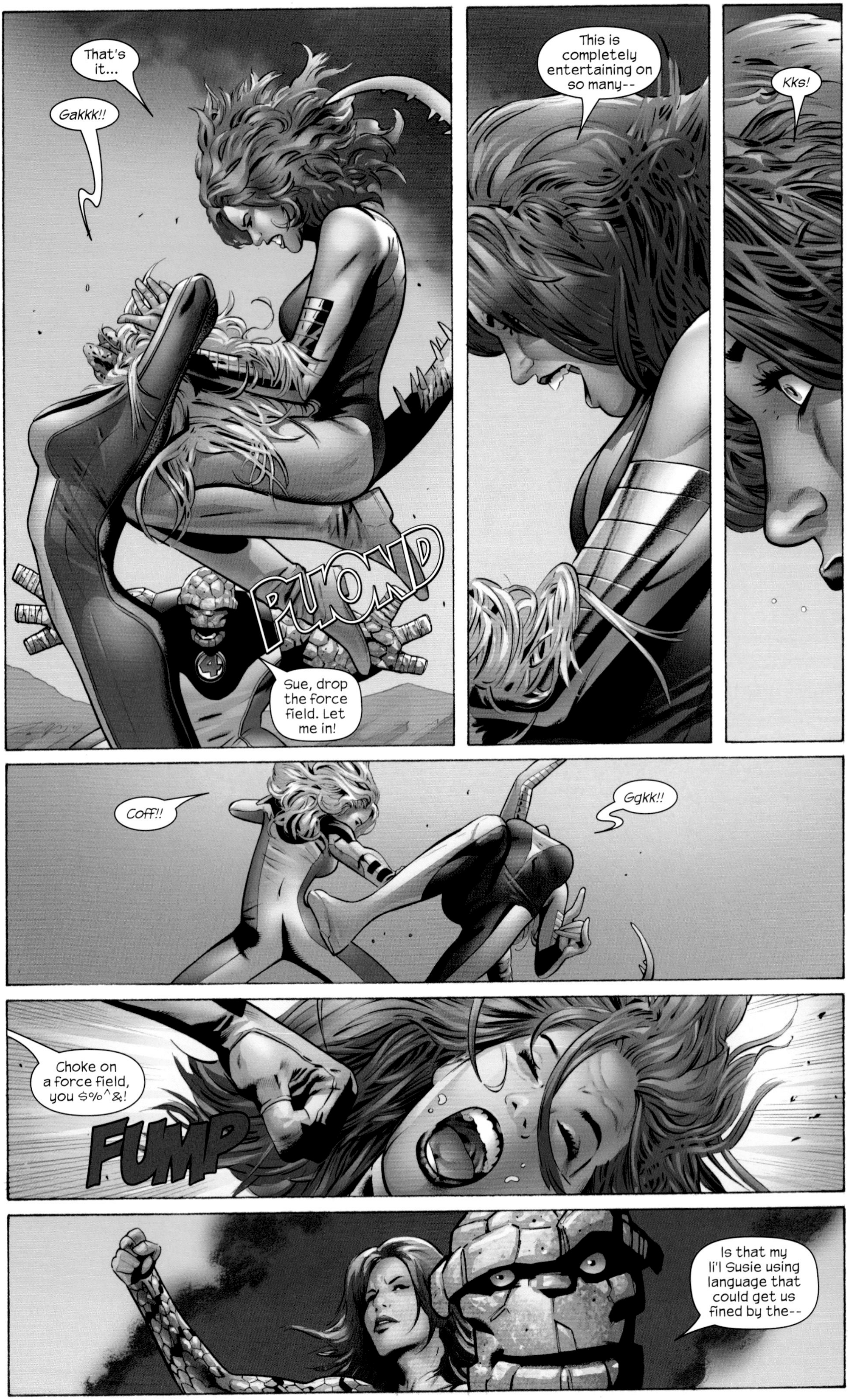
That's it...
Gakkk!!
PUOND
Sue, drop the force field. Let me in!
This is completely entertaining on so many--
Kks!
Coff!!
Ggkk!!
Choke on a force field, you $%^&!
FUMP
Is that my li'l Susie using language that could get us fined by the--

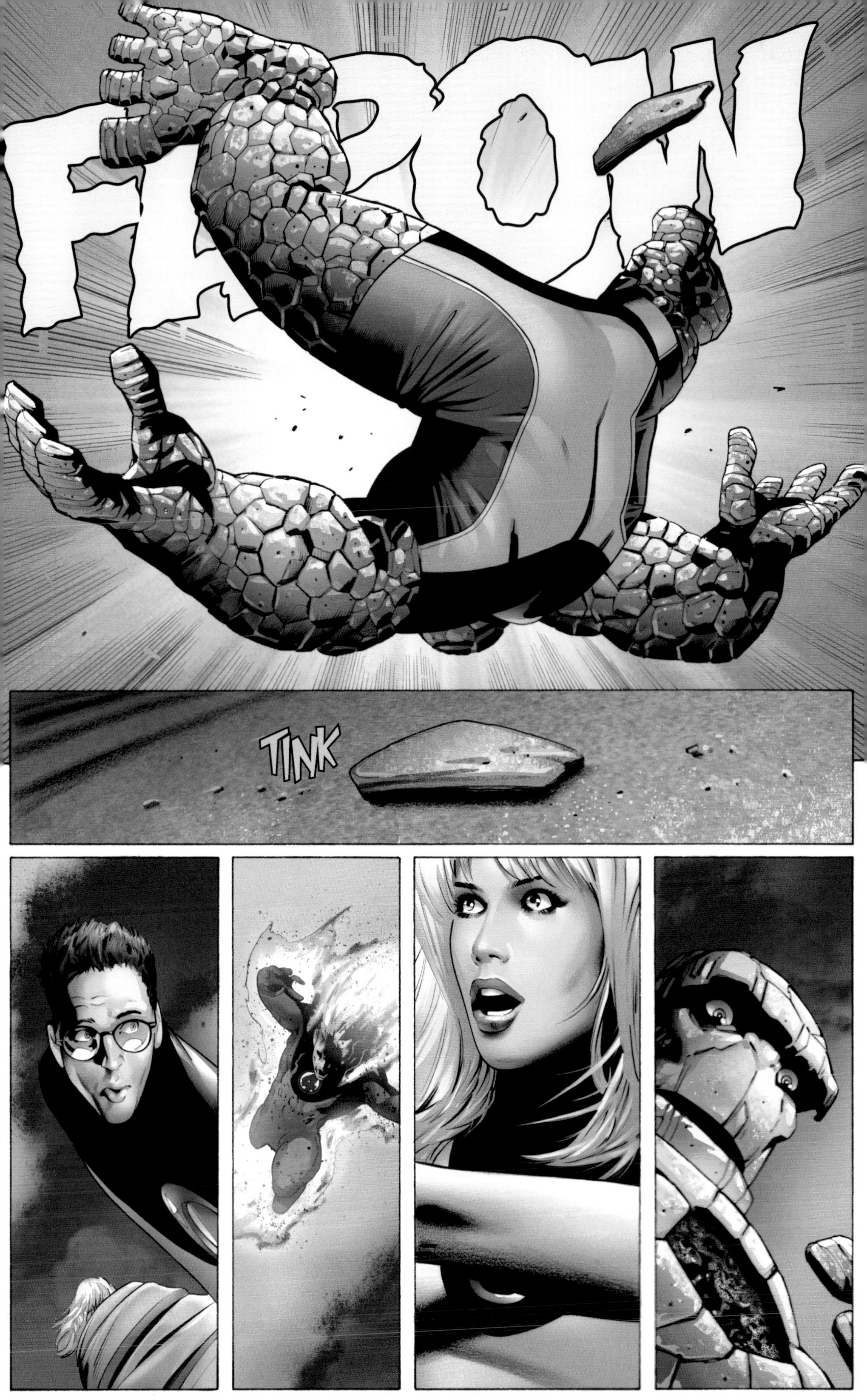
TINK

Don't touch it. No one touch it.

Settle down in there.

I'll kill you all!

Shush!

You...

...don't...

Night-night.

Reed?! Are you okay?

I'm okay, Johnny. The impact suit took most of it. It just stings.

I would never--

You didn't. It's okay.

Um--

Don't worry about it, Ben. We'll figure it out.

Am I breaking?

We'll figure it out.

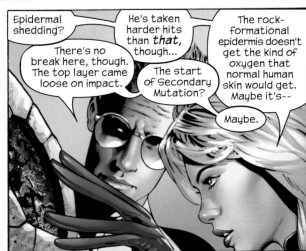

Epidermal shedding?

He's taken harder hits than *that*, though...

There's no break here, though. The top layer came loose on impact.

The start of Secondary Mutation?

The rock-formational epidermis doesn't get the kind of oxygen that normal human skin would get. Maybe it's--

Maybe.

I'll tell my dad to heat up the Starktech SD-1.

Yeah, yeah...

Hi, hi... I'm, uh, I'm S.H.I.E.L.D. Agent Wendell Vaughn.

I'm in charge of security here at the project but these serpent-women, man, they were *hammering* at us.

What was all this?

They said "Serpent Squad." Freaky cult.

I don't have all the info but they seem to think we have their Serpent Crown--

--which, I'm told, is some sort of unlawful energy source.

Do you *have* their Serpent Crown?

All Project Pegasus business is classified under the Gruenwald Doctrine.

I'm sorry.

What's Project Pegasus?

Off me!

Shush!

I'm sorry. I thought I just told you that all Project Pegasus business is classified under--

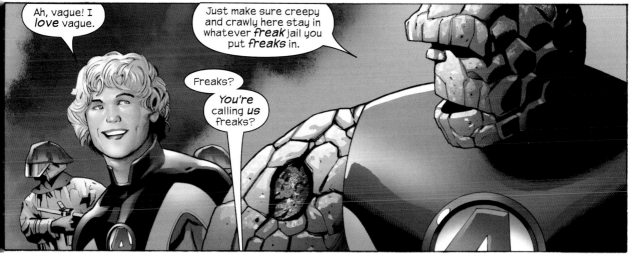

Ah, vague! I *love* vague.

Just make sure creepy and crawly here stay in whatever *freak* jail you put *freaks* in.

Freaks? *You're* calling *us* freaks?

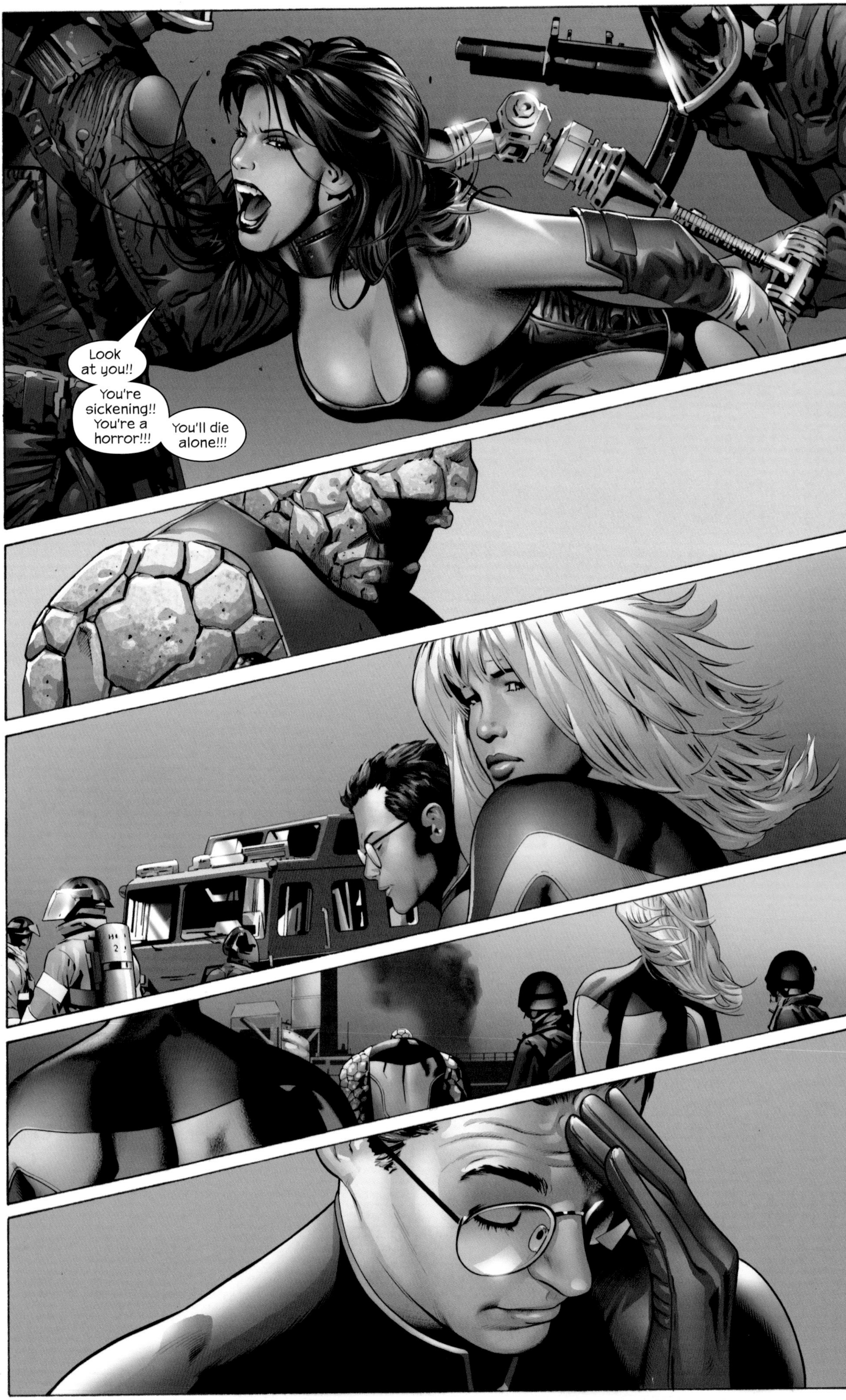
Look at you!!
You're sickening!! You're a horror!!!
You'll die alone!!!

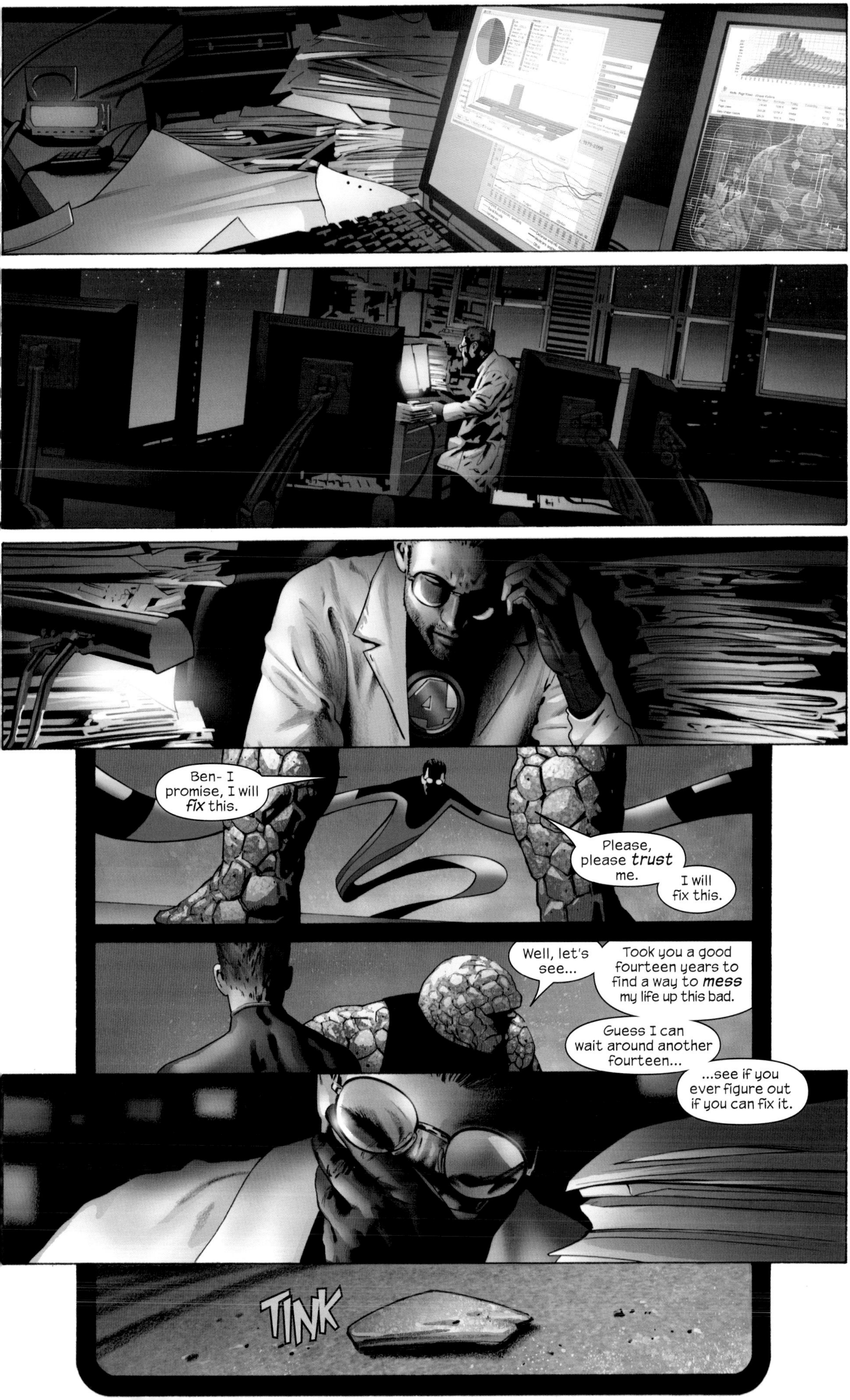

Ben- I promise, I will *fix* this.
Please, please **trust** me.
I will fix this.
Well, let's see...
Took you a good fourteen years to find a way to *mess* my life up this bad.
Guess I can wait around another fourteen...
...see if you ever figure out if you can fix it.
TINK

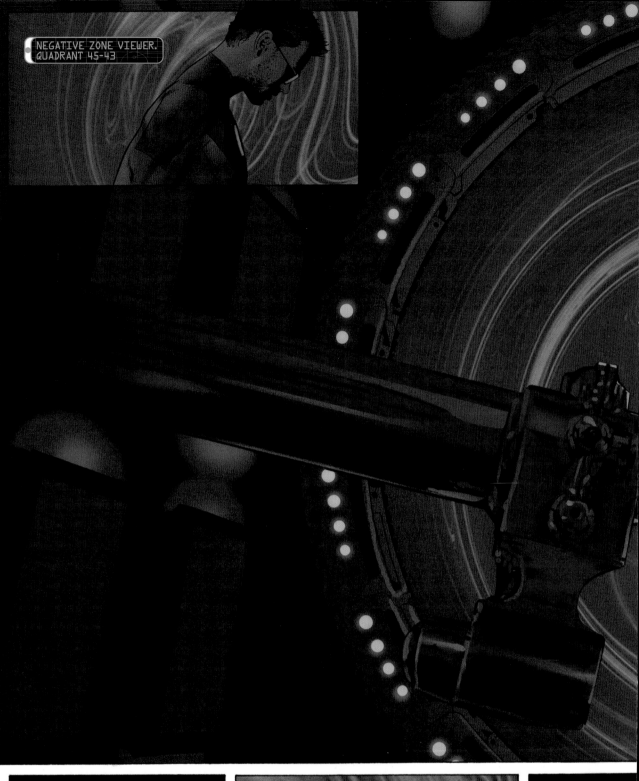

NEGATIVE ZONE VIEWER.
QUADRANT 45-43

Damn it!

SMASH

Why can't I *do* this?!!

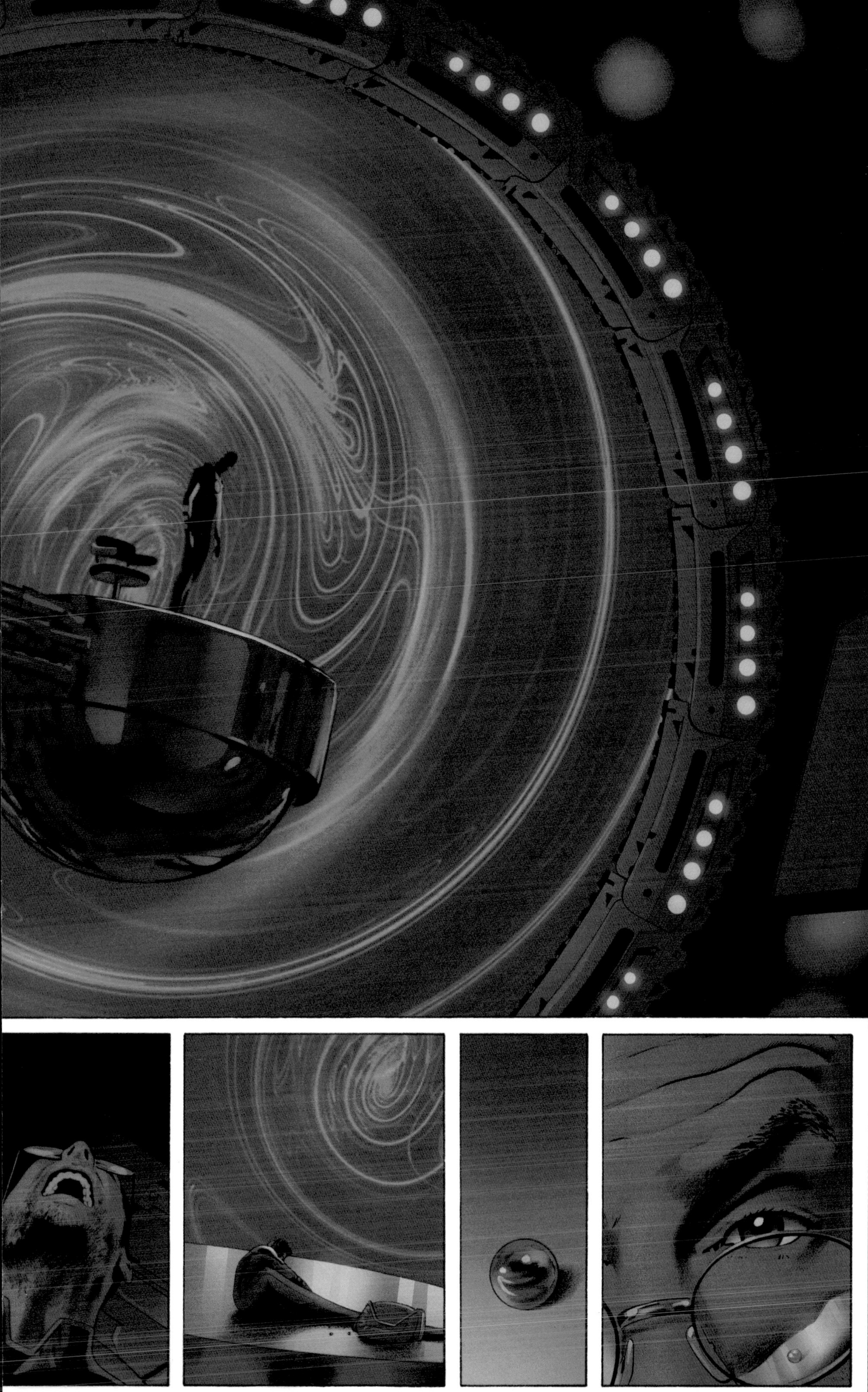

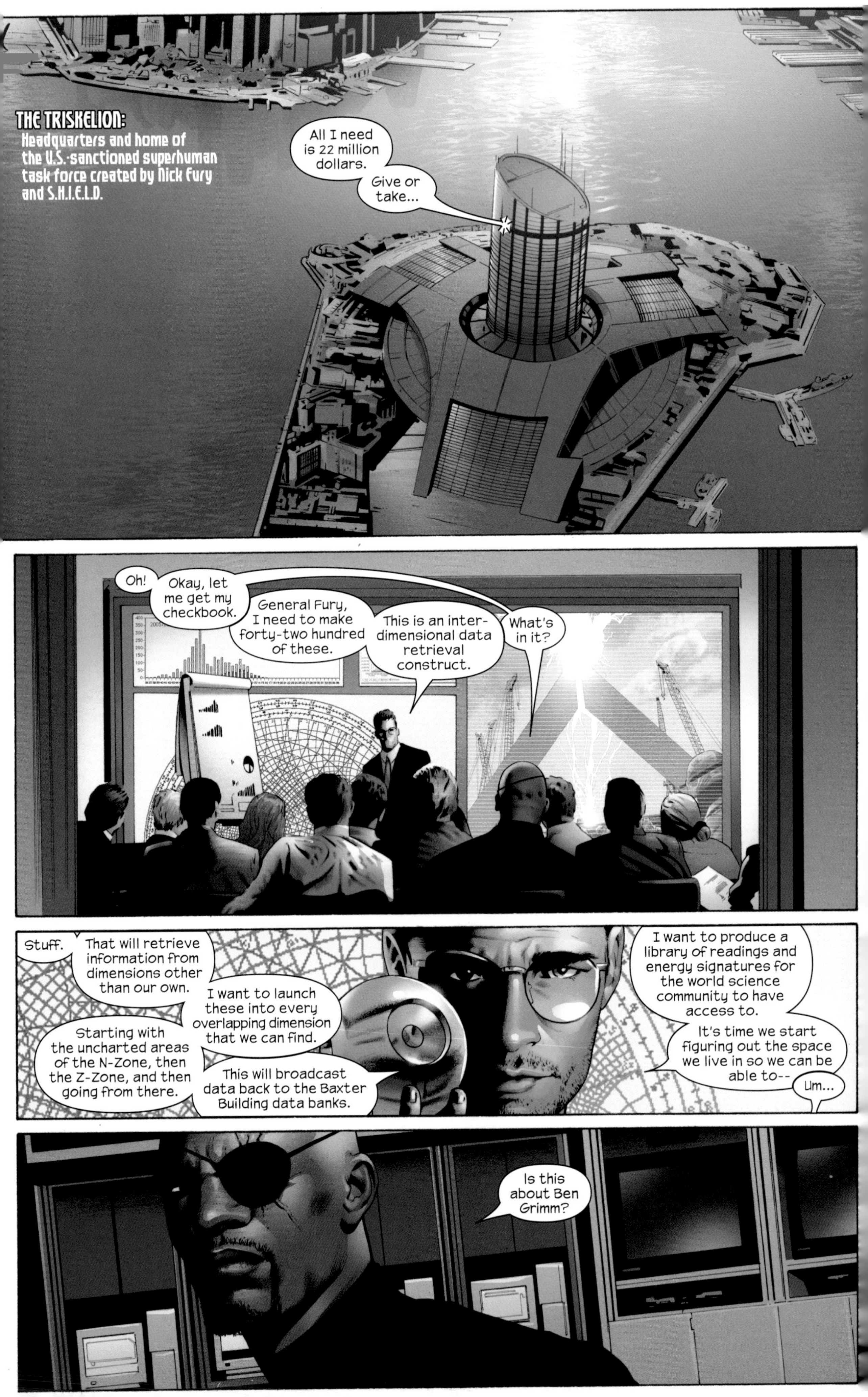
THE TRISKELION:
Headquarters and home of the U.S.-sanctioned superhuman task force created by Nick Fury and S.H.I.E.L.D.
All I need is 22 million dollars.
Give or take...
Oh!
Okay, let me get my checkbook.
General Fury, I need to make forty-two hundred of these.
This is an inter-dimensional data retrieval construct.
What's in it?
Stuff.
That will retrieve information from dimensions other than our own.
I want to launch these into every overlapping dimension that we can find.
Starting with the uncharted areas of the N-Zone, then the Z-Zone, and then going from there.
This will broadcast data back to the Baxter Building data banks.
I want to produce a library of readings and energy signatures for the world science community to have access to.
It's time we start figuring out the space we live in so we can be able to--
Um...
Is this about Ben Grimm?

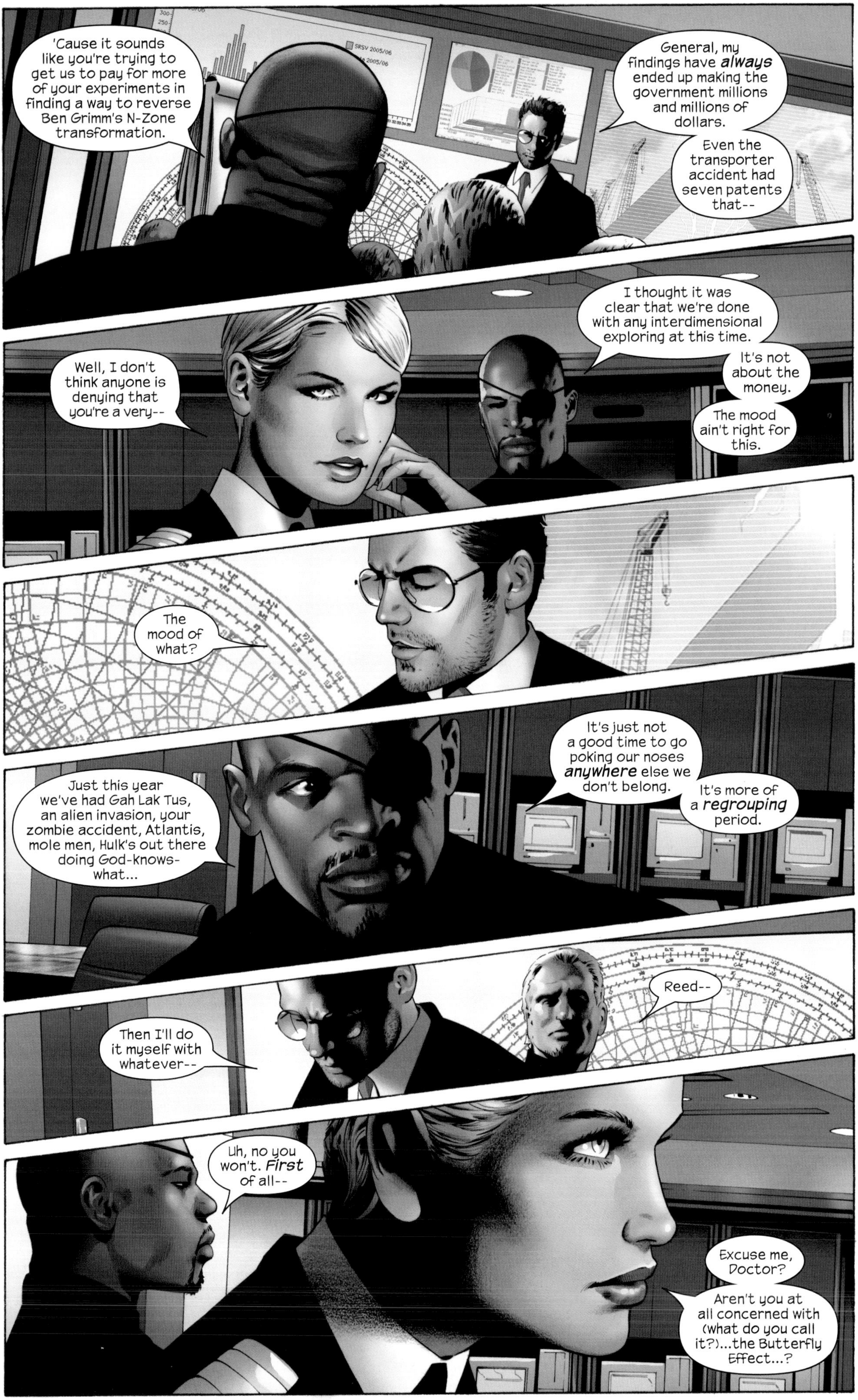

'Cause it sounds like you're trying to get us to pay for more of your experiments in finding a way to reverse Ben Grimm's N-Zone transformation.
General, my findings have *always* ended up making the government millions and millions of dollars.
Even the transporter accident had seven patents that--
Well, I don't think anyone is denying that you're a very--
I thought it was clear that we're done with any interdimensional exploring at this time.
It's not about the money.
The mood ain't right for this.
The mood of what?
Just this year we've had Gah Lak Tus, an alien invasion, your zombie accident, Atlantis, mole men, Hulk's out there doing God-knows-what...
It's just not a good time to go poking our noses *anywhere* else we don't belong.
It's more of a *regrouping* period.
Then I'll do it myself with whatever--
Reed--
Uh, no you won't. *First* of all--
Excuse me, Doctor?
Aren't you at all concerned with (what do you call it?)...the Butterfly Effect...?

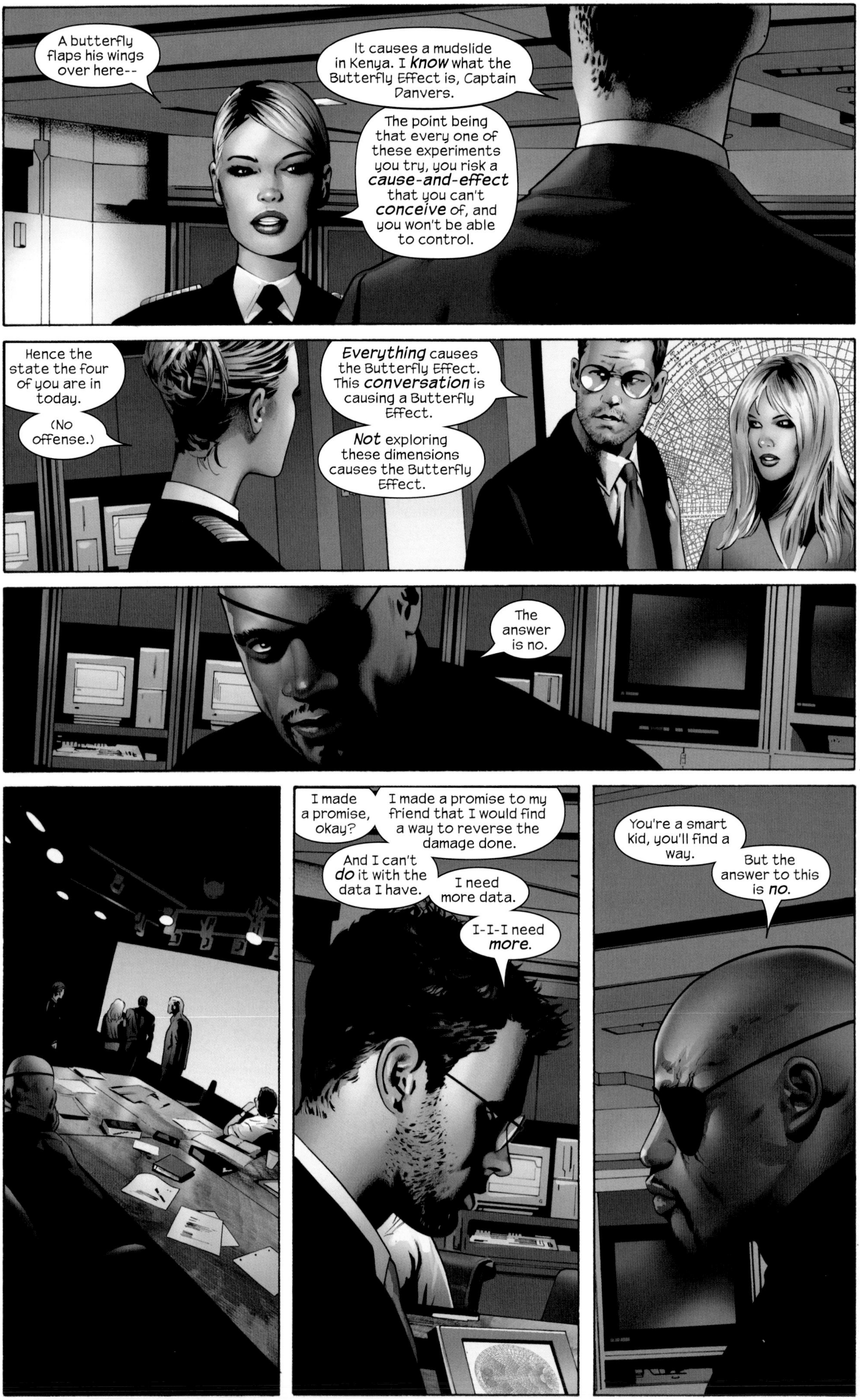

A butterfly flaps his wings over here--
It causes a mudslide in Kenya. I *know* what the Butterfly Effect is, Captain Danvers.
The point being that every one of these experiments you try, you risk a *cause-and-effect* that you can't *conceive* of, and you won't be able to control.
Hence the state the four of you are in today.
(No offense.)
Everything causes the Butterfly Effect. This *conversation* is causing a Butterfly Effect.
Not exploring these dimensions causes the Butterfly Effect.
The answer is no.
I made a promise, okay?
I made a promise to my friend that I would find a way to reverse the damage done.
And I can't *do* it with the data I have.
I need more data.
I-I-I need *more*.
You're a smart kid, you'll find a way.
But the answer to this is *no*.

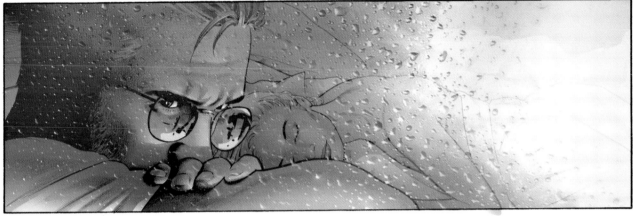

REED RICHARDS: IDENTIF...
...CURITY CLEARANCE 23R2...

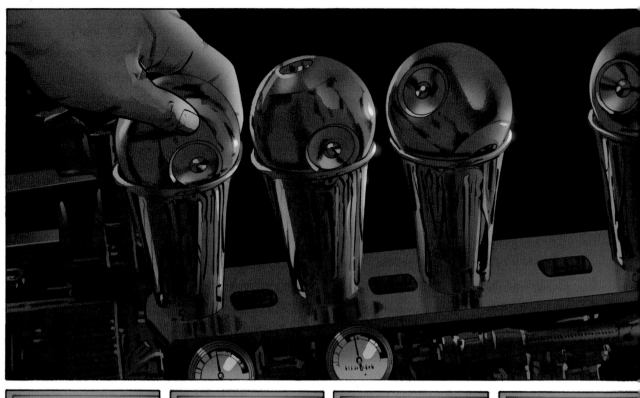

DESTINATION N-ZONE 24525252
CONFIRM? _

DESTINATION E-ZONE E3T3635
CONFIRM? _

DESTINATION R-ZONE DG363635T3
CONFIRM? _

DESTINATION A-ZONE E5T34GE4
CONFIRM? _

TAP

SPAK CRAKLE SPAK

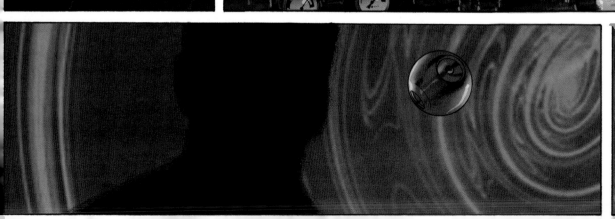

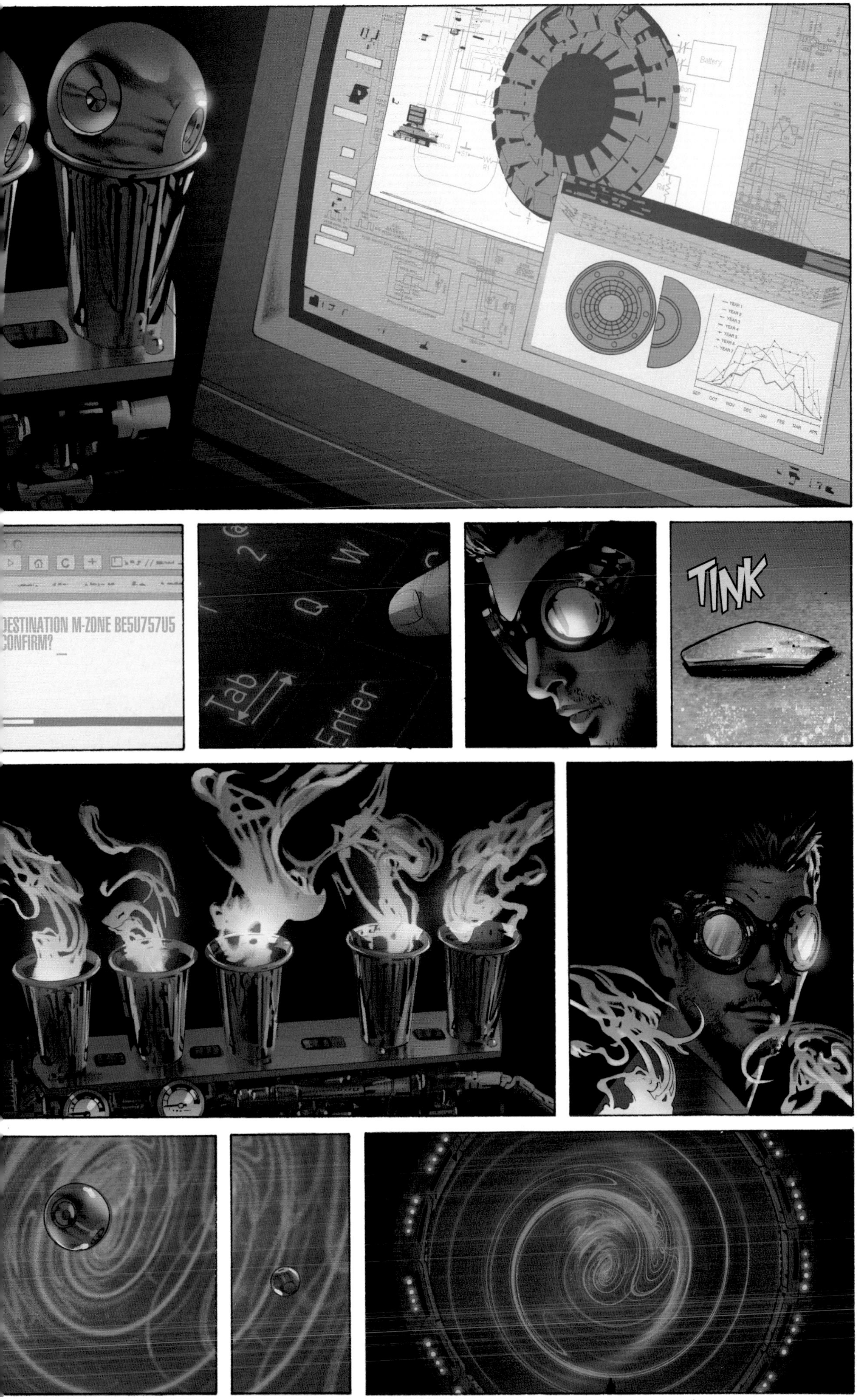
Battery
YEAR 1
YEAR 2
YEAR 3
YEAR 4
YEAR 5
YEAR 6
YEAR 7
SEP OCT NOV DEC JAN FEB MAR APR
DESTINATION M-ZONE BE5U757U5
CONFIRM? _
Tab
Enter
TINK

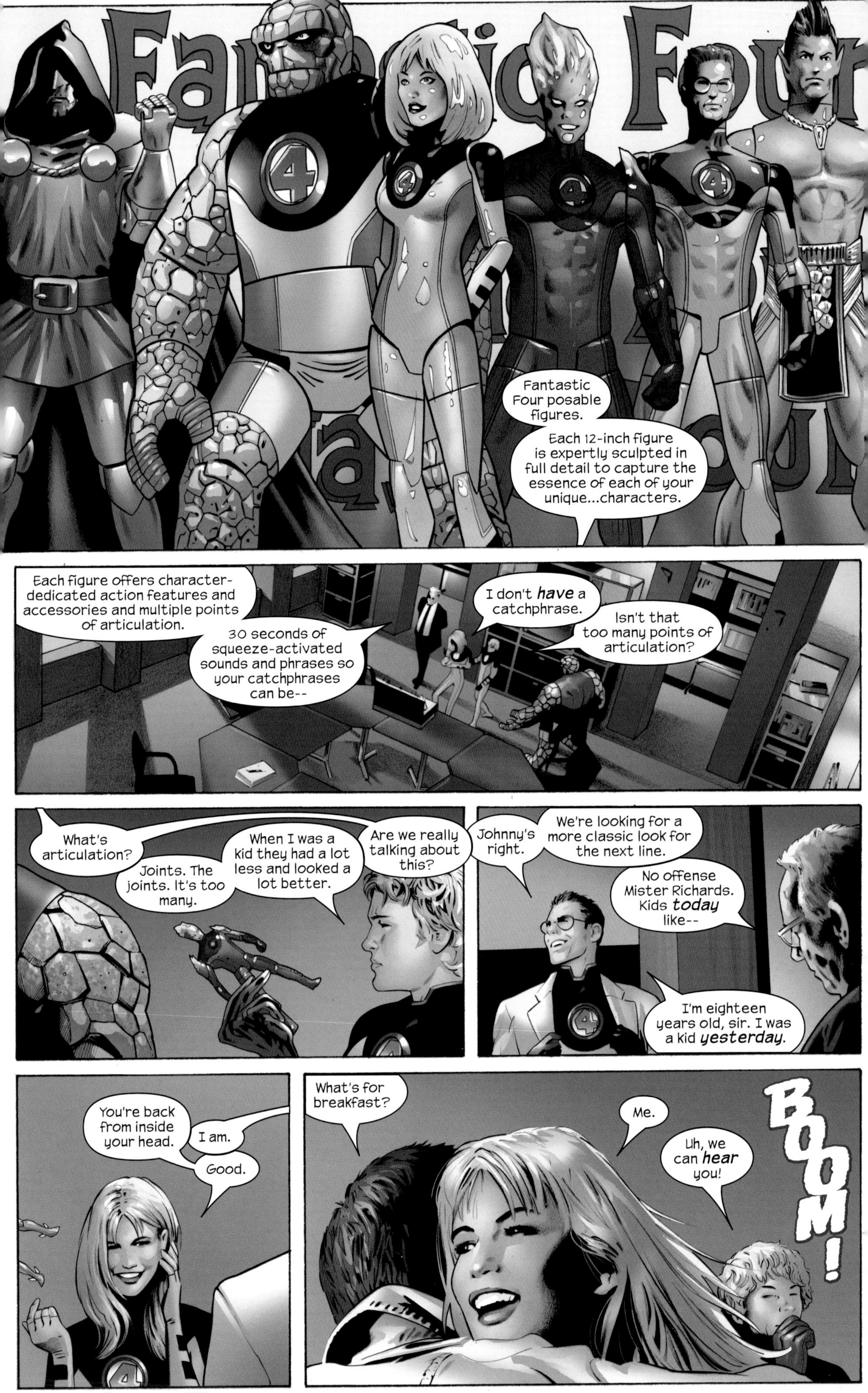
Fantastic Four posable figures.
Each 12-inch figure is expertly sculpted in full detail to capture the essence of each of your unique...characters.
Each figure offers character-dedicated action features and accessories and multiple points of articulation.
30 seconds of squeeze-activated sounds and phrases so your catchphrases can be--
I don't *have* a catchphrase.
Isn't that too many points of articulation?
What's articulation?
Joints. The joints. It's too many.
When I was a kid they had a lot less and looked a lot better.
Are we really talking about this?
Johnny's right.
We're looking for a more classic look for the next line.
No offense Mister Richards. Kids *today* like--
I'm eighteen years old, sir. I was a kid *yesterday*.
You're back from inside your head.
I am.
Good.
What's for breakfast?
Me.
Uh, we can *hear* you!
BOOM!

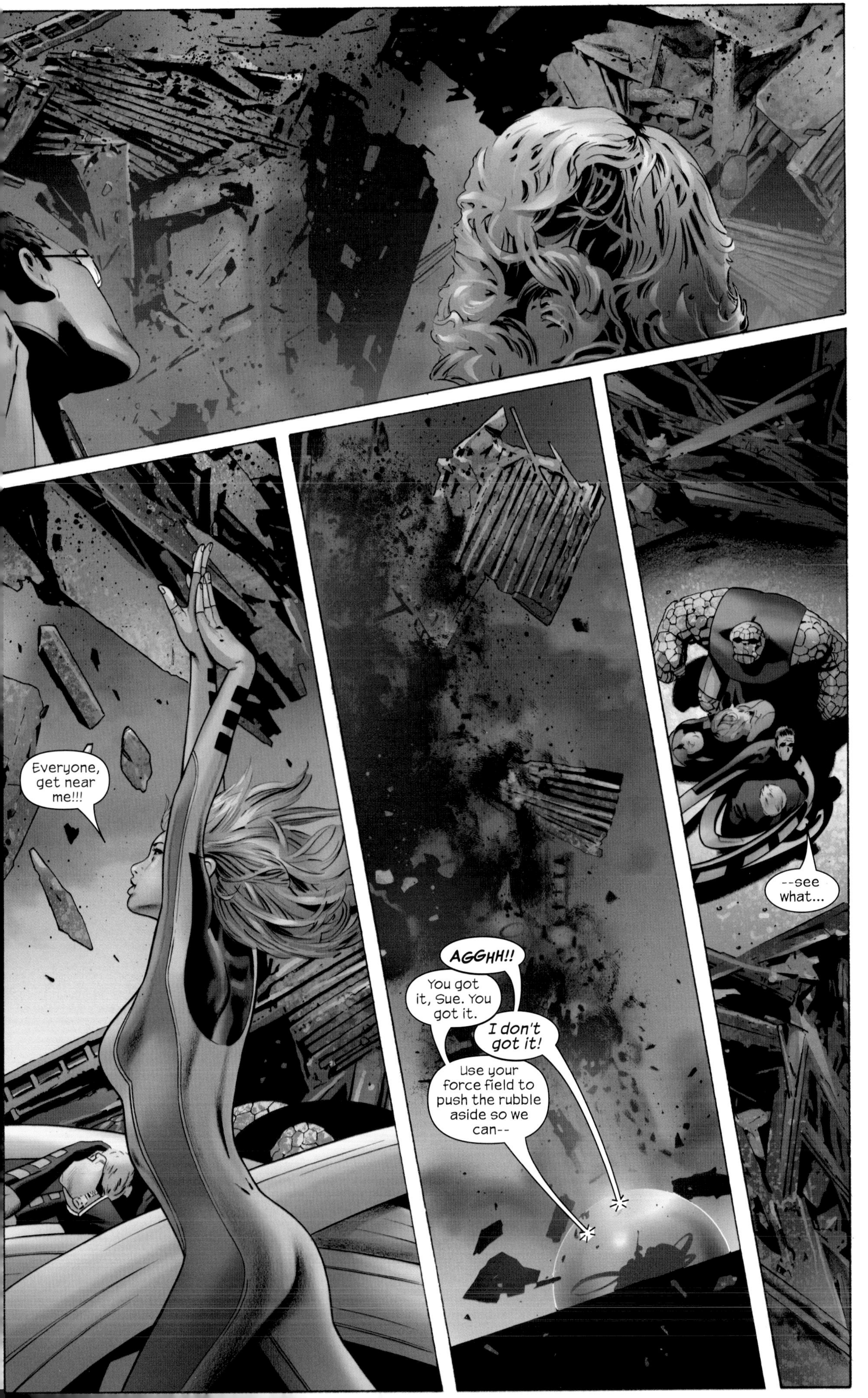
Everyone, get near me!!!
AGGHH!!
You got it, Sue. You got it.
I don't got it!
Use your force field to push the rubble aside so we can--
--see what...

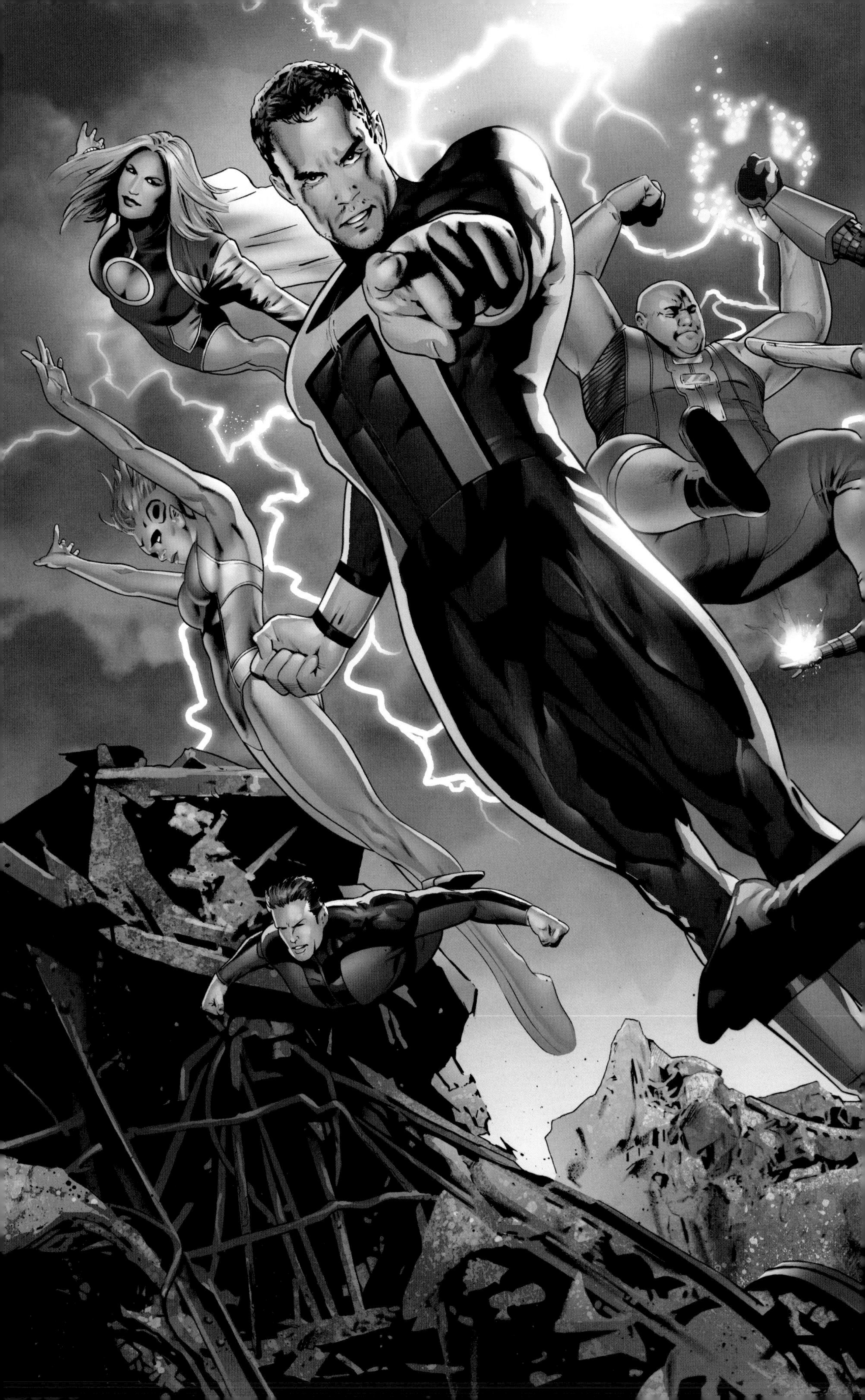

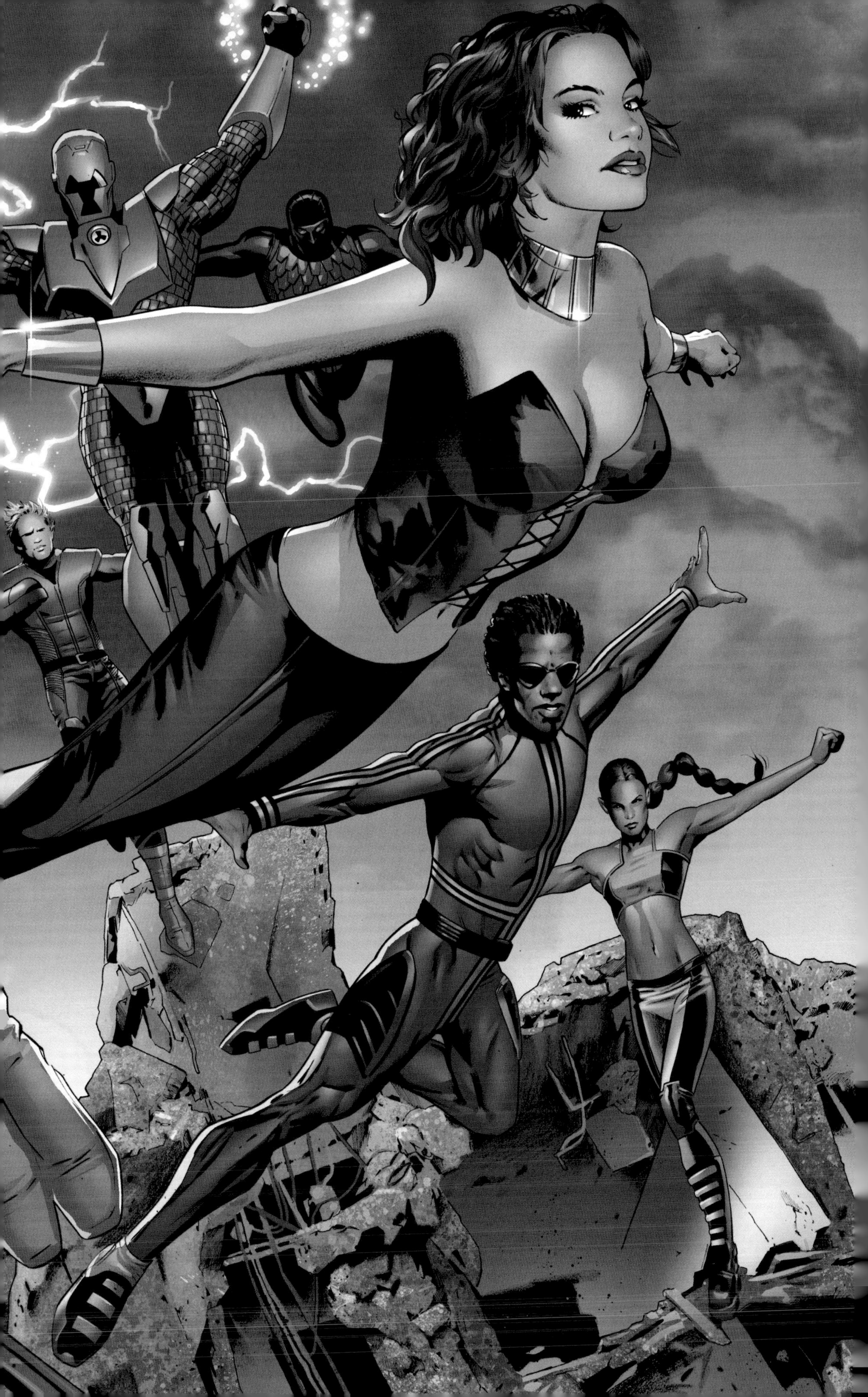

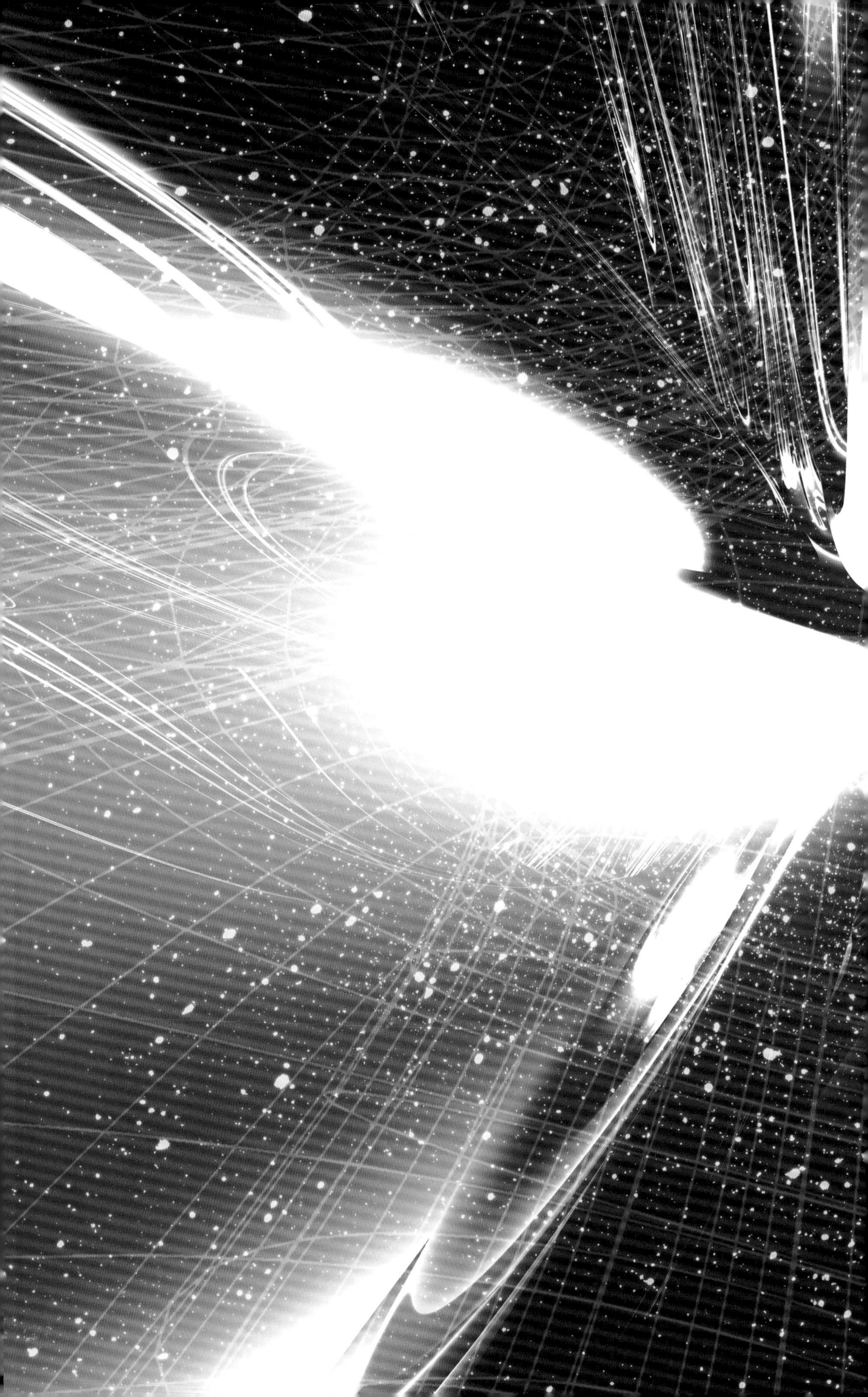

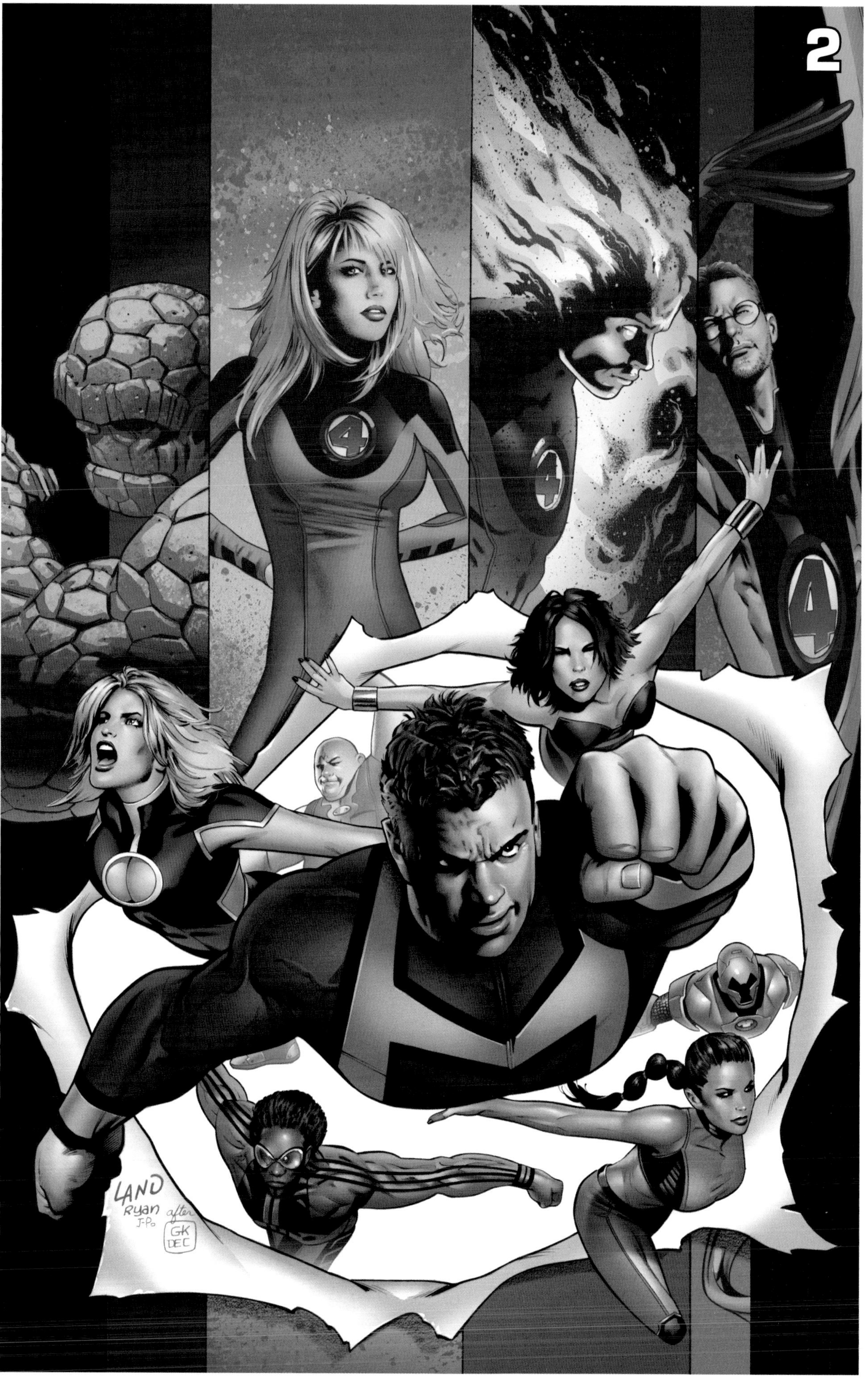
2
LAND
Ryan
J-Po
after
GK
DEC

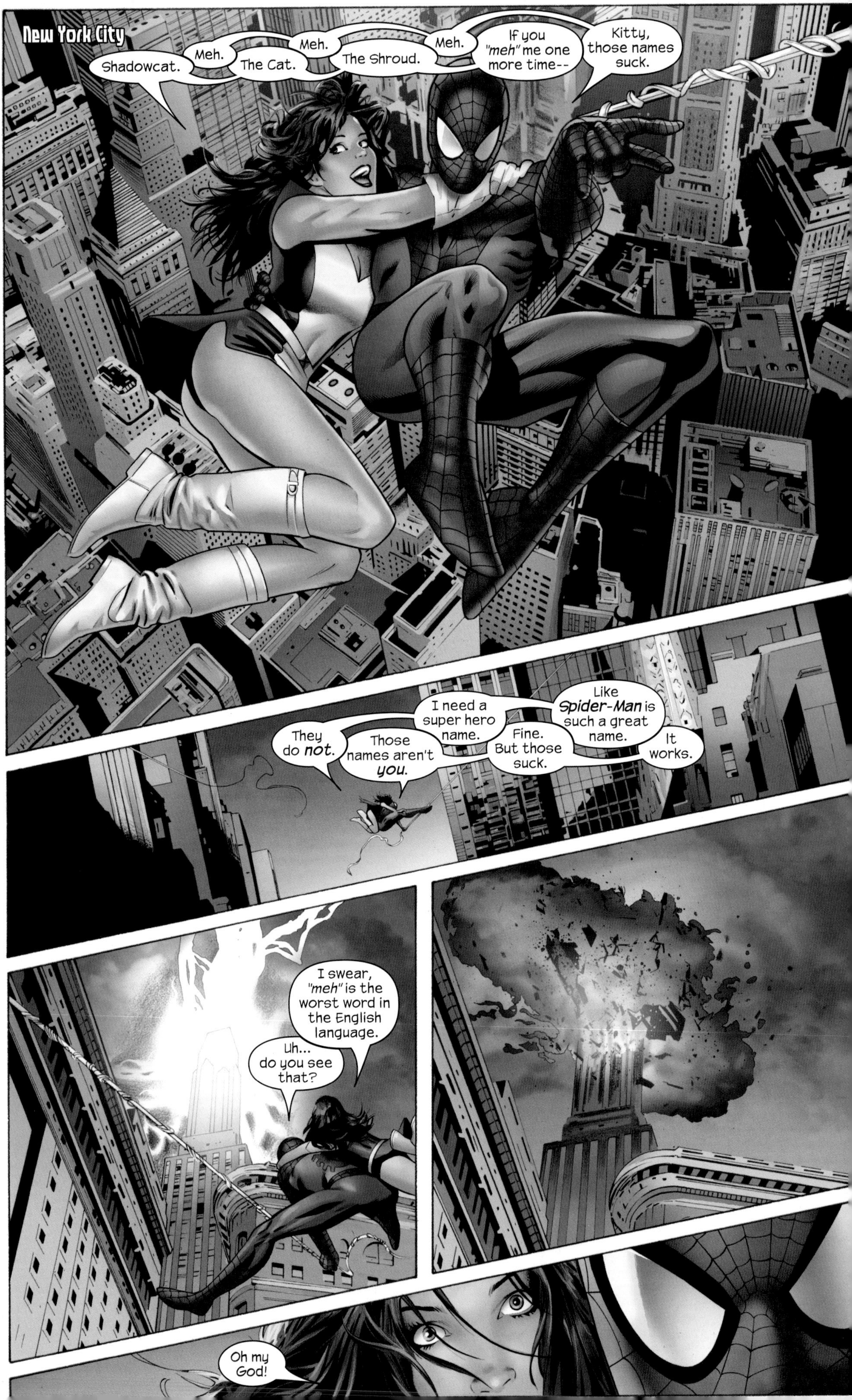

New York City
Shadowcat.
Meh.
The Cat.
Meh.
The Shroud.
Meh.
If you "meh" me one more time--
Kitty, those names suck.
They do not.
Those names aren't you.
I need a super hero name.
Fine. But those suck.
Like Spider-Man is such a great name.
It works.
I swear, "meh" is the worst word in the English language.
Uh... do you see that?
Oh my God!

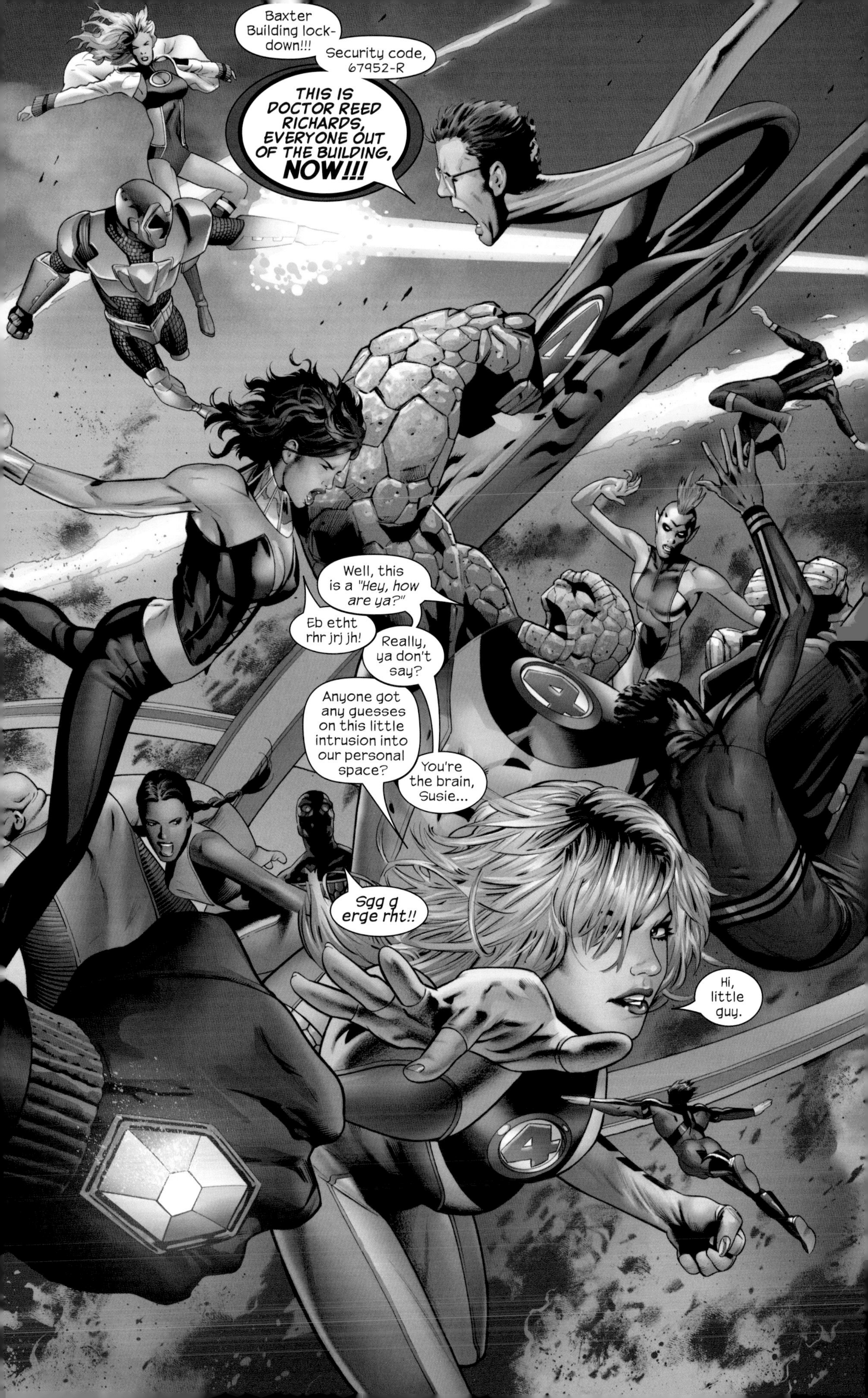
Baxter Building lock-down!!!
Security code, 67952-R
THIS IS DOCTOR REED RICHARDS, EVERYONE OUT OF THE BUILDING, NOW!!!
Well, this is a "Hey, how are ya?"
Eb etht rhr jrj jh!
Really, ya don't say?
Anyone got any guesses on this little intrusion into our personal space?
You're the brain, Susie...
Sgg g erge rht!!
Hi, little guy.

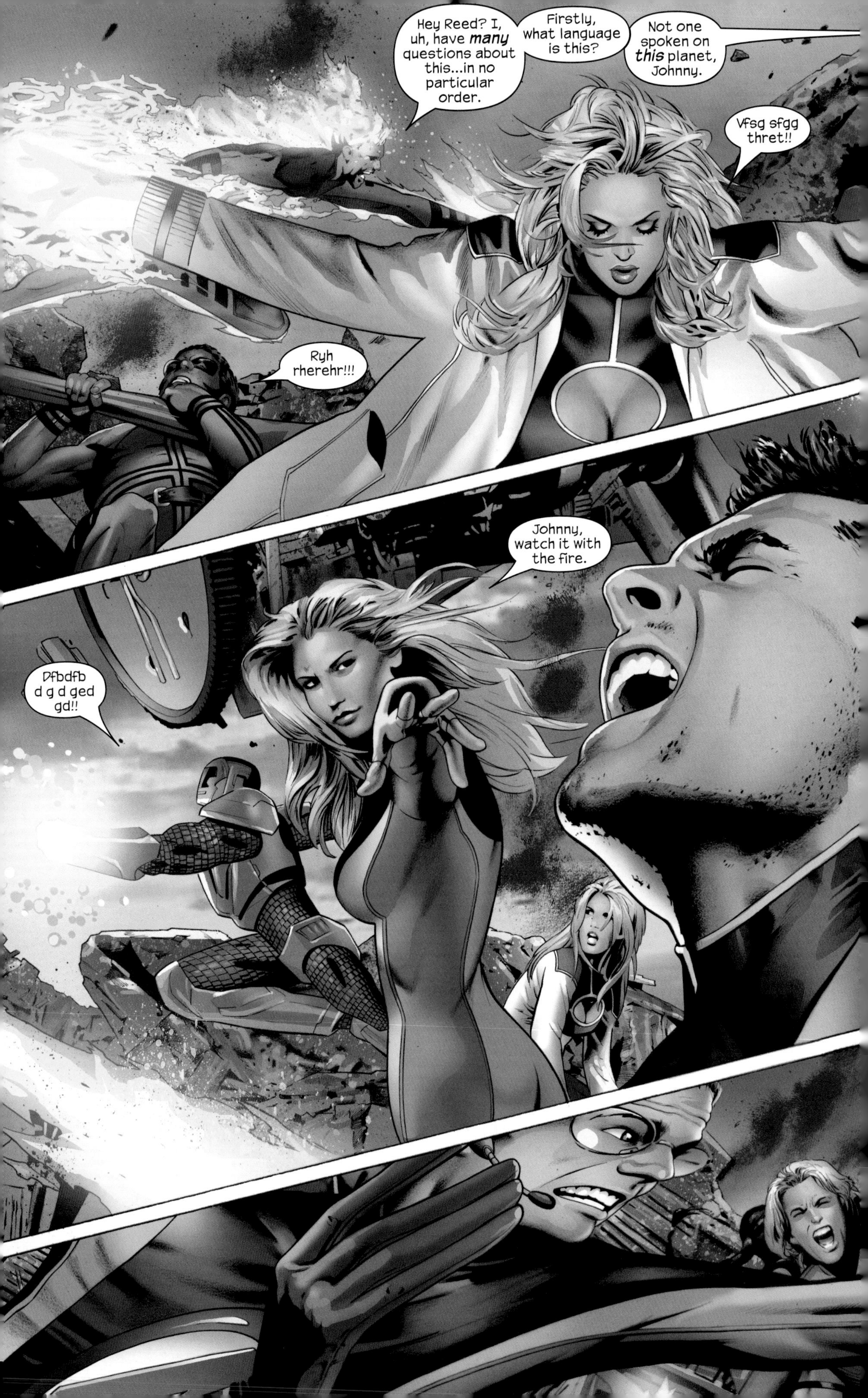
Hey Reed? I, uh, have *many* questions about this...in no particular order.
Firstly, what language is this?
Not one spoken on *this* planet, Johnny.
Vfsg sfgg thret!!
Ryh rherehr!!!
Johnny, watch it with the fire.
Dfbdfb d g d ged gd!!

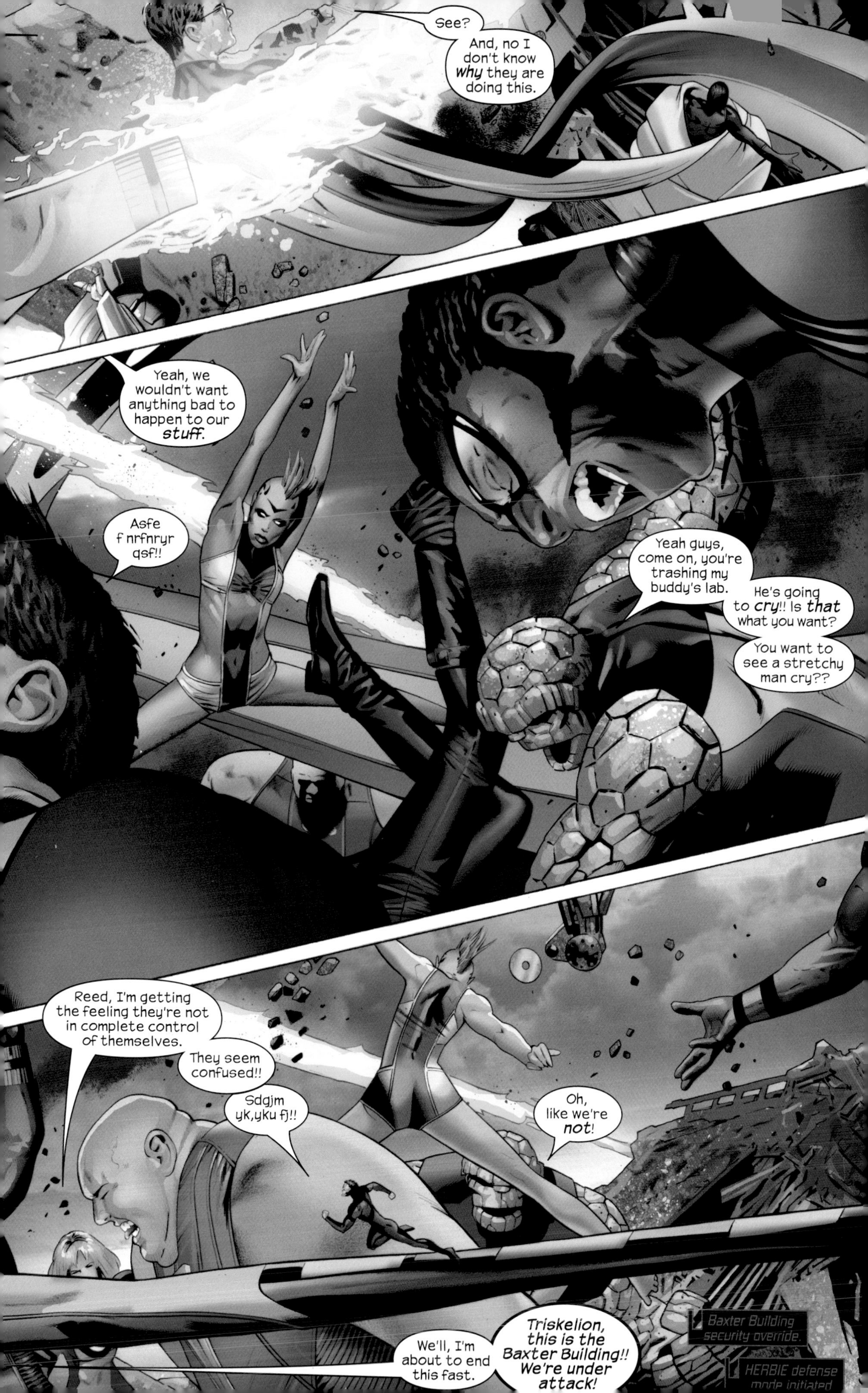
See?
And, no I don't know *why* they are doing this.
Yeah, we wouldn't want anything bad to happen to our *stuff*.
Asfe f nrfnryr qsf!!
Yeah guys, come on, you're trashing my buddy's lab.
He's going to *cry*!! Is *that* what you want?
You want to see a stretchy man cry??
Reed, I'm getting the feeling they're not in complete control of themselves.
They seem confused!!
Sdgjm yk,yku fj!!
Oh, like we're *not*!
We'll, I'm about to end this fast.
Triskelion, this is the Baxter Building!! We're under attack!
Baxter Building security override.
HERBIE defense mode initiated

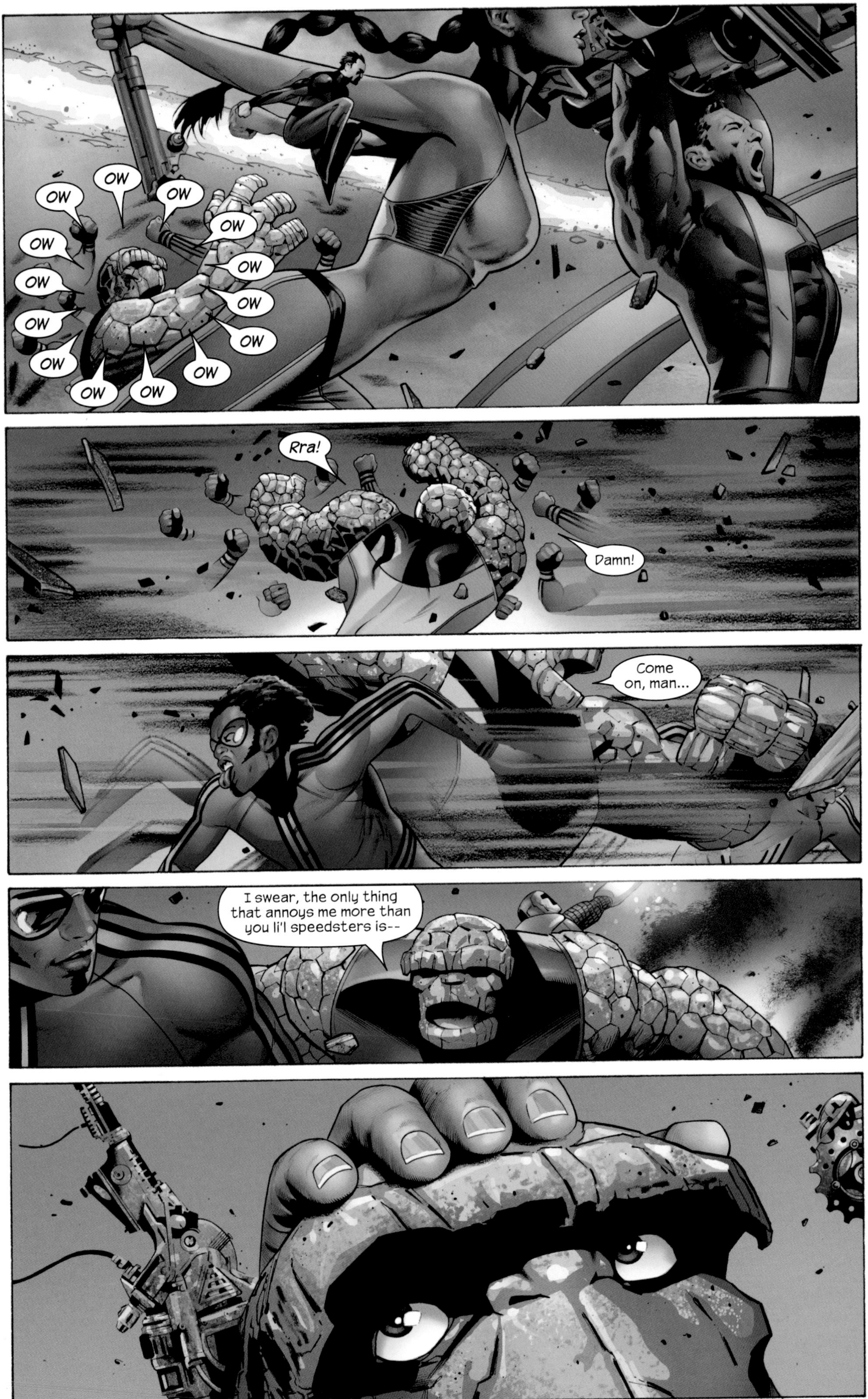
OW
OW
OW
OW
OW
OW
OW
OW
OW
OW
OW
OW
OW
OW
OW
Rra!
Damn!
Come on, man...
I swear, the only thing that annoys me more than you li'l speedsters is--

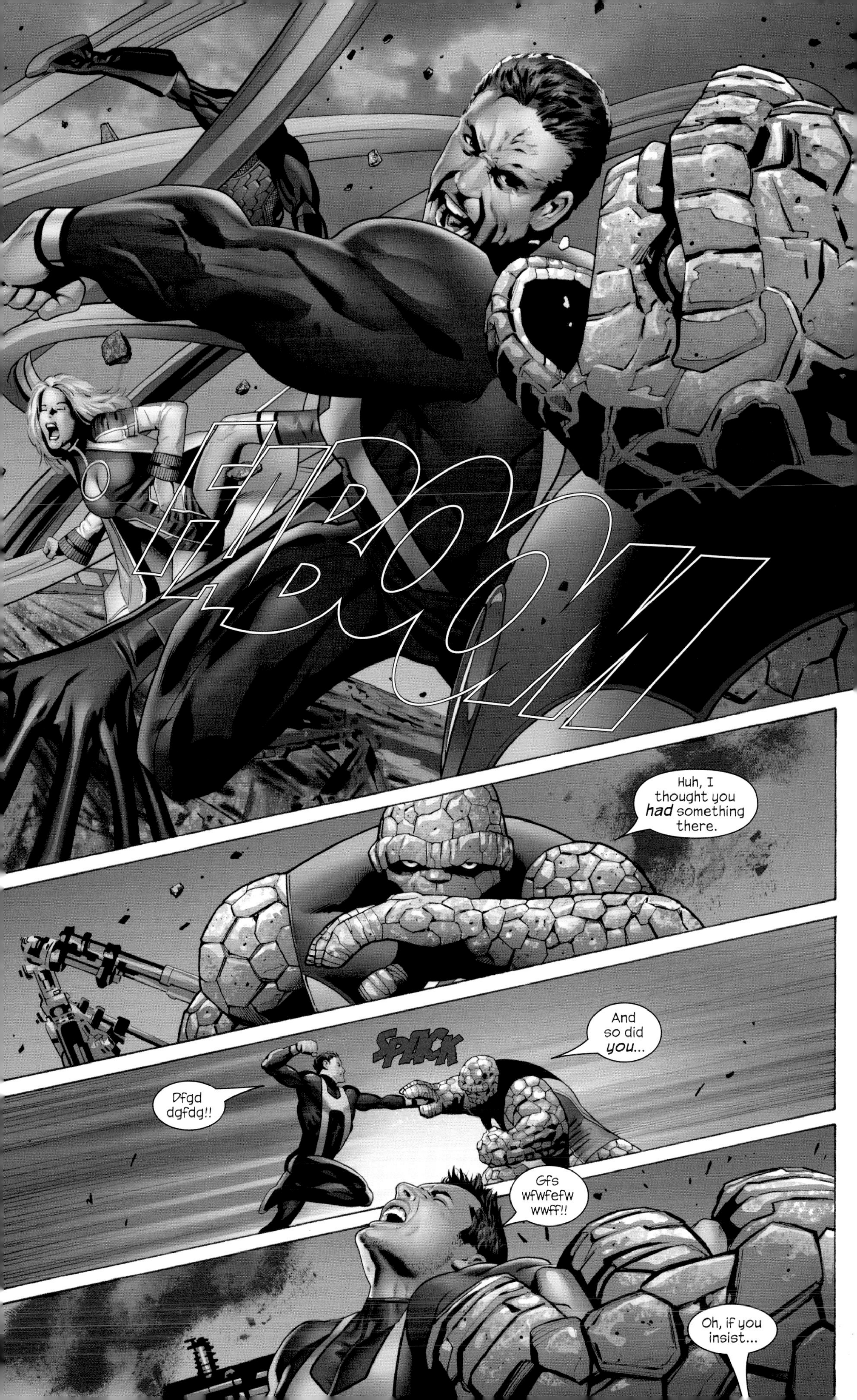
FFROOM
Huh, I thought you had something there.
And so did you...
SPACK
Dfgd dgfdg!!
Gfs wfwfefw wwff!!
Oh, if you insist...

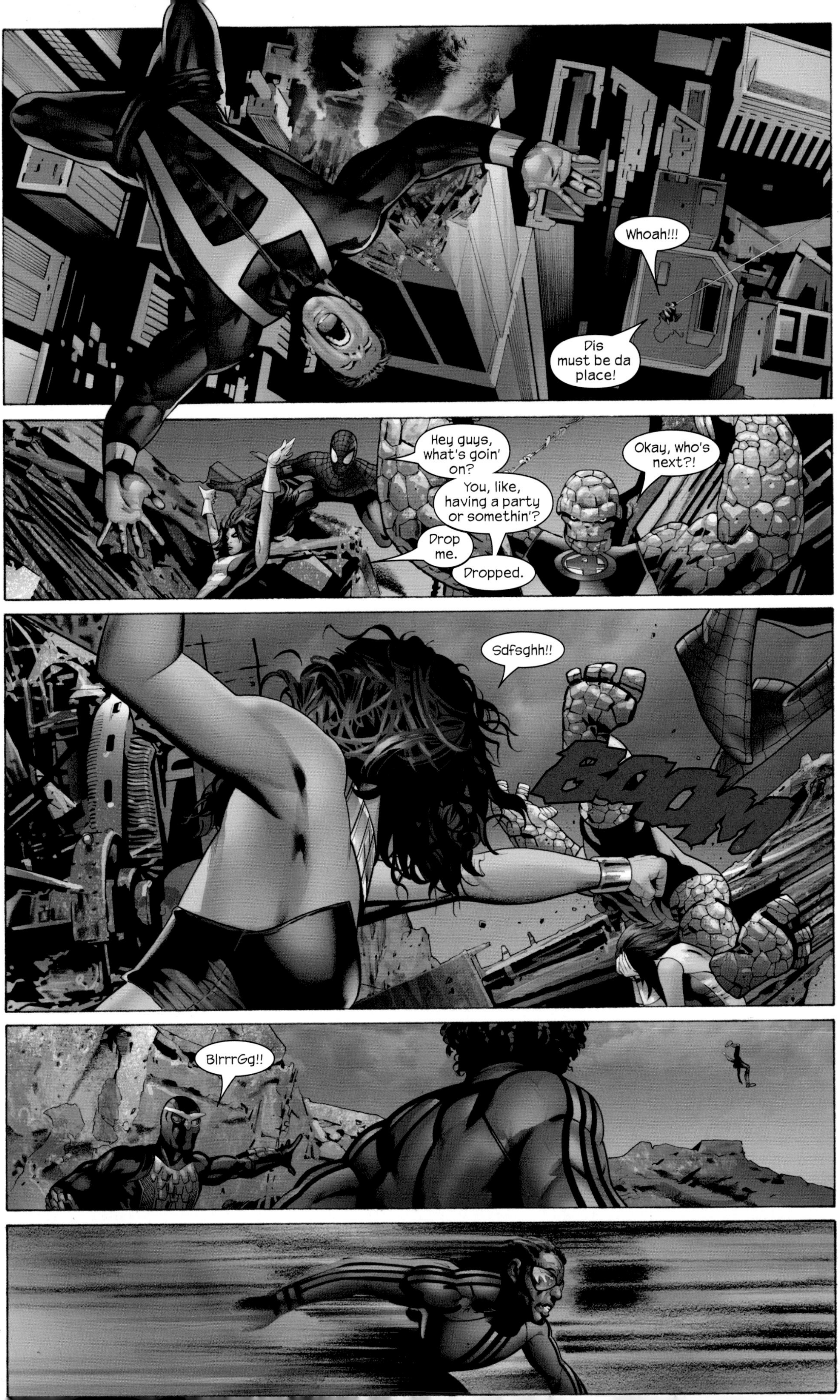
Whoah!!!
Dis must be da place!
Hey guys, what's goin' on?
You, like, having a party or somethin'?
Okay, who's next?!
Drop me.
Dropped.
Sdfsghh!!
Blrrrgg!!

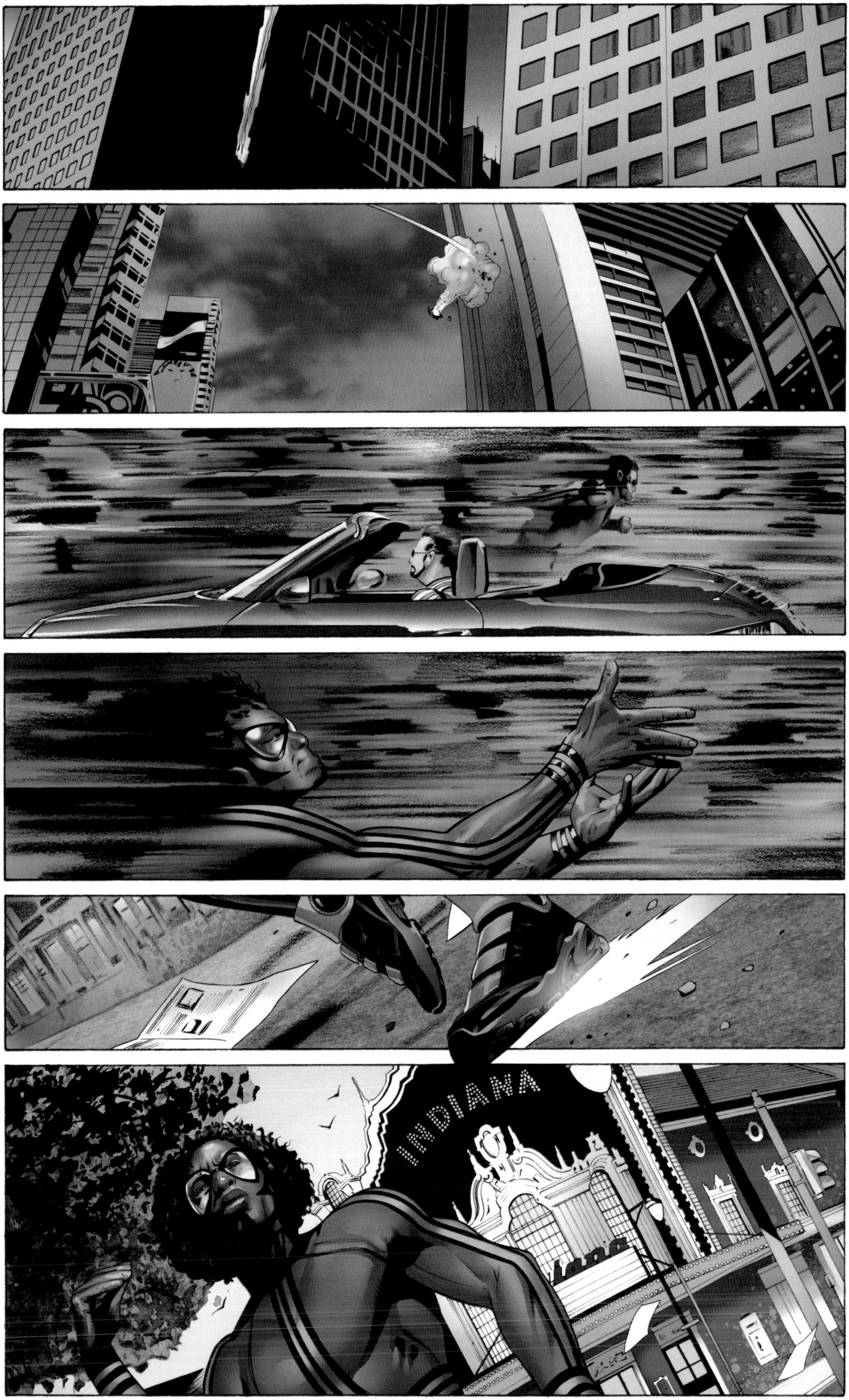
INDIANA

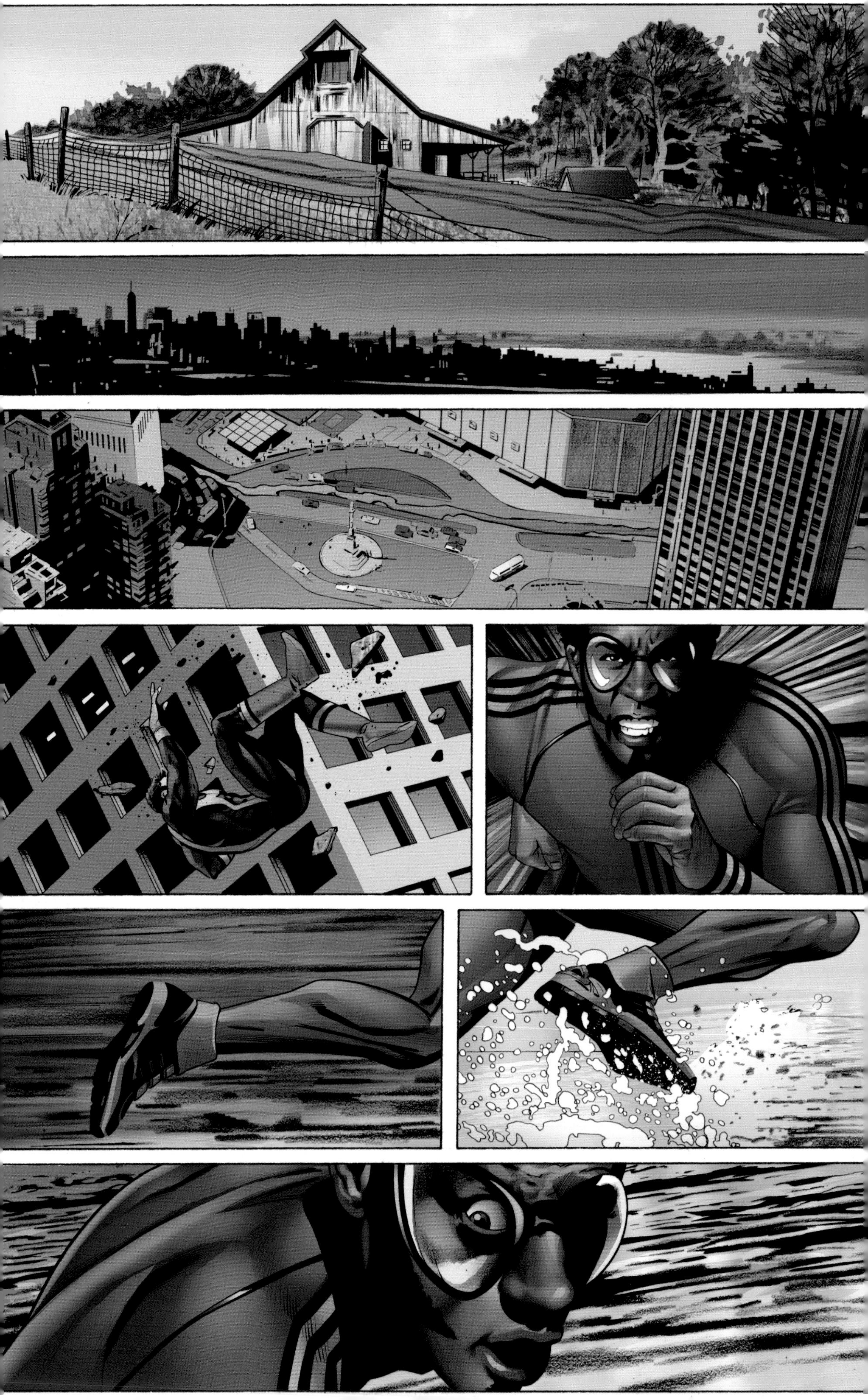

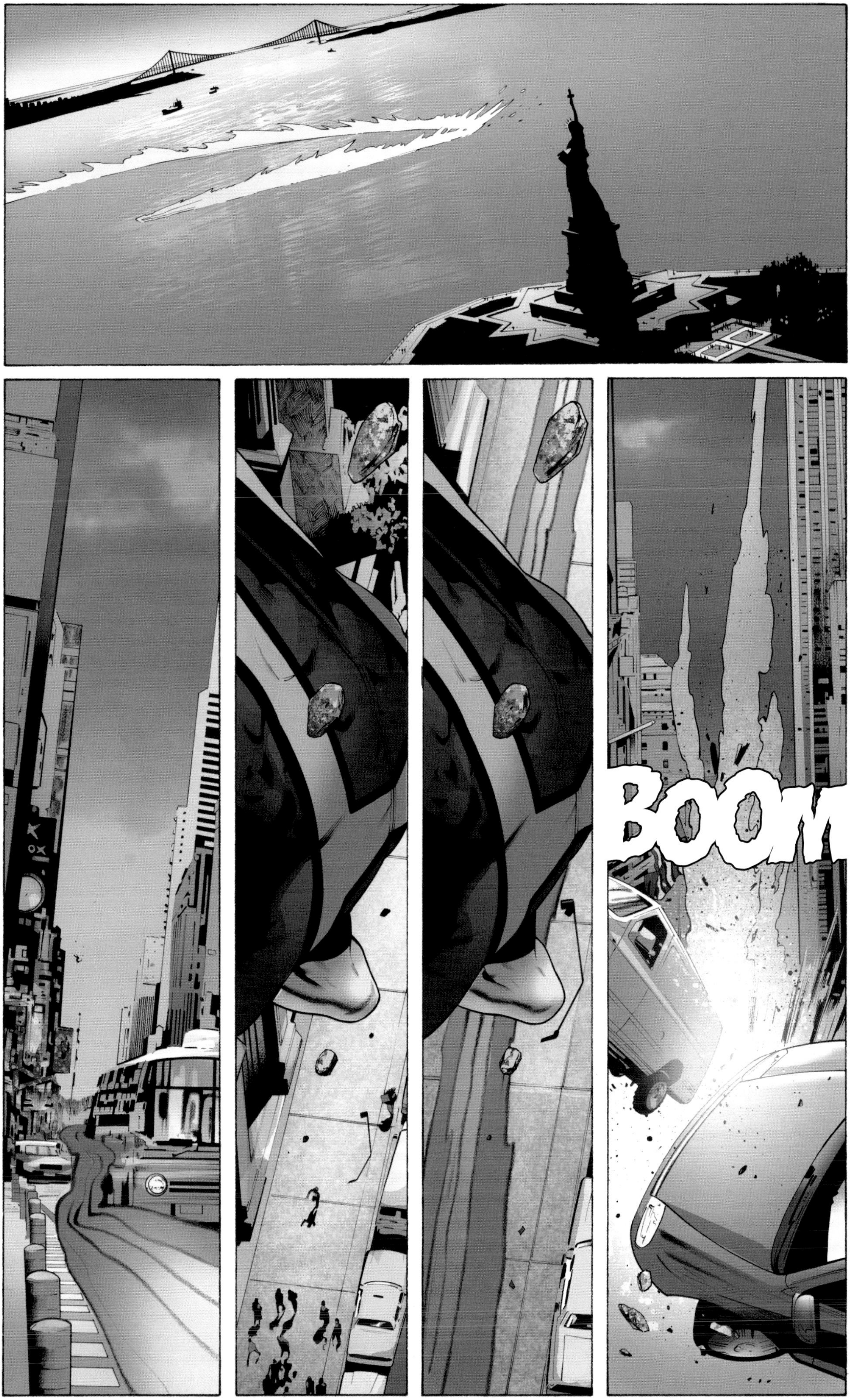
BOOM

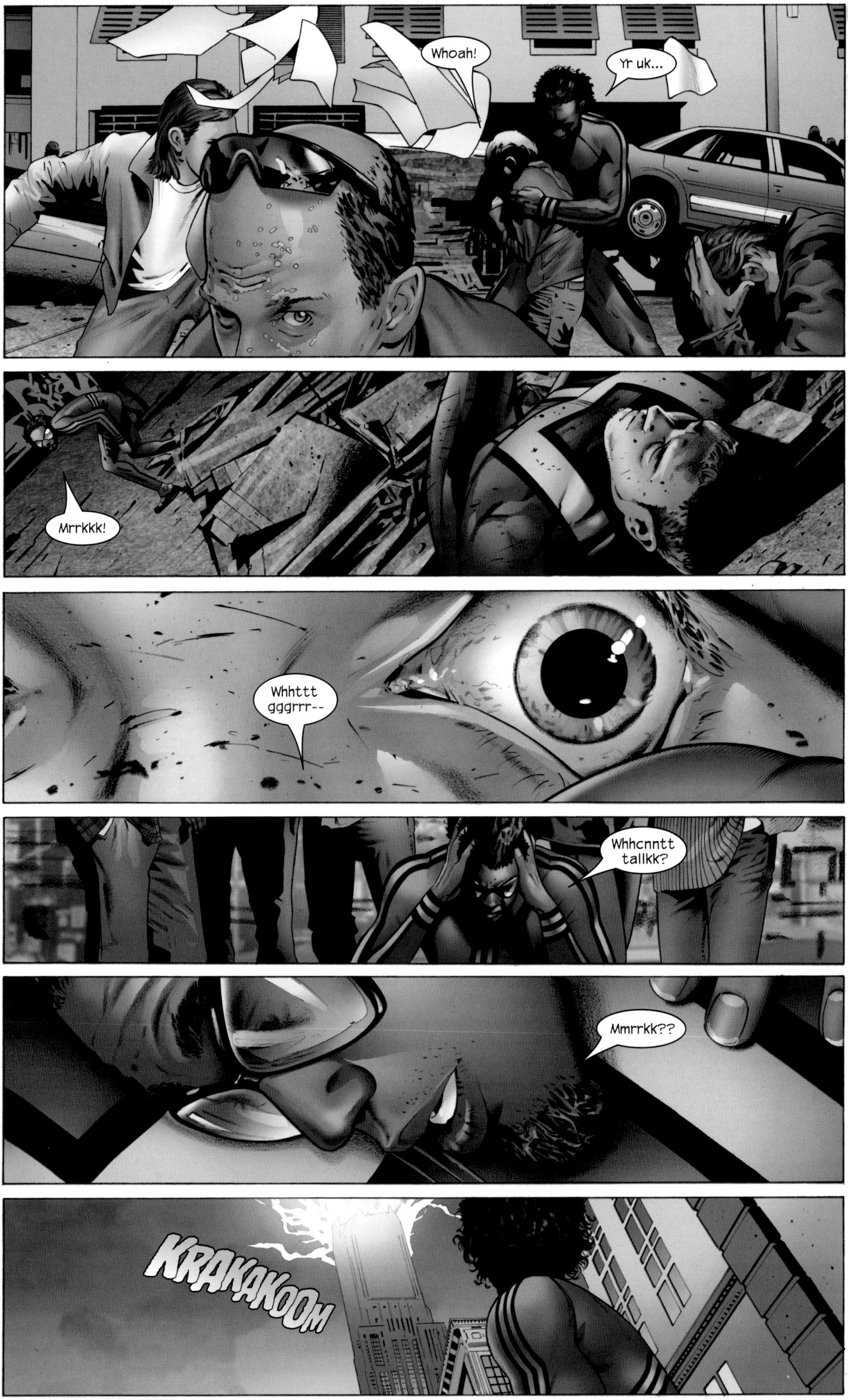
Whoah!
Yr uk...
Mrrkkk!
Whhttt gggrrr--
Whhcnntt tallkk?
Mmrrkk??
KRAKAKOOM

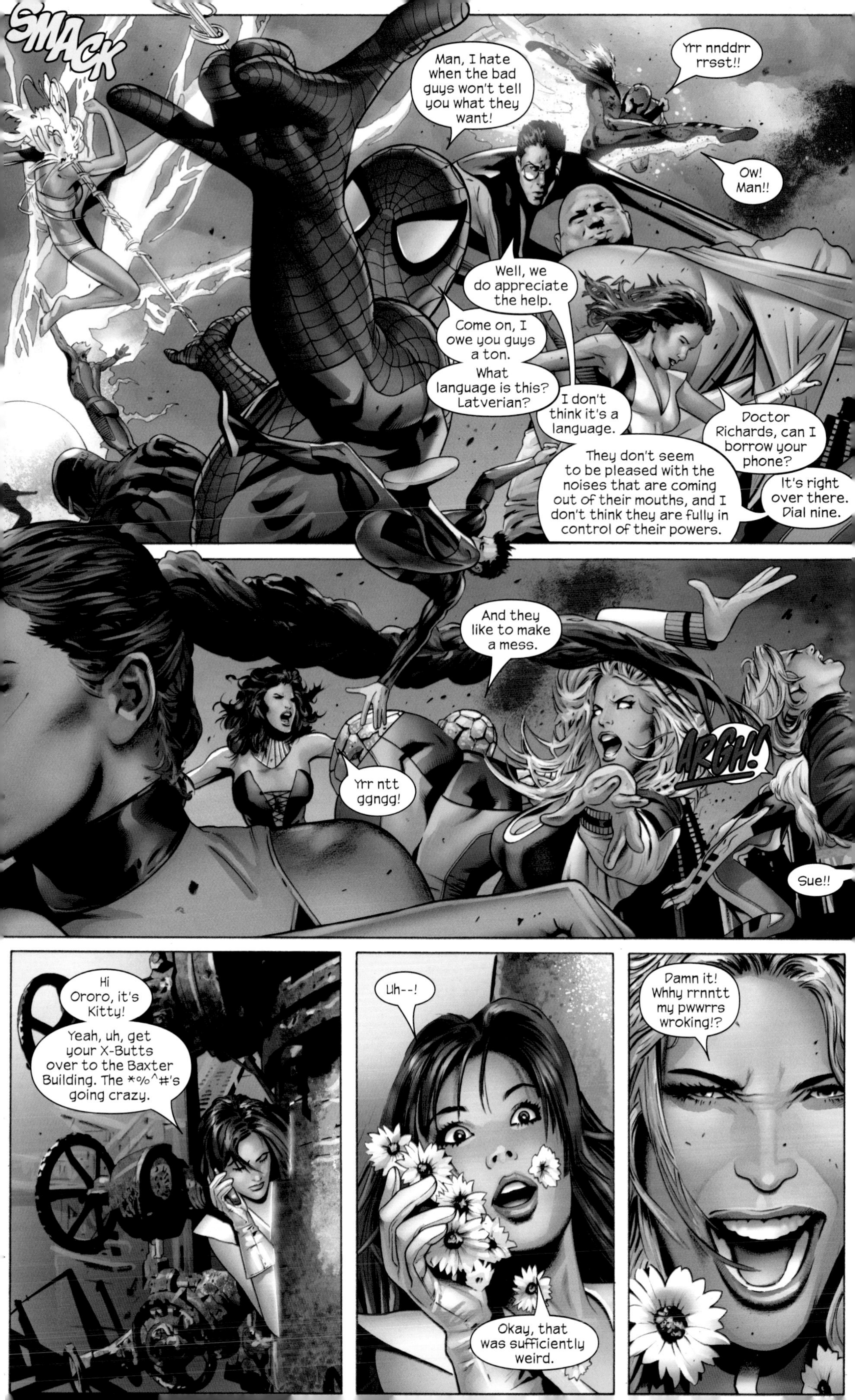
SMACK
Man, I hate when the bad guys won't tell you what they want!
Yrr nnddrr rrsst!!
Ow! Man!!
Well, we do appreciate the help.
Come on, I owe you guys a ton.
What language is this? Latverian?
I don't think it's a language.
Doctor Richards, can I borrow your phone?
They don't seem to be pleased with the noises that are coming out of their mouths, and I don't think they are fully in control of their powers.
It's right over there. Dial nine.
And they like to make a mess.
Yrr ntt ggngg!
ARGH!
Sue!!
Hi Ororo, it's Kitty!
Yeah, uh, get your X-Butts over to the Baxter Building. The *%^#'s going crazy.
Uh--!
Okay, that was sufficiently weird.
Damn it! Whhy rrnntt my pwwrrs wroking!?

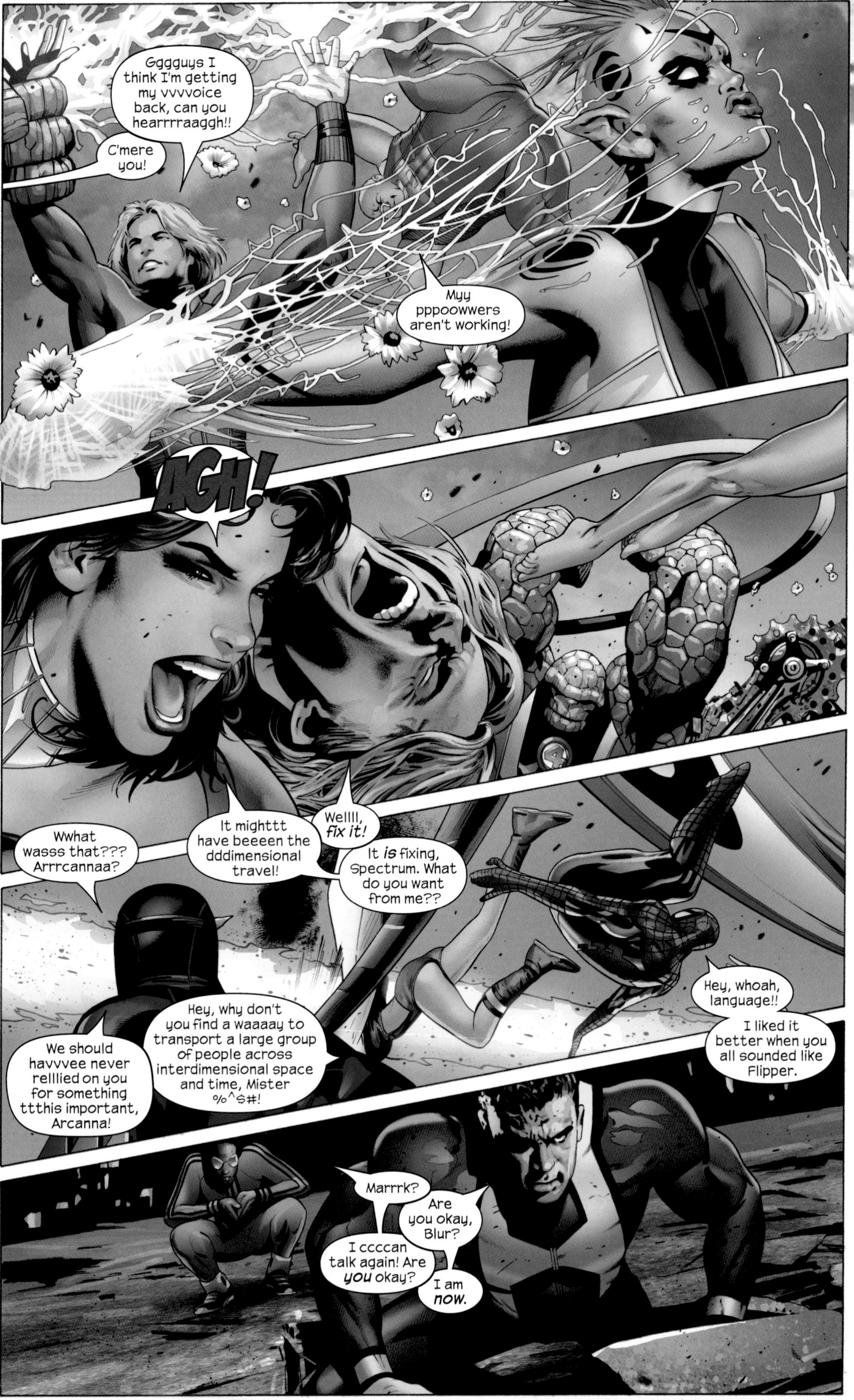
Ggguys I think I'm getting my vvvvoice back, can you hearrrraaggh!!
C'mere you!
Myy pppoowwers aren't working!
AGH!
Wwhat wasss that??? Arrrcannaa?
It mighttt have beeeen the dddimensional travel!
Wellll, fix it!
It is fixing, Spectrum. What do you want from me??
Hey, why don't you find a waaaay to transport a large group of people across interdimensional space and time, Mister %^$#!
We should havvvee never relllied on you for something ttthis important, Arcanna!
Hey, whoah, language!!
I liked it better when you all sounded like Flipper.
Marrrk?
Are you okay, Blur?
I ccccan talk again! Are you okay?
I am now.

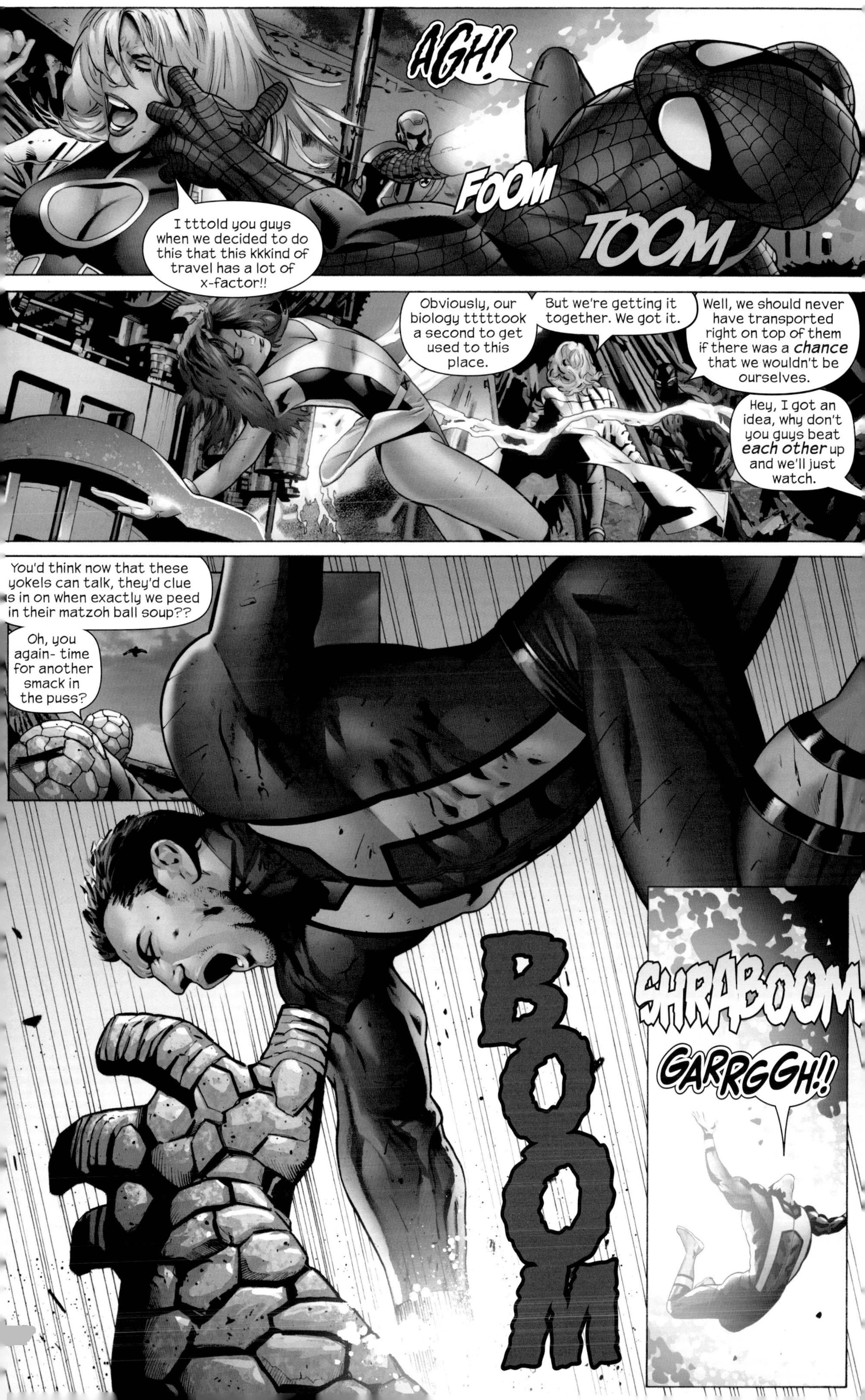
AGH!
FOOM
TOOM
I tttold you guys when we decided to do this that this kkkind of travel has a lot of x-factor!!
Obviously, our biology tttttook a second to get used to this place.
But we're getting it together. We got it.
Well, we should never have transported right on top of them if there was a *chance* that we wouldn't be ourselves.
Hey, I got an idea, why don't you guys beat *each other* up and we'll just watch.
You'd think now that these yokels can talk, they'd clue us in on when exactly we peed in their matzoh ball soup??
Oh, you again- time for another smack in the puss?
BOOM
SHRABOOM
GARRGGH!!

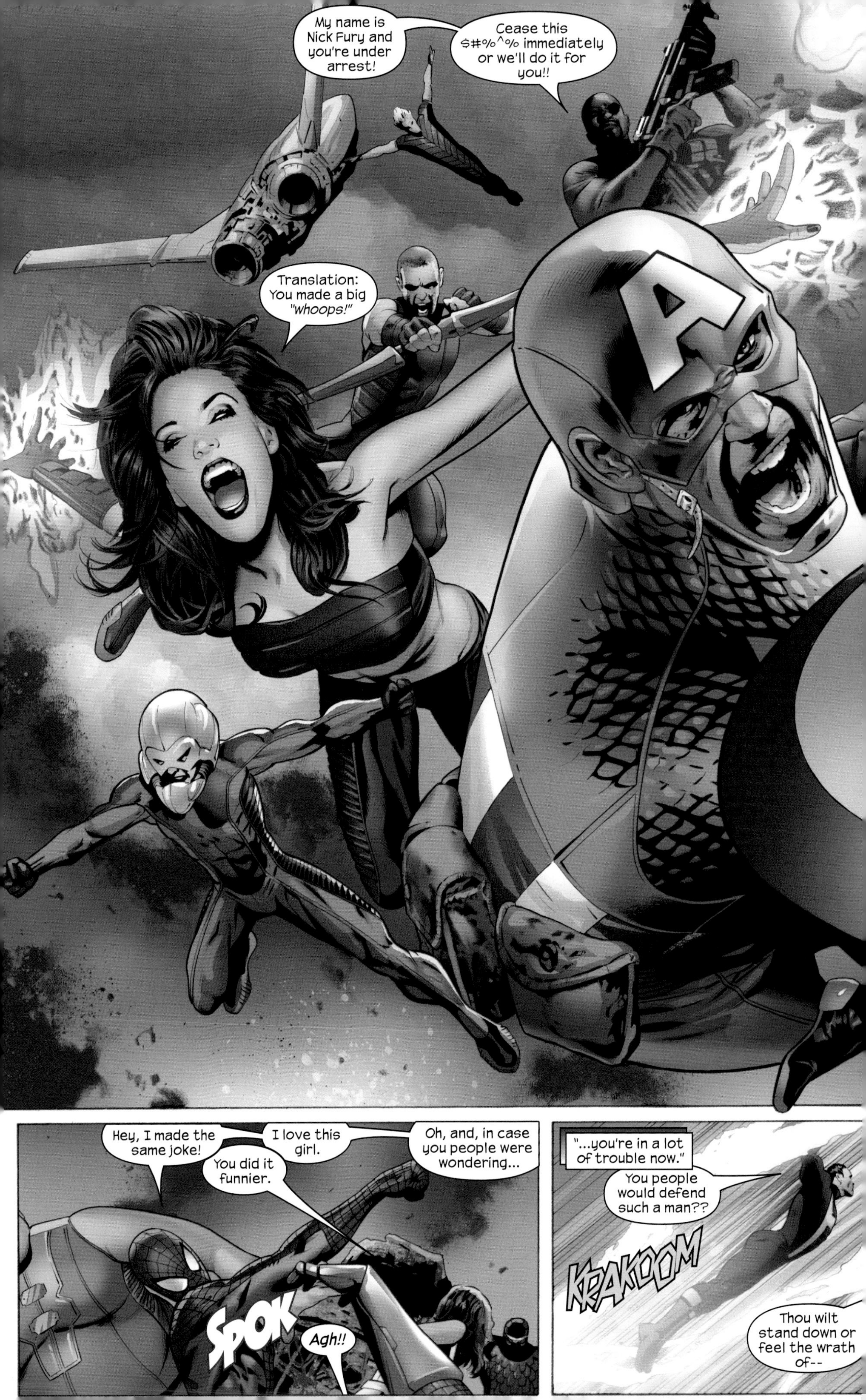
My name is Nick Fury and you're under arrest!
Cease this $#%^% immediately or we'll do it for you!!
Translation: You made a big "whoops!"
Hey, I made the same joke!
I love this girl.
You did it funnier.
Oh, and, in case you people were wondering...
SPOK
Agh!!
"...you're in a lot of trouble now."
You people would defend such a man??
KRAKOOM
Thou wilt stand down or feel the wrath of--

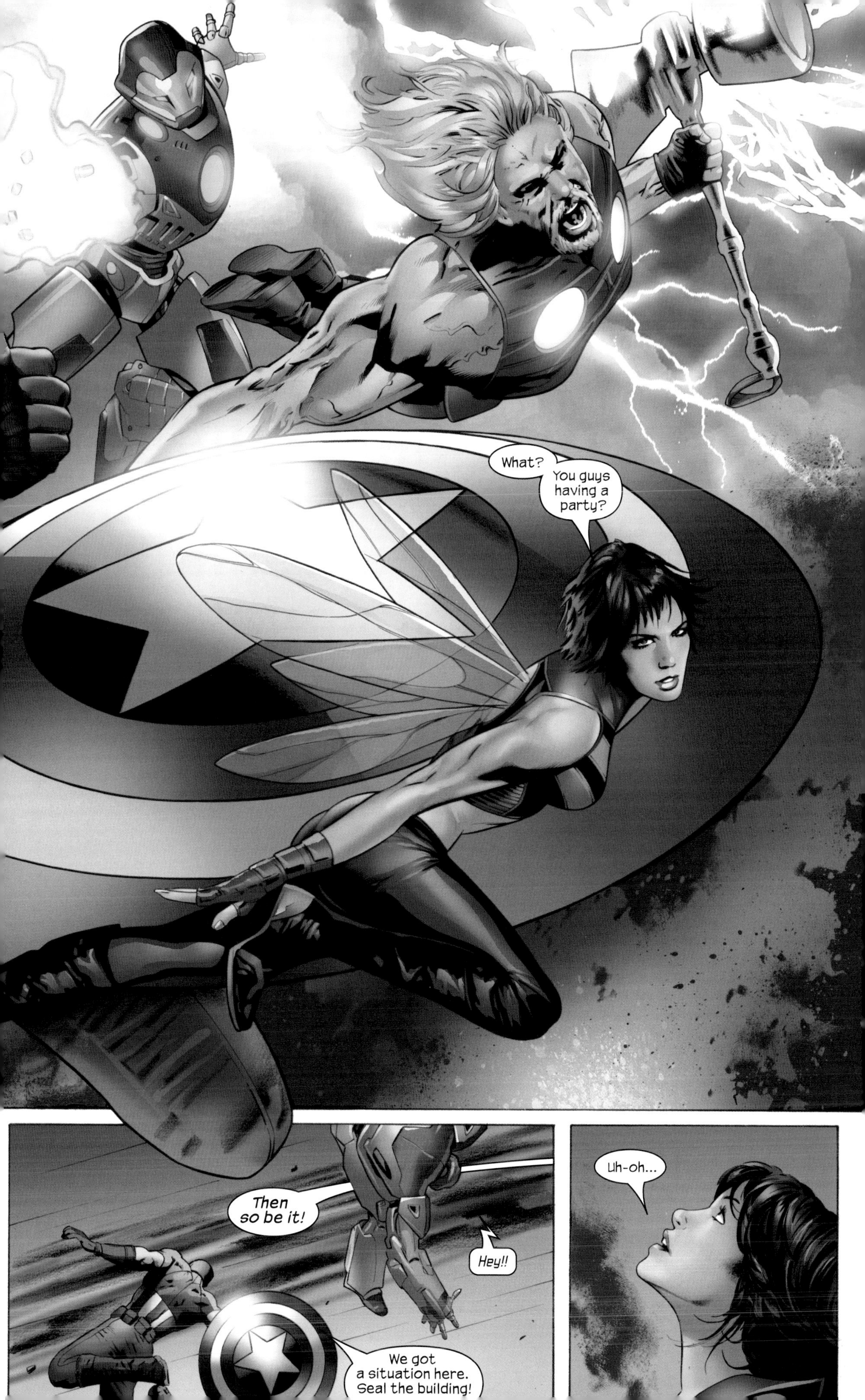
What?
You guys having a party?
Then so be it!
Hey!!
We got a situation here. Seal the building!
Uh-oh...

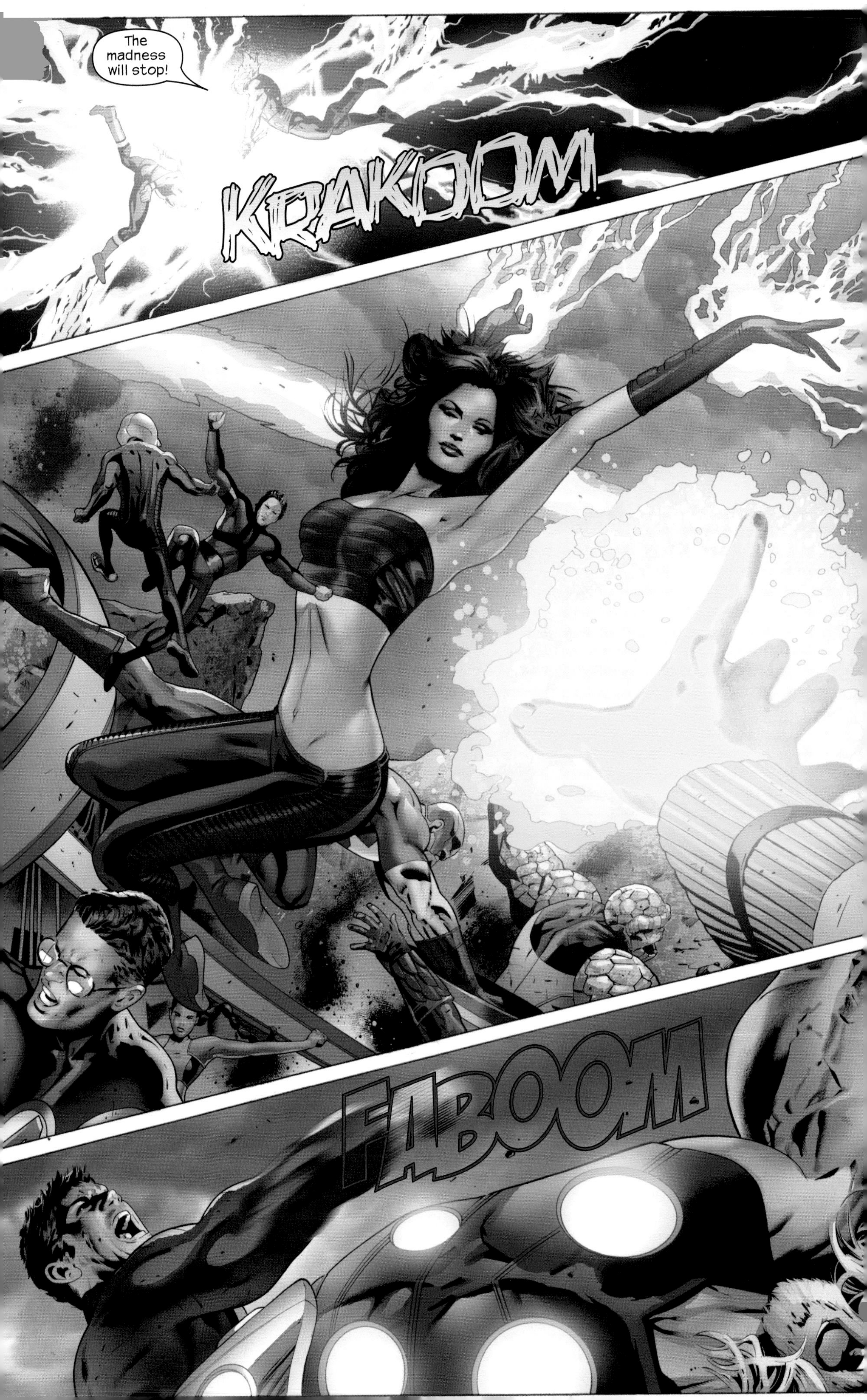
The madness will stop!
KRAKOOM
FABOOM

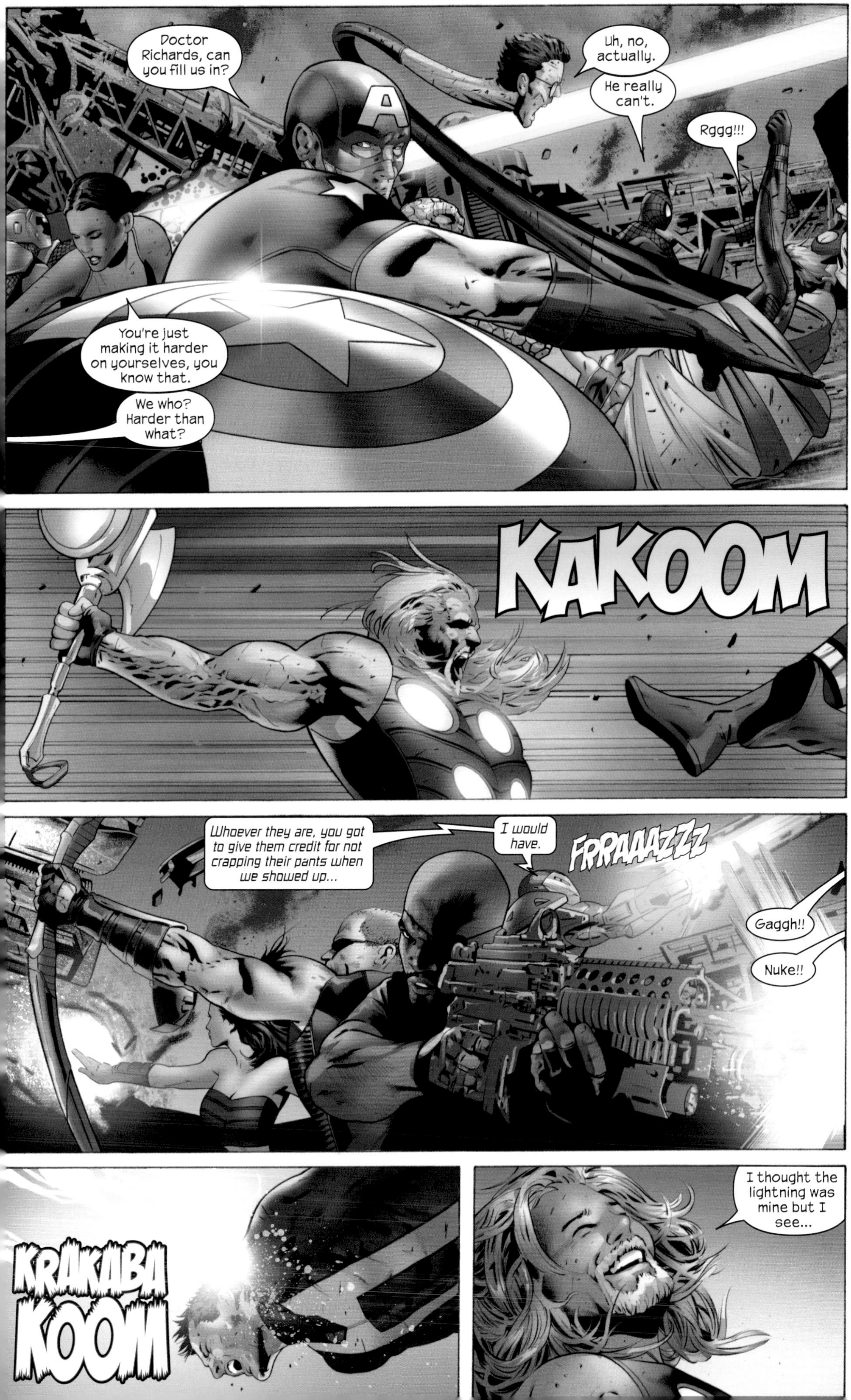
Doctor Richards, can you fill us in?
Uh, no, actually.
He really can't.
Rggg!!!
You're just making it harder on yourselves, you know that.
We who? Harder than what?
KAKOOM
Whoever they are, you got to give them credit for not crapping their pants when we showed up...
I would have.
FRRAAAZZZ
Gaggh!!
Nuke!!
KRAKABA KOOM
I thought the lightning was mine but I see...

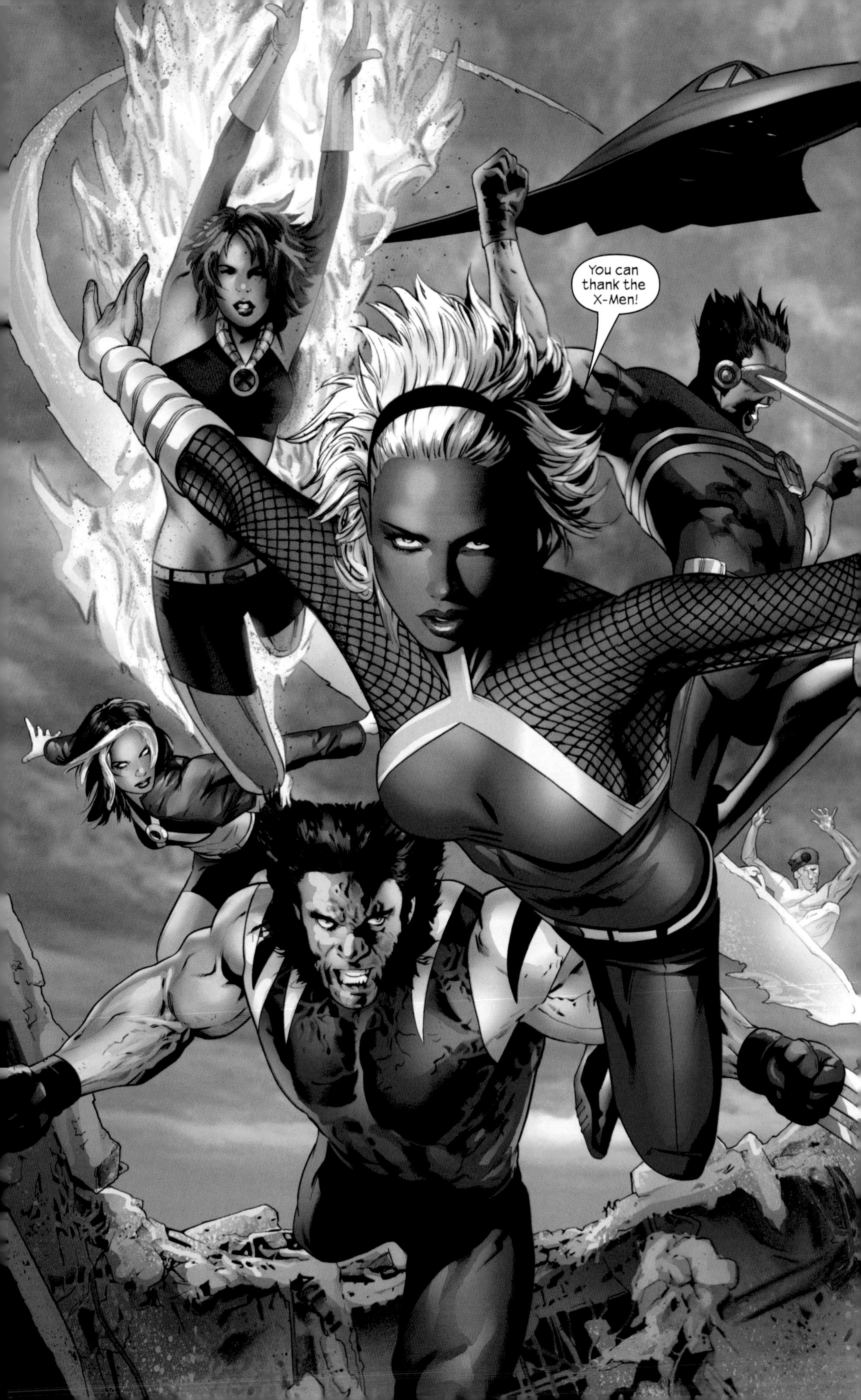
You can thank the X-Men!

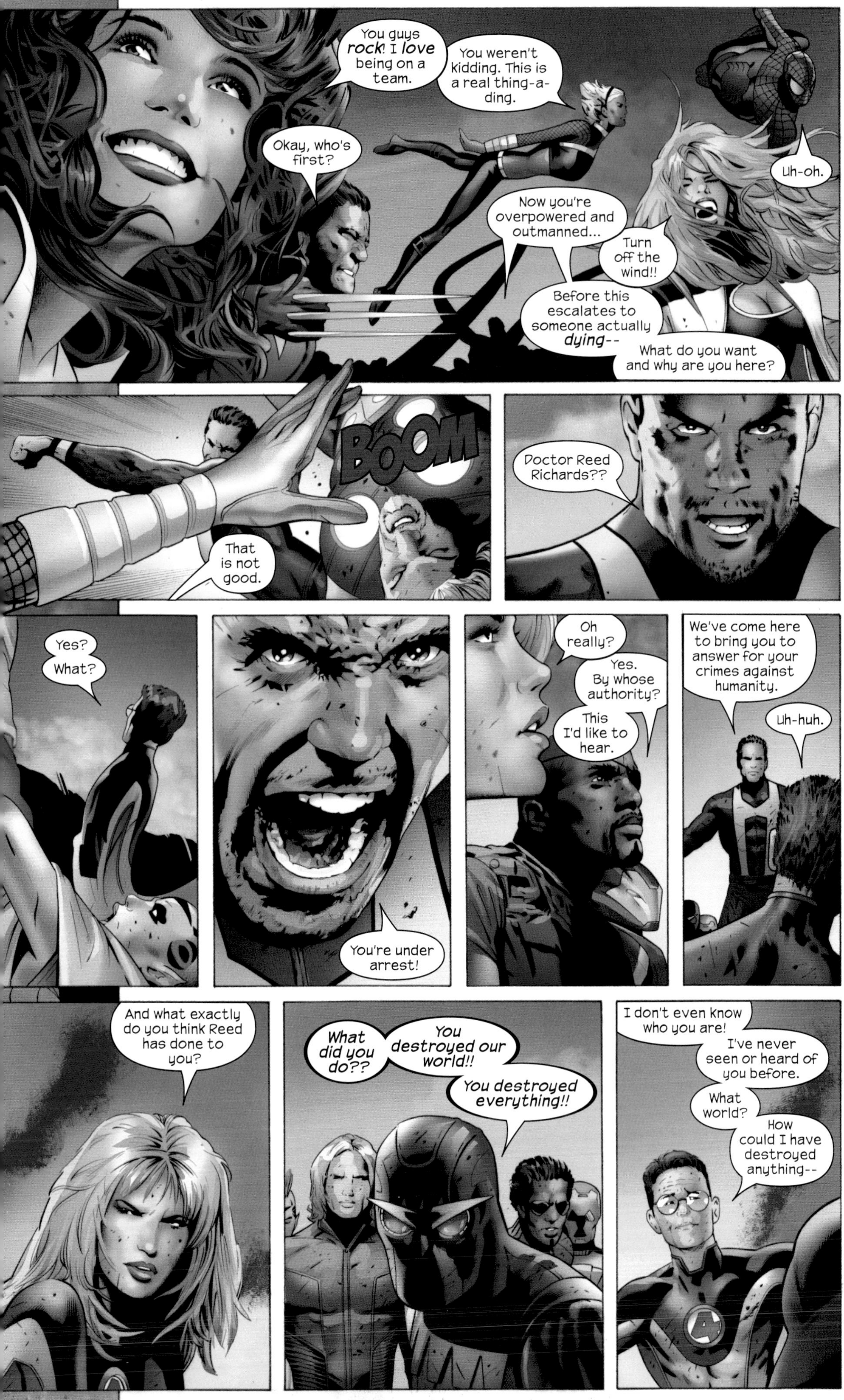

You guys rock! I love being on a team.
You weren't kidding. This is a real thing-a-ding.
Okay, who's first?
Uh-oh.
Now you're overpowered and outmanned...
Turn off the wind!!
Before this escalates to someone actually dying--
What do you want and why are you here?
BOOM
That is not good.
Doctor Reed Richards??
Yes?
What?
You're under arrest!
Oh really?
Yes. By whose authority?
This I'd like to hear.
We've come here to bring you to answer for your crimes against humanity.
Uh-huh.
And what exactly do you think Reed has done to you?
What did you do??
You destroyed our world!!
You destroyed everything!!
I don't even know who you are!
I've never seen or heard of you before.
What world?
How could I have destroyed anything--

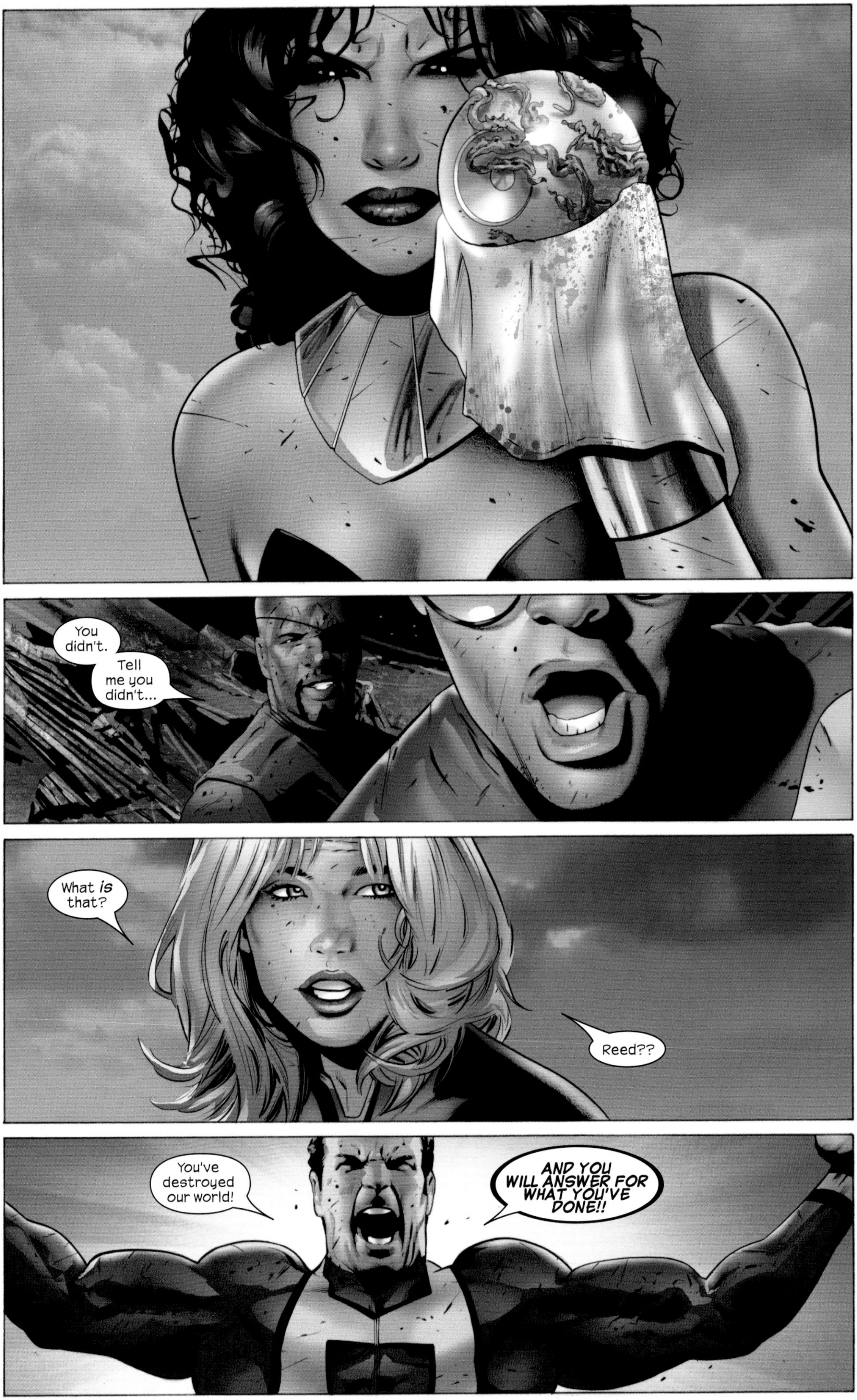

You didn't.
Tell me you didn't...
What *is* that?
Reed??
You've destroyed our world!
AND YOU WILL ANSWER FOR WHAT YOU'VE DONE!!

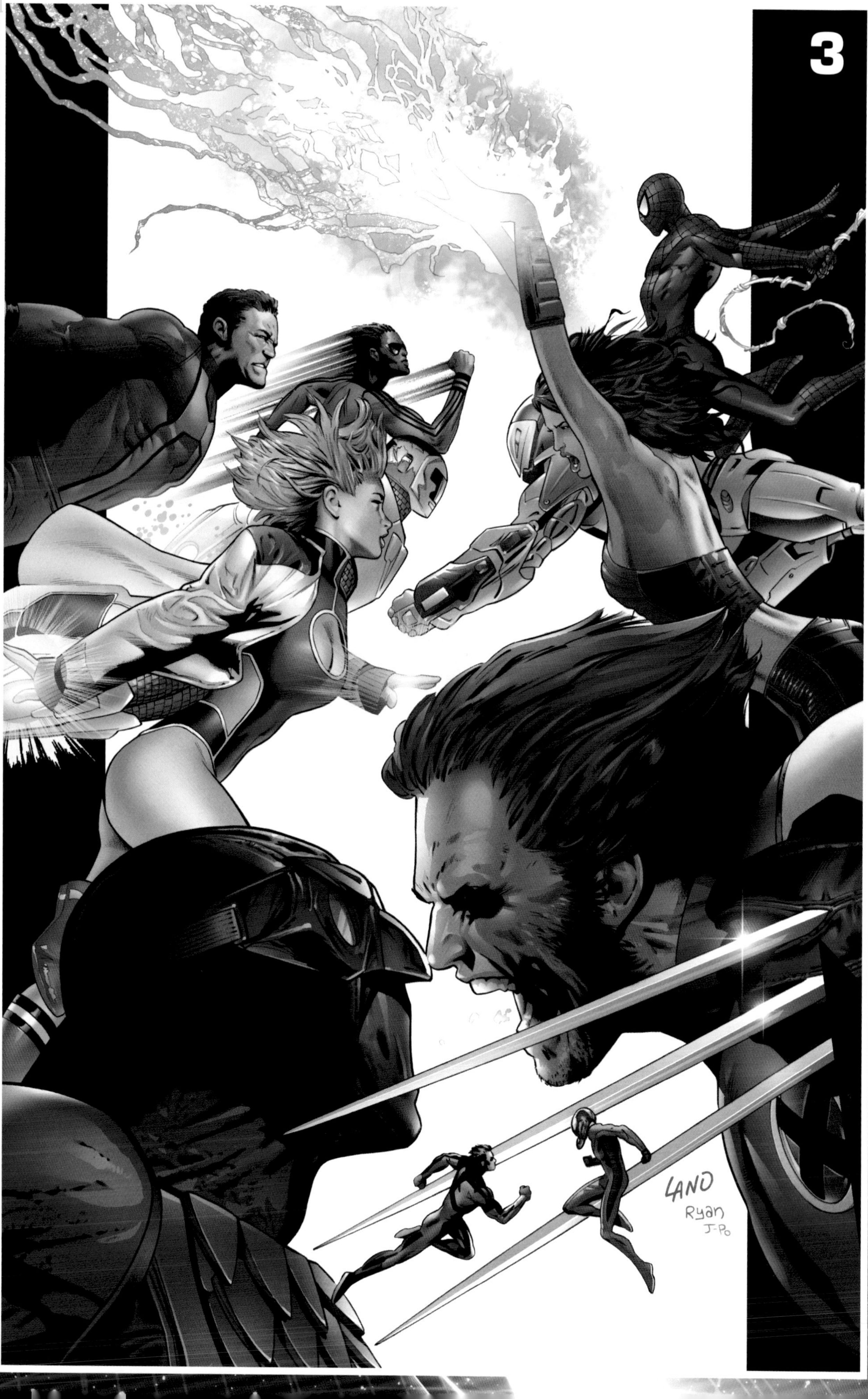
3
LAND
Ryan
J-Po

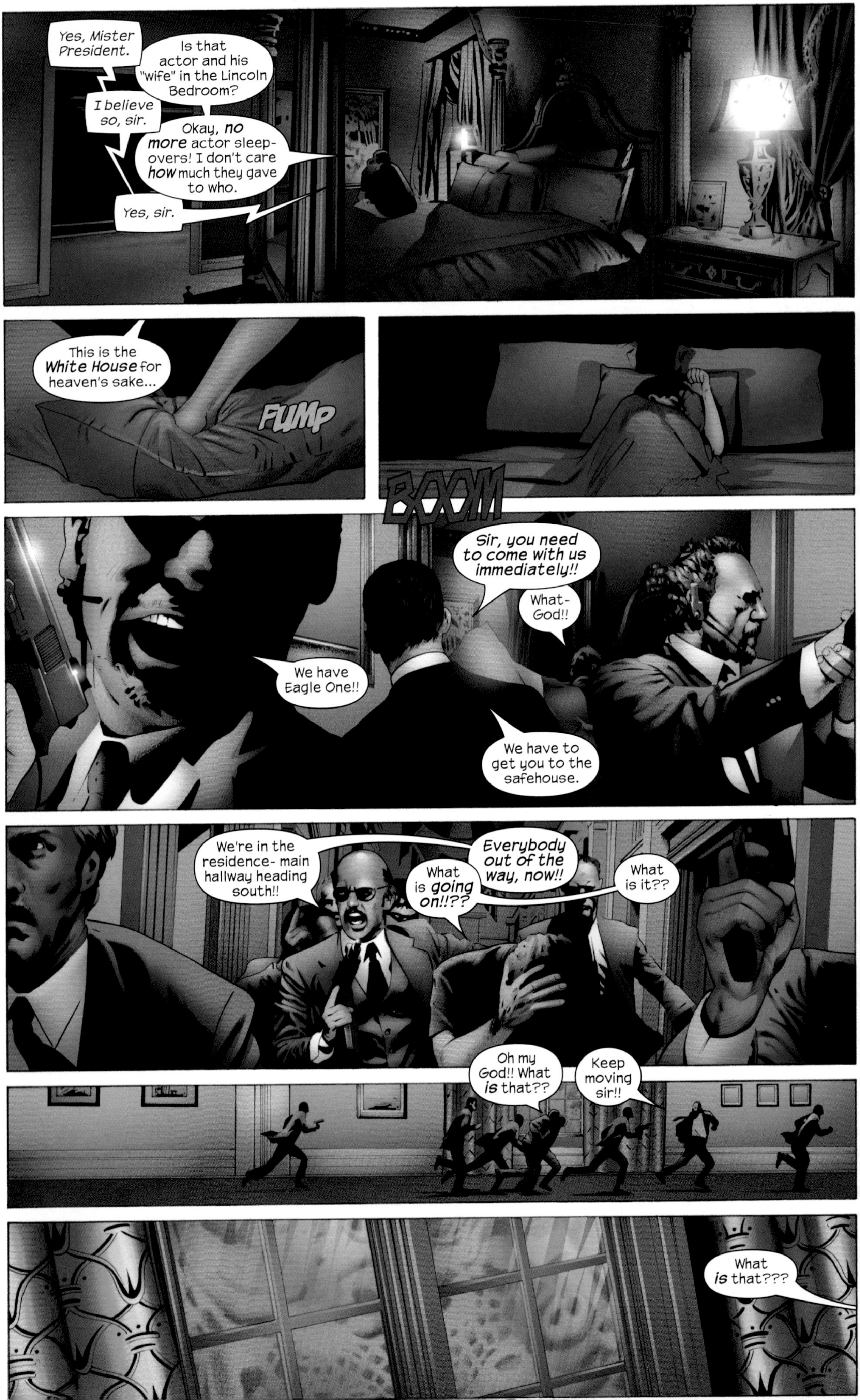
Yes, Mister President.
Is that actor and his "wife" in the Lincoln Bedroom?
I believe so, sir.
Okay, no more actor sleep-overs! I don't care how much they gave to who.
Yes, sir.
This is the White House for heaven's sake...
FUMP
BOOM
Sir, you need to come with us immediately!!
What- God!!
We have Eagle One!!
We have to get you to the safehouse.
We're in the residence- main hallway heading south!!
Everybody out of the way, now!!
What is going on!!??
What is it??
Oh my God!! What is that??
Keep moving sir!!
What is that???

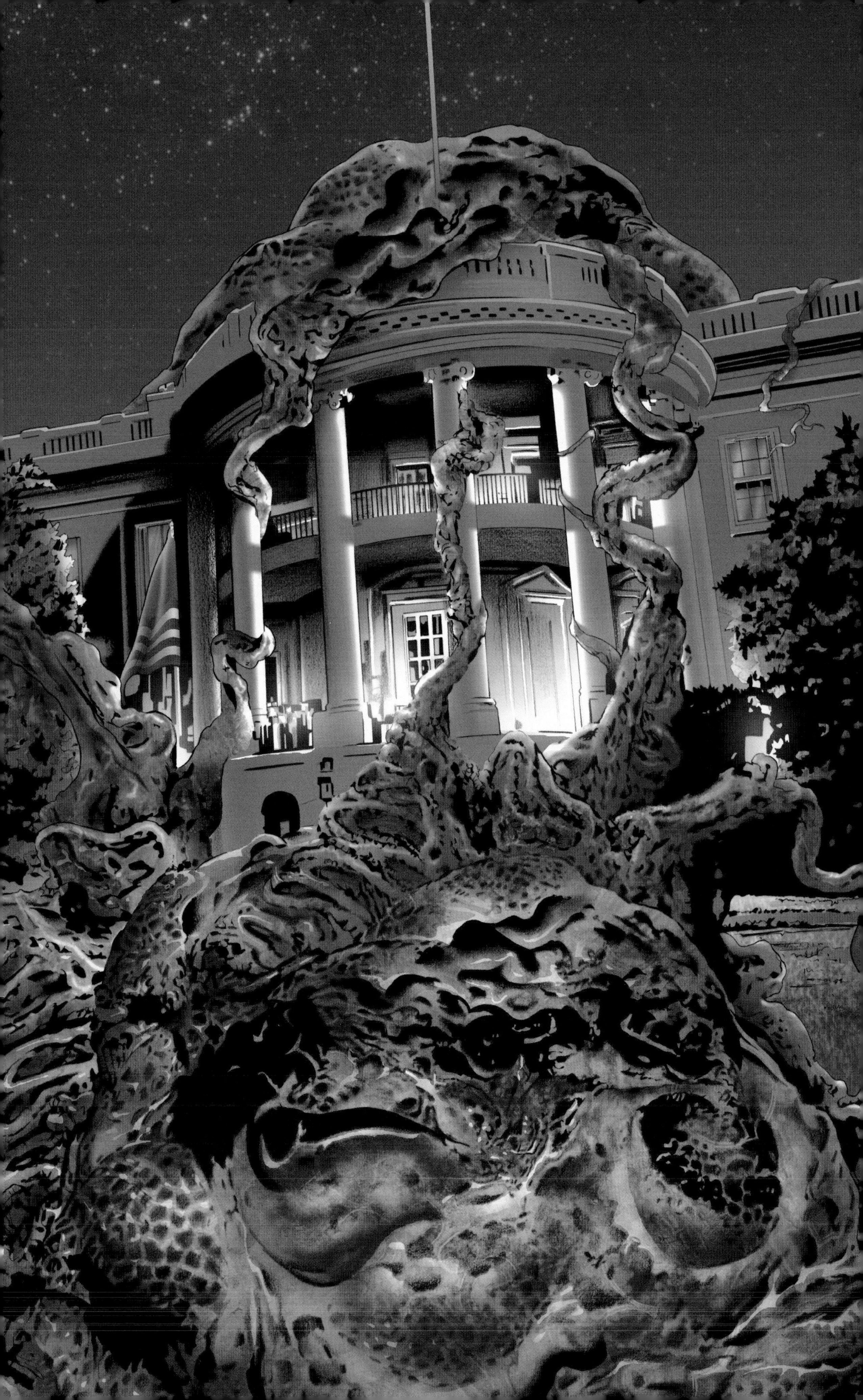

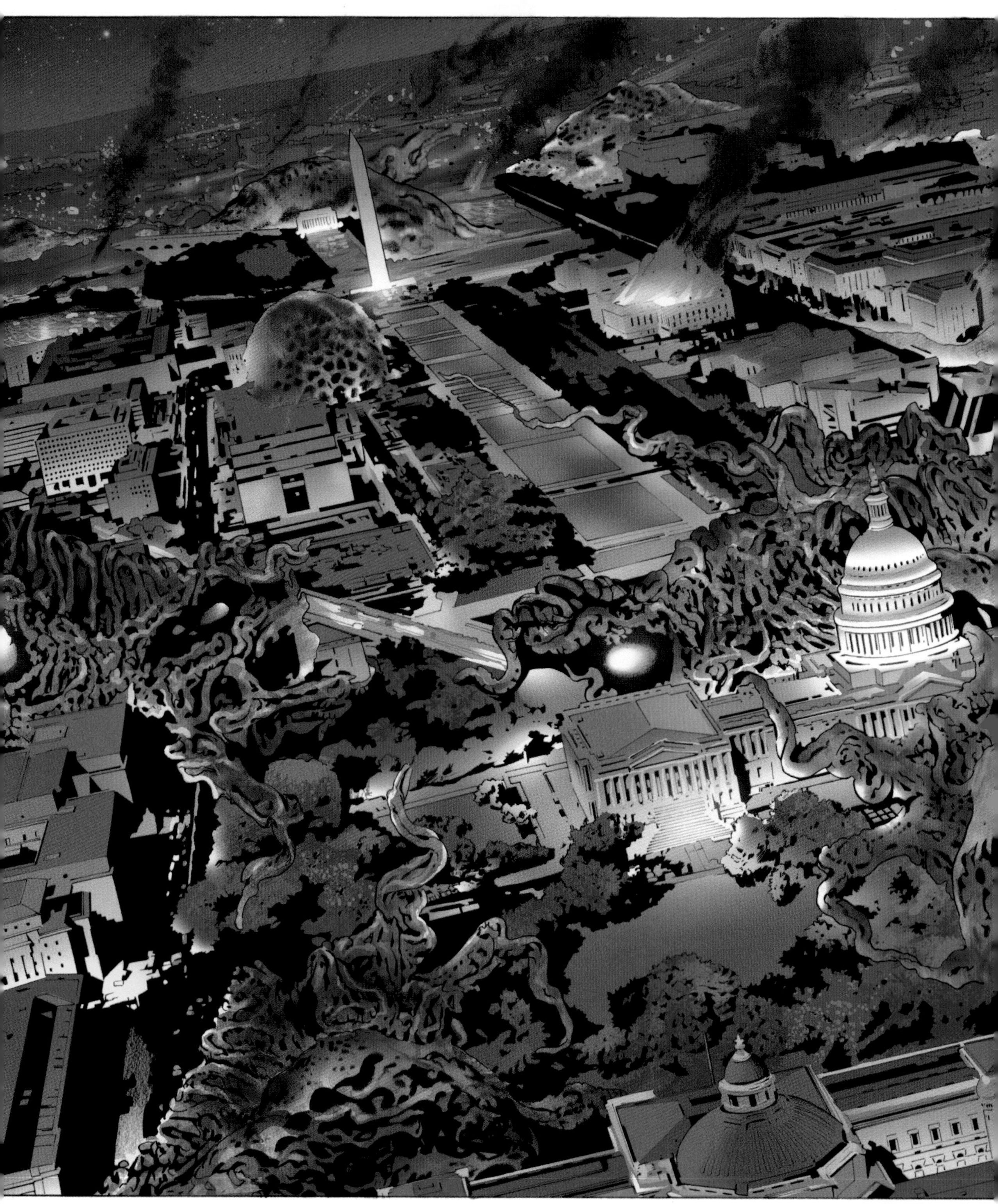
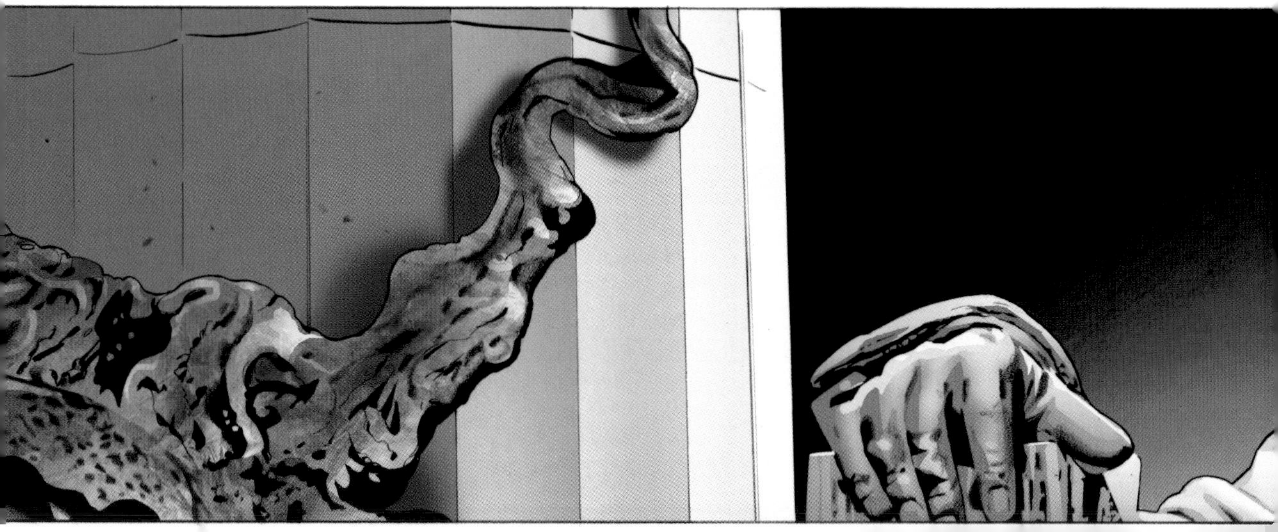

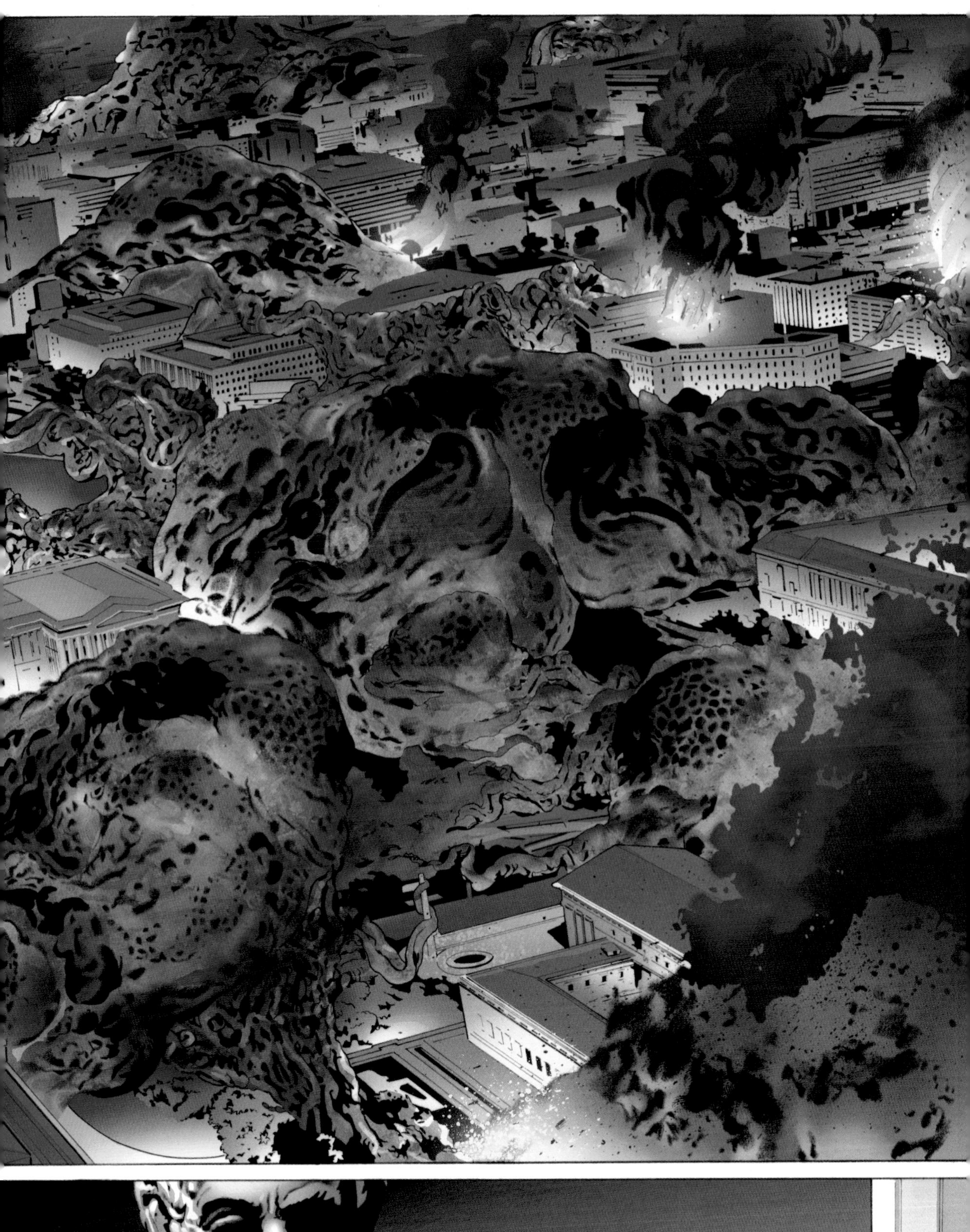

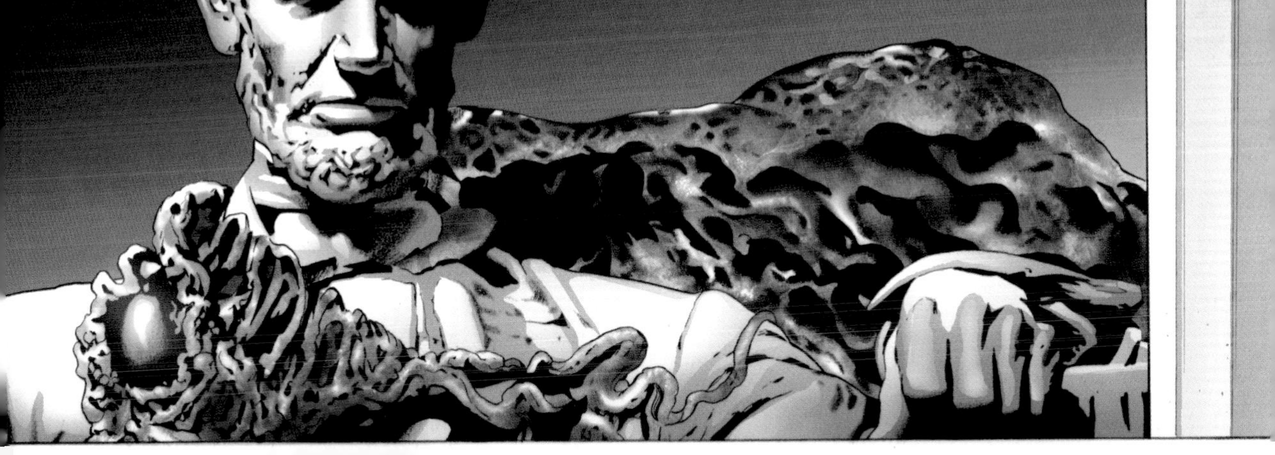

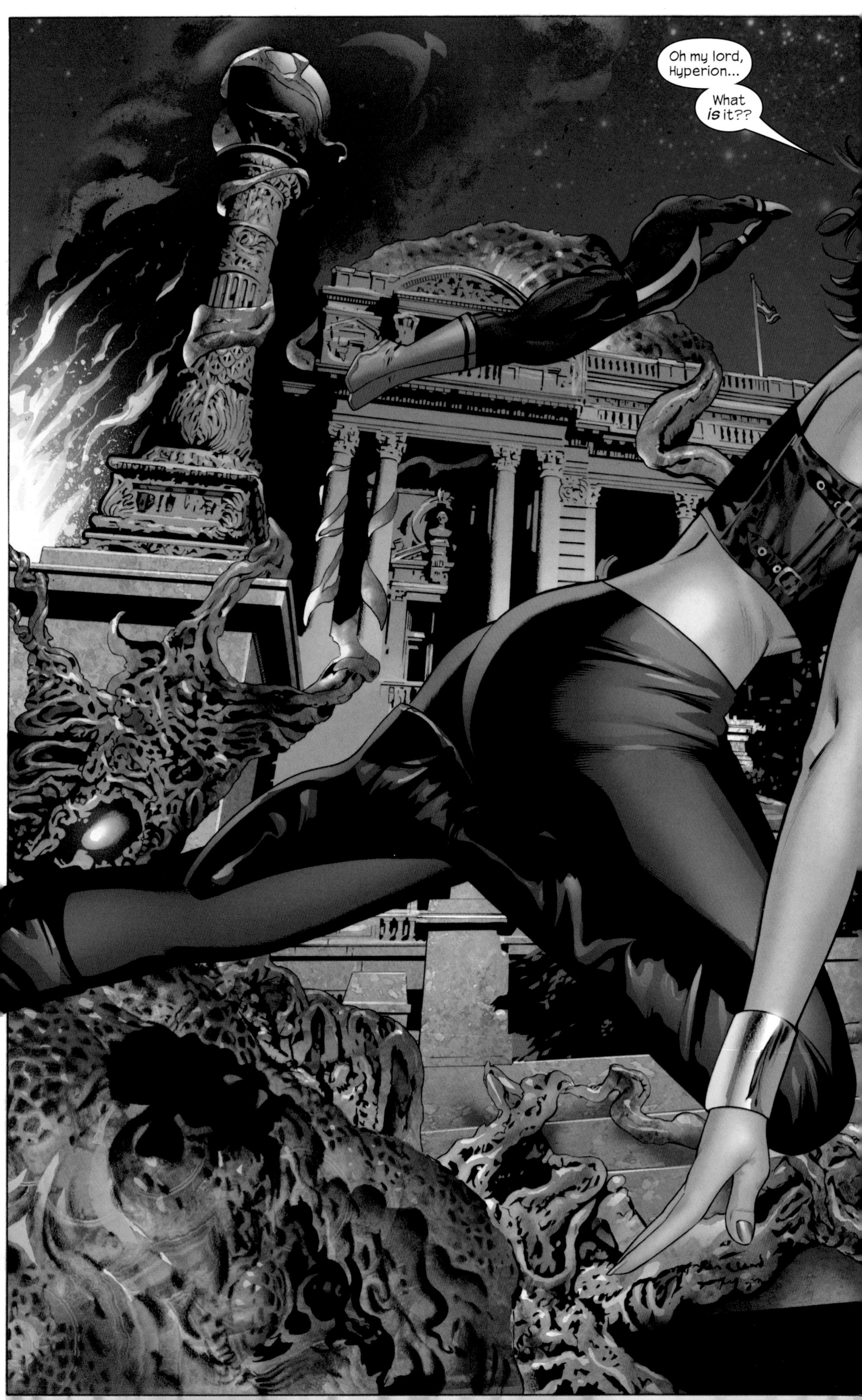
Oh my lord, Hyperion...
What *is* it??

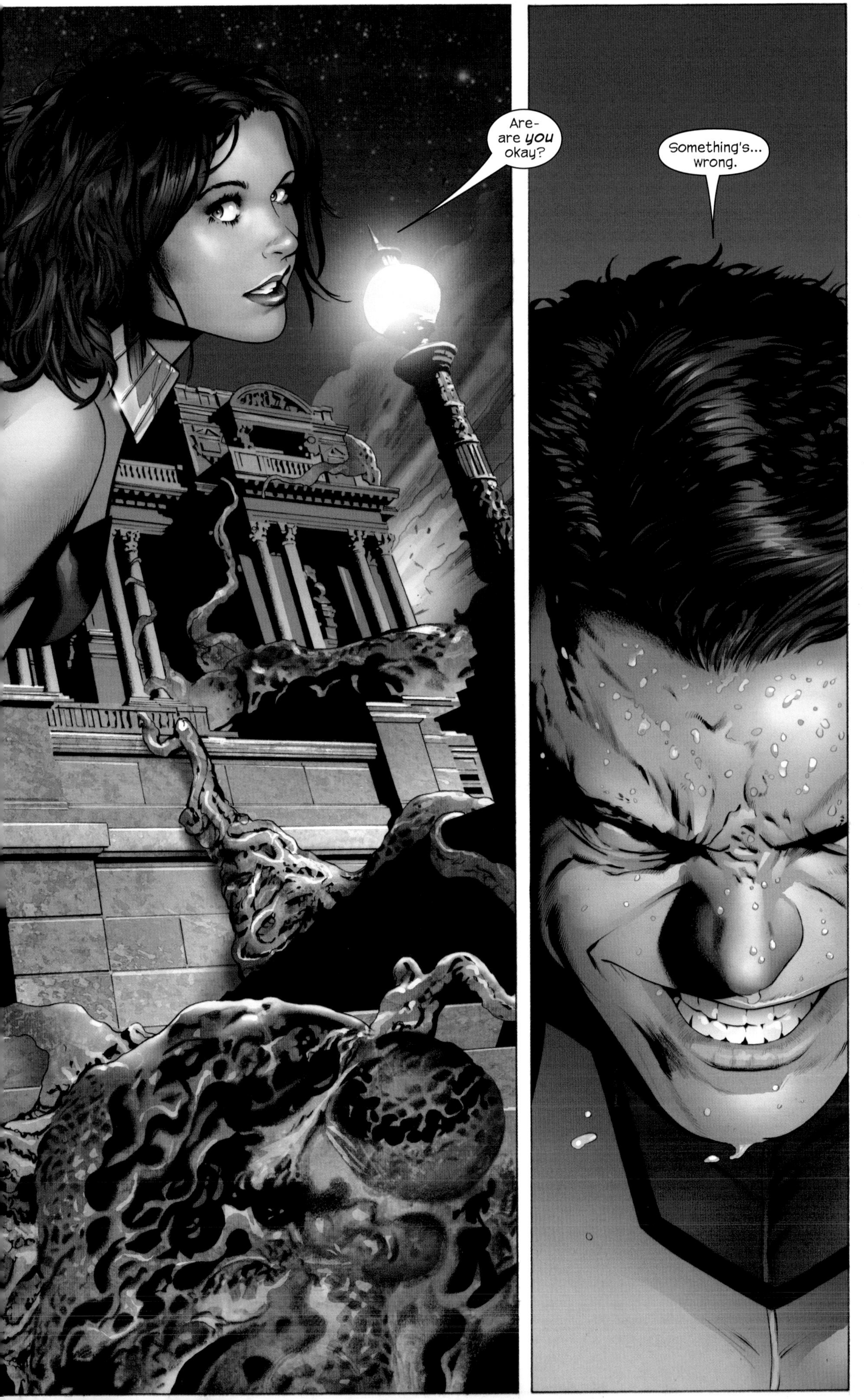
Are-
are *you* okay?
Something's... wrong.

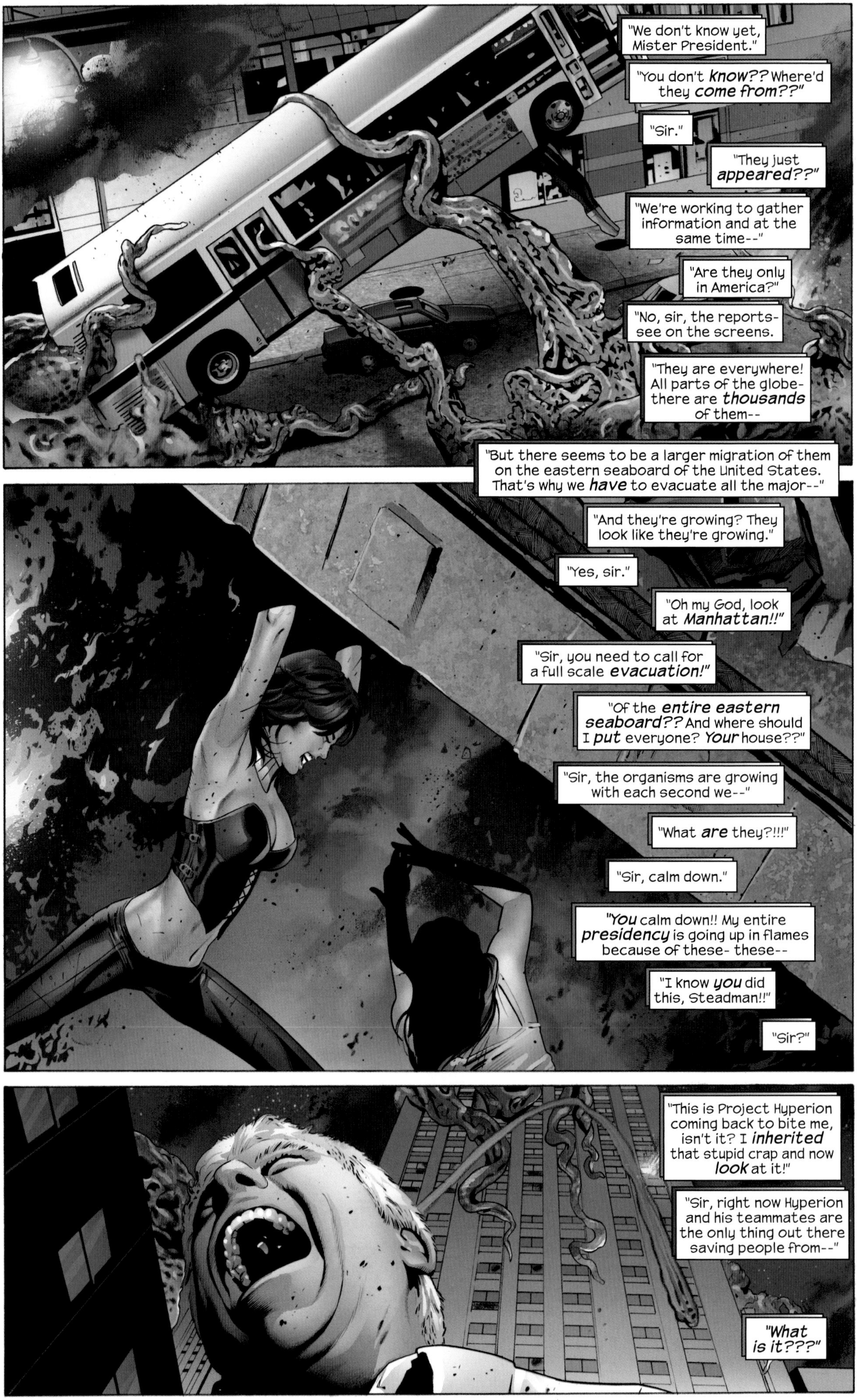
"We don't know yet, Mister President."
"You don't know?? Where'd they come from??"
"Sir."
"They just appeared??"
"We're working to gather information and at the same time--"
"Are they only in America?"
"No, sir, the reports- see on the screens.
"They are everywhere! All parts of the globe- there are thousands of them--
"But there seems to be a larger migration of them on the eastern seaboard of the United States. That's why we have to evacuate all the major--"
"And they're growing? They look like they're growing."
"Yes, sir."
"Oh my God, look at Manhattan!!"
"Sir, you need to call for a full scale evacuation!"
"Of the entire eastern seaboard?? And where should I put everyone? Your house??"
"Sir, the organisms are growing with each second we--"
"What are they?!!!"
"Sir, calm down."
"You calm down!! My entire presidency is going up in flames because of these- these--
"I know you did this, Steadman!!"
"Sir?"
"This is Project Hyperion coming back to bite me, isn't it? I inherited that stupid crap and now look at it!"
"Sir, right now Hyperion and his teammates are the only thing out there saving people from--"
"What is it???"

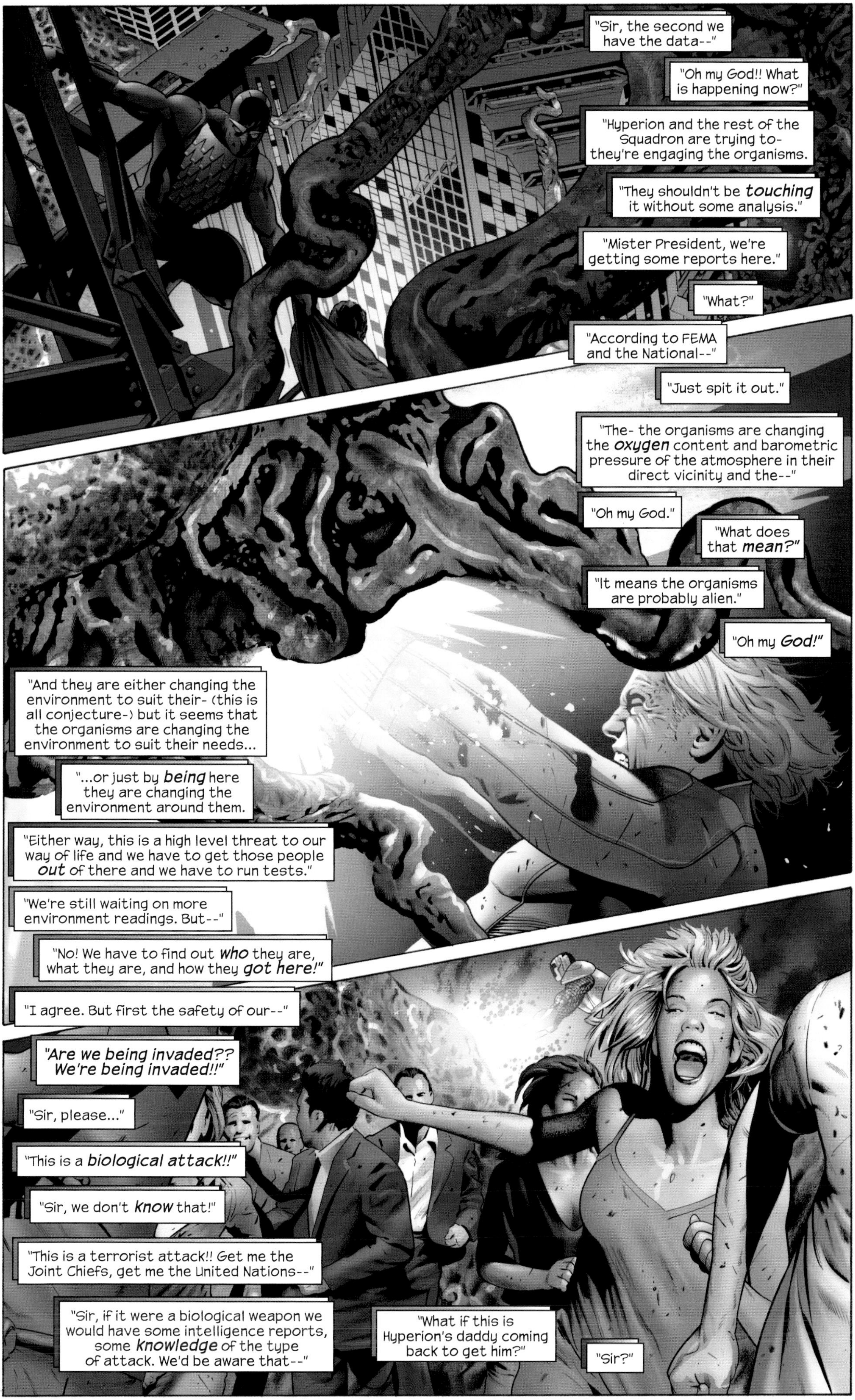
"Sir, the second we have the data--"
"Oh my God!! What is happening now?"
"Hyperion and the rest of the Squadron are trying to- they're engaging the organisms.
"They shouldn't be *touching* it without some analysis."
"Mister President, we're getting some reports here."
"What?"
"According to FEMA and the National--"
"Just spit it out."
"The- the organisms are changing the *oxygen* content and barometric pressure of the atmosphere in their direct vicinity and the--"
"Oh my God."
"What does that *mean?*"
"It means the organisms are probably alien."
"Oh my *God!*"
"And they are either changing the environment to suit their- (this is all conjecture-) but it seems that the organisms are changing the environment to suit their needs...
"...or just by *being* here they are changing the environment around them.
"Either way, this is a high level threat to our way of life and we have to get those people *out* of there and we have to run tests."
"We're still waiting on more environment readings. But--"
"No! We have to find out *who* they are, what they are, and how they *got here!*"
"I agree. But first the safety of our--"
"Are we being invaded?? We're being invaded!!"
"Sir, please..."
"This is a *biological attack!!"*
"Sir, we don't *know* that!"
"This is a terrorist attack!! Get me the Joint Chiefs, get me the United Nations--"
"Sir, if it were a biological weapon we would have some intelligence reports, some *knowledge* of the type of attack. We'd be aware that--"
"What if this is Hyperion's daddy coming back to get him?"
"Sir?"

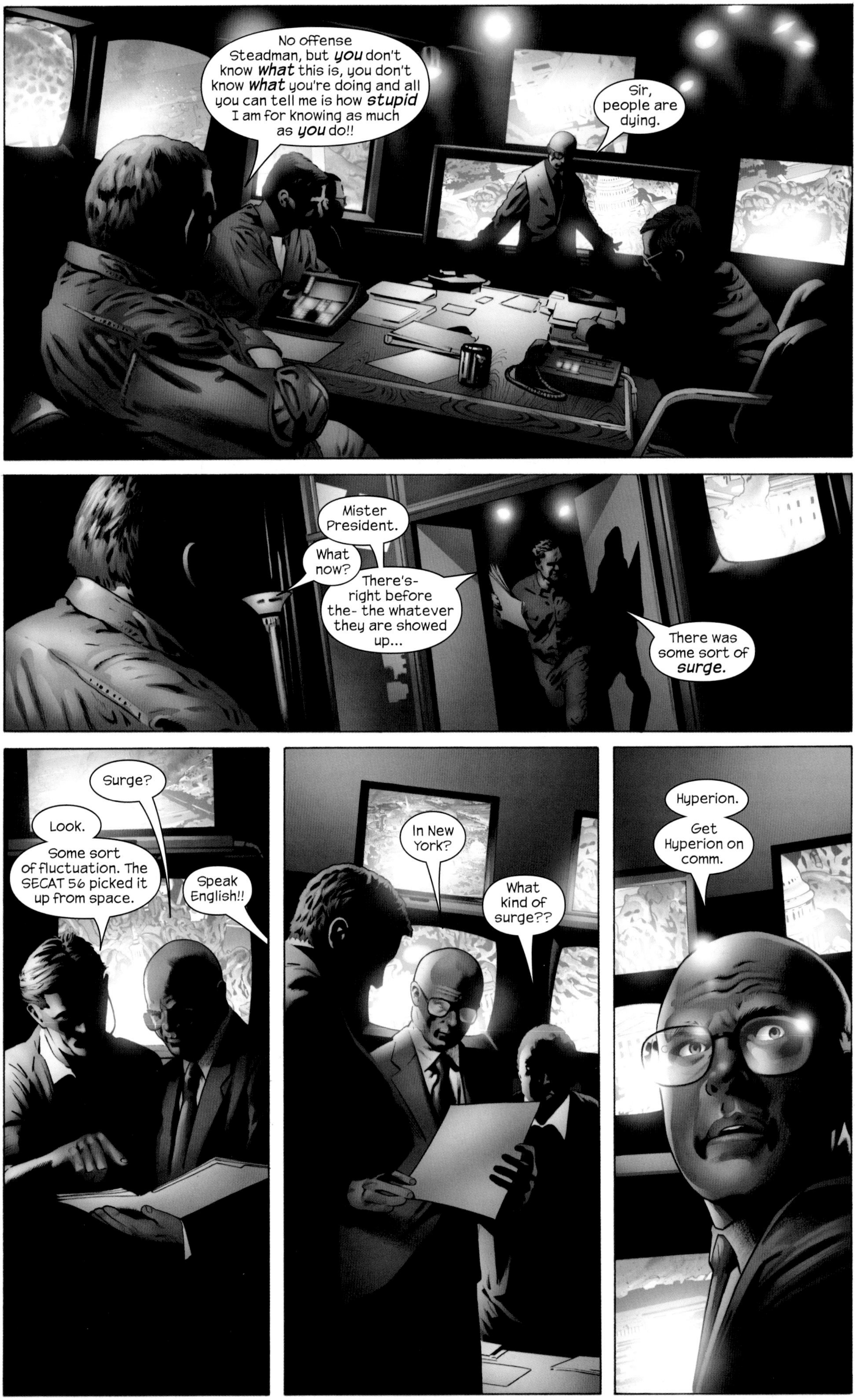
No offense Steadman, but *you* don't know *what* this is, you don't know *what* you're doing and all you can tell me is how *stupid* I am for knowing as much as *you* do!!
Sir, people are dying.
Mister President.
What now?
There's- right before the- the whatever they are showed up...
There was some sort of *surge.*
Surge?
Look.
Some sort of fluctuation. The SECAT 56 picked it up from space.
Speak English!!
In New York?
What kind of surge??
Hyperion.
Get Hyperion on comm.

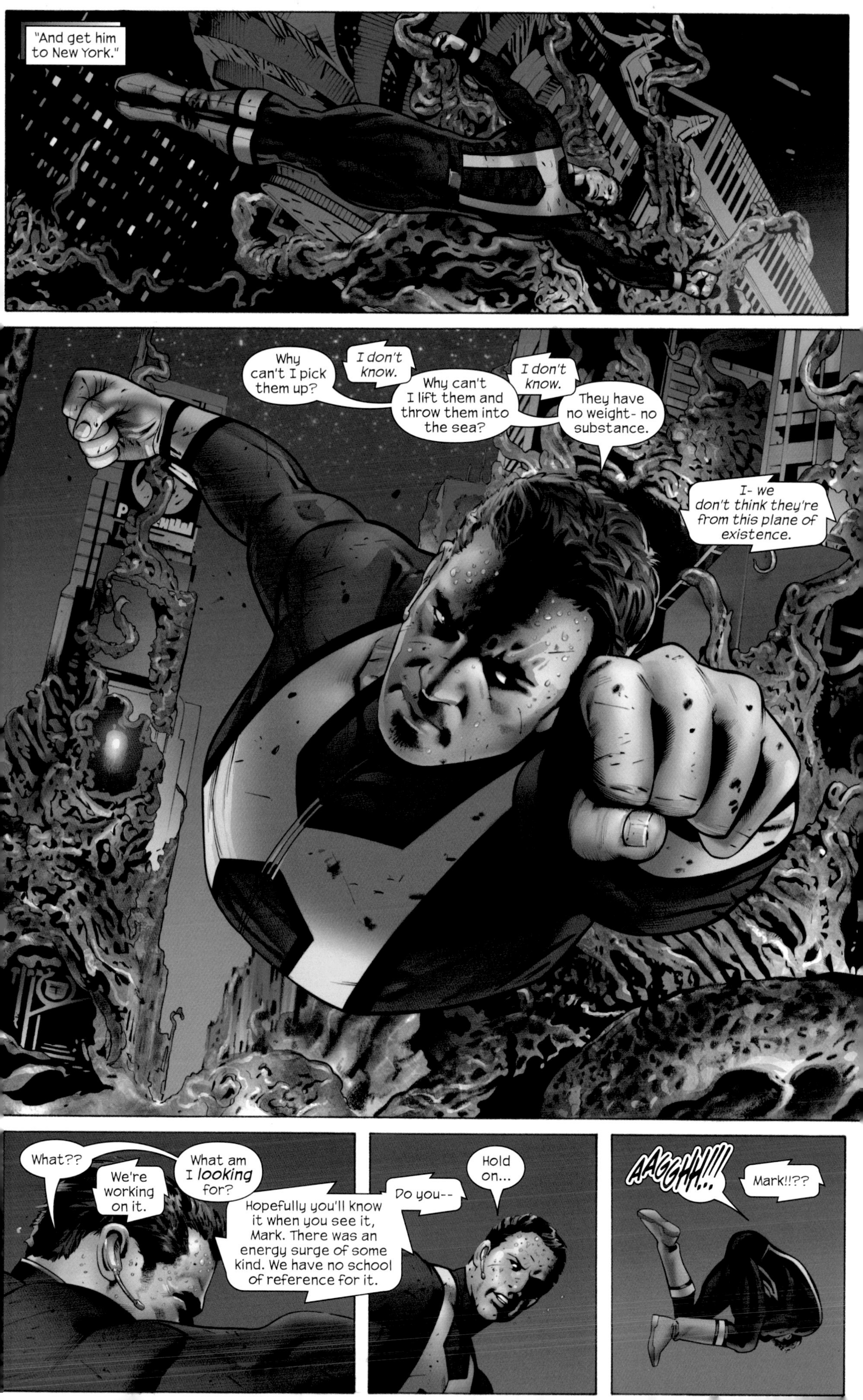
"And get him to New York."
Why can't I pick them up?
I don't know.
Why can't I lift them and throw them into the sea?
I don't know.
They have no weight- no substance.
I- we don't think they're from this plane of existence.
What??
We're working on it.
What am I *looking* for?
Hopefully you'll know it when you see it, Mark. There was an energy surge of some kind. We have no school of reference for it.
Do you--
Hold on...
AAGGHH!!!
Mark!!??

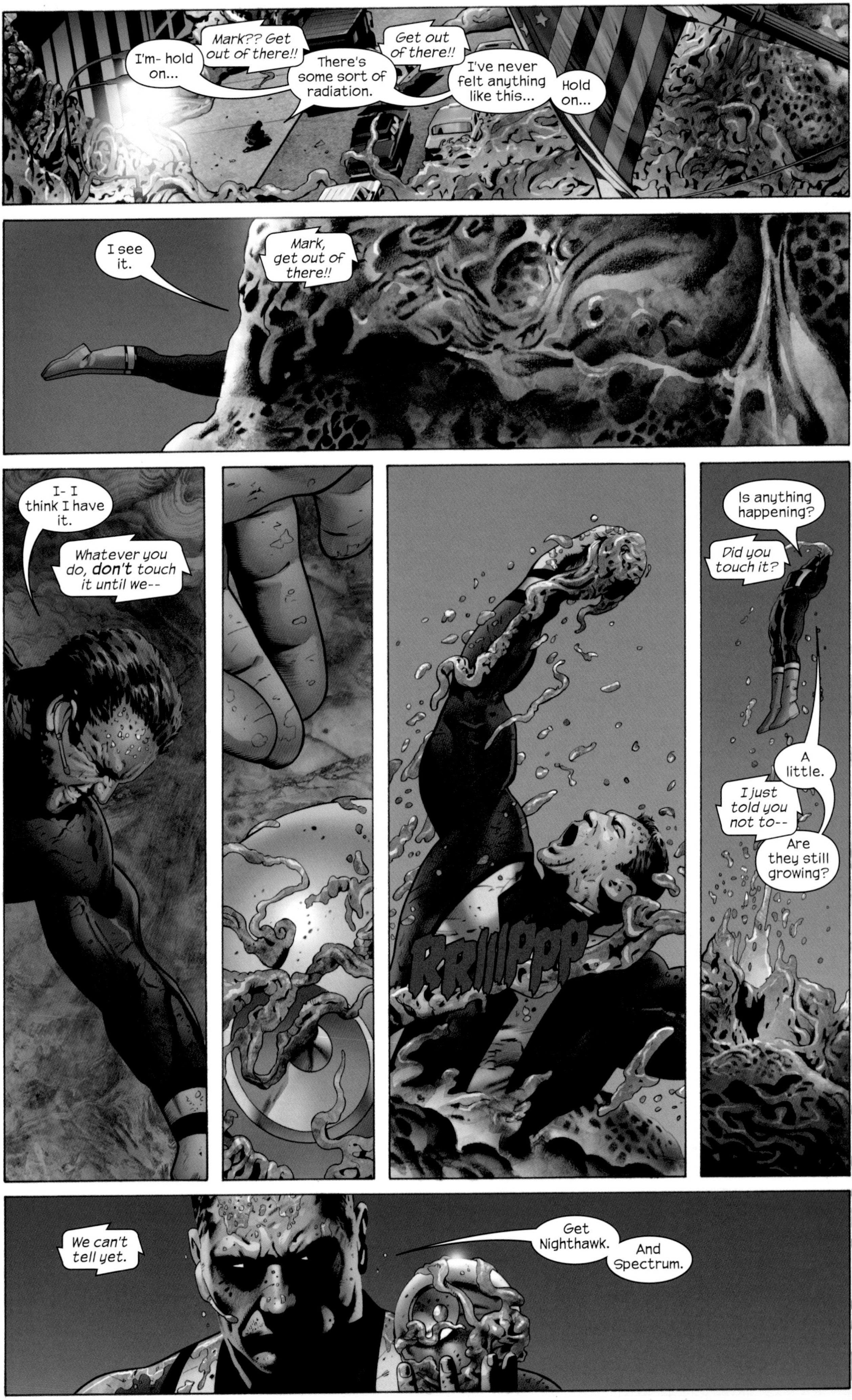
I'm- hold on...
Mark?? Get out of there!!
There's some sort of radiation.
Get out of there!!
I've never felt anything like this...
Hold on...
I see it.
Mark, get out of there!!
I- I think I have it.
Whatever you do, **don't** touch it until we--
RRIIIPPP
Is anything happening?
Did you touch it?
A little.
I just told you not to--
Are they still growing?
We can't tell yet.
Get Nighthawk.
And Spectrum.

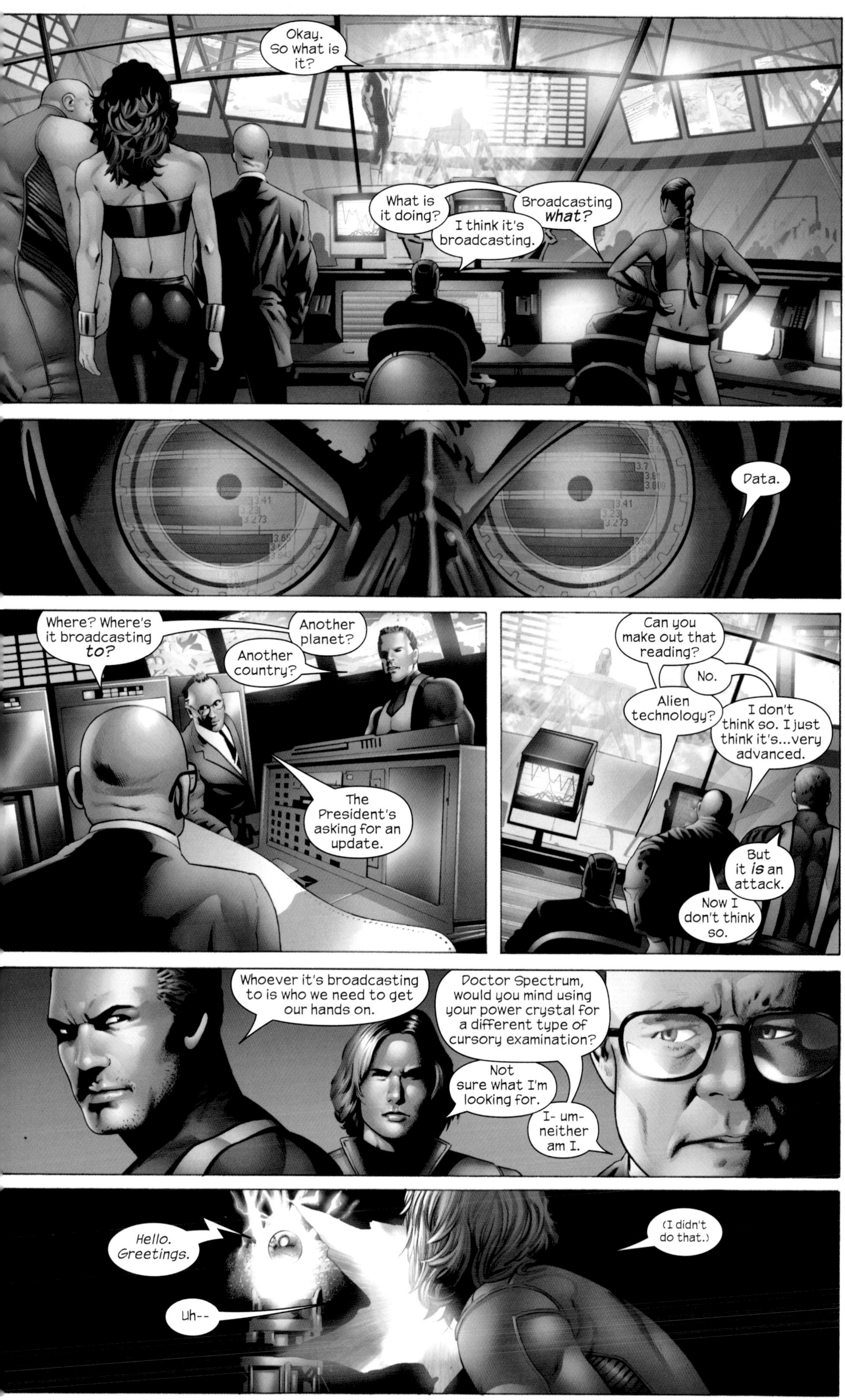
Okay. So what is it?
What is it doing?
I think it's broadcasting.
Broadcasting *what?*
Data.
Where? Where's it broadcasting *to?*
Another planet?
Another country?
The President's asking for an update.
Can you make out that reading?
No.
Alien technology?
I don't think so. I just think it's...very advanced.
But it *is* an attack.
Now I don't think so.
Whoever it's broadcasting to is who we need to get our hands on.
Doctor Spectrum, would you mind using your power crystal for a different type of cursory examination?
Not sure what I'm looking for.
I- um- neither am I.
Hello. Greetings.
(I didn't do that.)
Uh--

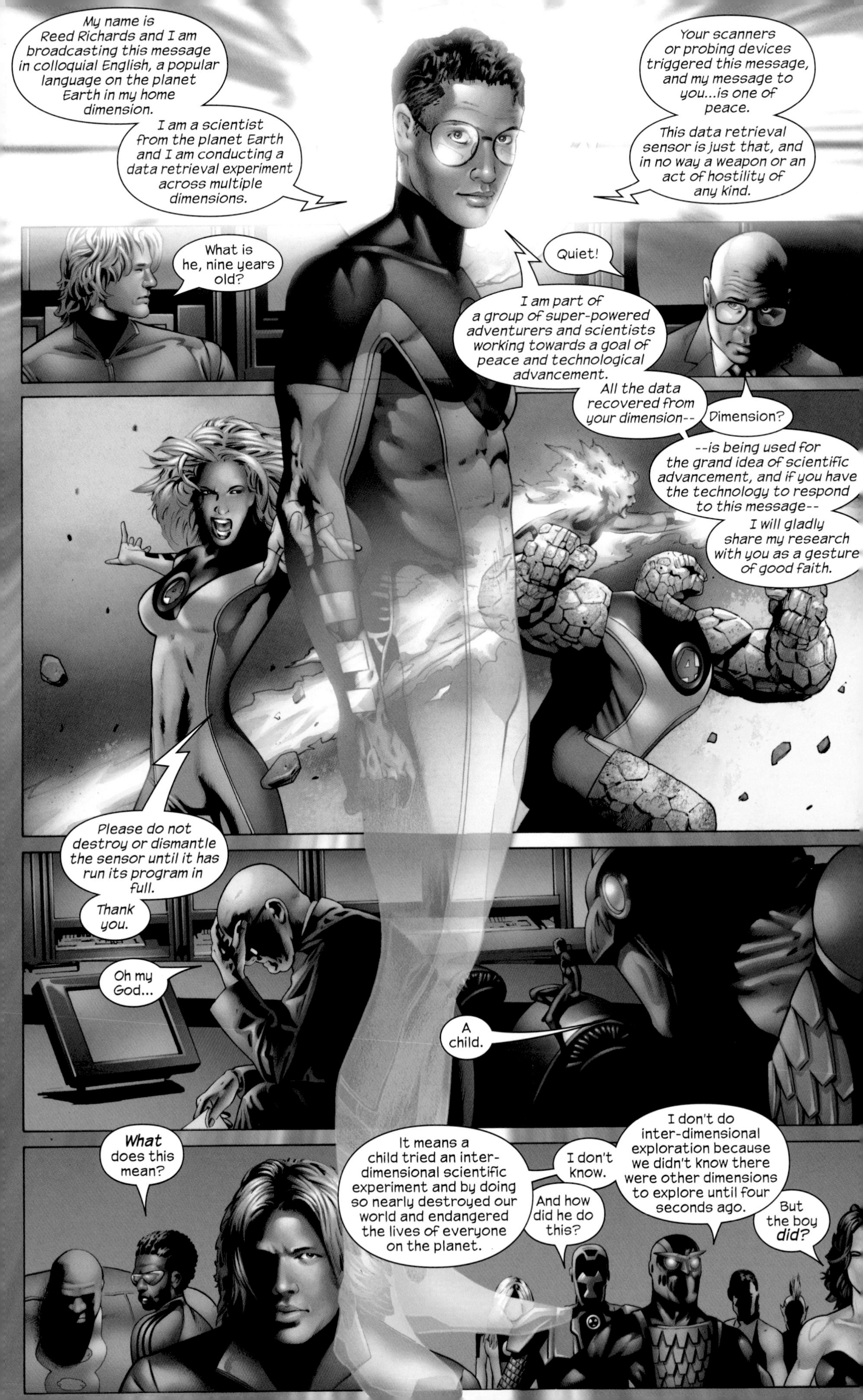
My name is Reed Richards and I am broadcasting this message in colloquial English, a popular language on the planet Earth in my home dimension.
I am a scientist from the planet Earth and I am conducting a data retrieval experiment across multiple dimensions.
Your scanners or probing devices triggered this message, and my message to you...is one of peace.
This data retrieval sensor is just that, and in no way a weapon or an act of hostility of any kind.
What is he, nine years old?
Quiet!
I am part of a group of super-powered adventurers and scientists working towards a goal of peace and technological advancement.
All the data recovered from your dimension--
Dimension?
--is being used for the grand idea of scientific advancement, and if you have the technology to respond to this message--
I will gladly share my research with you as a gesture of good faith.
Please do not destroy or dismantle the sensor until it has run its program in full.
Thank you.
Oh my God...
A child.
What does this mean?
It means a child tried an inter-dimensional scientific experiment and by doing so nearly destroyed our world and endangered the lives of everyone on the planet.
I don't know.
And how did he do this?
I don't do inter-dimensional exploration because we didn't know there were other dimensions to explore until four seconds ago.
But the boy *did?*

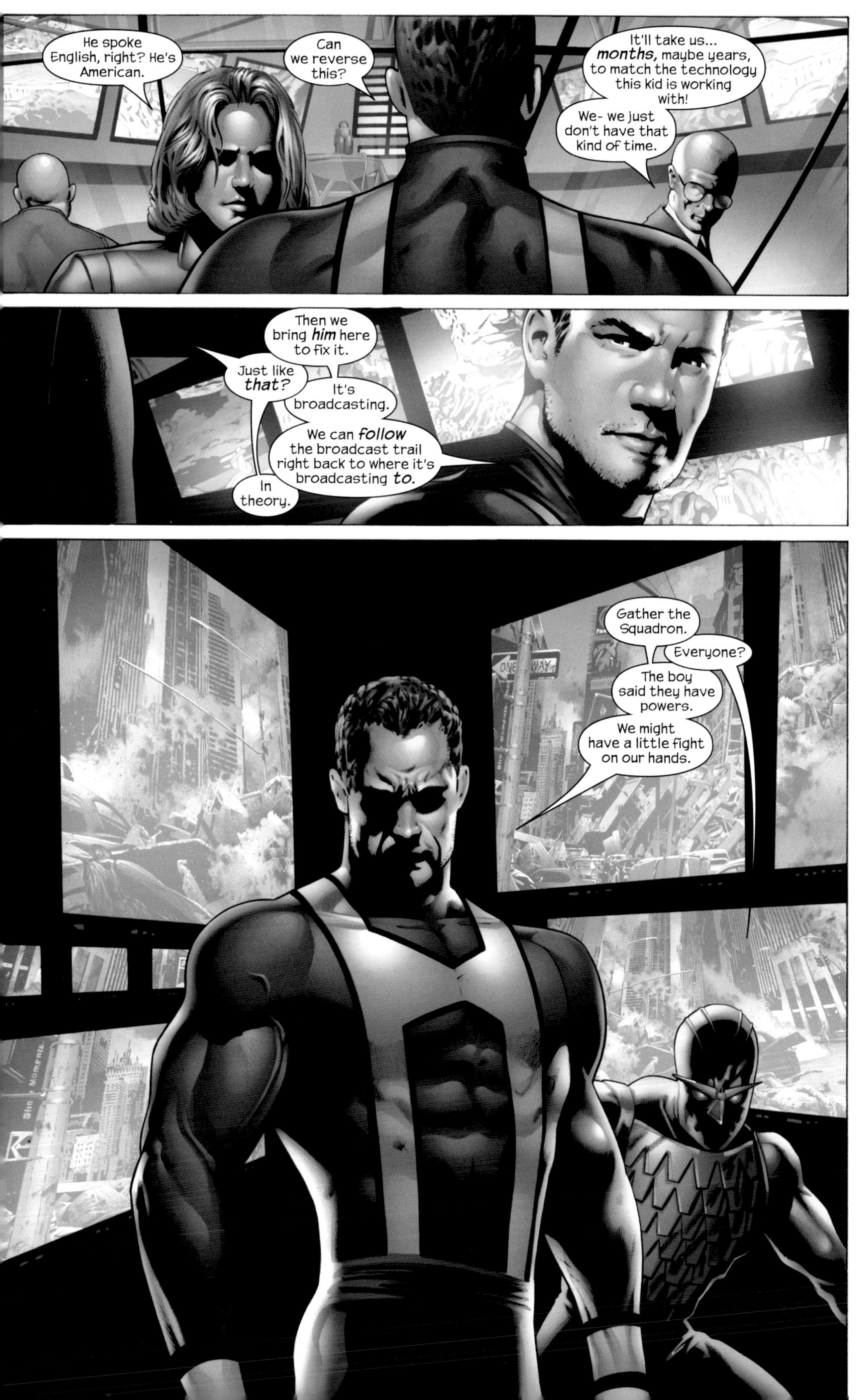
He spoke English, right? He's American.
Can we reverse this?
It'll take us... ***months,*** maybe years, to match the technology this kid is working with!
We- we just don't have that kind of time.
Then we bring ***him*** here to fix it.
Just like ***that?***
It's broadcasting.
We can ***follow*** the broadcast trail right back to where it's broadcasting ***to.***
In theory.
Gather the Squadron.
Everyone?
The boy said they have powers.
We might have a little fight on our hands.

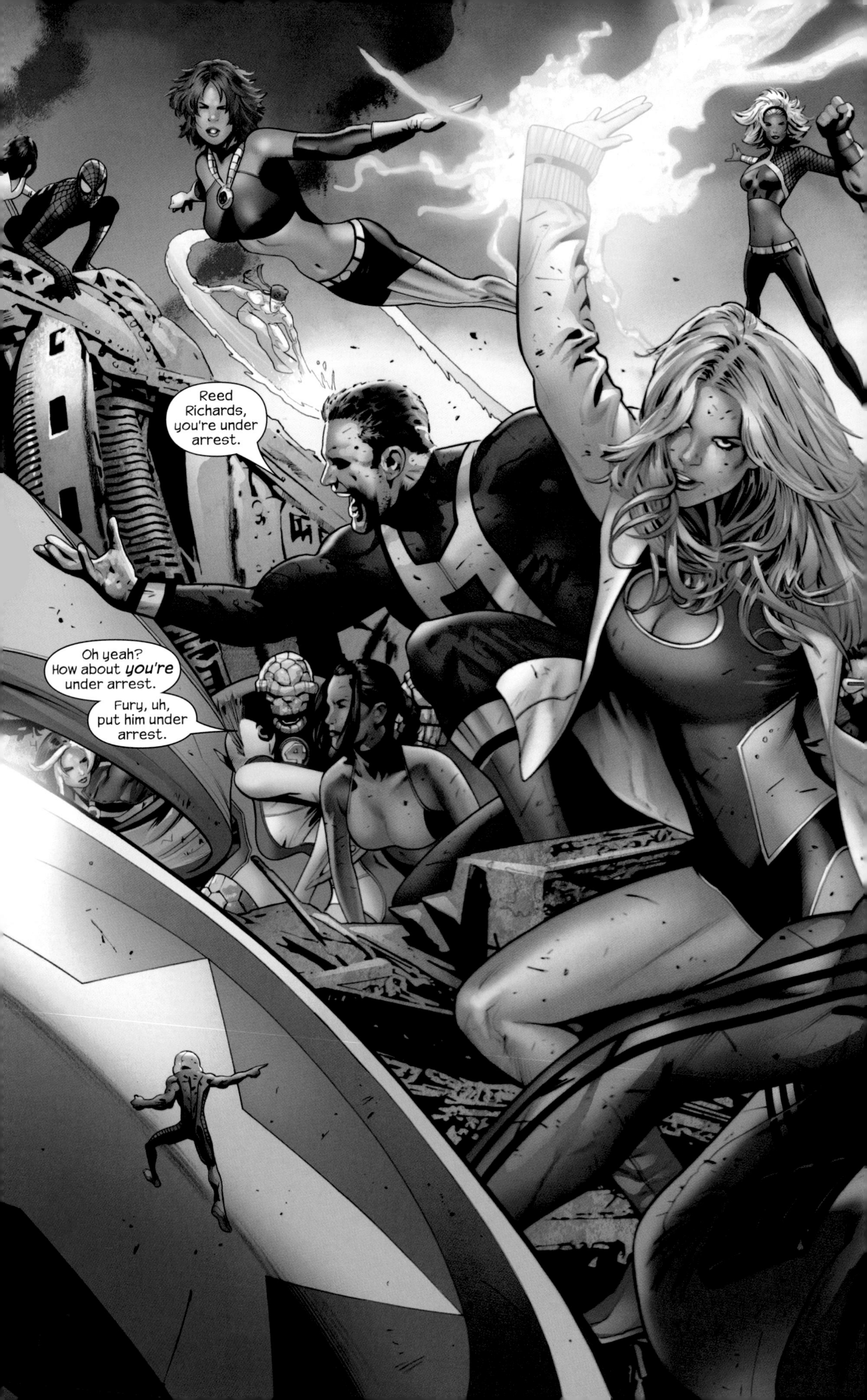
Reed Richards, you're under arrest.
Oh yeah? How about *you're* under arrest.
Fury, uh, put him under arrest.

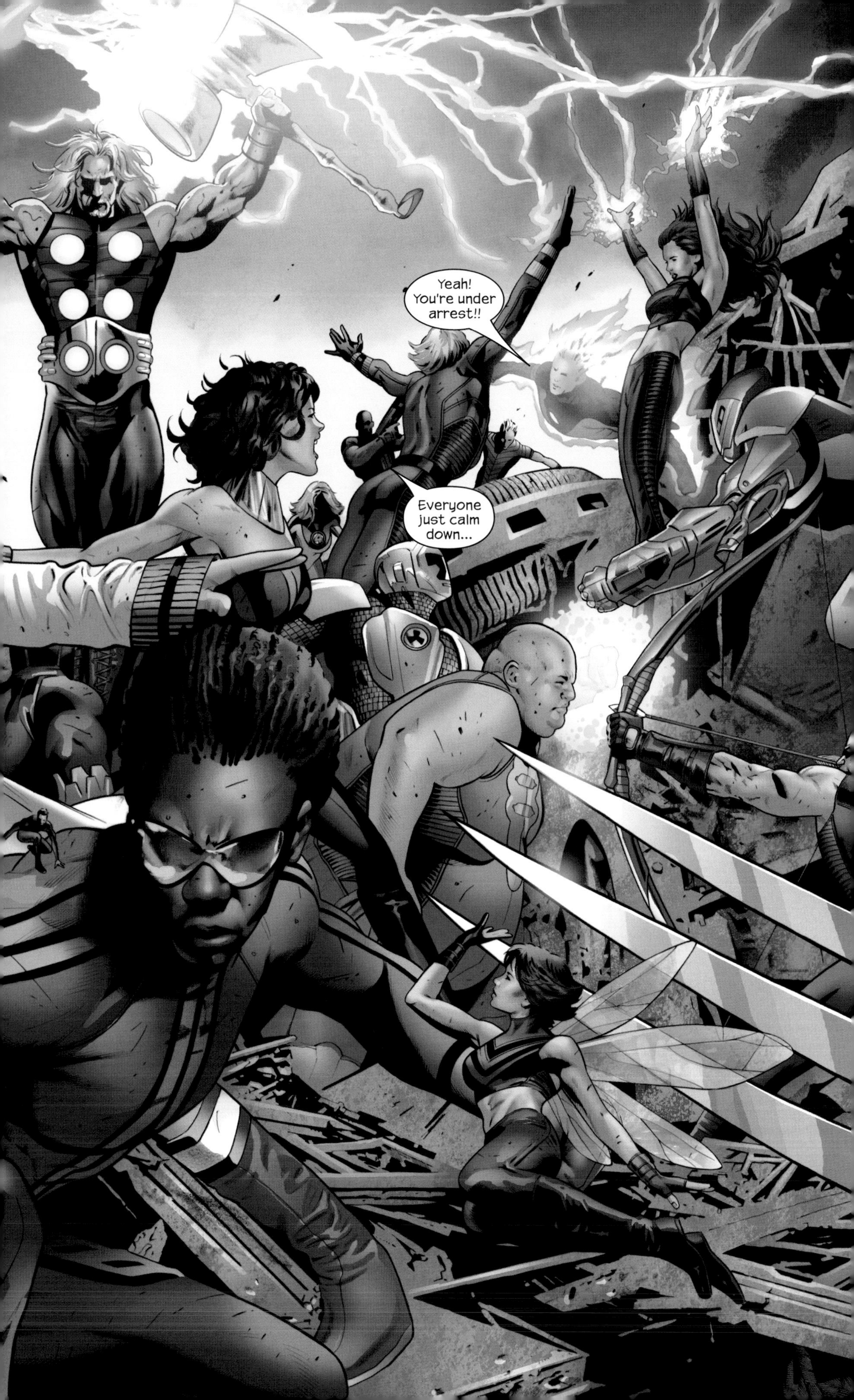
Yeah! You're under arrest!!
Everyone just calm down...

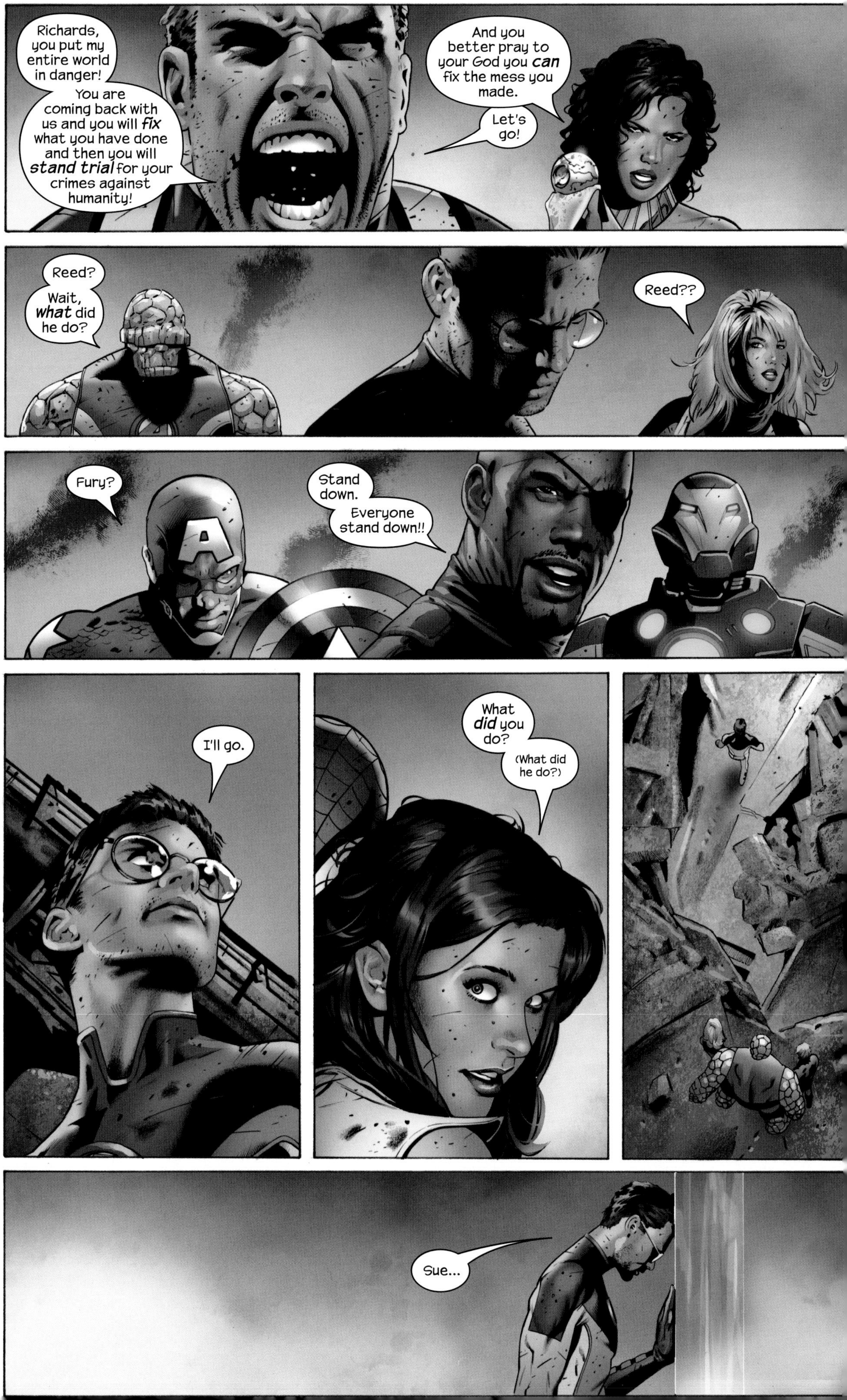
Richards, you put my entire world in danger!
You are coming back with us and you will *fix* what you have done and then you will ***stand trial*** for your crimes against humanity!
And you better pray to your God you ***can*** fix the mess you made.
Let's go!
Reed?
Wait, ***what*** did he do?
Reed??
Fury?
Stand down.
Everyone stand down!!
I'll go.
What ***did*** you do?
(What did he do?)
Sue...

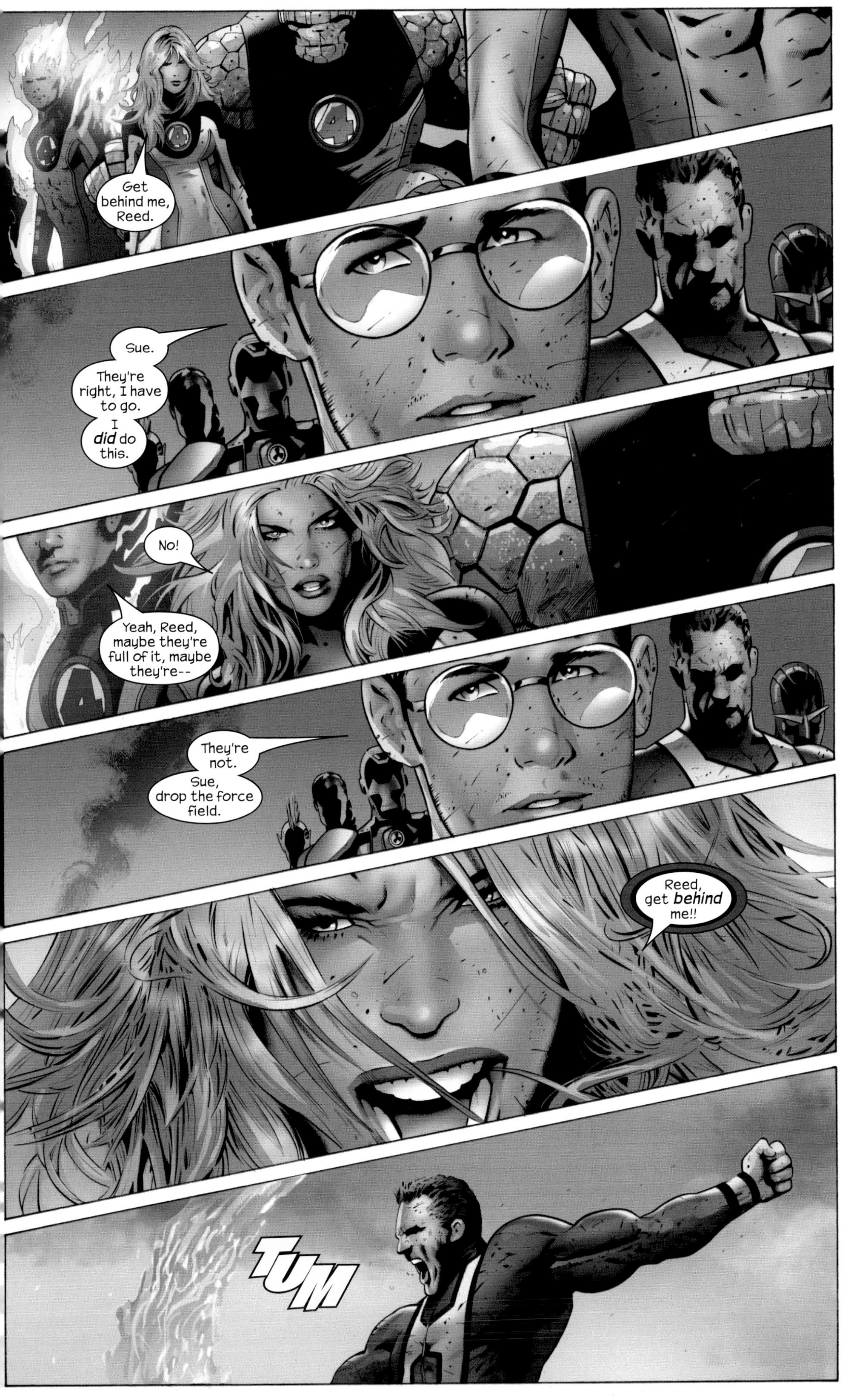
Get behind me, Reed.
Sue.
They're right, I have to go.
I *did* do this.
No!
Yeah, Reed, maybe they're full of it, maybe they're--
They're not.
Sue, drop the force field.
Reed, get *behind* me!!
TUM

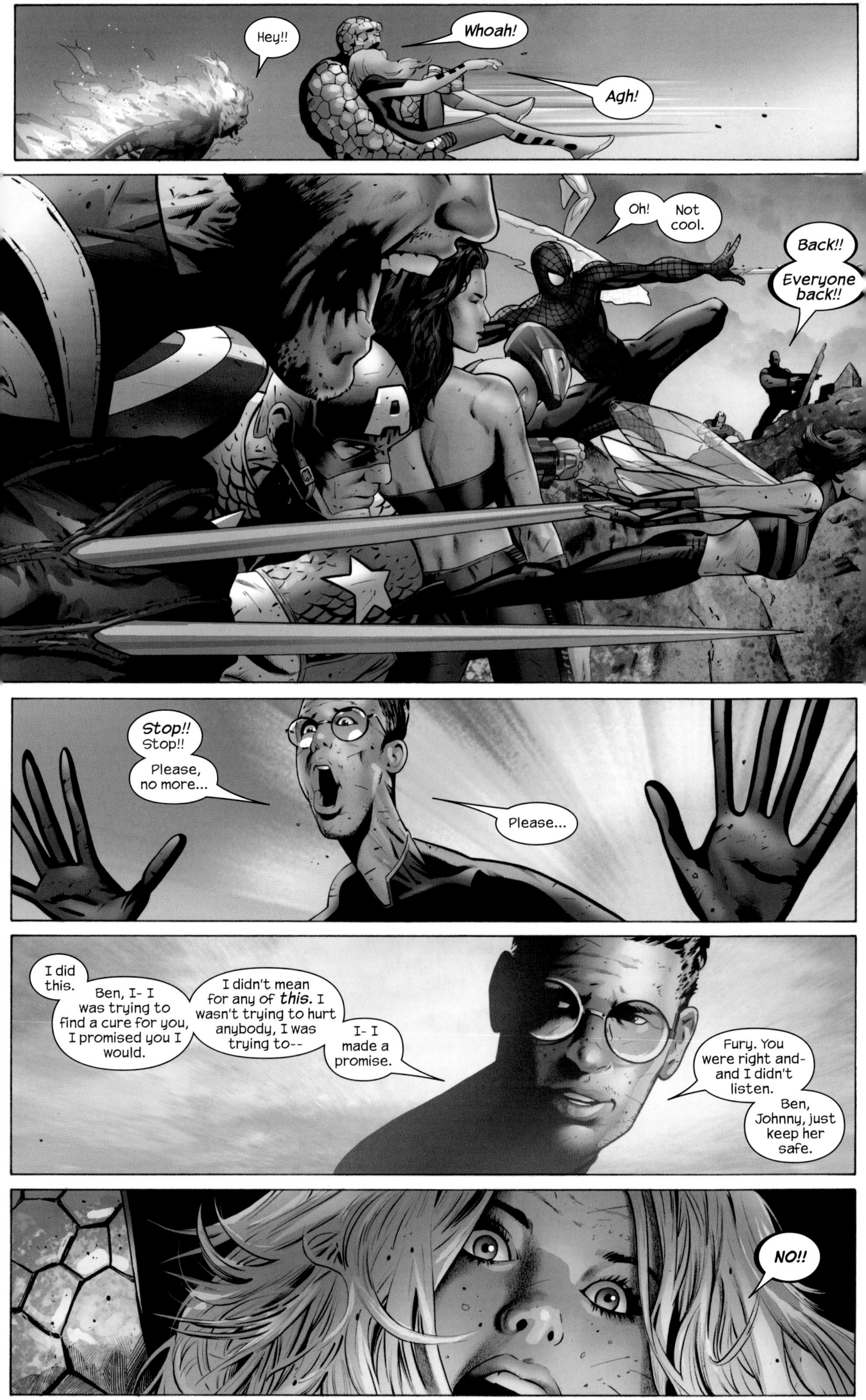
Hey!!
Whoah!
Agh!
Oh!
Not cool.
Back!!
Everyone back!!
Stop!! Stop!!
Please, no more...
Please...
I did this.
Ben, I- I was trying to find a cure for you, I promised you I would.
I didn't mean for any of this. I wasn't trying to hurt anybody, I was trying to--
I- I made a promise.
Fury. You were right and- and I didn't listen.
Ben, Johnny, just keep her safe.
NO!!

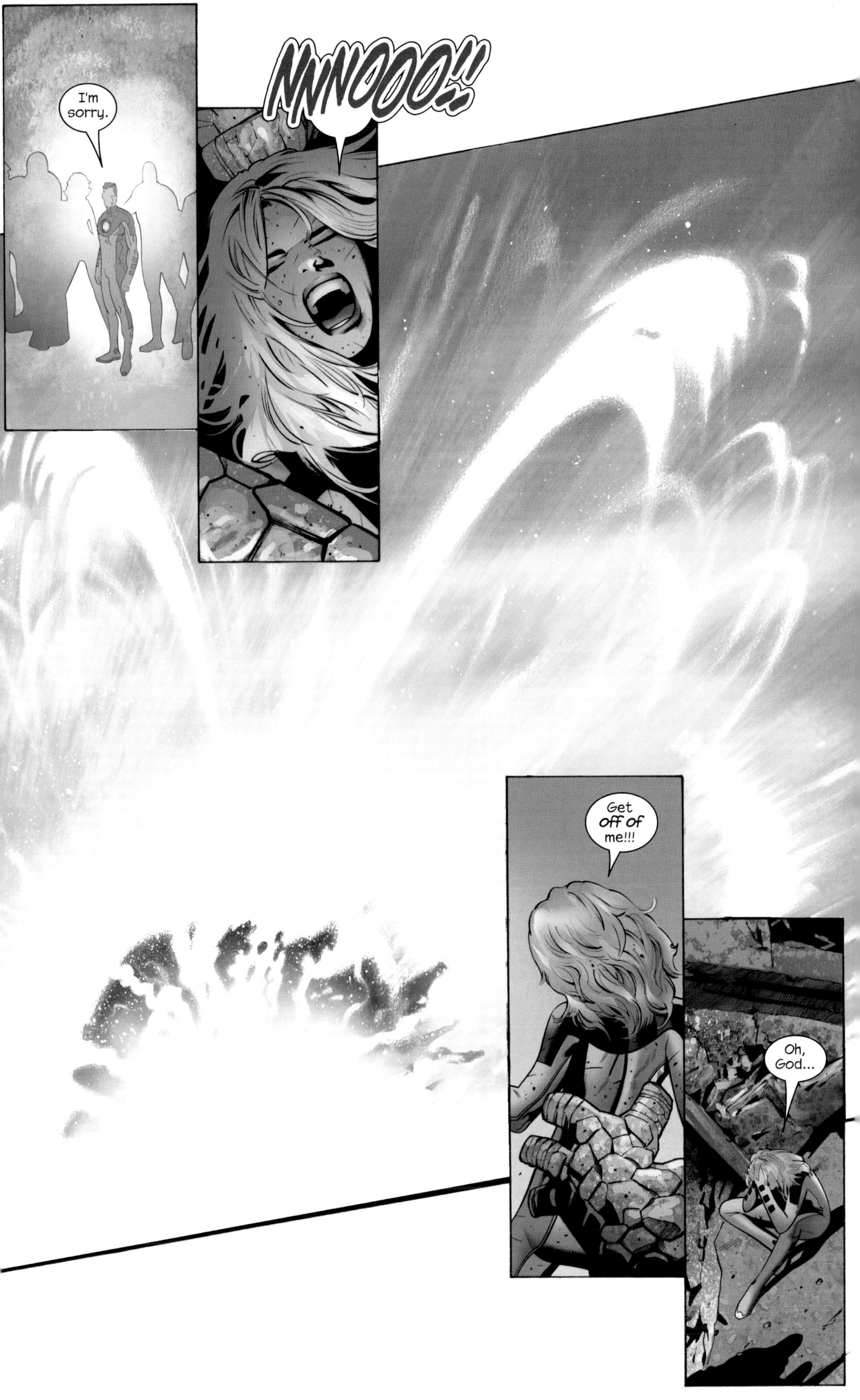
I'm sorry.
NNNOOO!!
Get off of me!!!
Oh, God...

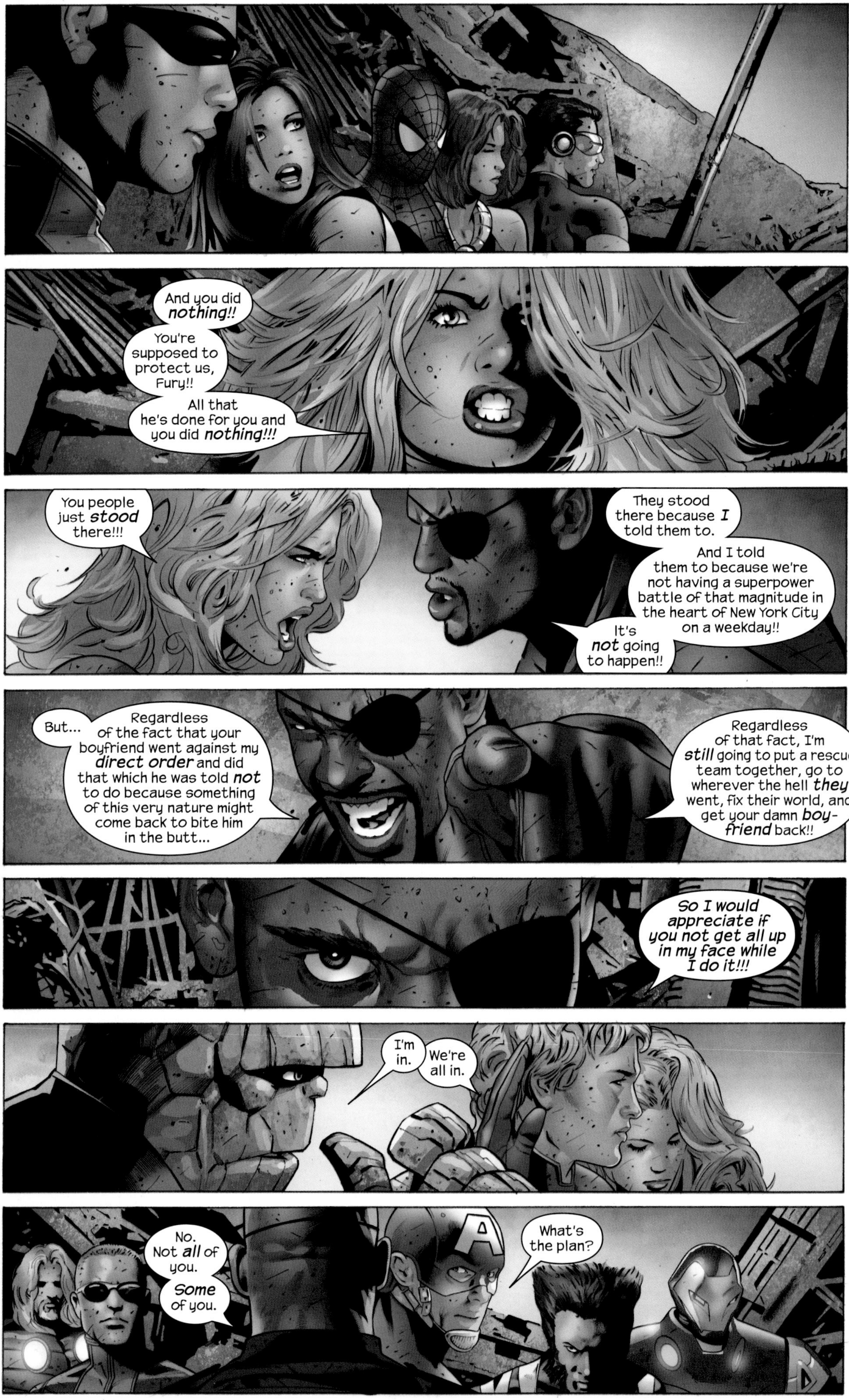

And you did nothing!!
You're supposed to protect us, Fury!!
All that he's done for you and you did nothing!!!
You people just stood there!!!
They stood there because I told them to.
And I told them to because we're not having a superpower battle of that magnitude in the heart of New York City on a weekday!!
It's not going to happen!!
But...
Regardless of the fact that your boyfriend went against my direct order and did that which he was told not to do because something of this very nature might come back to bite him in the butt...
Regardless of that fact, I'm still going to put a rescue team together, go to wherever the hell they went, fix their world, and get your damn boy-friend back!!
So I would appreciate if you not get all up in my face while I do it!!!
I'm in.
We're all in.
No. Not all of you.
Some of you.
What's the plan?

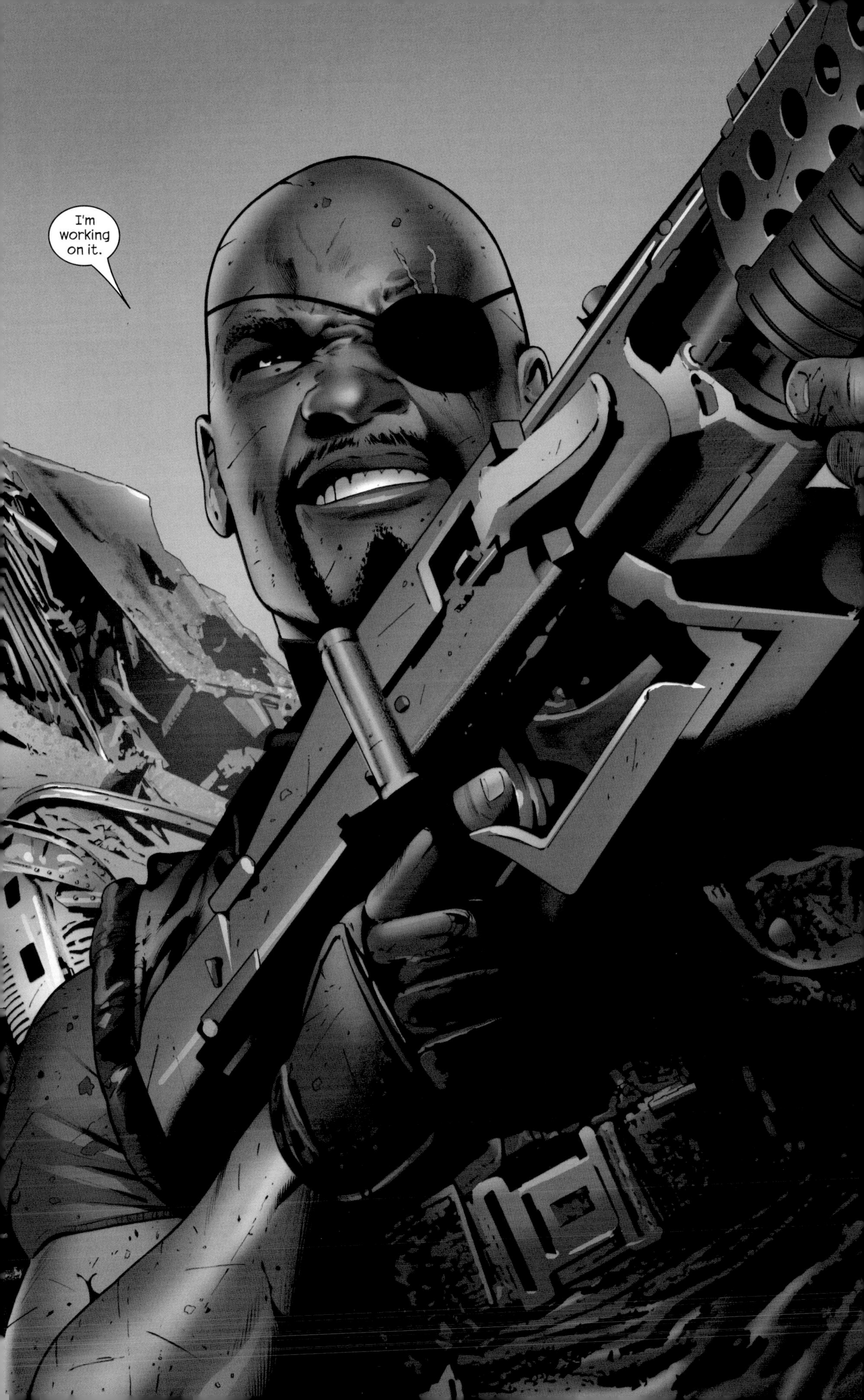
I'm working on it.

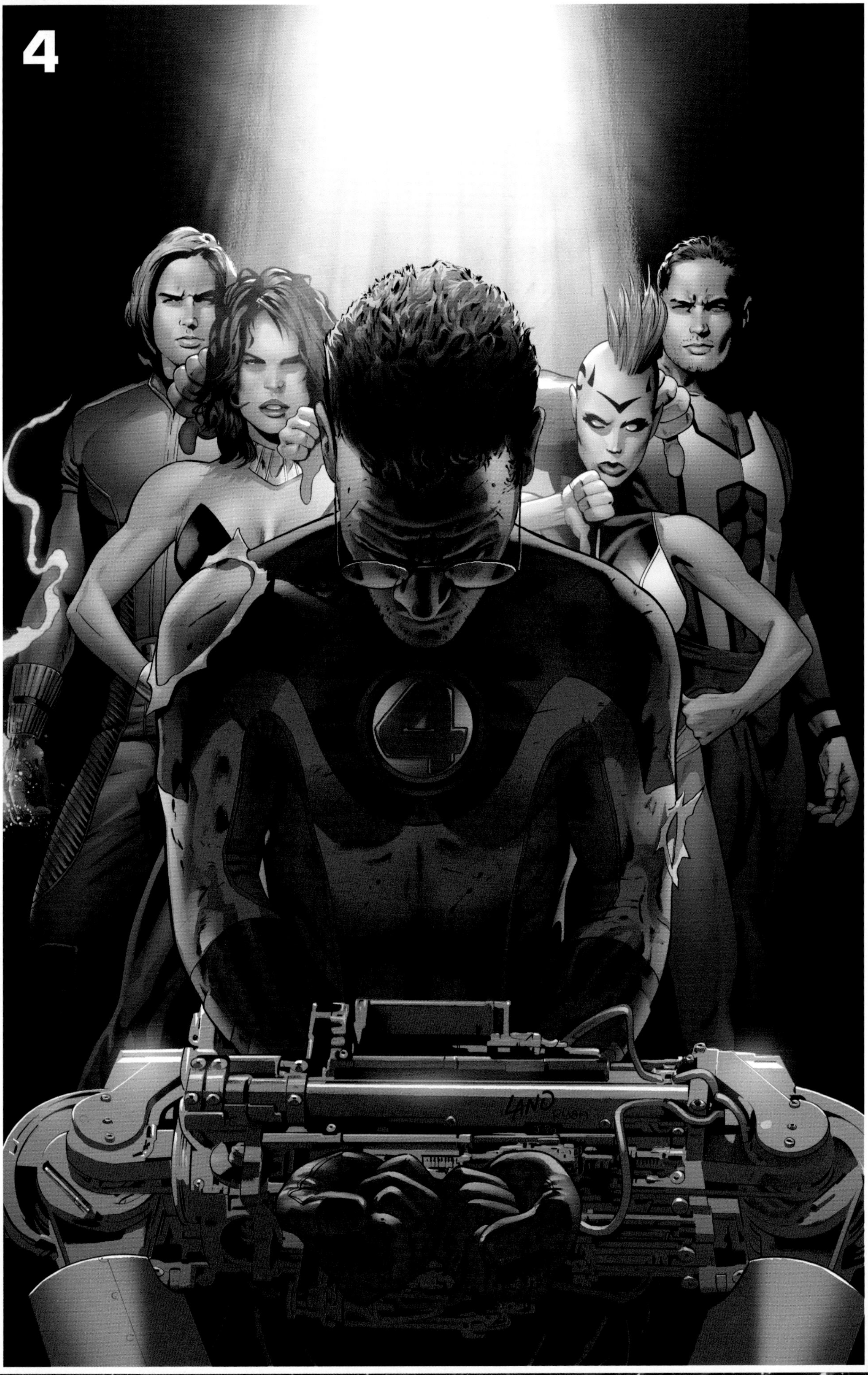
4

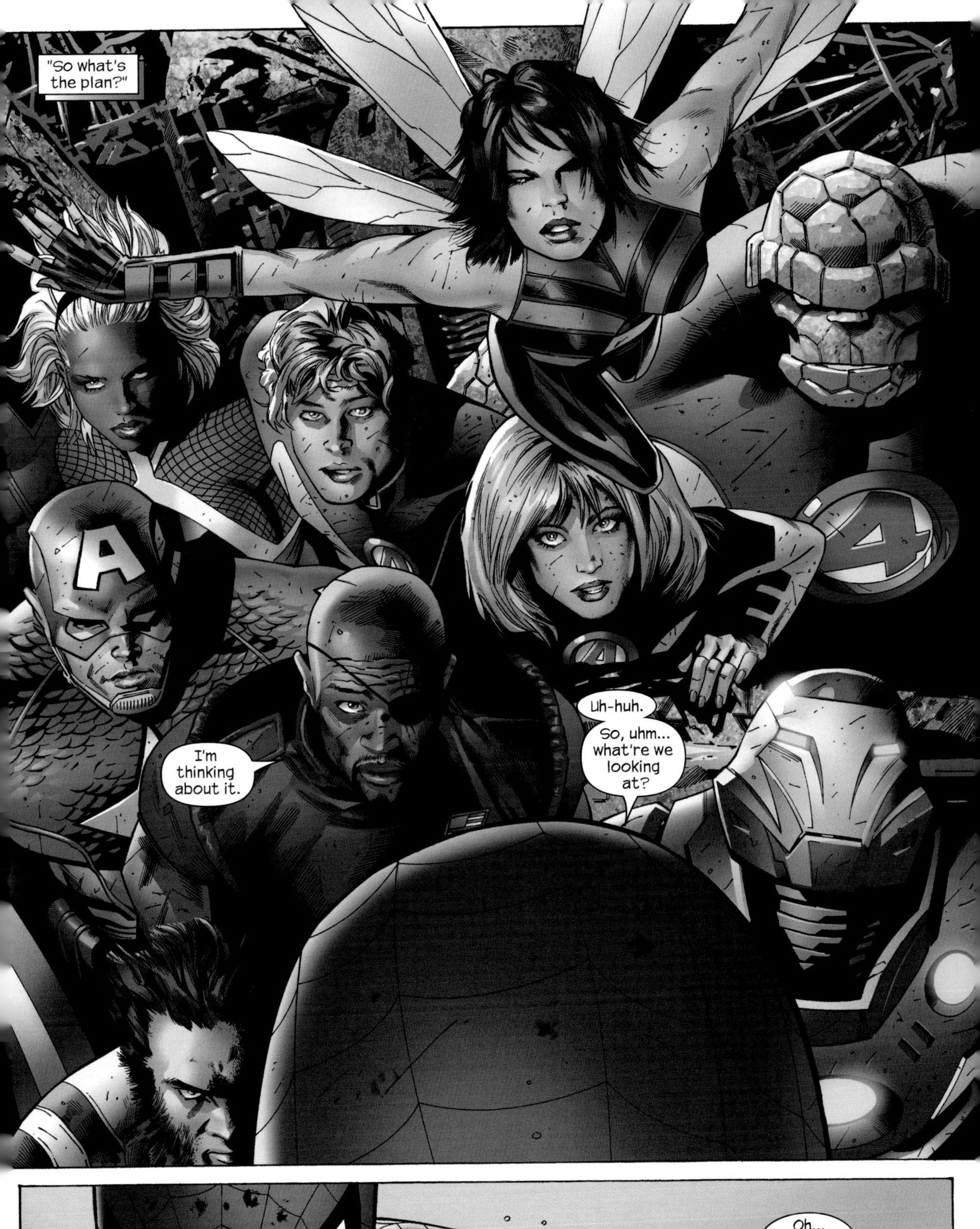
"So what's the plan?"
I'm thinking about it.
Uh-huh.
So, uhm... what're we looking at?

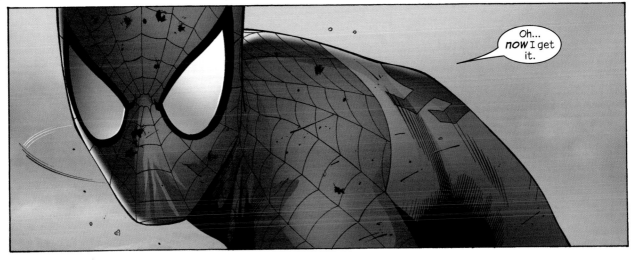

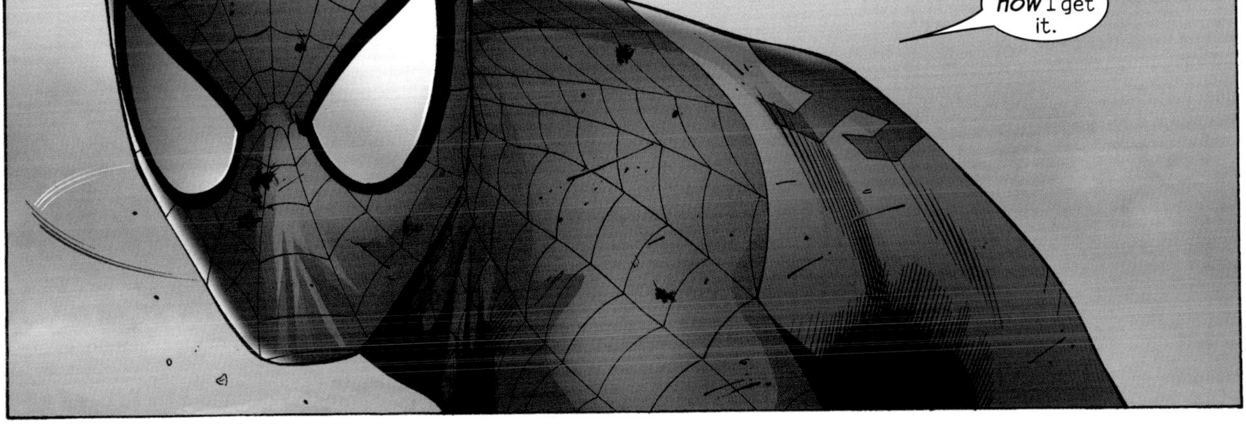
Oh... NOW I get it.

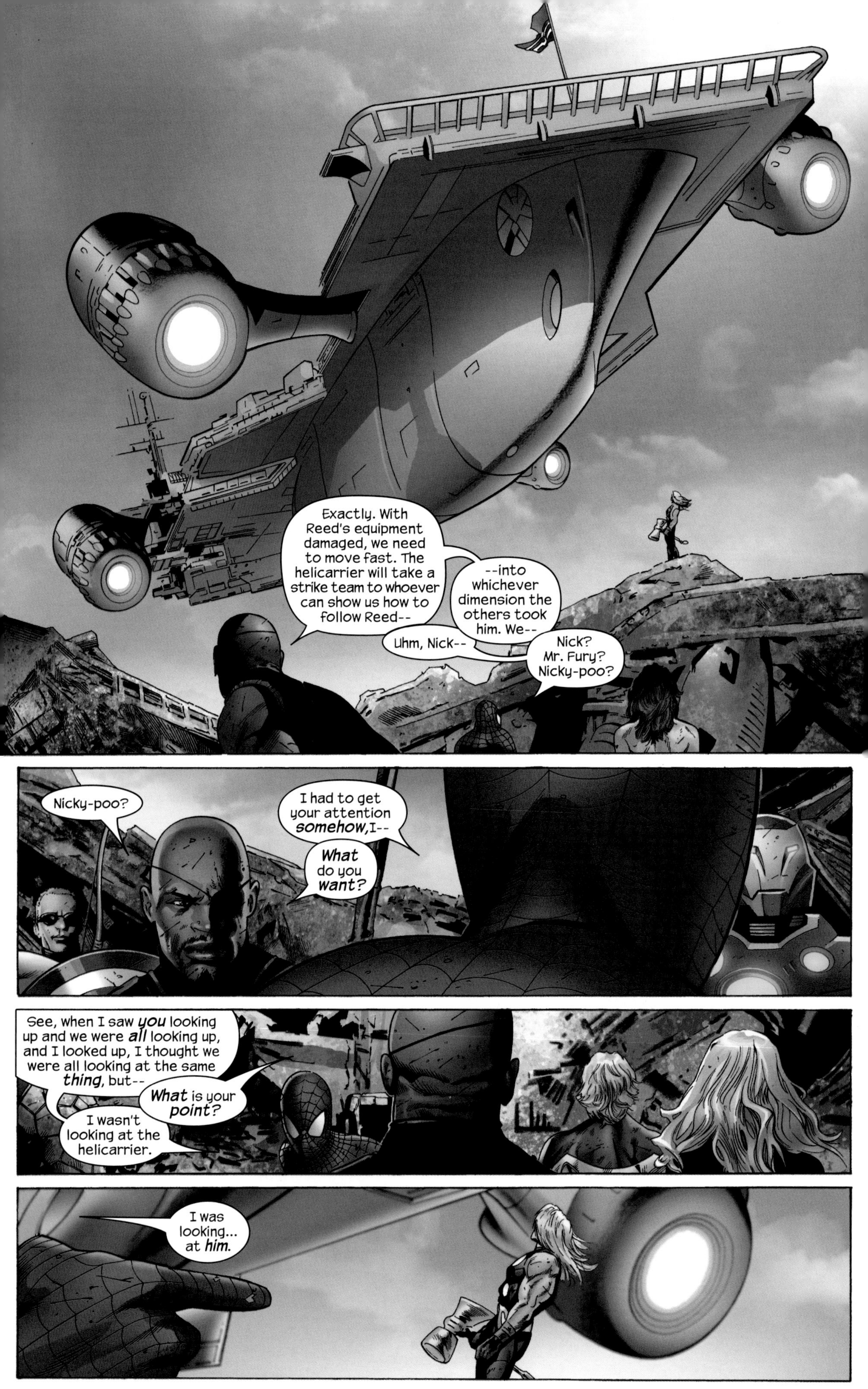
Exactly. With Reed's equipment damaged, we need to move fast. The helicarrier will take a strike team to whoever can show us how to follow Reed--
--into whichever dimension the others took him. We--
Uhm, Nick--
Nick? Mr. Fury? Nicky-poo?
Nicky-poo?
I had to get your attention somehow, I--
What do you want?
See, when I saw you looking up and we were all looking up, and I looked up, I thought we were all looking at the same thing, but--
What is your point?
I wasn't looking at the helicarrier.
I was looking... at him.

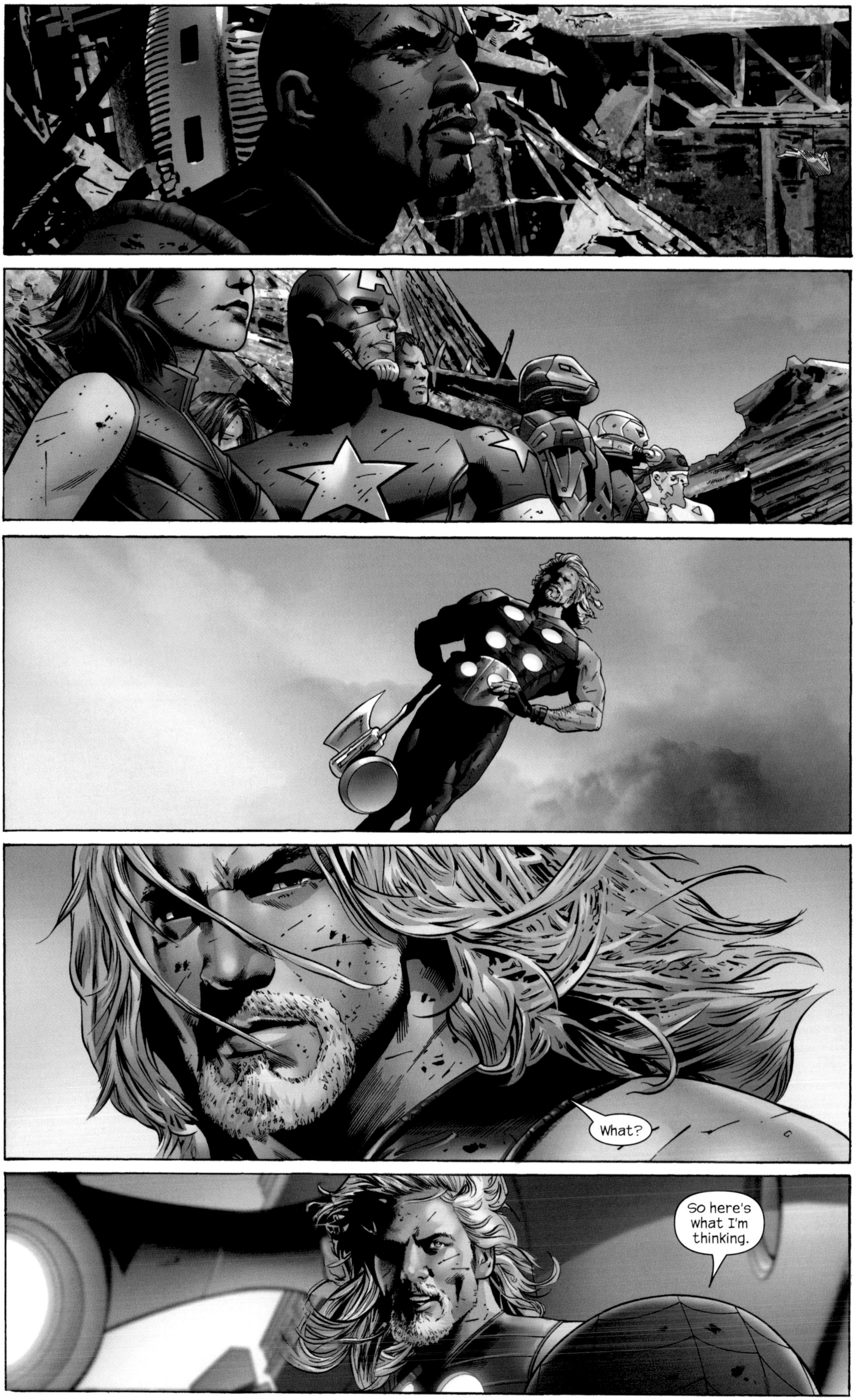
What?
So here's what I'm thinking.

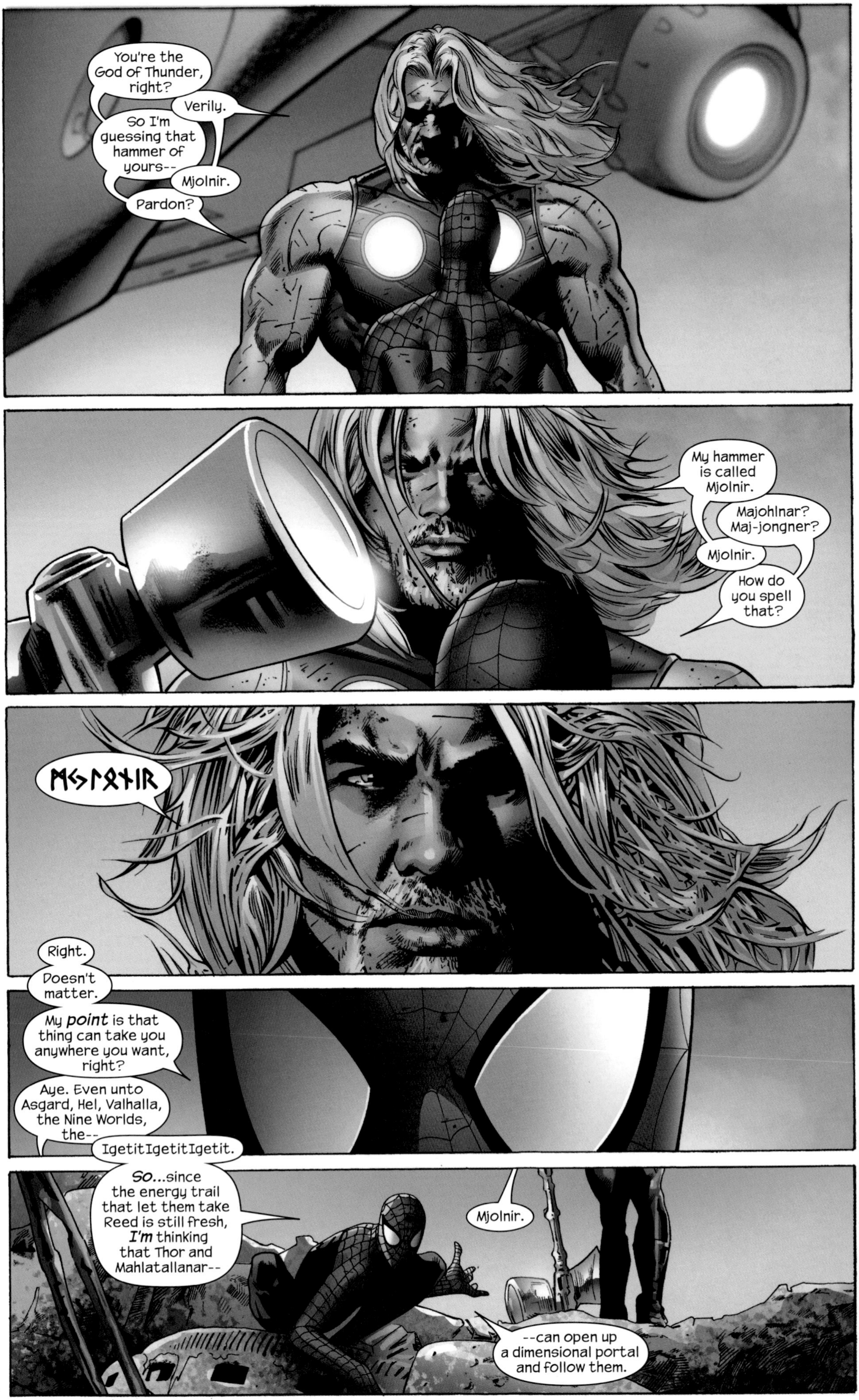

You're the God of Thunder, right?
Verily.
So I'm guessing that hammer of yours--
Mjolnir.
Pardon?
My hammer is called Mjolnir.
Majohlnar? Maj-jongner?
Mjolnir.
How do you spell that?
Right.
Doesn't matter.
My *point* is that thing can take you anywhere you want, right?
Aye. Even unto Asgard, Hel, Valhalla, the Nine Worlds, the--
IgetitIgetitIgetit.
So...since the energy trail that let them take Reed is still fresh, *I'm* thinking that Thor and Mahlatallanar--
Mjolnir.
--can open up a dimensional portal and follow them.

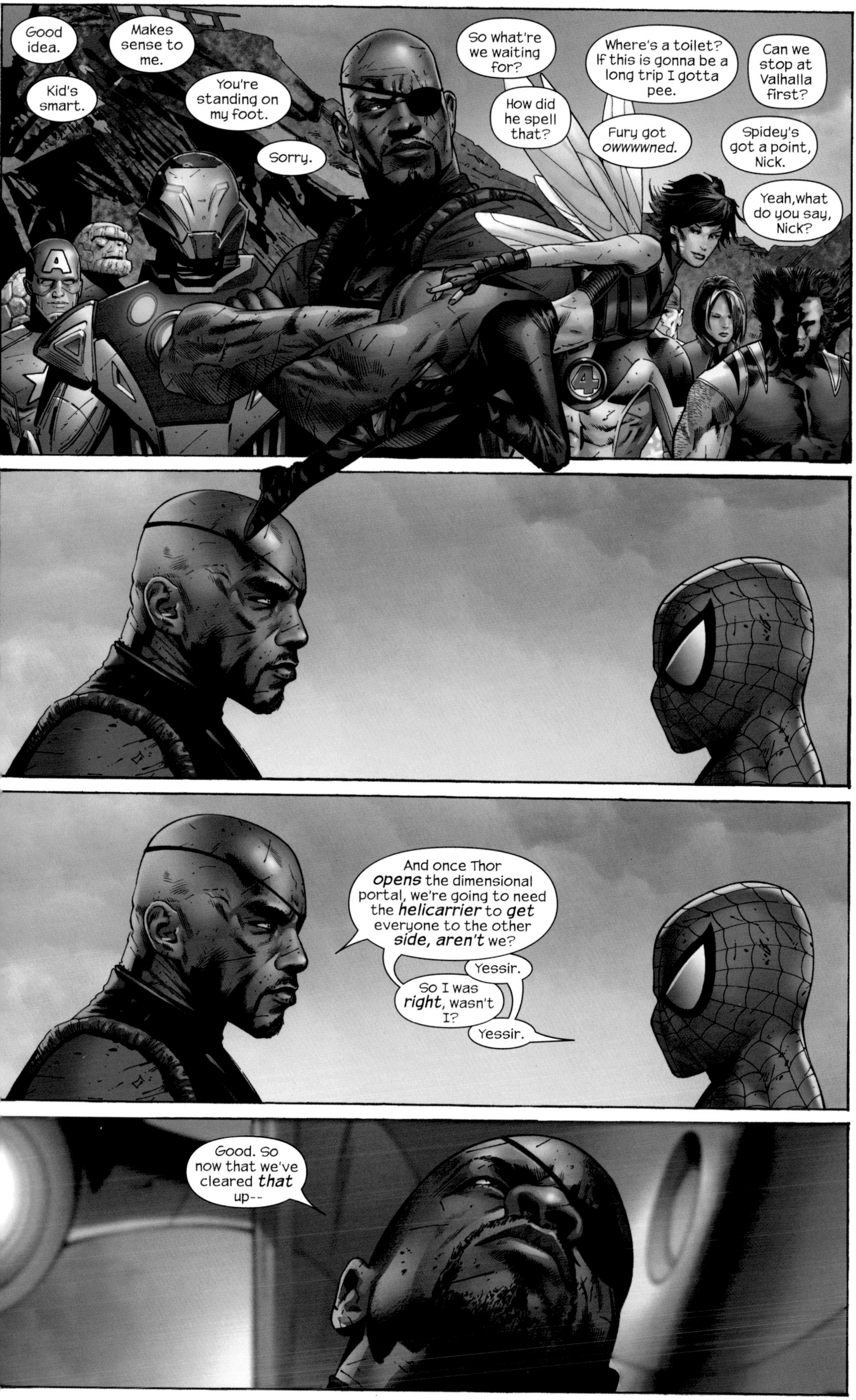
Good idea.
Makes sense to me.
Kid's smart.
You're standing on my foot.
Sorry.
So what're we waiting for?
How did he spell that?
Where's a toilet? If this is gonna be a long trip I gotta pee.
Fury got *owwwwned.*
Can we stop at Valhalla first?
Spidey's got a point, Nick.
Yeah,what do you say, Nick?
And once Thor ***opens*** the dimensional portal, we're going to need the ***helicarrier*** to ***get*** everyone to the other ***side, aren't*** we?
Yessir.
So I was ***right***, wasn't I?
Yessir.
Good. So now that we've cleared ***that*** up--

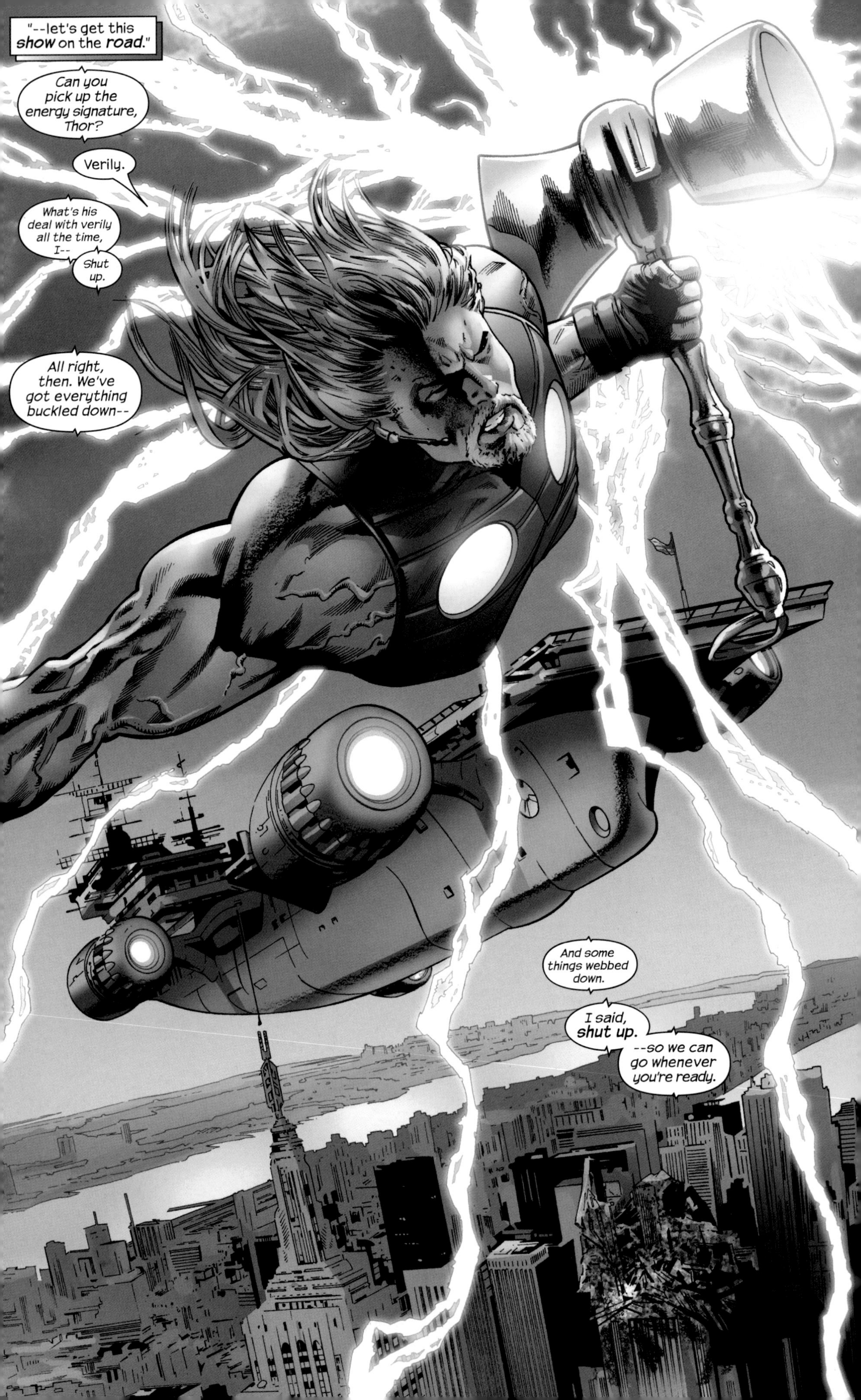
"--let's get this **show** on the **road**."
Can you pick up the energy signature, Thor?
Verily.
What's his deal with verily all the time, I--
Shut up.
All right, then. We've got everything buckled down--
And some things webbed down.
I said, **shut up.**
--so we can go whenever you're ready.

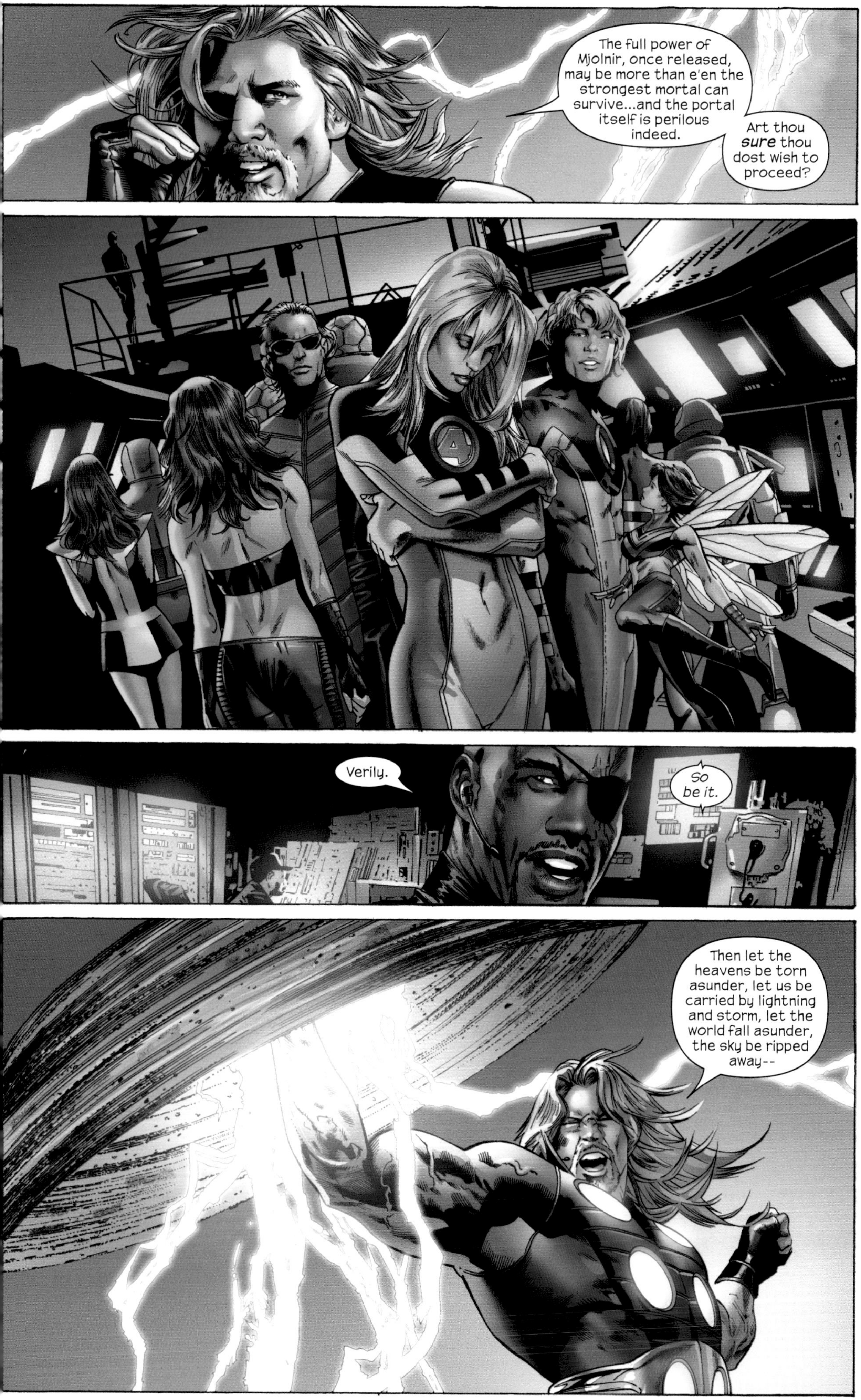
The full power of Mjolnir, once released, may be more than e'en the strongest mortal can survive...and the portal itself is perilous indeed.
Art thou *sure* thou dost wish to proceed?
Verily.
So be it.
Then let the heavens be torn asunder, let us be carried by lightning and storm, let the world fall asunder, the sky be ripped away--

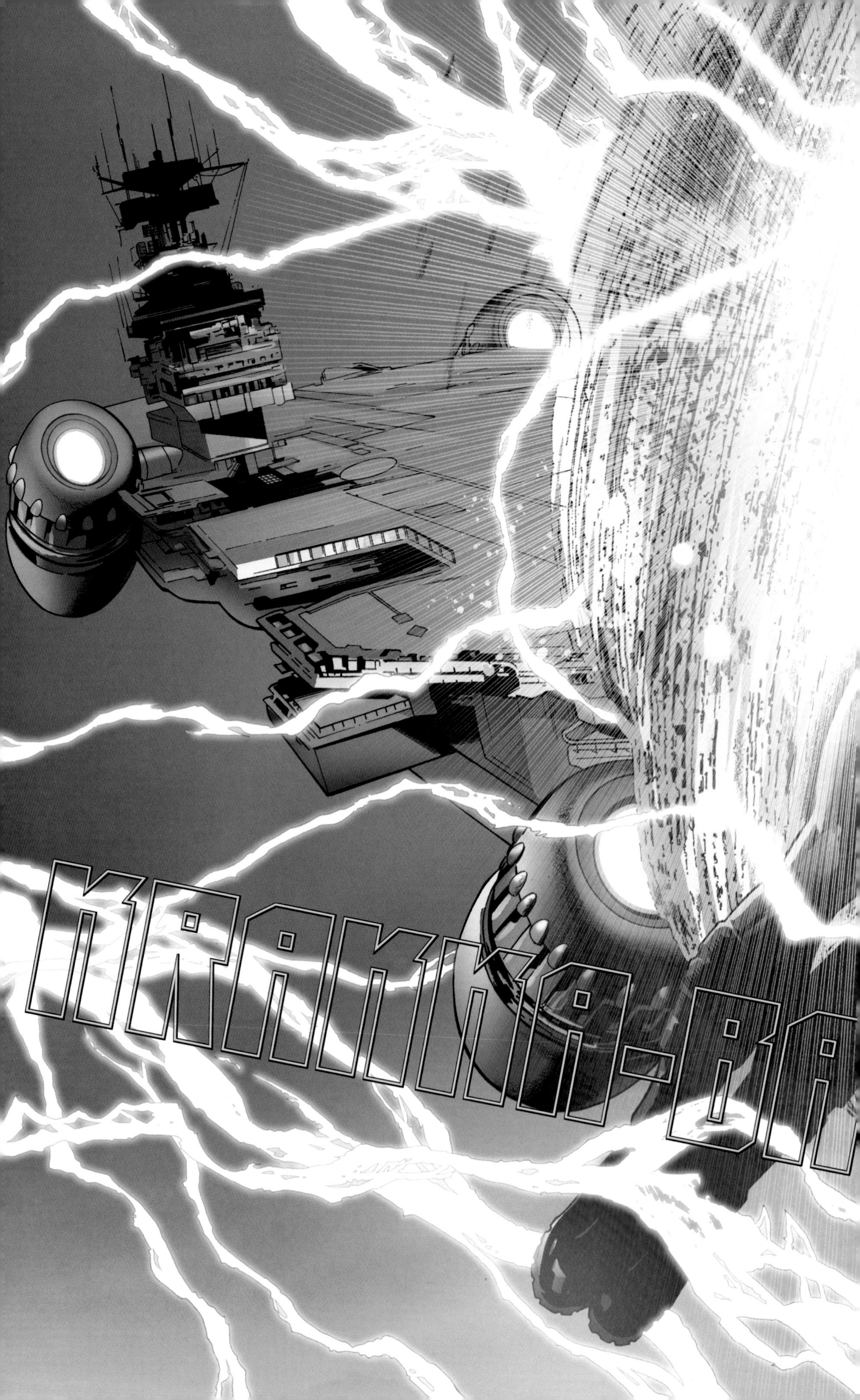
KRAKKA-BA

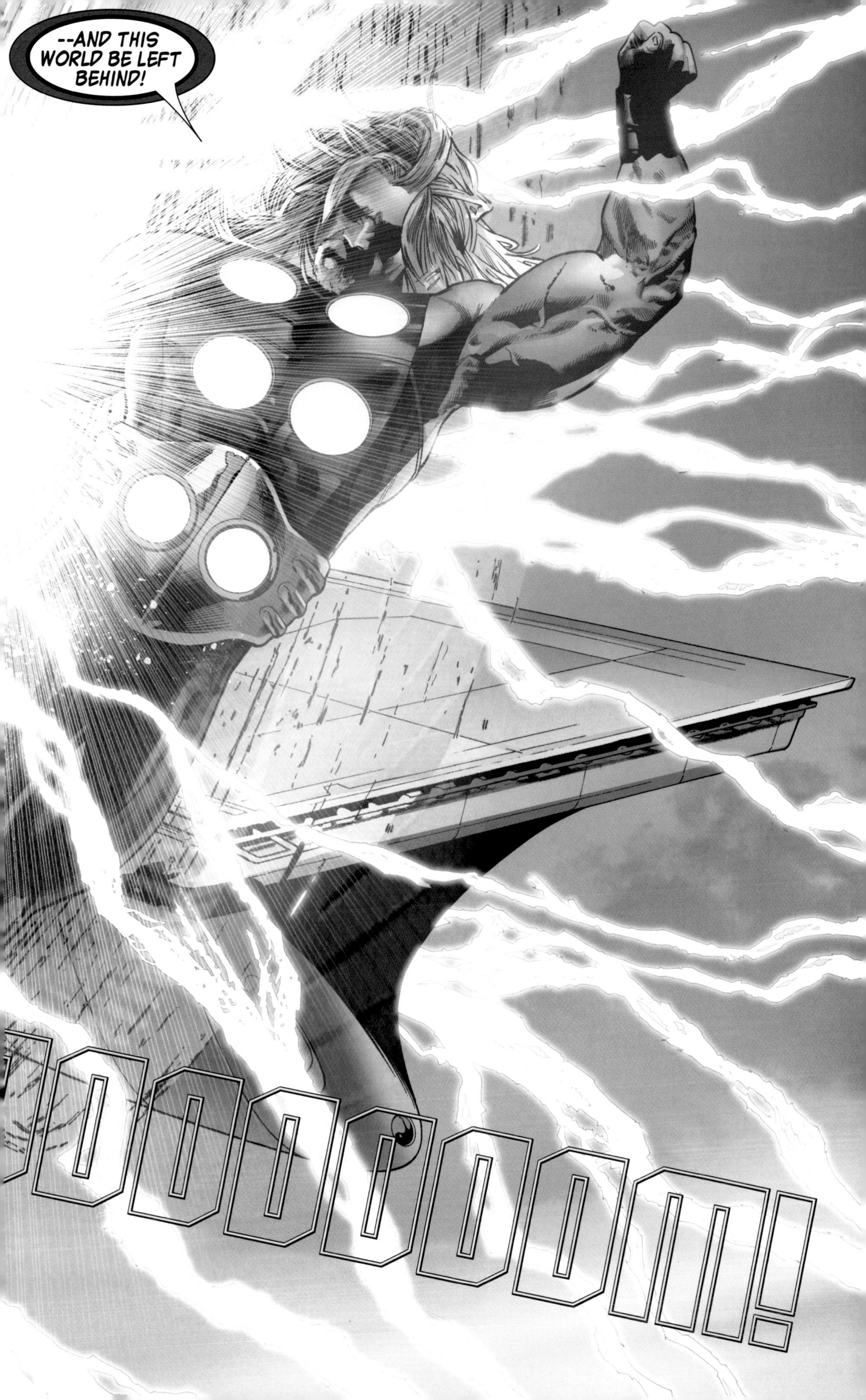
--AND THIS WORLD BE LEFT BEHIND!
DOOOOOOOM!

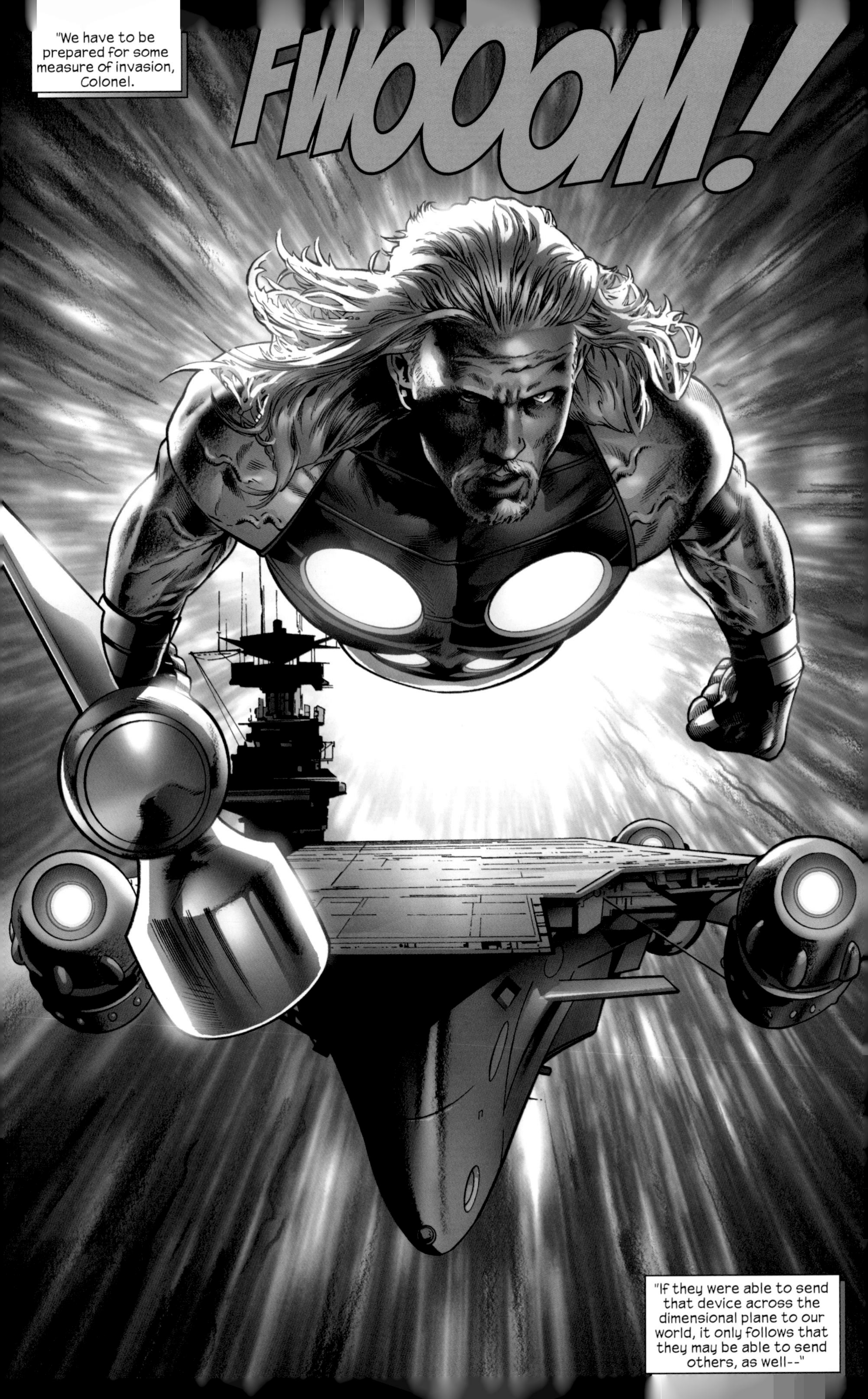
"We have to be prepared for some measure of invasion, Colonel.
FWOOOM!
"If they were able to send that device across the dimensional plane to our world, it only follows that they may be able to send others, as well--"

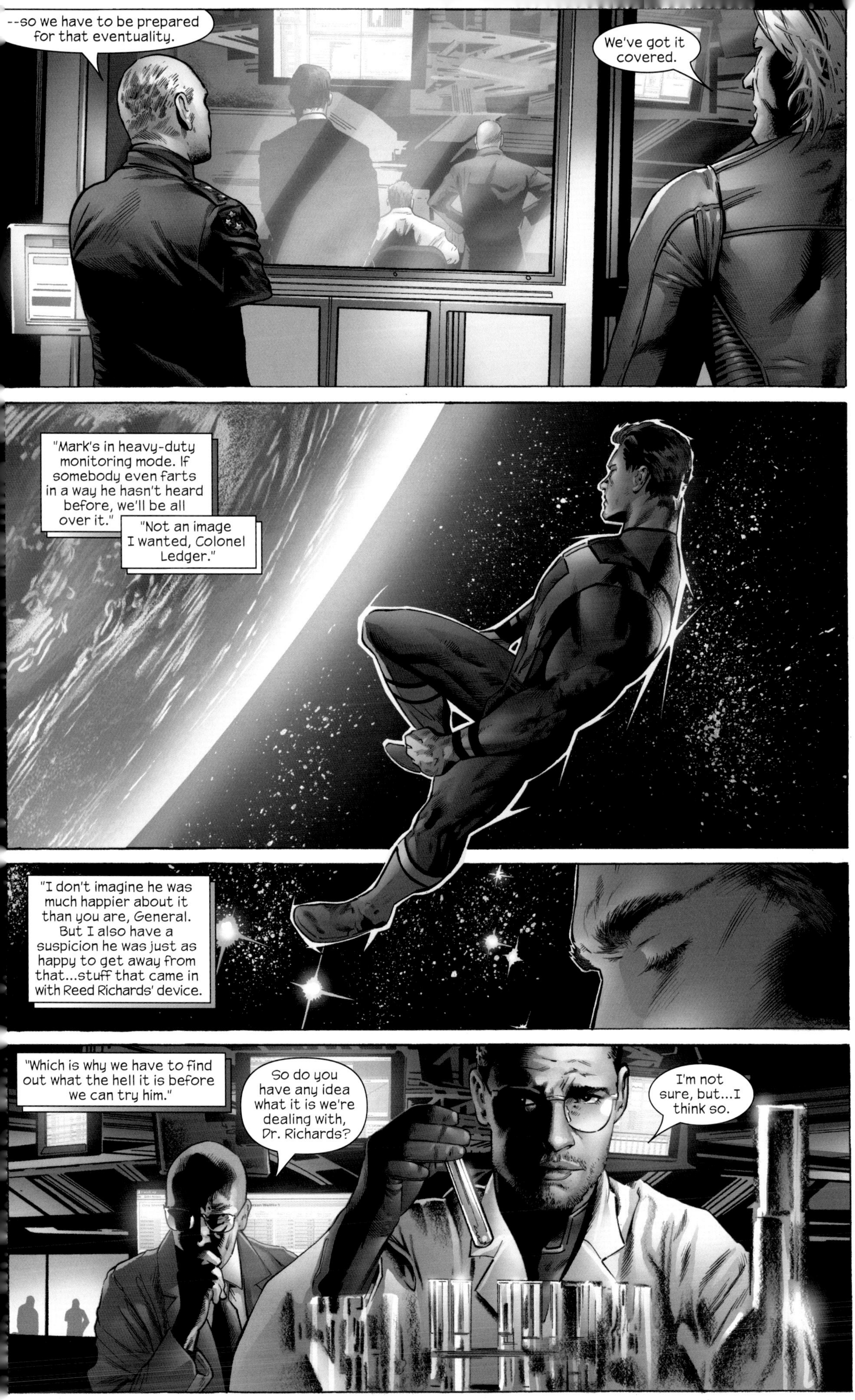
--so we have to be prepared for that eventuality.
We've got it covered.
"Mark's in heavy-duty monitoring mode. If somebody even farts in a way he hasn't heard before, we'll be all over it."
"Not an image I wanted, Colonel Ledger."
"I don't imagine he was much happier about it than you are, General. But I also have a suspicion he was just as happy to get away from that...stuff that came in with Reed Richards' device.
"Which is why we have to find out what the hell it is before we can try him."
So do you have any idea what it is we're dealing with, Dr. Richards?
I'm not sure, but...I think so.

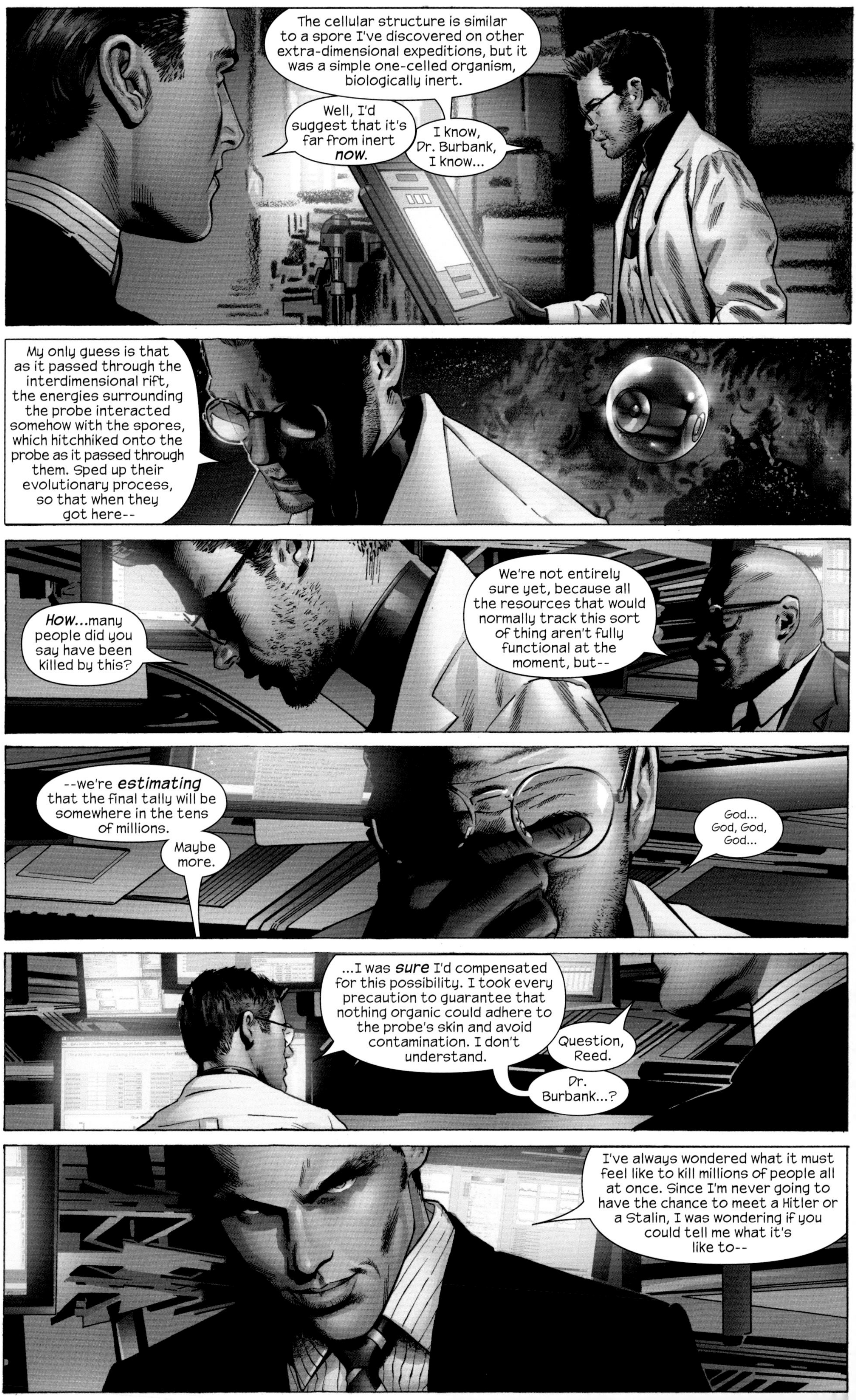
The cellular structure is similar to a spore I've discovered on other extra-dimensional expeditions, but it was a simple one-celled organism, biologically inert.
Well, I'd suggest that it's far from inert *now.*
I know, Dr. Burbank, I know...
My only guess is that as it passed through the interdimensional rift, the energies surrounding the probe interacted somehow with the spores, which hitchhiked onto the probe as it passed through them. Sped up their evolutionary process, so that when they got here--
*How...*many people did you say have been killed by this?
We're not entirely sure yet, because all the resources that would normally track this sort of thing aren't fully functional at the moment, but--
--we're *estimating* that the final tally will be somewhere in the tens of millions.
Maybe more.
God... God, God, God...
...I was *sure* I'd compensated for this possibility. I took every precaution to guarantee that nothing organic could adhere to the probe's skin and avoid contamination. I don't understand.
Question, Reed.
Dr. Burbank...?
I've always wondered what it must feel like to kill millions of people all at once. Since I'm never going to have the chance to meet a Hitler or a Stalin, I was wondering if you could tell me what it's like to--

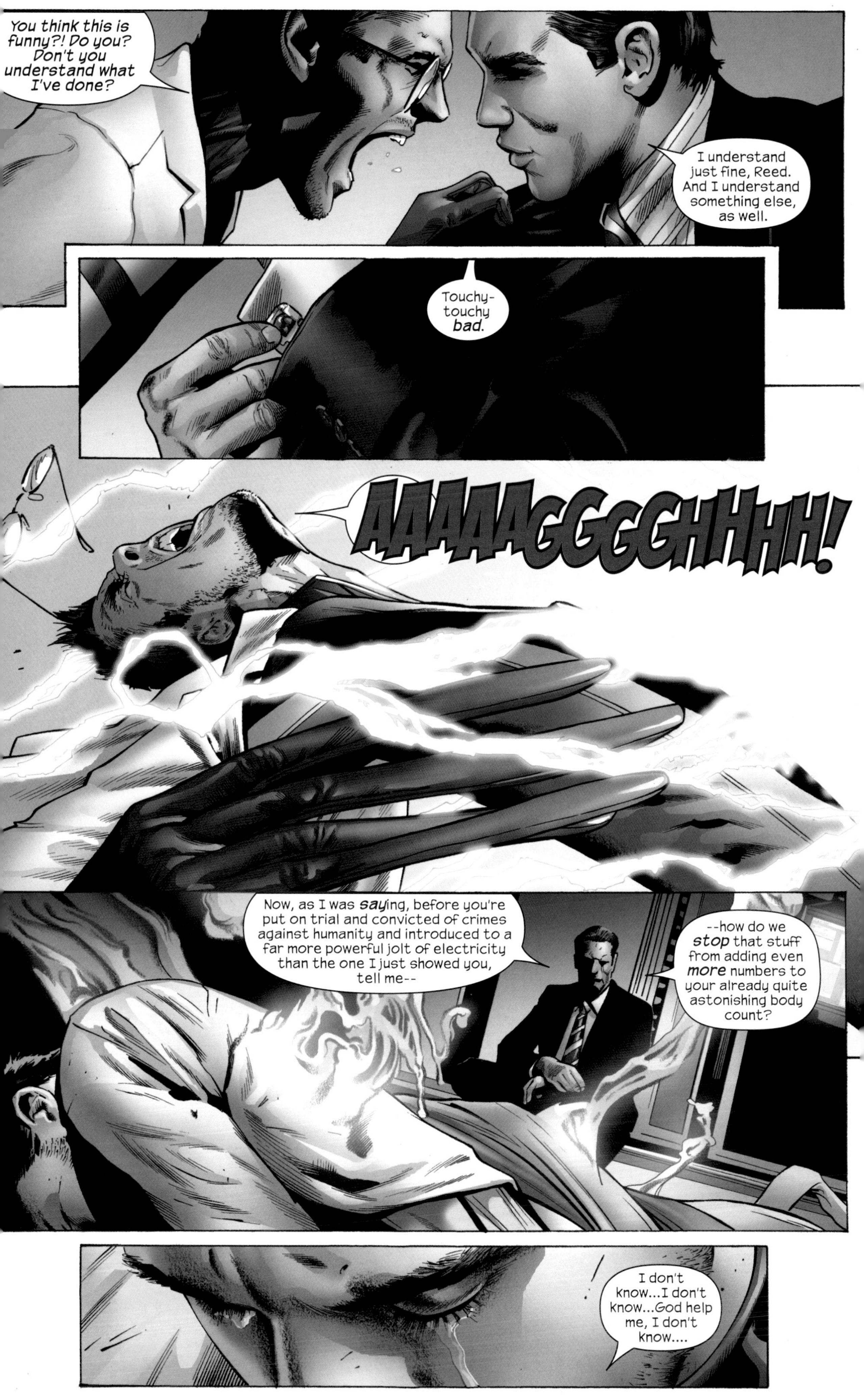
You think this is funny?! Do you? Don't you understand what I've done?
I understand just fine, Reed. And I understand something else, as well.
Touchy-touchy bad.
AAAAAGGGGHHHH!
Now, as I was saying, before you're put on trial and convicted of crimes against humanity and introduced to a far more powerful jolt of electricity than the one I just showed you, tell me--
--how do we stop that stuff from adding even more numbers to your already quite astonishing body count?
I don't know...I don't know...God help me, I don't know....

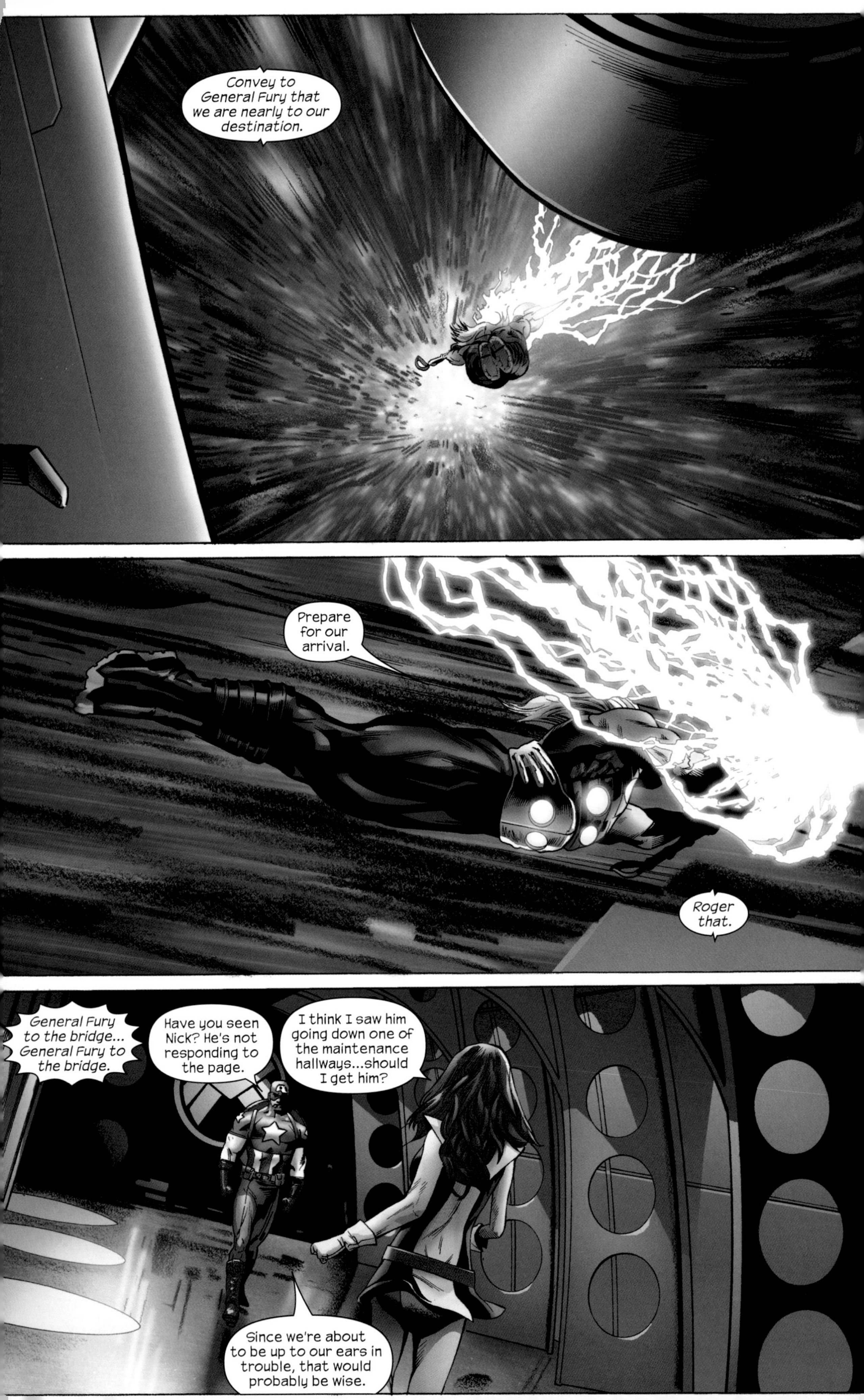

Convey to General Fury that we are nearly to our destination.
Prepare for our arrival.
Roger that.
General Fury to the bridge... General Fury to the bridge.
Have you seen Nick? He's not responding to the page.
I think I saw him going down one of the maintenance hallways...should I get him?
Since we're about to be up to our ears in trouble, that would probably be wise.

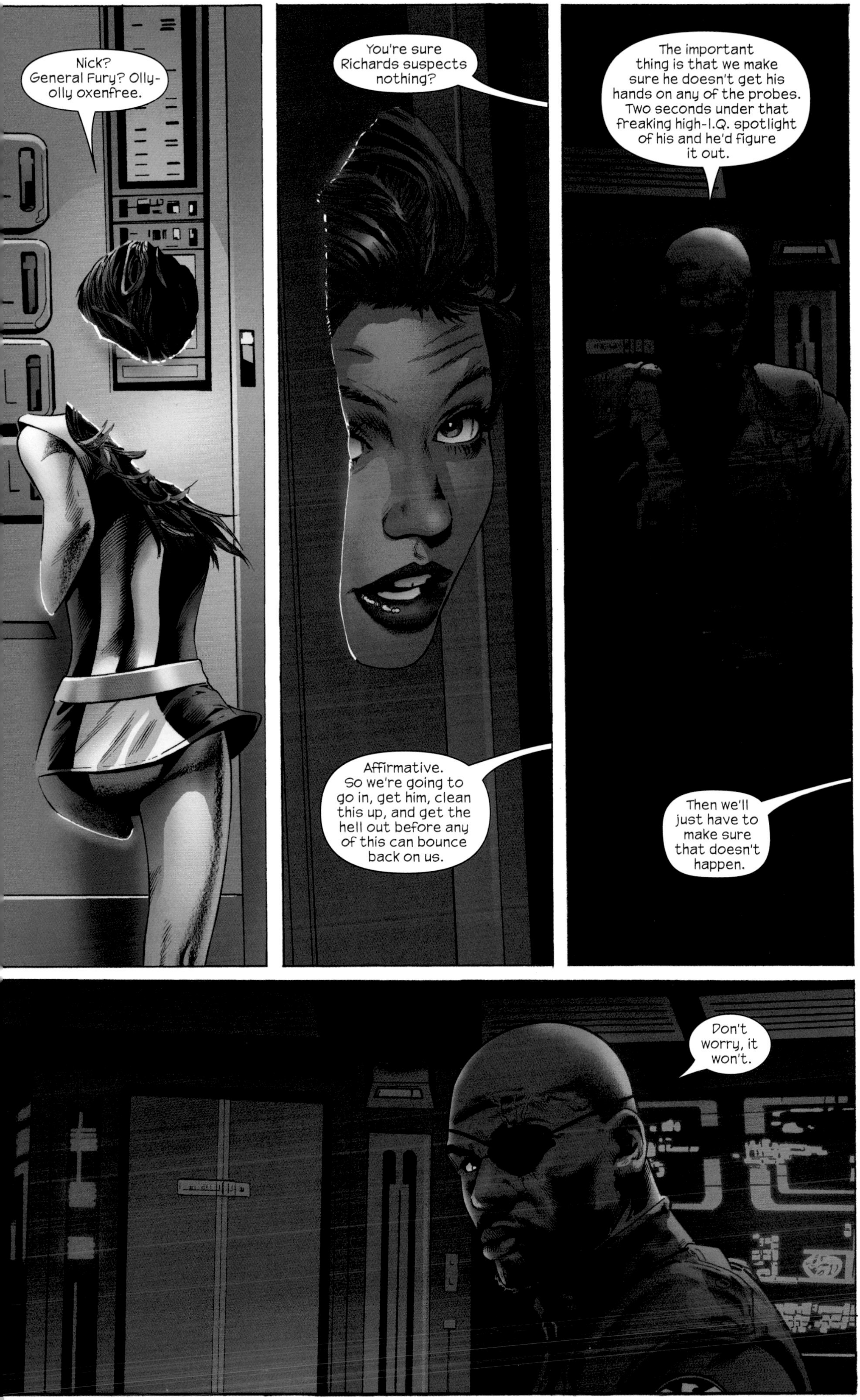

Nick? General Fury? Olly-olly oxenfree.
You're sure Richards suspects nothing?
The important thing is that we make sure he doesn't get his hands on any of the probes. Two seconds under that freaking high-I.Q. spotlight of his and he'd figure it out.
Affirmative. So we're going to go in, get him, clean this up, and get the hell out before any of this can bounce back on us.
Then we'll just have to make sure that doesn't happen.
Don't worry, it won't.

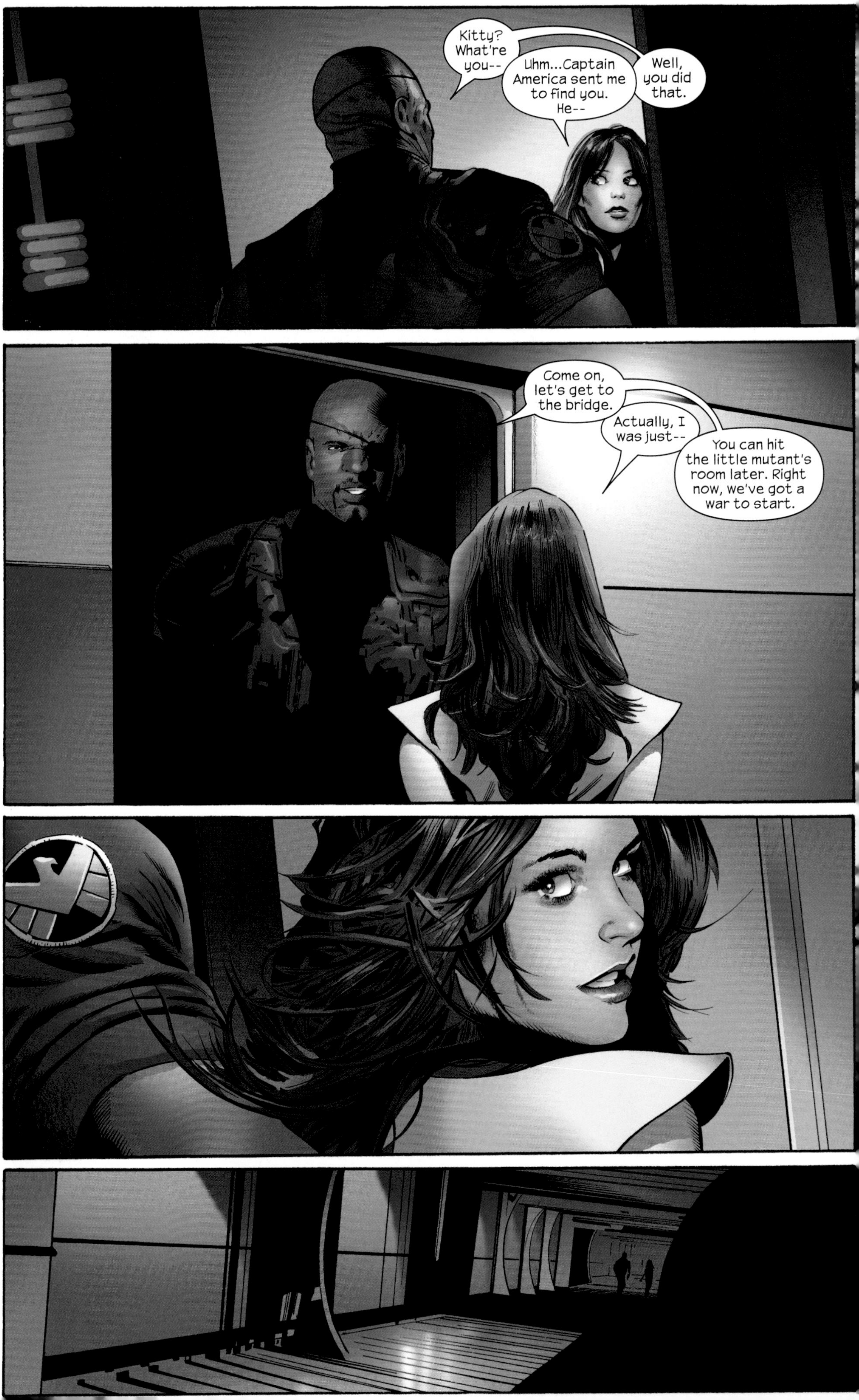
Kitty? What're you--
Uhm...Captain America sent me to find you. He--
Well, you did that.
Come on, let's get to the bridge.
Actually, I was just--
You can hit the little mutant's room later. Right now, we've got a war to start.

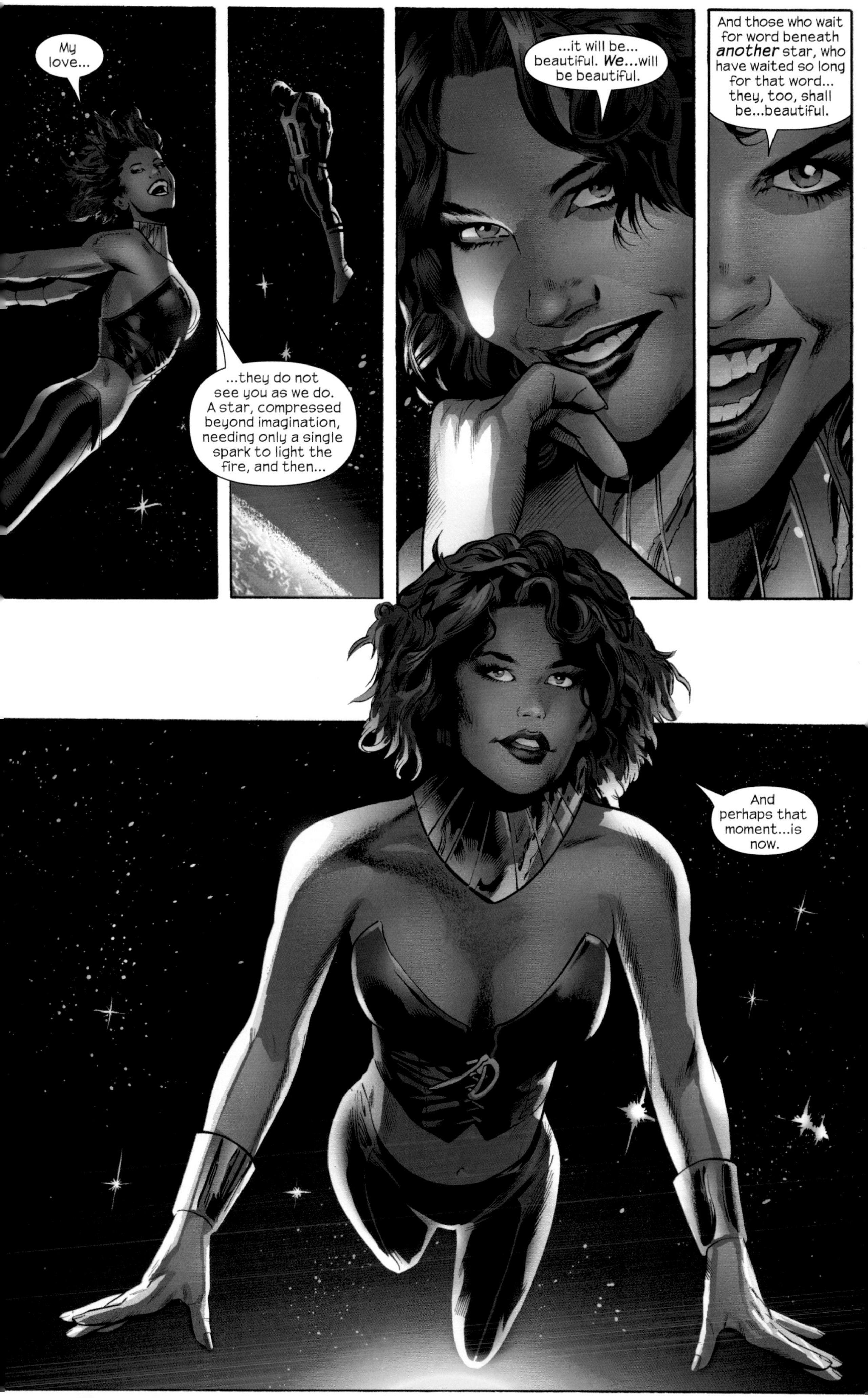
My love...
...they do not see you as we do. A star, compressed beyond imagination, needing only a single spark to light the fire, and then...
...it will be... beautiful. We...will be beautiful.
And those who wait for word beneath another star, who have waited so long for that word... they, too, shall be...beautiful.
And perhaps that moment...is now.

Do not open your eyes, my love. But continue to listen...not for the approach of the enemy, but to those below.

Listen to those that crawl across the broken rind of the world below, denied flight, denied the sky, denied the stars... listen...

...what do you hear?

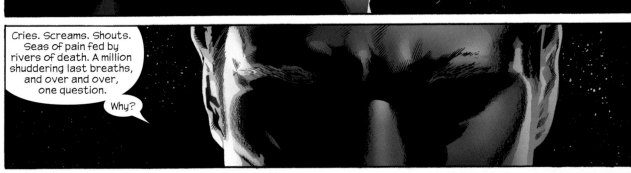

Cries. Screams. Shouts. Seas of pain fed by rivers of death. A million shuddering last breaths, and over and over, one question.

Why?

It is the question we have awaited, my love. Because now we can give them the answer they have always known, but needed to be told before they could truly understand it.

Why are they dying?

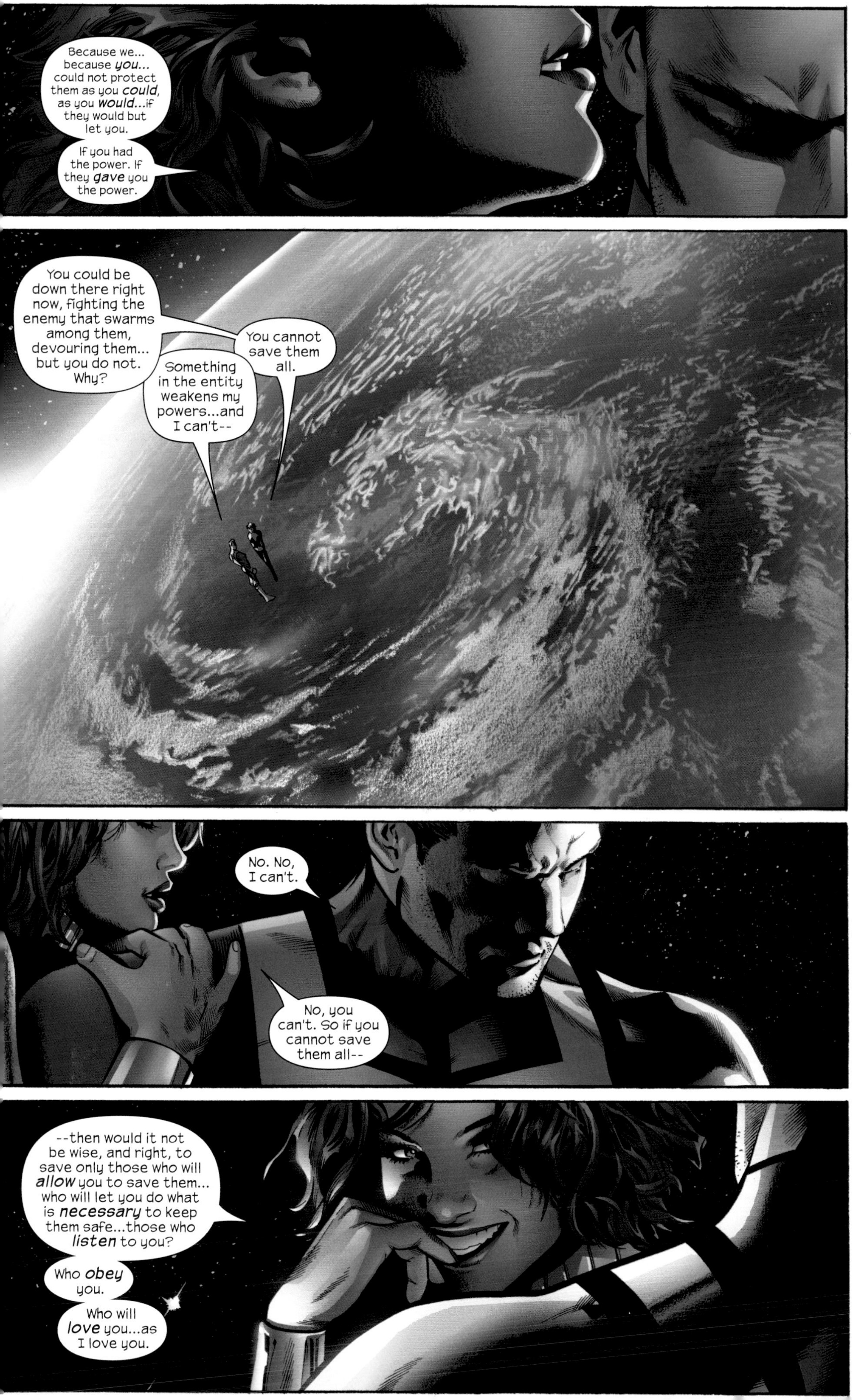

Because we... because *you*... could not protect them as you *could*, as you *would*...if they would but let you.
If you had the power. If they *gave* you the power.
You could be down there right now, fighting the enemy that swarms among them, devouring them... but you do not. Why?
Something in the entity weakens my powers...and I can't--
You cannot save them all.
No. No, I can't.
No, you can't. So if you cannot save them all--
--then would it not be wise, and right, to save only those who will *allow* you to save them... who will let you do what is *necessary* to keep them safe...those who *listen* to you?
Who *obey* you.
Who will *love* you...as I love you.

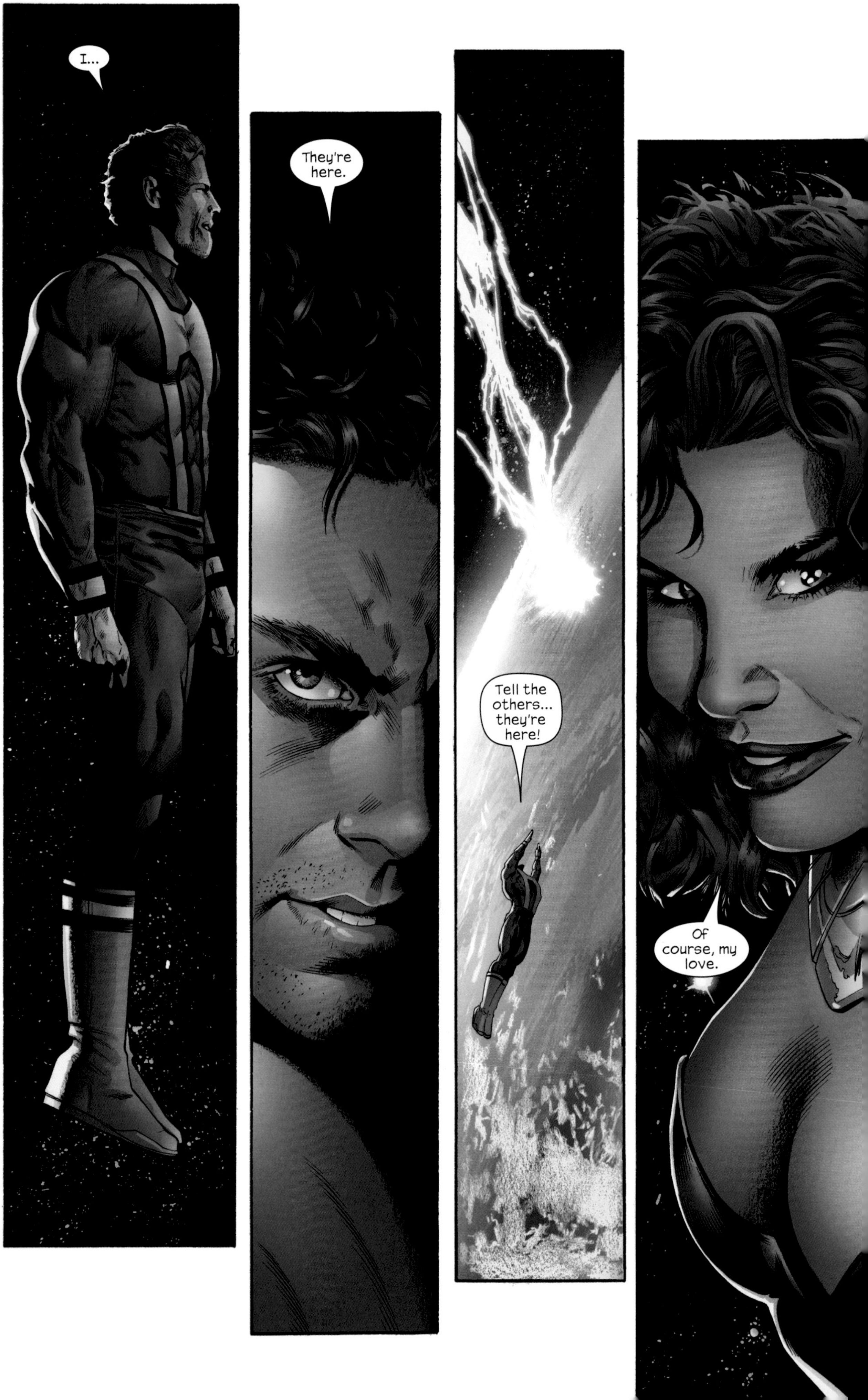
I...
They're here.
Tell the others... they're here!
Of course, my love.

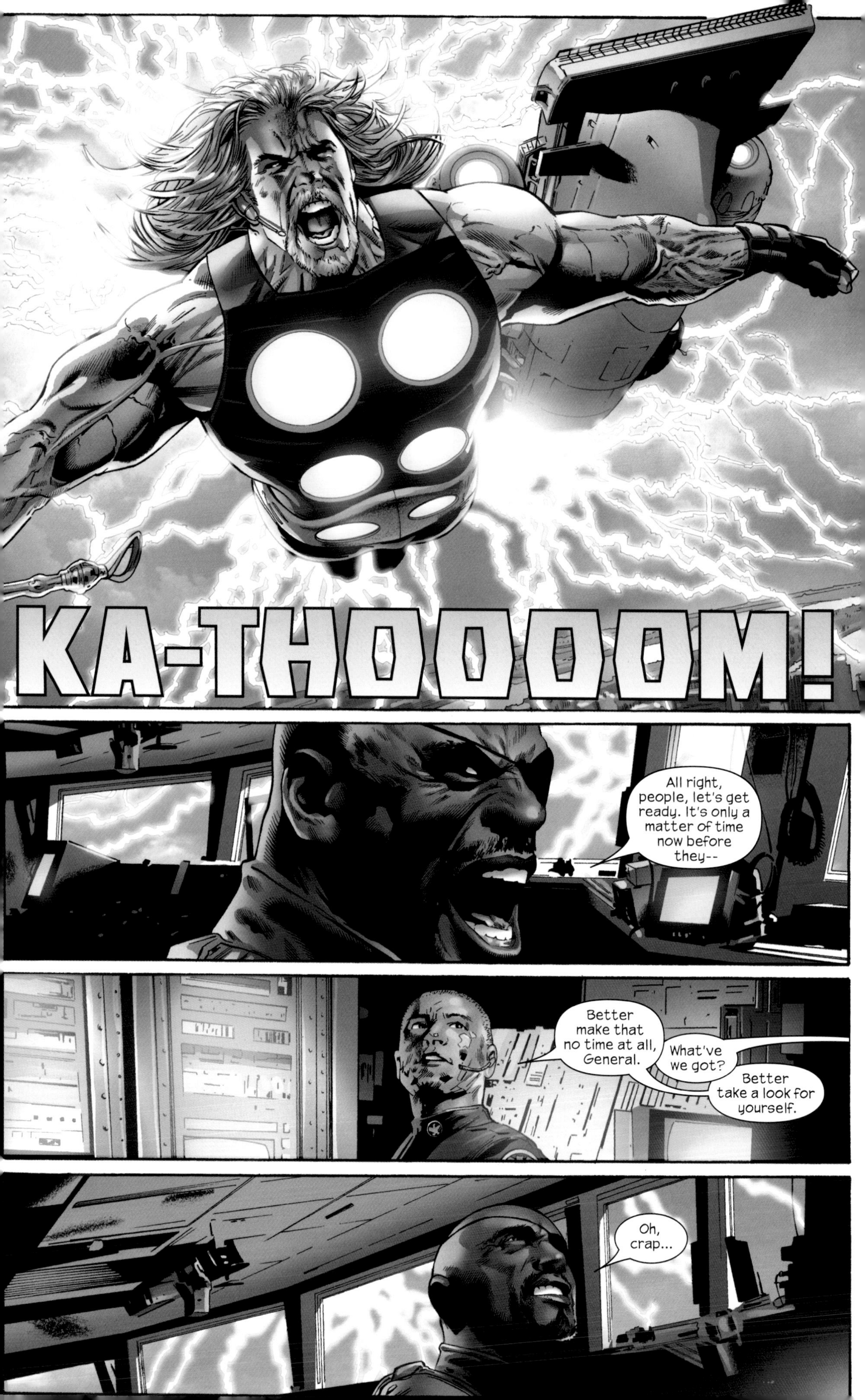
KA-THOOOOM!
All right, people, let's get ready. It's only a matter of time now before they--
Better make that no time at all, General.
What've we got?
Better take a look for yourself.
Oh, crap...

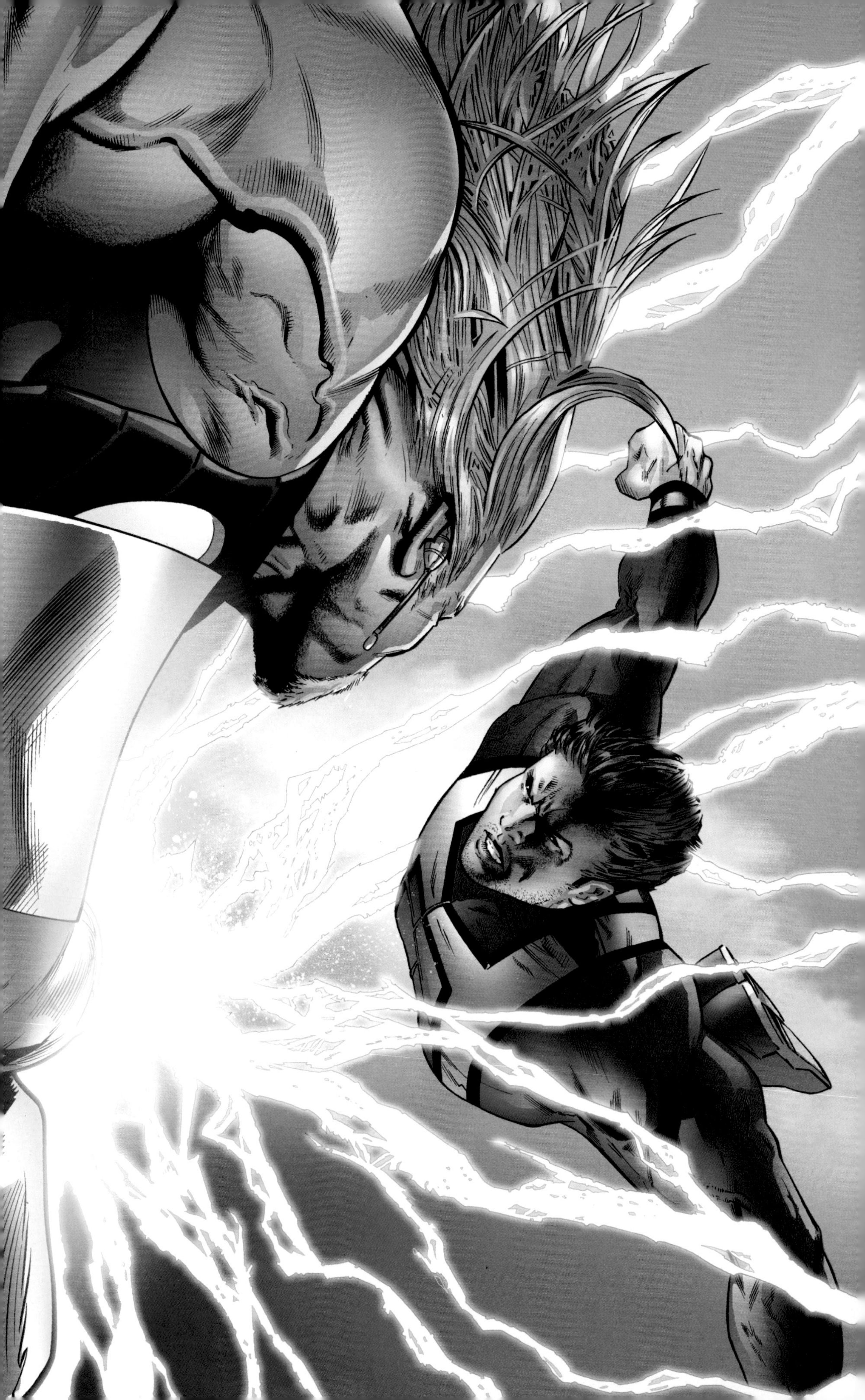

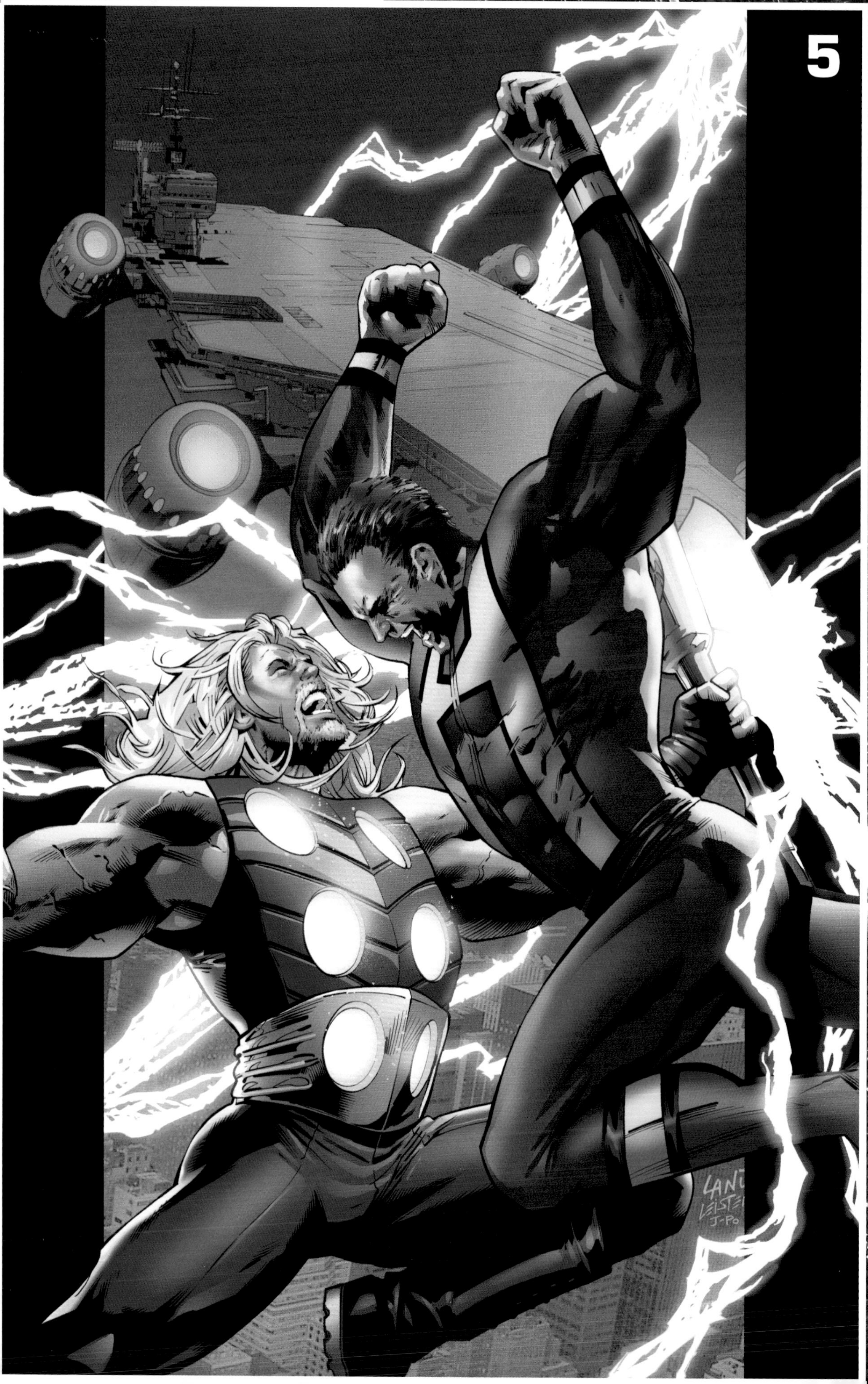
5

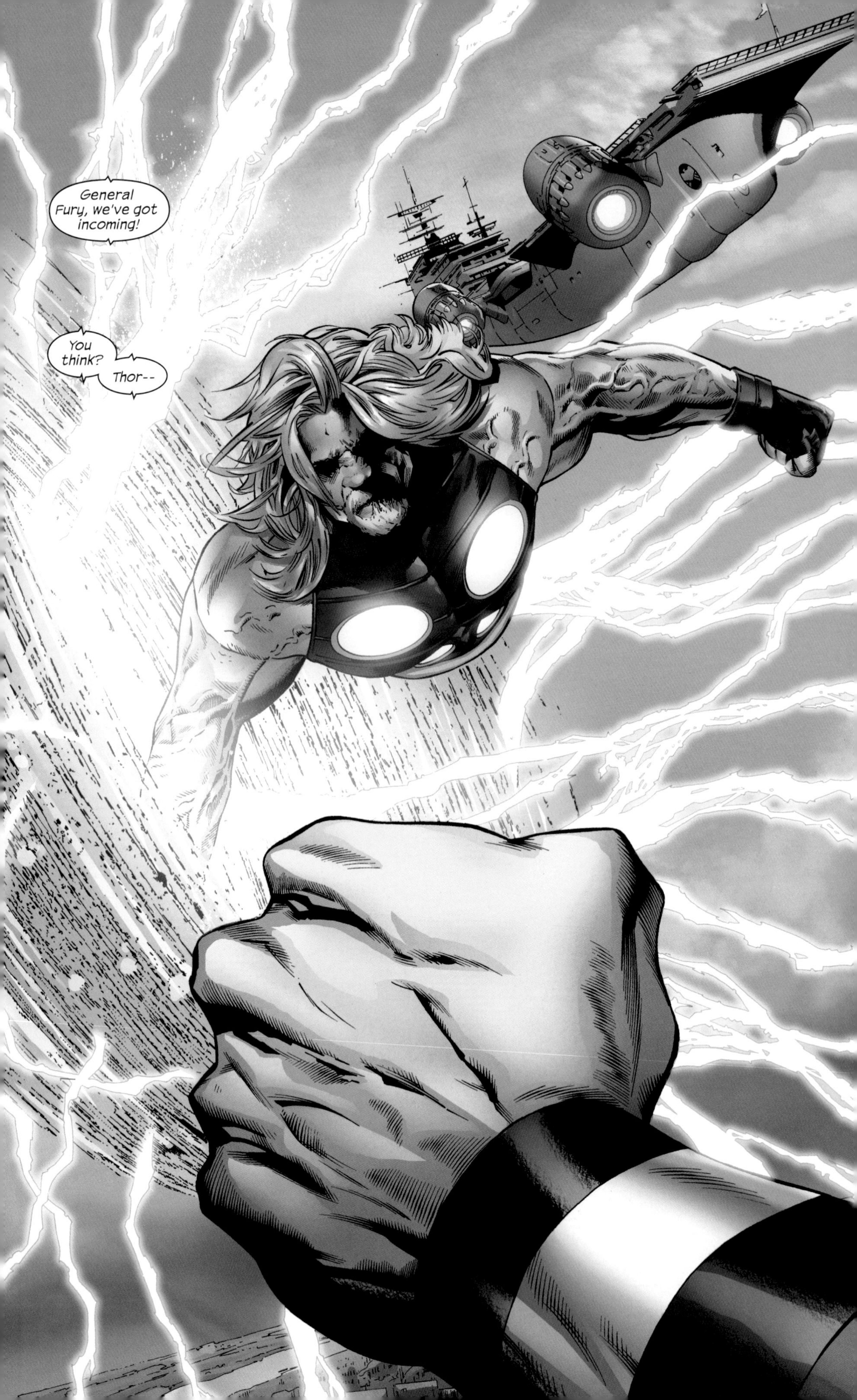
General Fury, we've got incoming!
You think?
Thor--

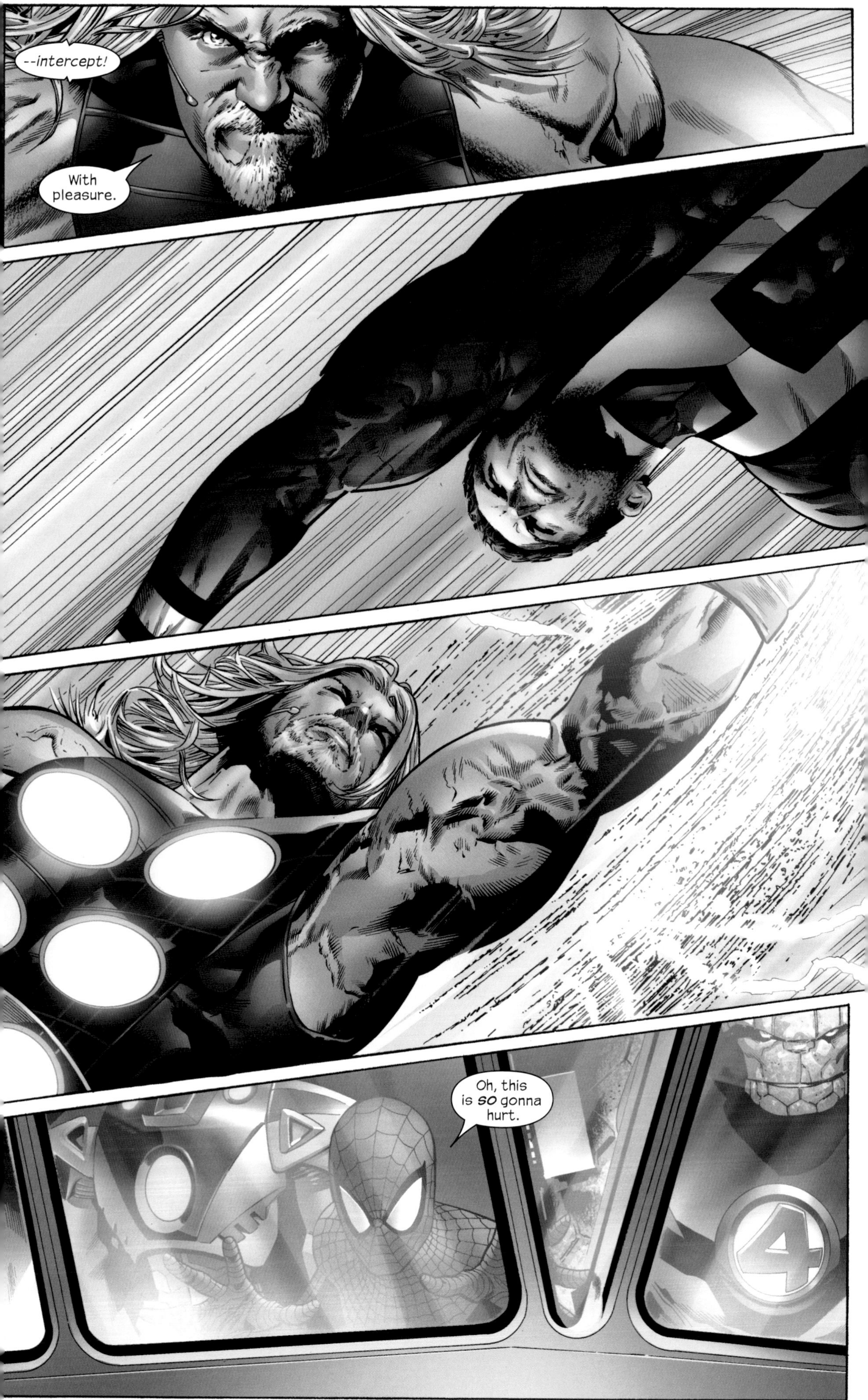
--intercept!
With pleasure.
Oh, this is *SO* gonna hurt.

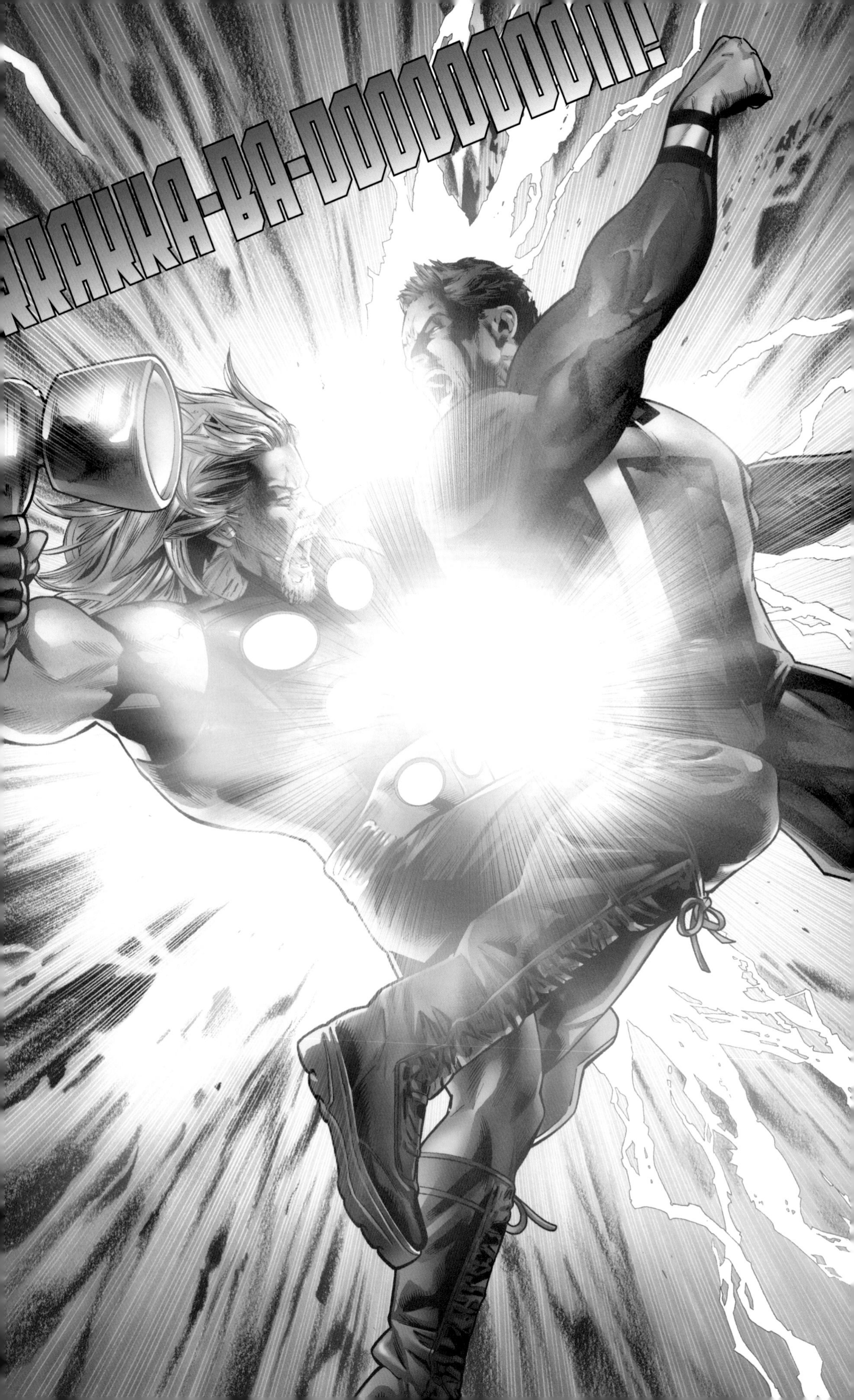
RRAKKA-BA-DOOOOOOOOM!

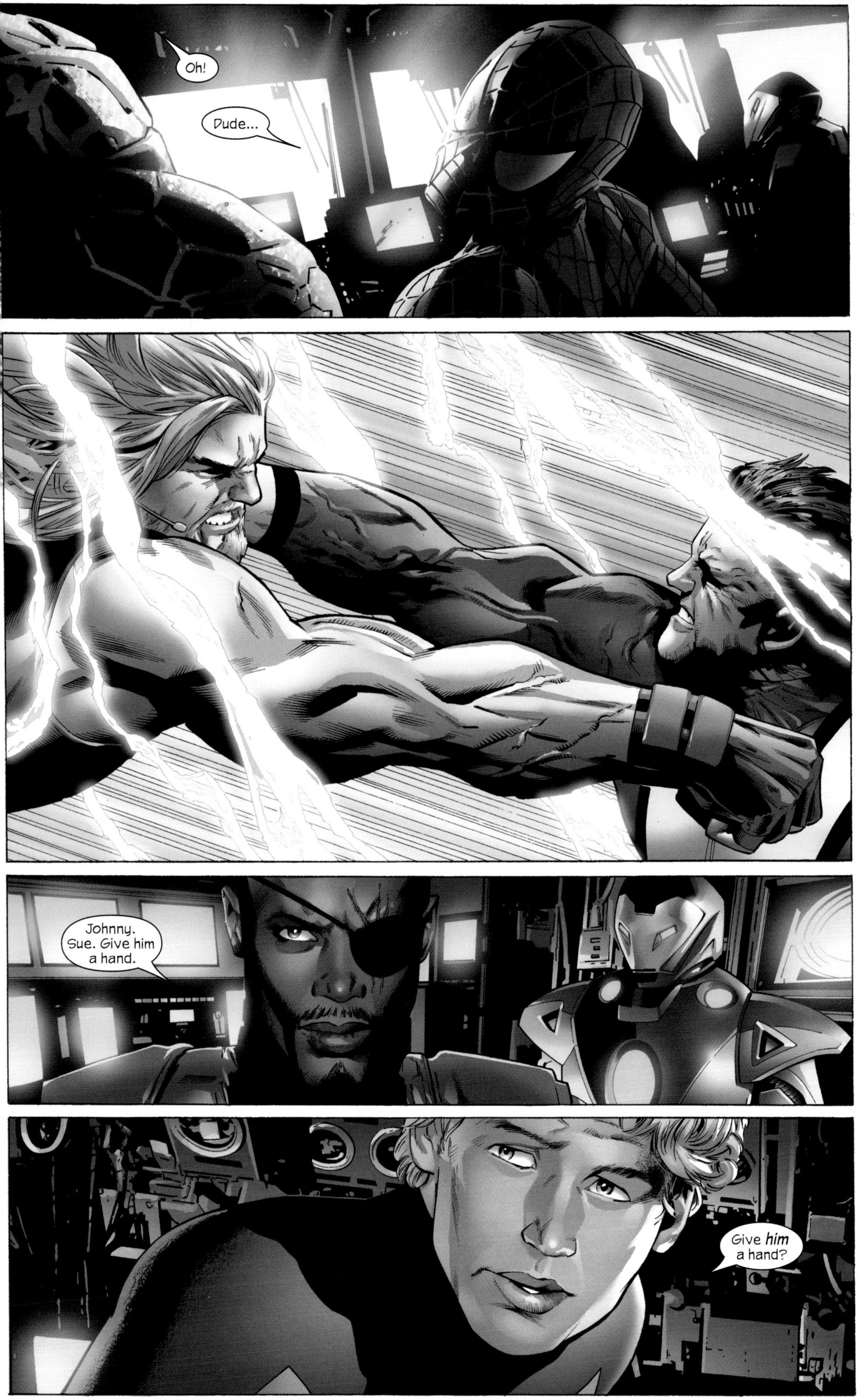
Oh!
Dude...
Johnny. Sue. Give him a hand.
Give *him* a hand?

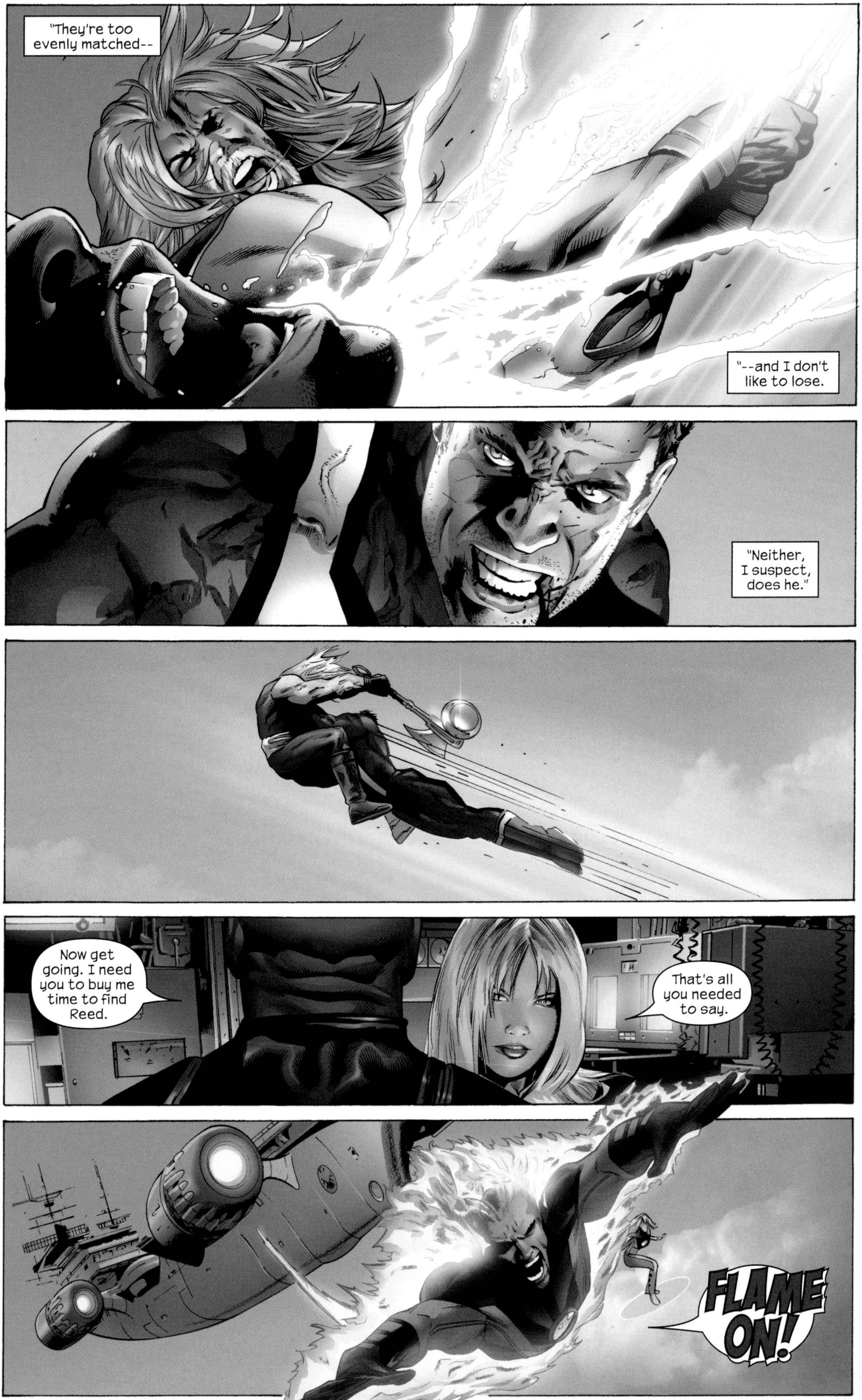
"They're too evenly matched--
"--and I don't like to lose.
"Neither, I suspect, does he."
Now get going. I need you to buy me time to find Reed.
That's all you needed to say.
FLAME ON!

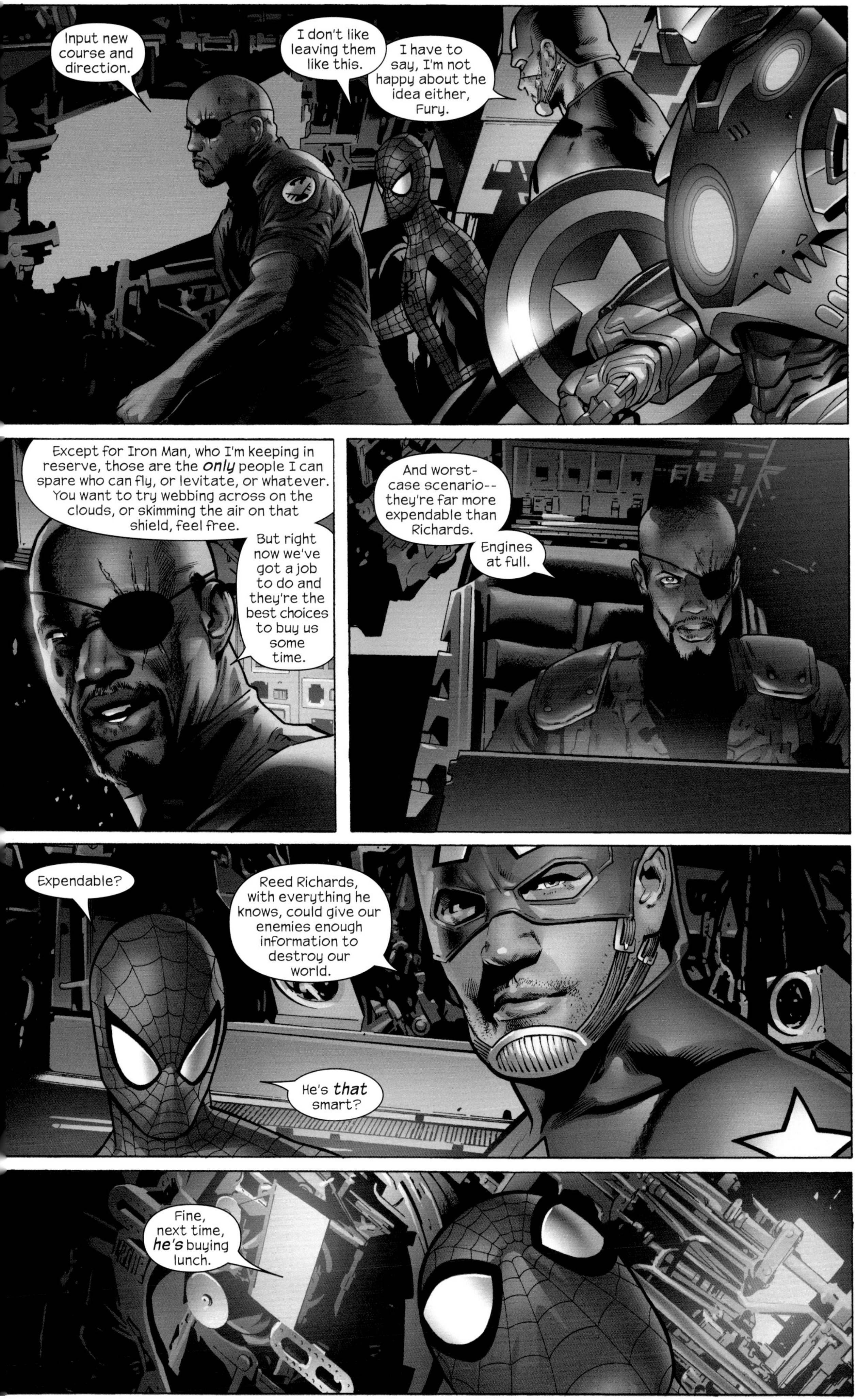

Input new course and direction.
I don't like leaving them like this.
I have to say, I'm not happy about the idea either, Fury.
Except for Iron Man, who I'm keeping in reserve, those are the *only* people I can spare who can fly, or levitate, or whatever. You want to try webbing across on the clouds, or skimming the air on that shield, feel free.
But right now we've got a job to do and they're the best choices to buy us some time.
And worst-case scenario--they're far more expendable than Richards.
Engines at full.
Expendable?
Reed Richards, with everything he knows, could give our enemies enough information to destroy our world.
He's *that* smart?
Fine, next time, ***he's*** buying lunch.

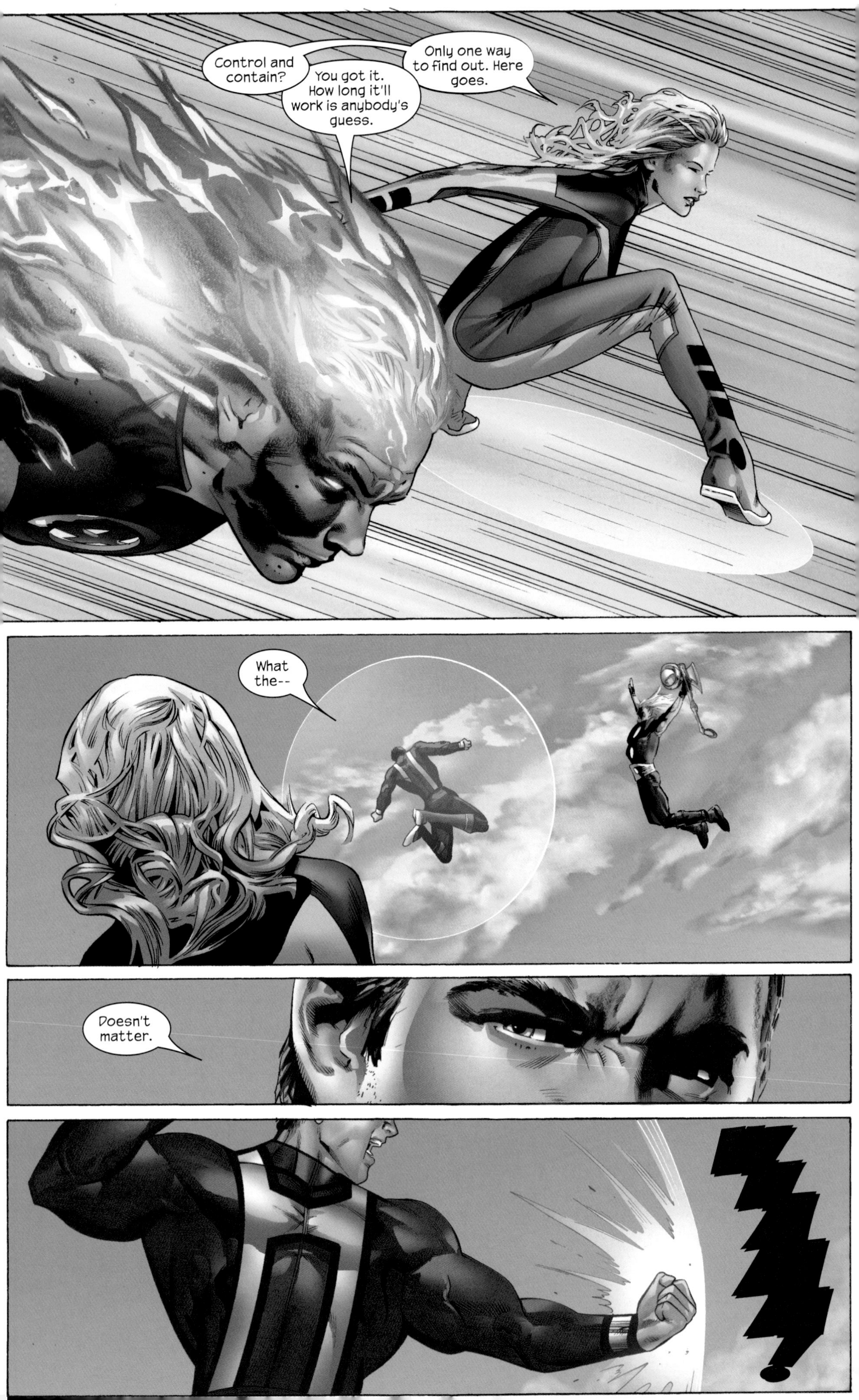
Control and contain?
You got it. How long it'll work is anybody's guess.
Only one way to find out. Here goes.
What the--
Doesn't matter.

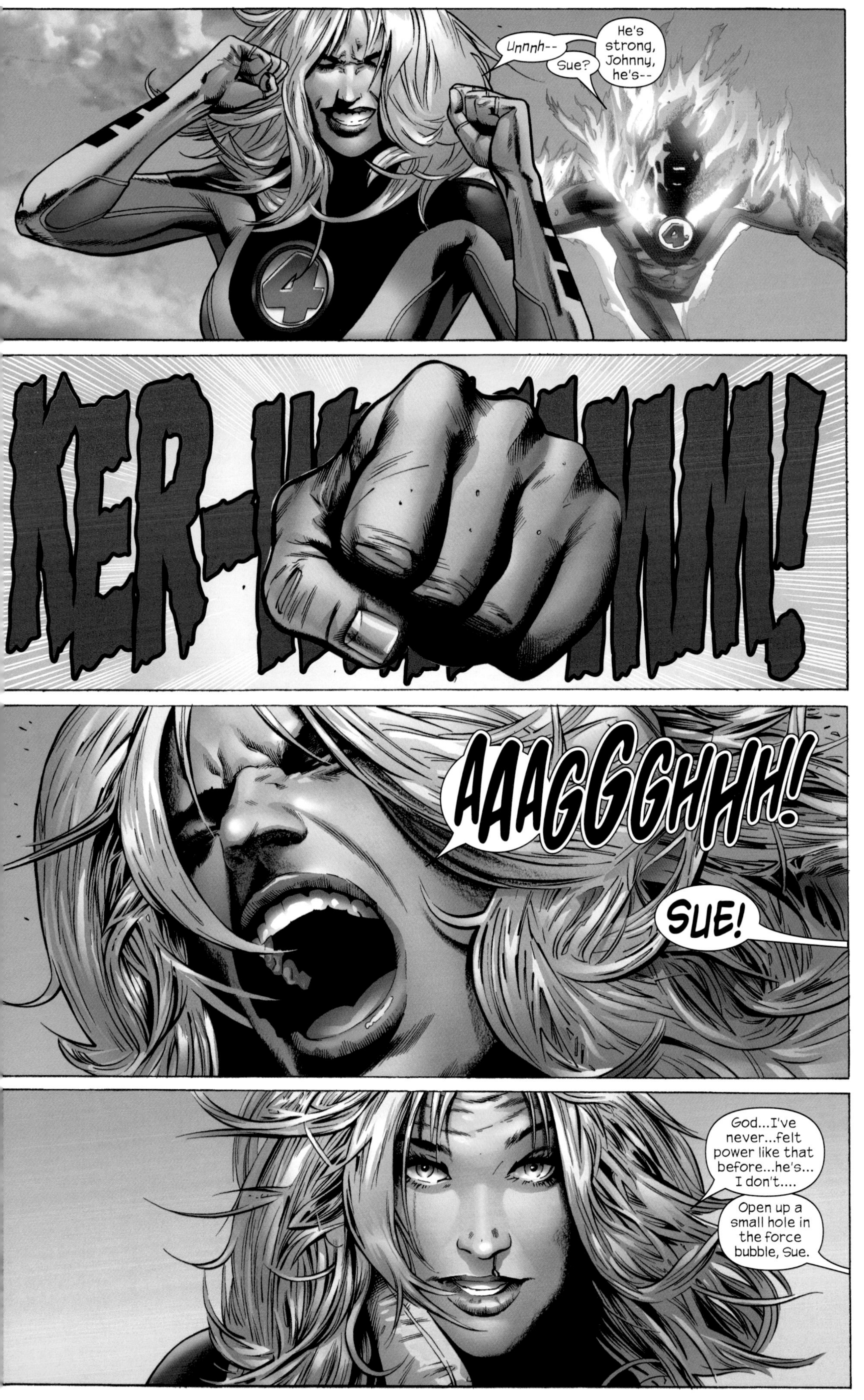
Unnnh--
Sue?
He's strong, Johnny, he's--
KER-
AAAGGGHHH!
SUE!
God...I've never...felt power like that before...he's... I don't....
Open up a small hole in the force bubble, Sue.

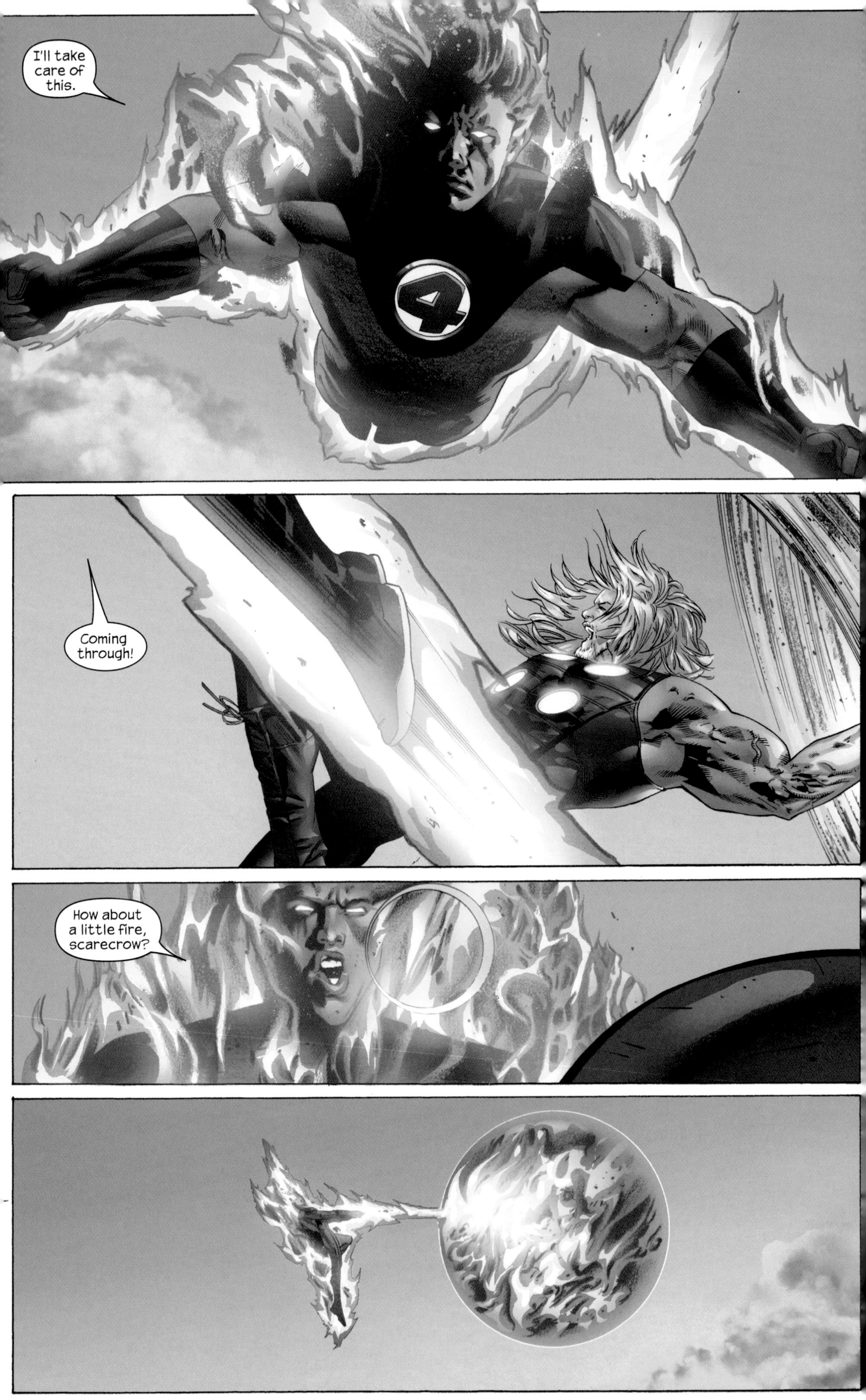
I'll take care of this.
Coming through!
How about a little fire, scarecrow?

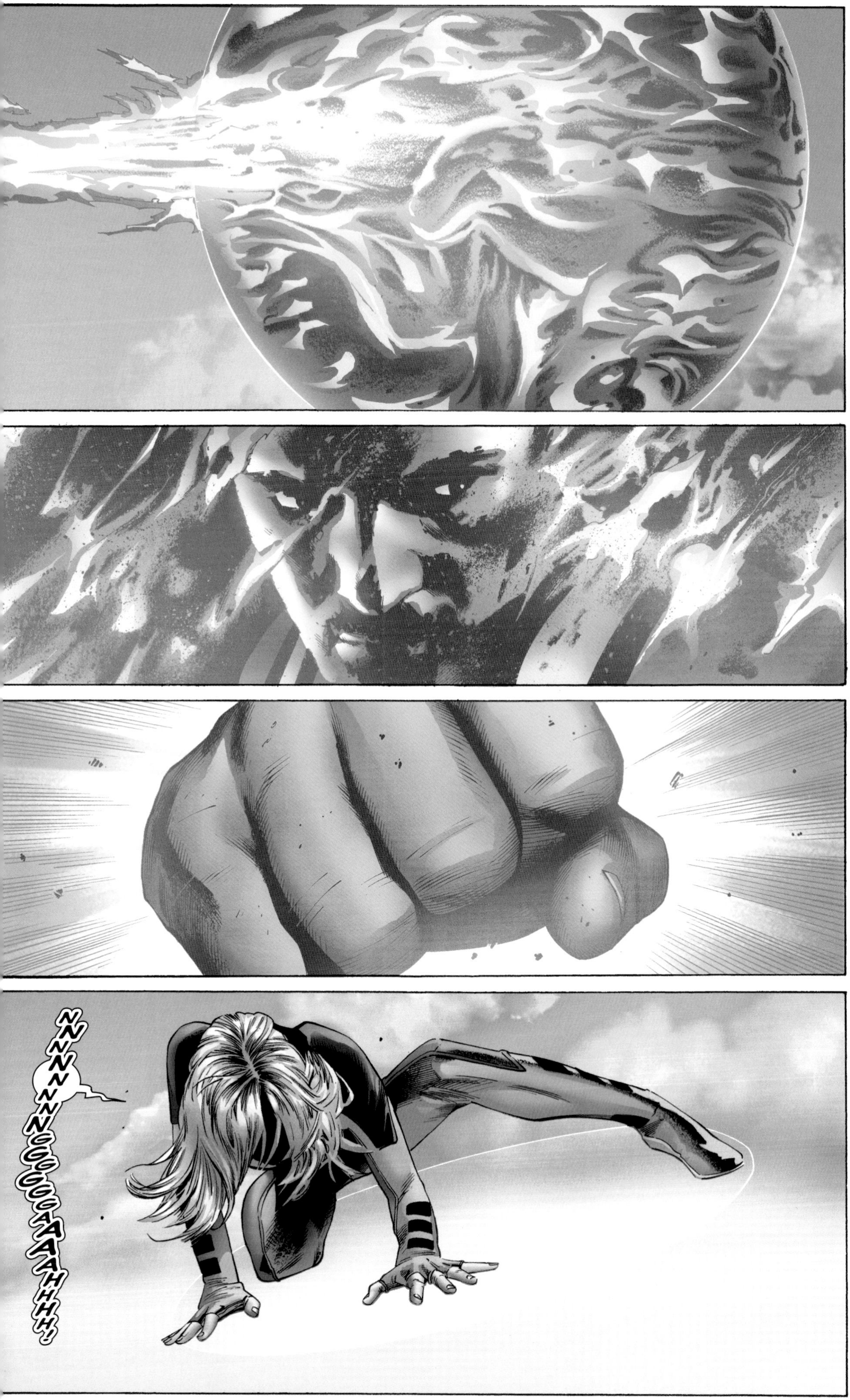
NNNNNNNGGGGAAAHHHH!

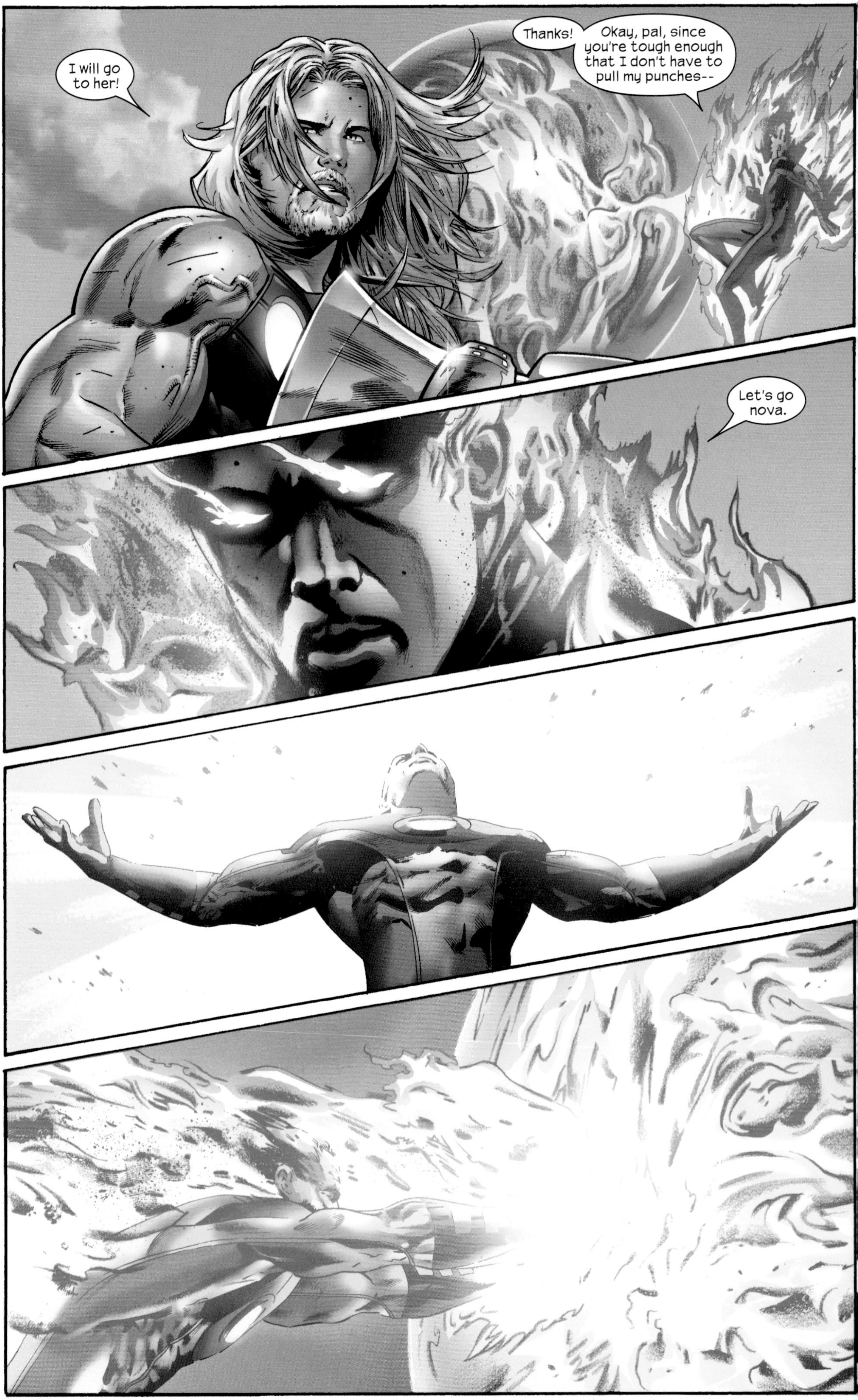
I will go to her!
Thanks!
Okay, pal, since you're tough enough that I don't have to pull my punches--
Let's go nova.

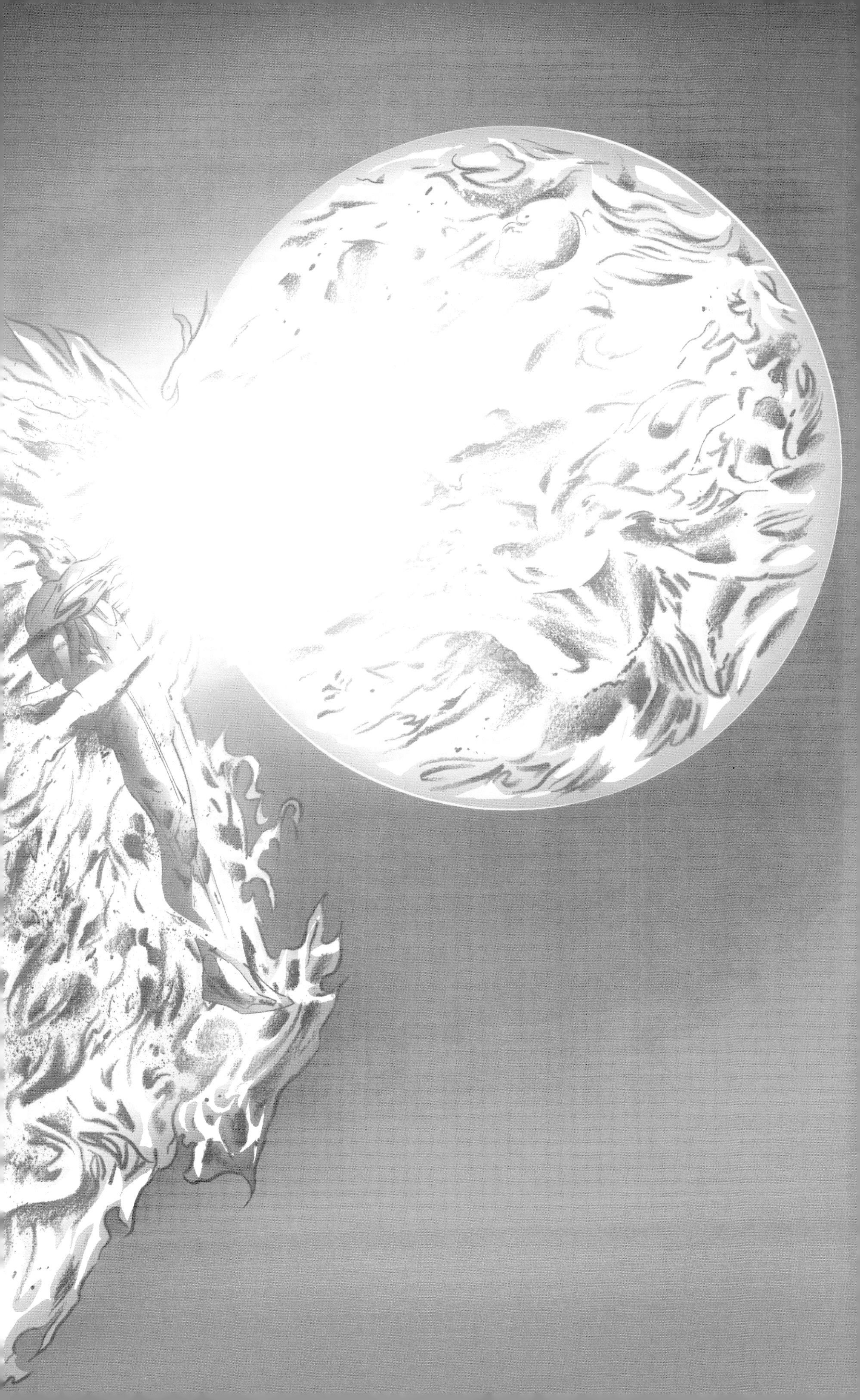

Don't want to kill him...but I don't know where to stop...can't keep this going forever, either, I--
--I--
Burn.

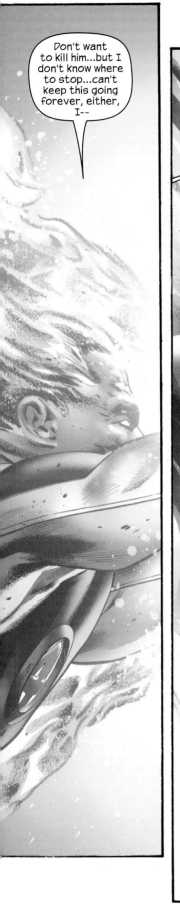

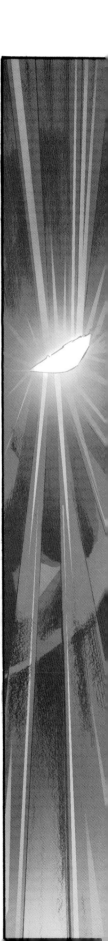

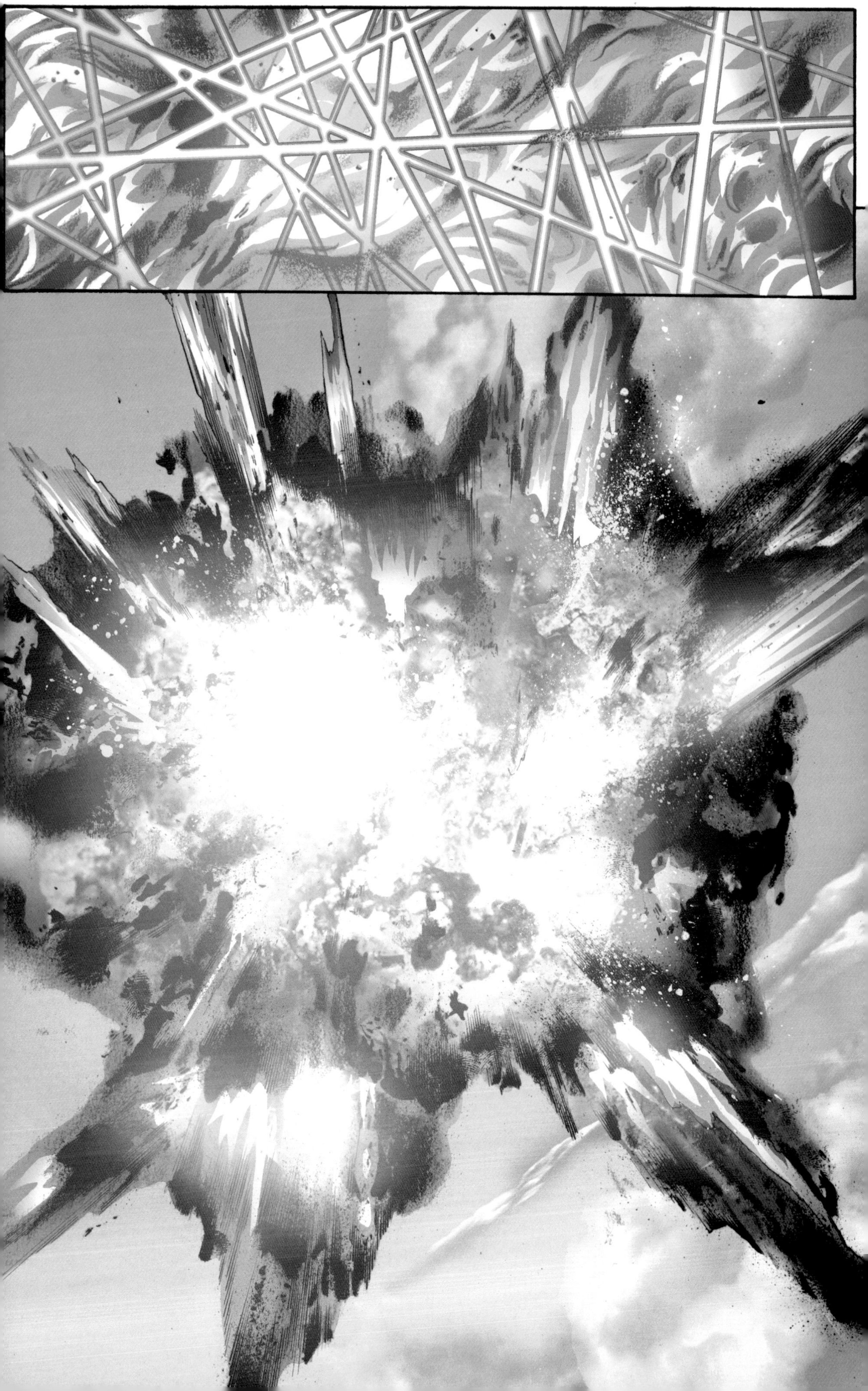

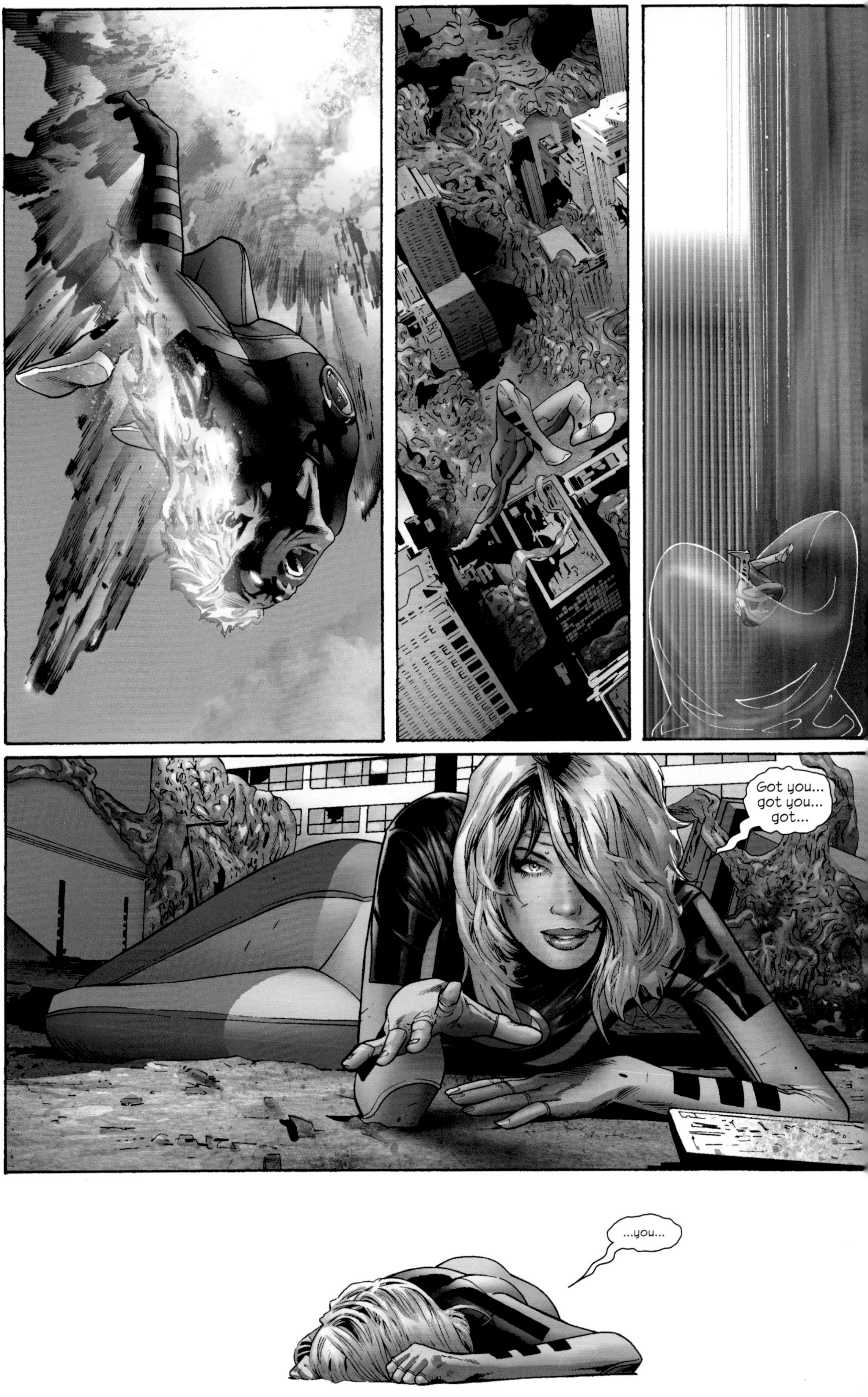
Got you...
got you...
got...
...you...

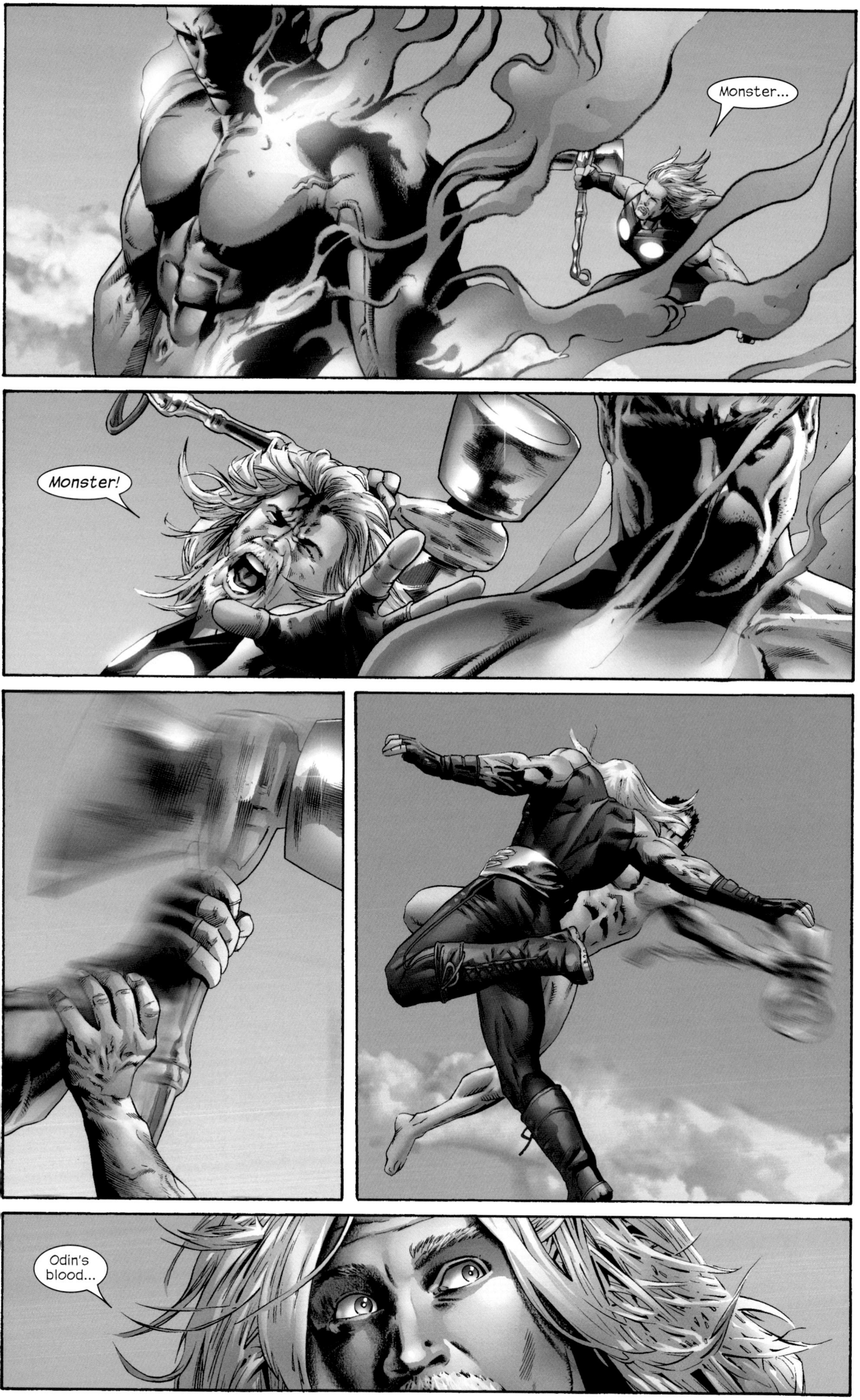
Monster...
Monster!
Odin's blood...

No. **Your** blood.

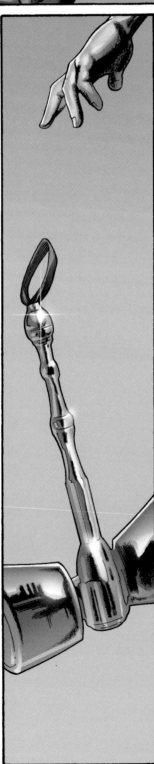

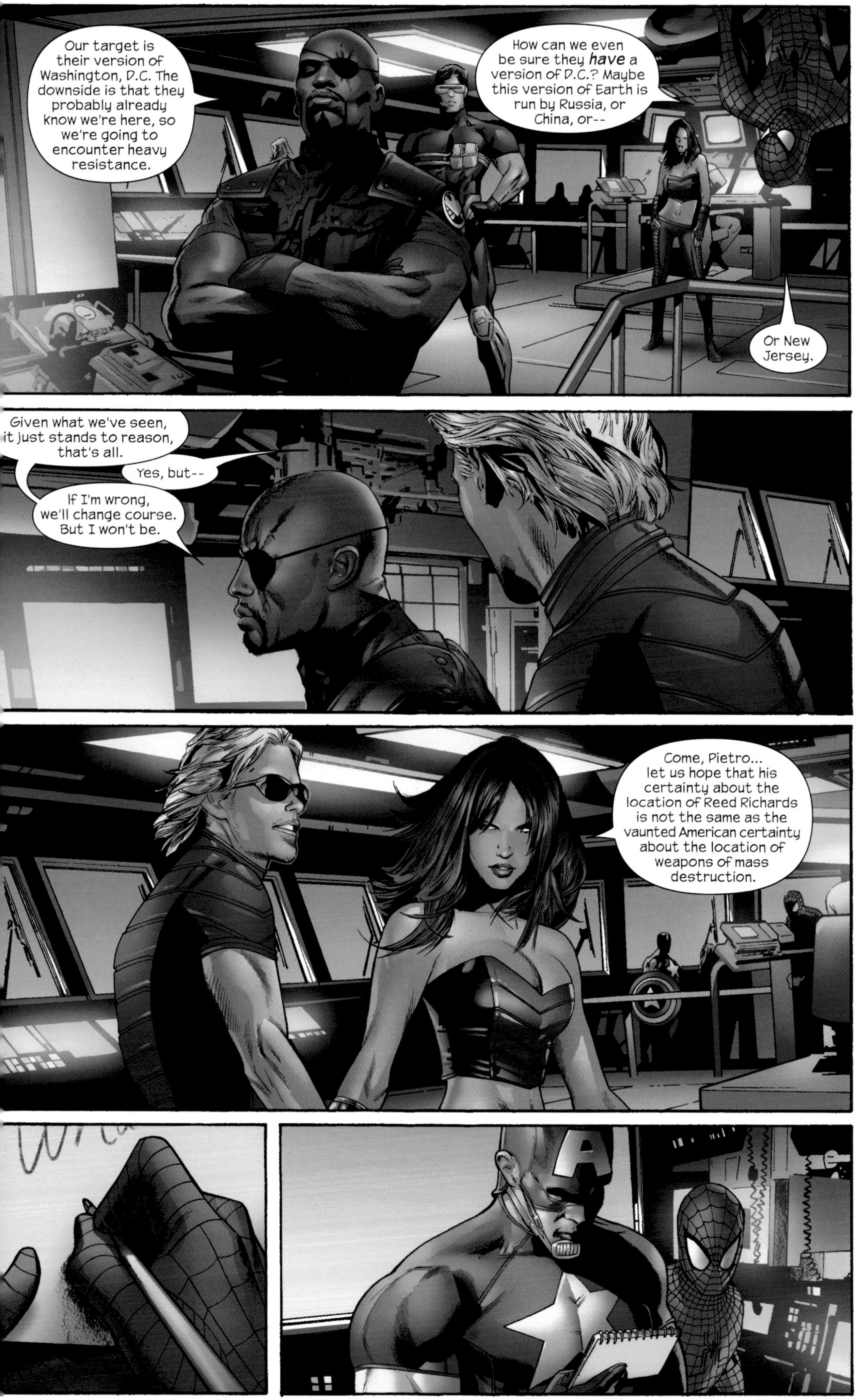
Our target is their version of Washington, D.C. The downside is that they probably already know we're here, so we're going to encounter heavy resistance.
How can we even be sure they *have* a version of D.C.? Maybe this version of Earth is run by Russia, or China, or--
Or New Jersey.
Given what we've seen, it just stands to reason, that's all.
Yes, but--
If I'm wrong, we'll change course. But I won't be.
Come, Pietro... let us hope that his certainty about the location of Reed Richards is not the same as the vaunted American certainty about the location of weapons of mass destruction.

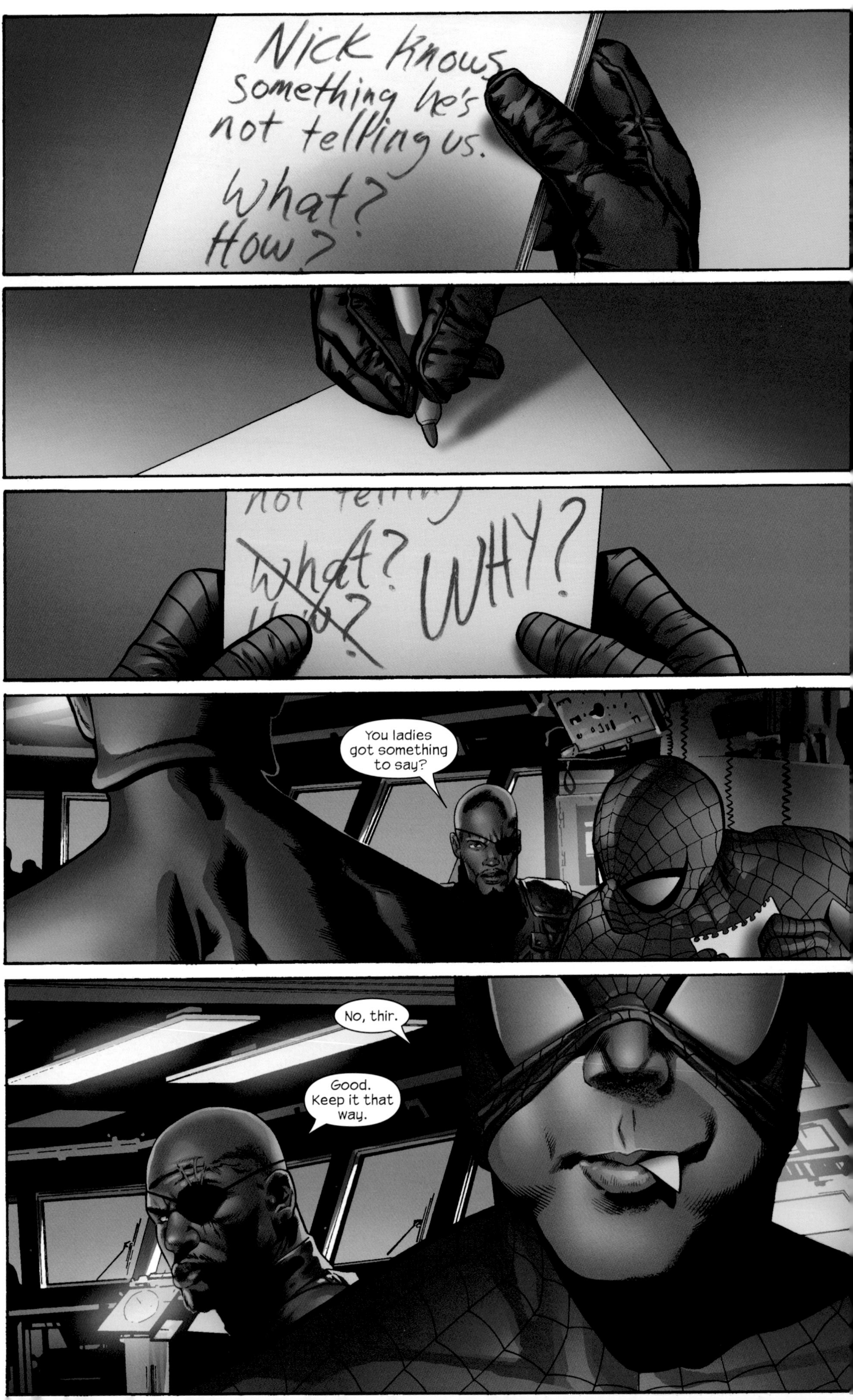
Nick knows something he's not telling us.
What?
How?
What?
How?
WHY?
You ladies got something to say?
No, thir.
Good. Keep it that way.

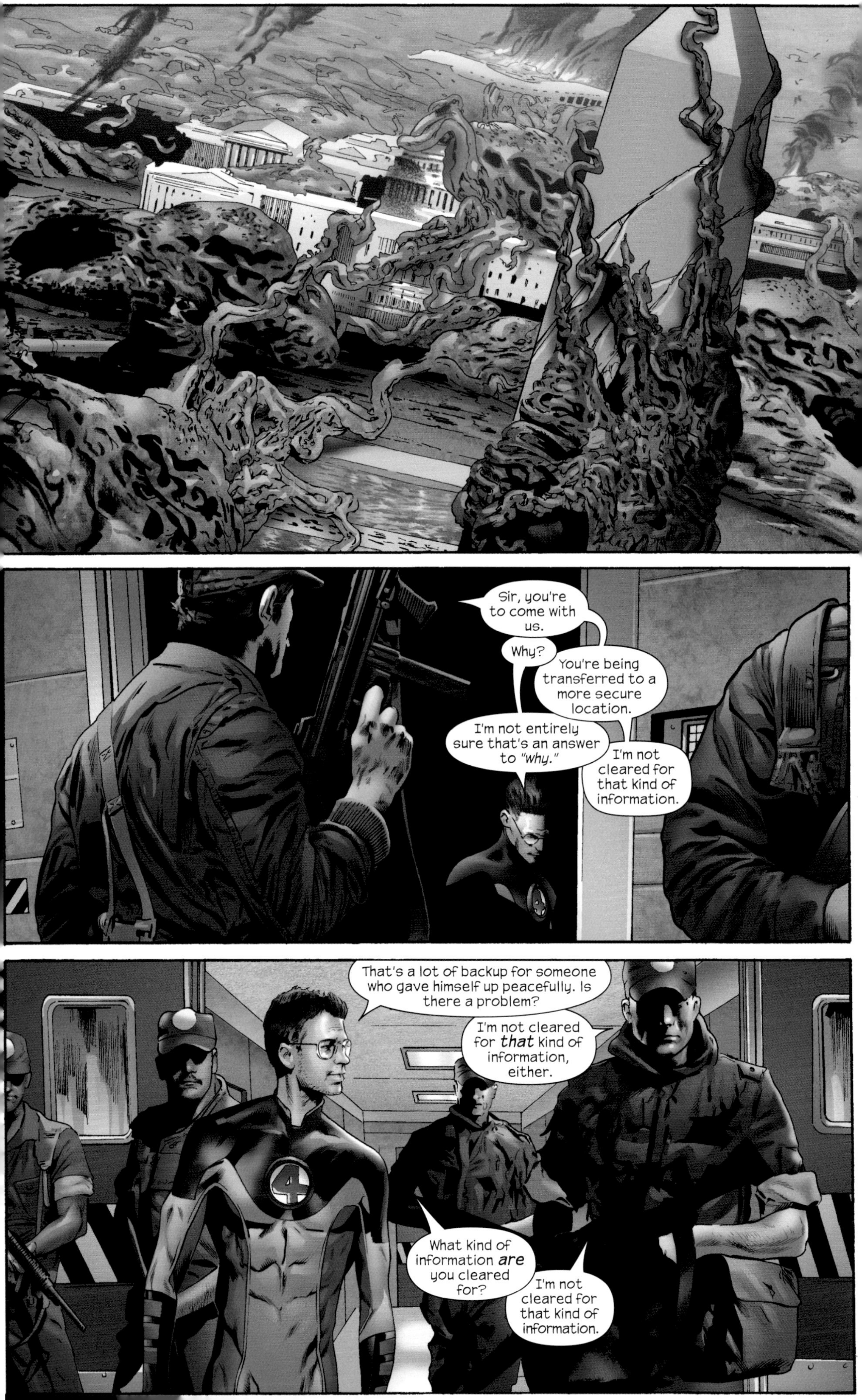

Sir, you're to come with us.
Why?
You're being transferred to a more secure location.
I'm not entirely sure that's an answer to "why."
I'm not cleared for that kind of information.
That's a lot of backup for someone who gave himself up peacefully. Is there a problem?
I'm not cleared for *that* kind of information, either.
What kind of information *are* you cleared for?
I'm not cleared for that kind of information.

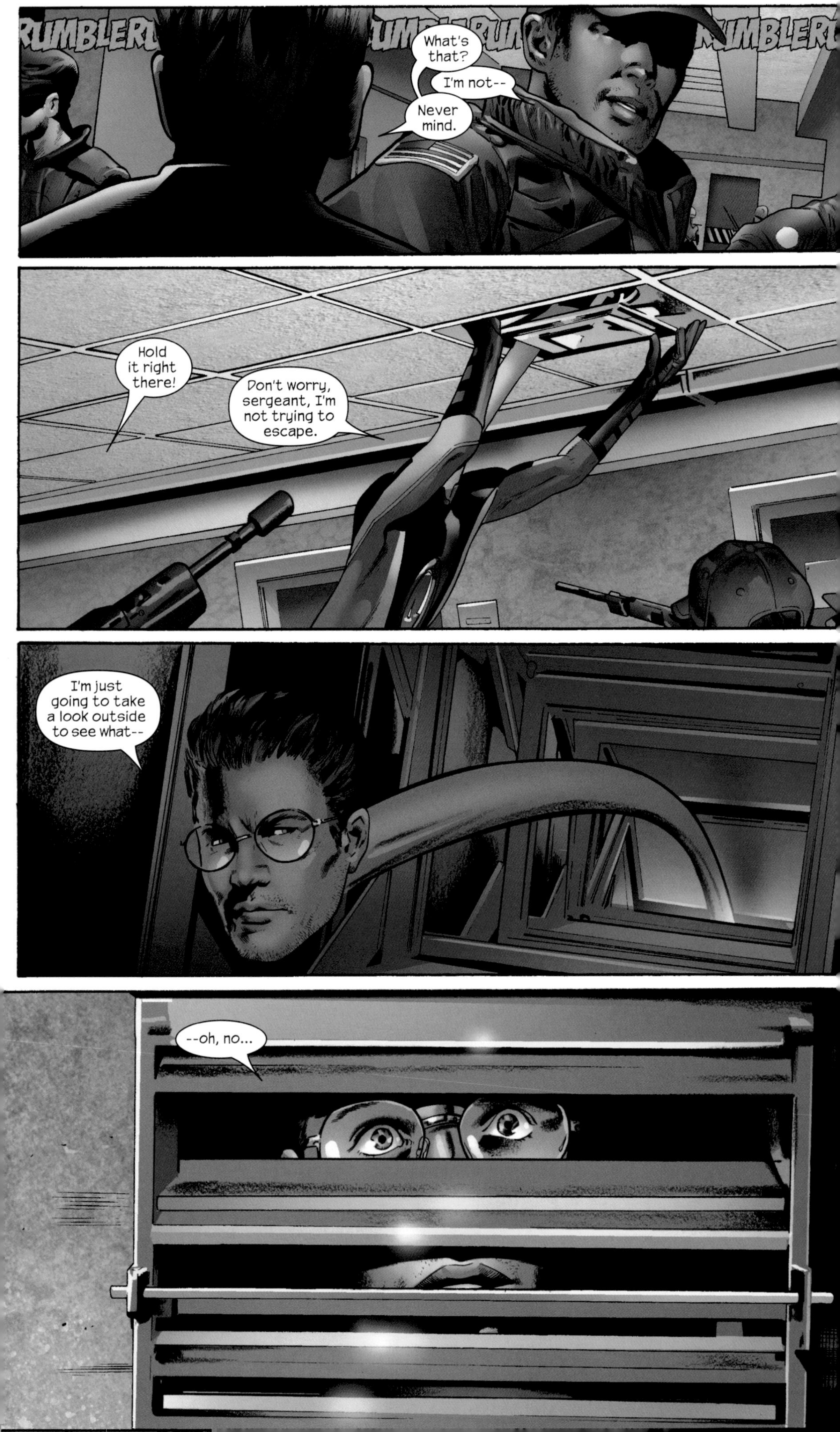
RUMBLERUMBLERUMBLERUMBLERU
What's that?
I'm not--
Never mind.
Hold it right there!
Don't worry, sergeant, I'm not trying to escape.
I'm just going to take a look outside to see what--
--oh, no...

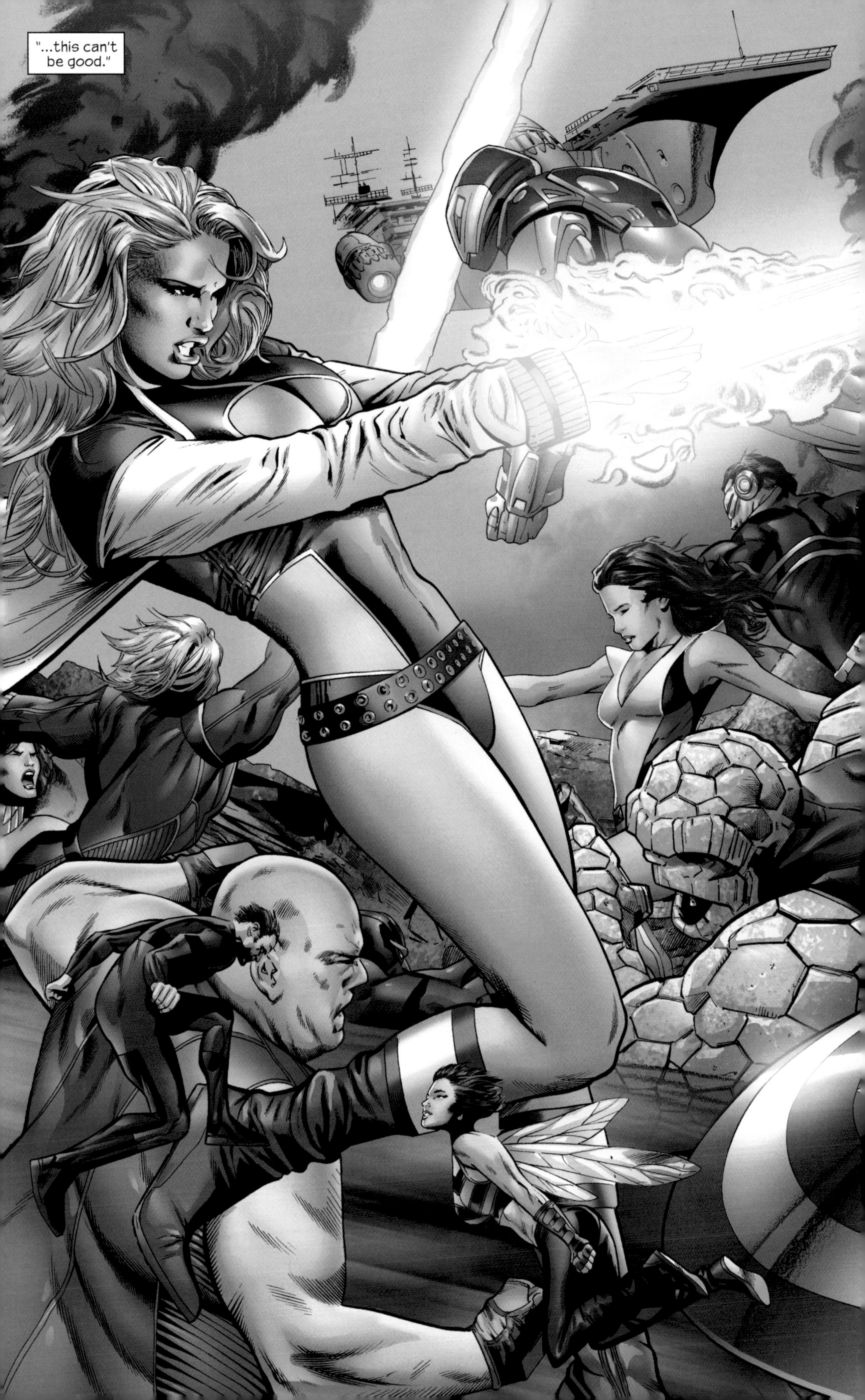
"...this can't be good."

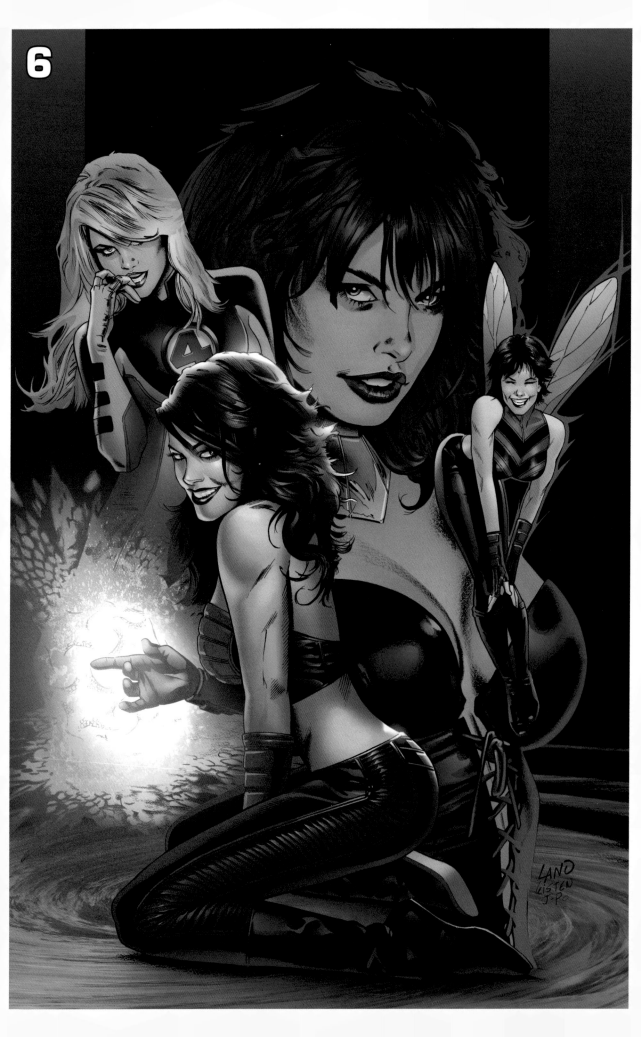

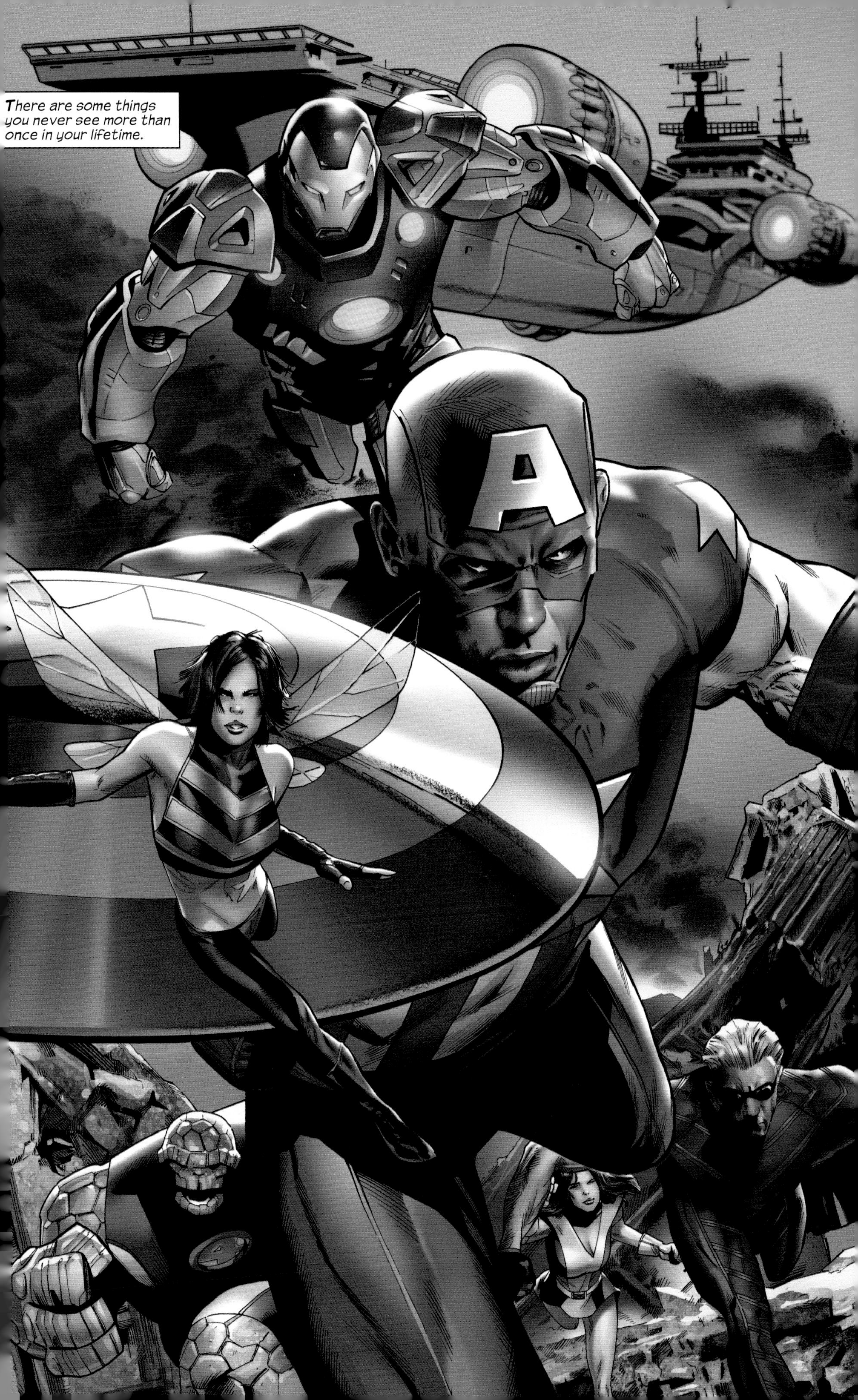
There are some things you never see more than once in your lifetime.

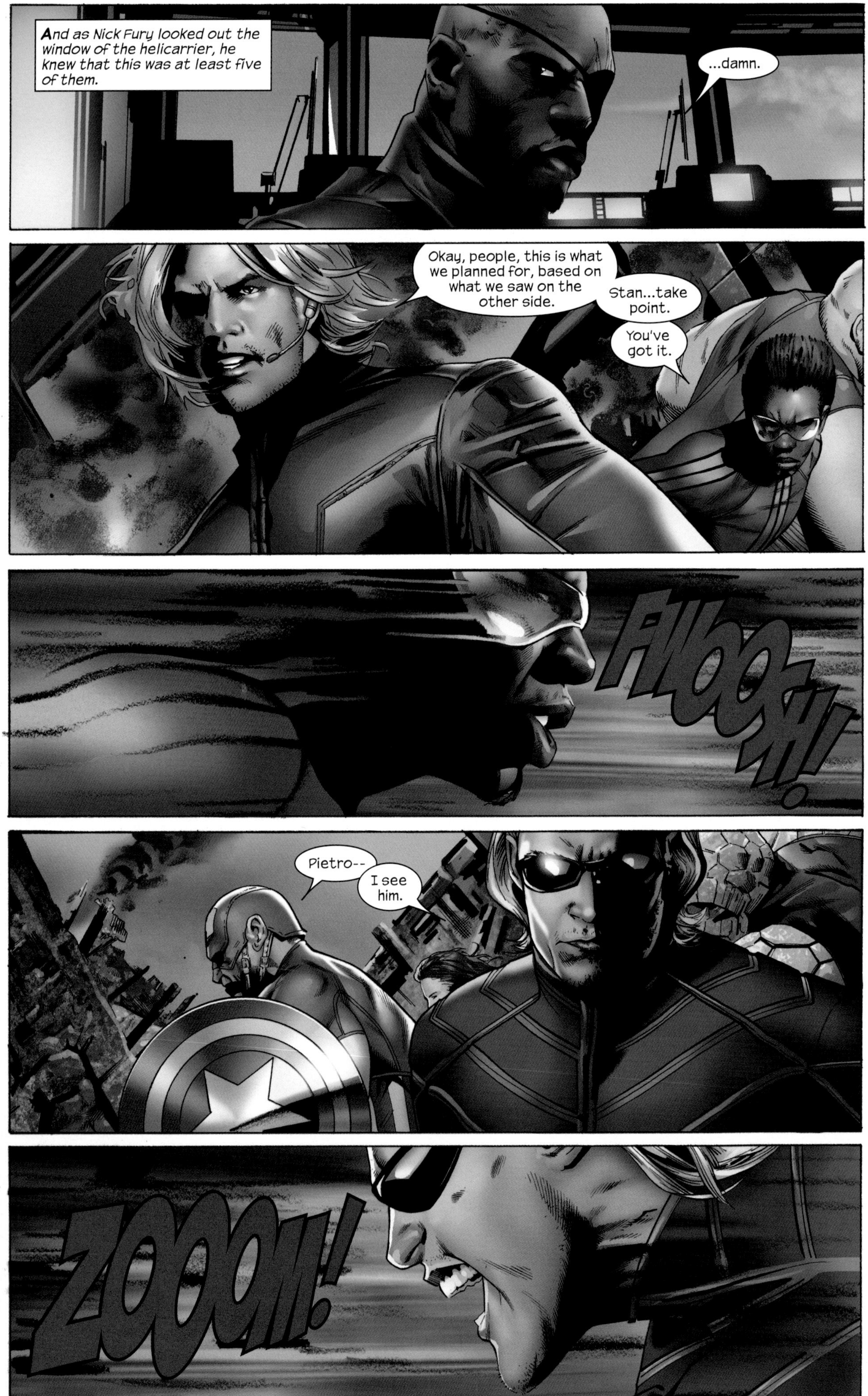

And as Nick Fury looked out the window of the helicarrier, he knew that this was at least five of them.
...damn.
Okay, people, this is what we planned for, based on what we saw on the other side.
Stan...take point.
You've got it.
FWOOSH!
Pietro--
I see him.
ZOOOM!

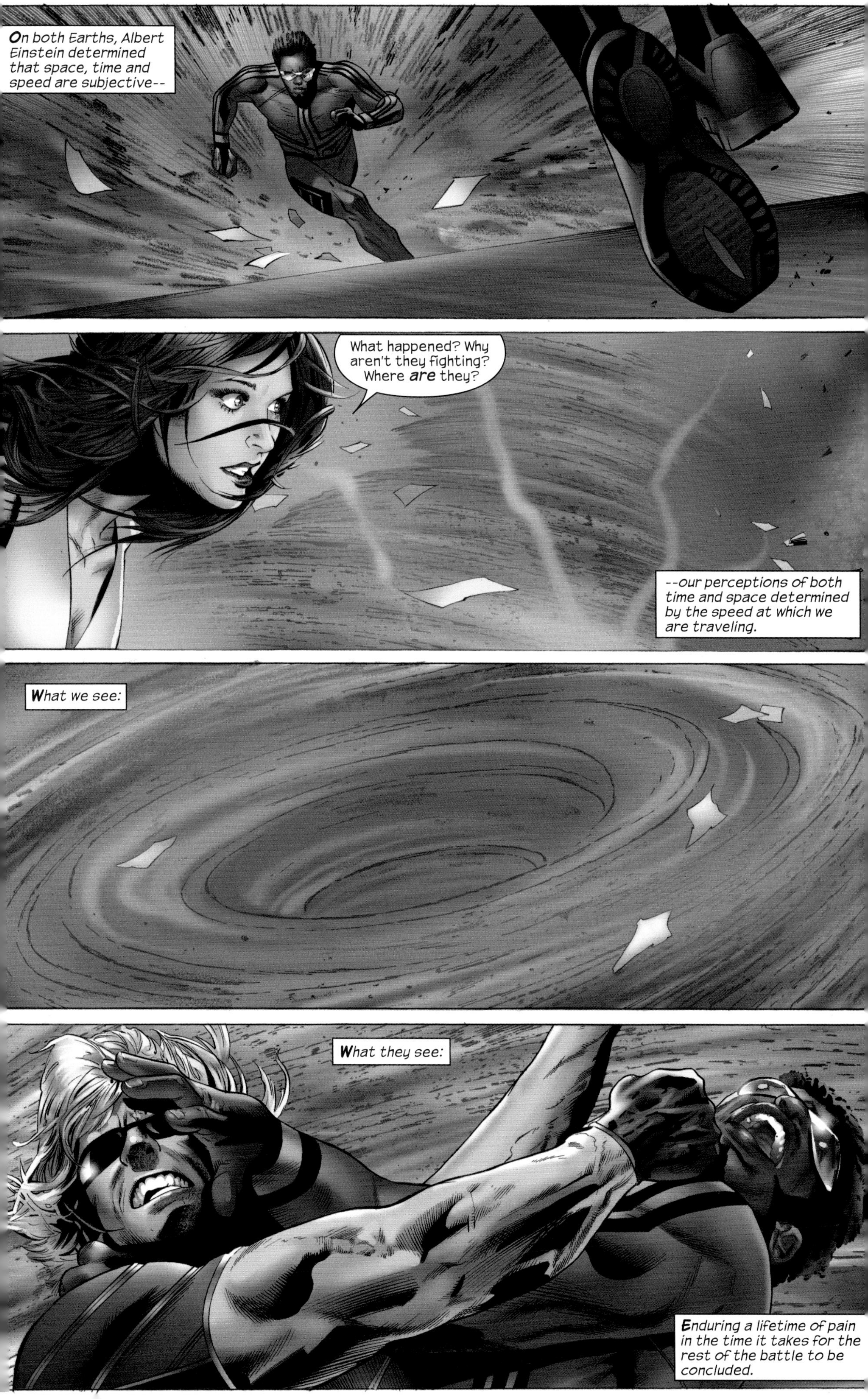
On both Earths, Albert Einstein determined that space, time and speed are subjective--
What happened? Why aren't they fighting? Where are they?
--our perceptions of both time and space determined by the speed at which we are traveling.
What we see:
What they see:
Enduring a lifetime of pain in the time it takes for the rest of the battle to be concluded.

Let's try and soften them up a little.

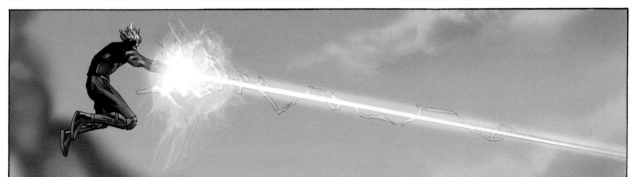

FSSSSSSSSH!!

Welcome to the majors.

So. Now that we've learned you like to accessorize with jewelry--

--what *else* you got?

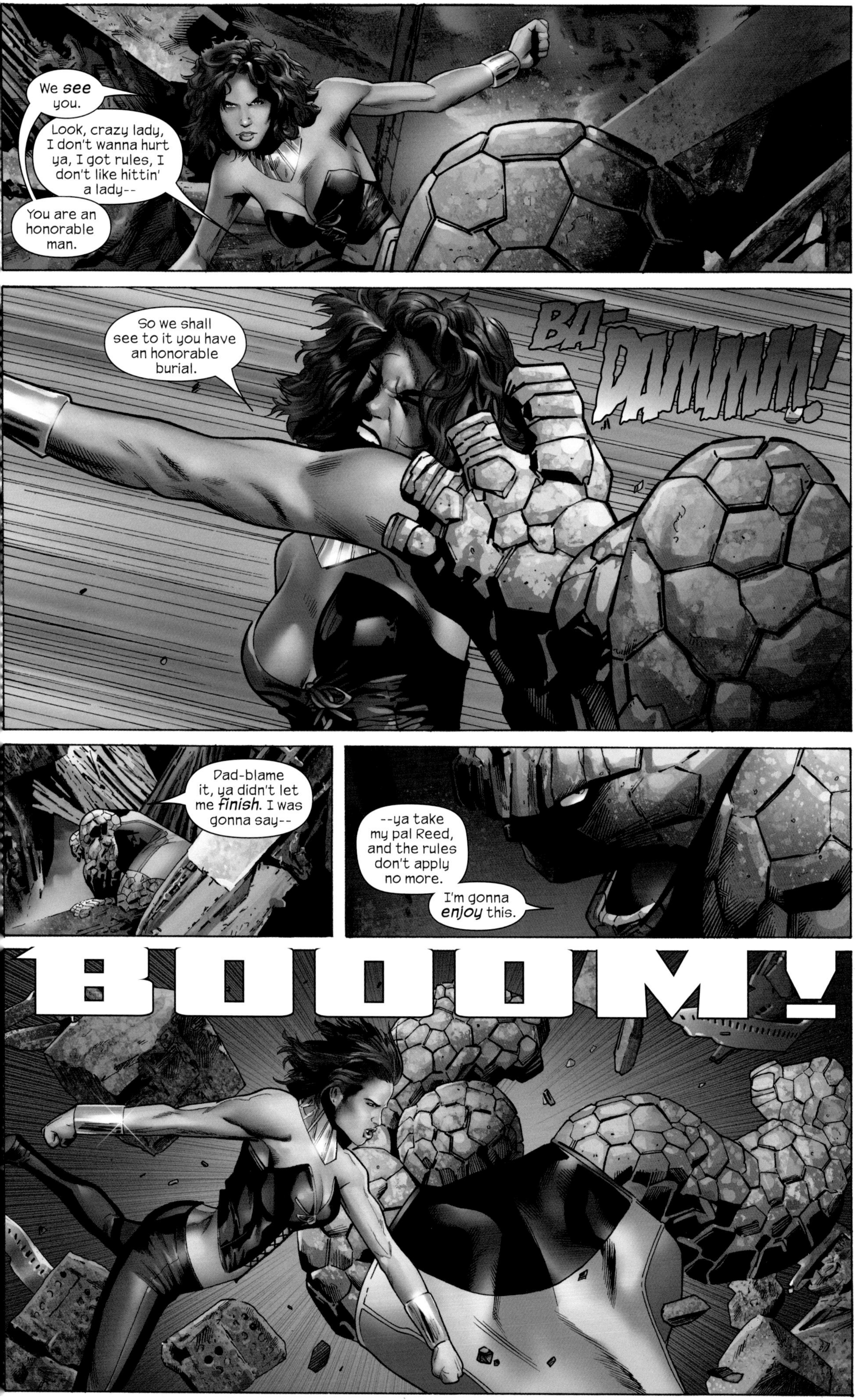
We see you.
Look, crazy lady, I don't wanna hurt ya, I got rules, I don't like hittin' a lady--
You are an honorable man.
So we shall see to it you have an honorable burial.
BA-DAMMM!
Dad-blame it, ya didn't let me finish. I was gonna say--
--ya take my pal Reed, and the rules don't apply no more.
I'm gonna enjoy this.
BOOOM!

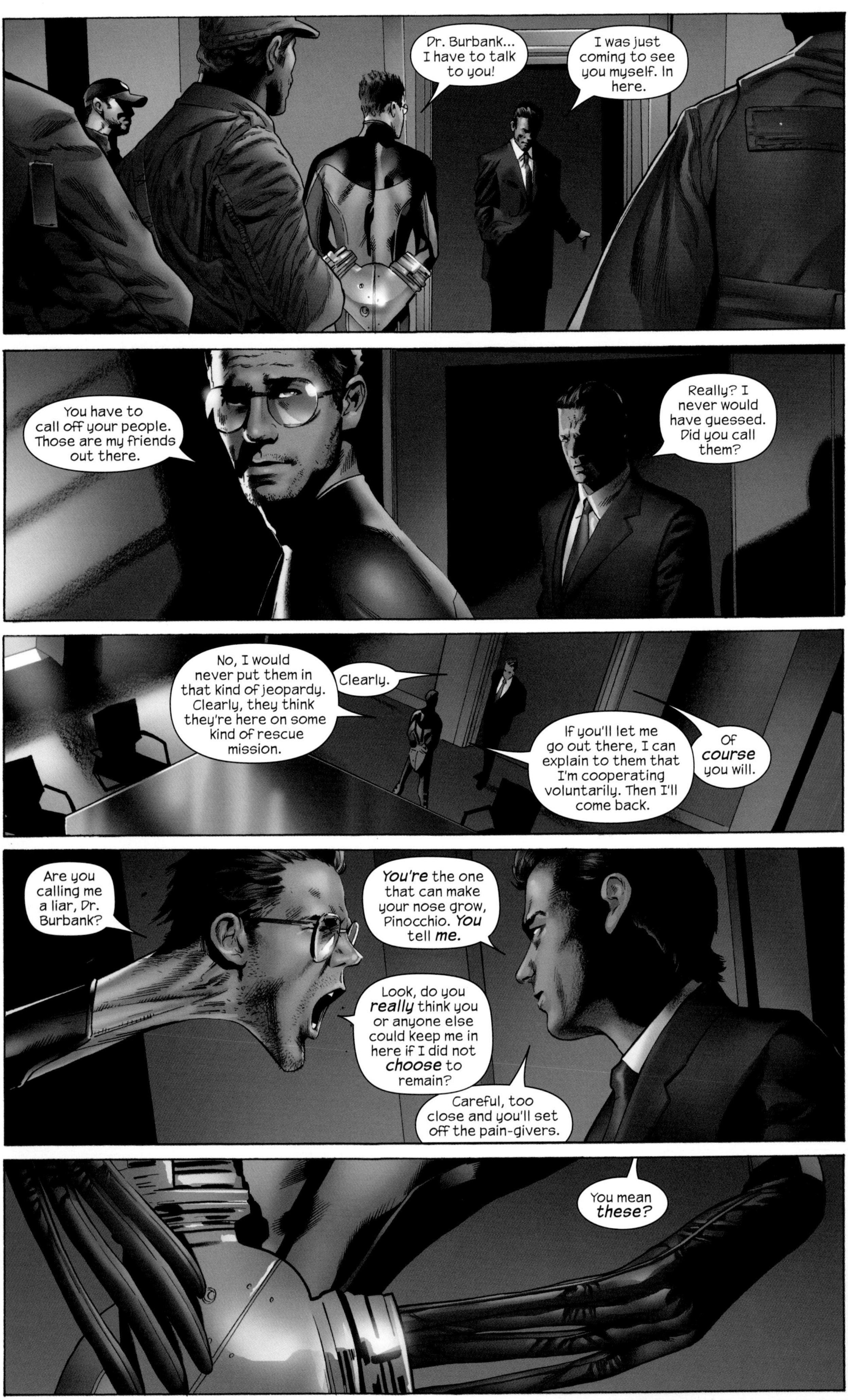
Dr. Burbank... I have to talk to you!
I was just coming to see you myself. In here.
You have to call off your people. Those are my friends out there.
Really? I never would have guessed. Did you call them?
No, I would never put them in that kind of jeopardy. Clearly, they think they're here on some kind of rescue mission.
Clearly.
If you'll let me go out there, I can explain to them that I'm cooperating voluntarily. Then I'll come back.
Of course you will.
Are you calling me a liar, Dr. Burbank?
You're the one that can make your nose grow, Pinocchio. You tell me.
Look, do you really think you or anyone else could keep me in here if I did not choose to remain?
Careful, too close and you'll set off the pain-givers.
You mean these?

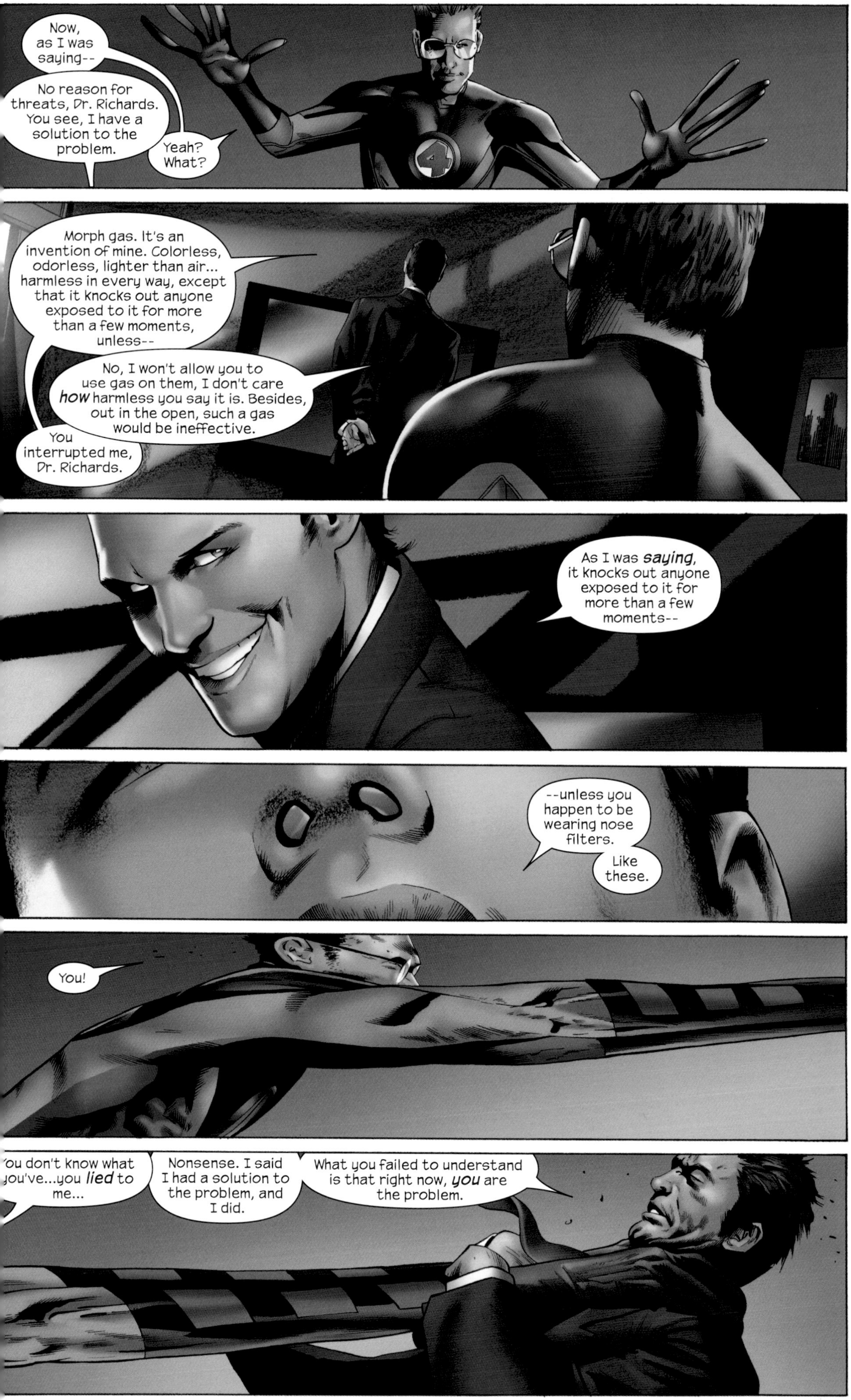
Now, as I was saying--
No reason for threats, Dr. Richards. You see, I have a solution to the problem.
Yeah? What?
Morph gas. It's an invention of mine. Colorless, odorless, lighter than air... harmless in every way, except that it knocks out anyone exposed to it for more than a few moments, unless--
No, I won't allow you to use gas on them, I don't care *how* harmless you say it is. Besides, out in the open, such a gas would be ineffective.
You interrupted me, Dr. Richards.
As I was *saying*, it knocks out anyone exposed to it for more than a few moments--
--unless you happen to be wearing nose filters.
Like these.
You!
You don't know what you've...you *lied* to me...
Nonsense. I said I had a solution to the problem, and I did.
What you failed to understand is that right now, *you* are the problem.

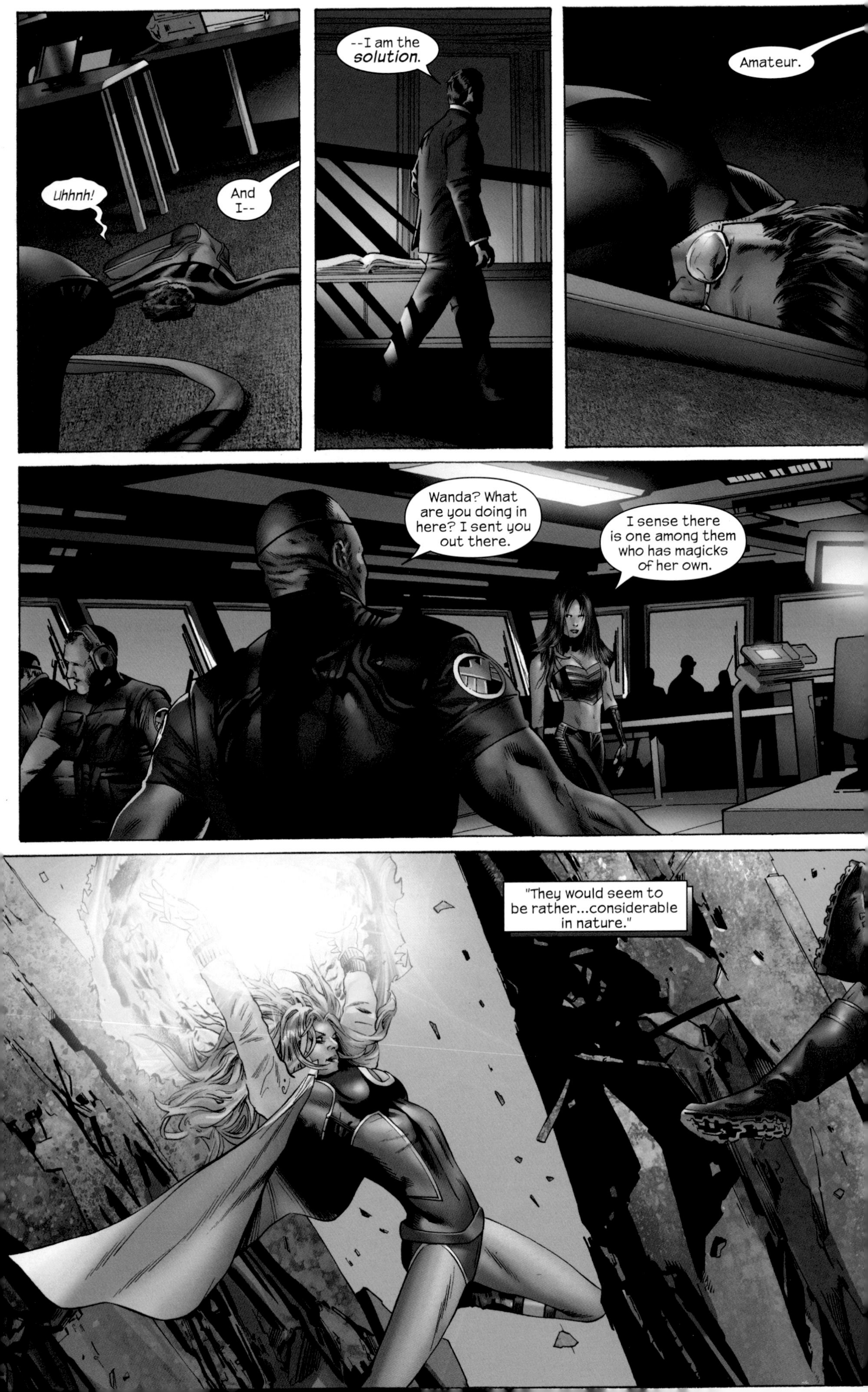

Uhhnh!
And I--
--I am the *solution*.
Amateur.
Wanda? What are you doing in here? I sent you out there.
I sense there is one among them who has magicks of her own.
"They would seem to be rather...considerable in nature."

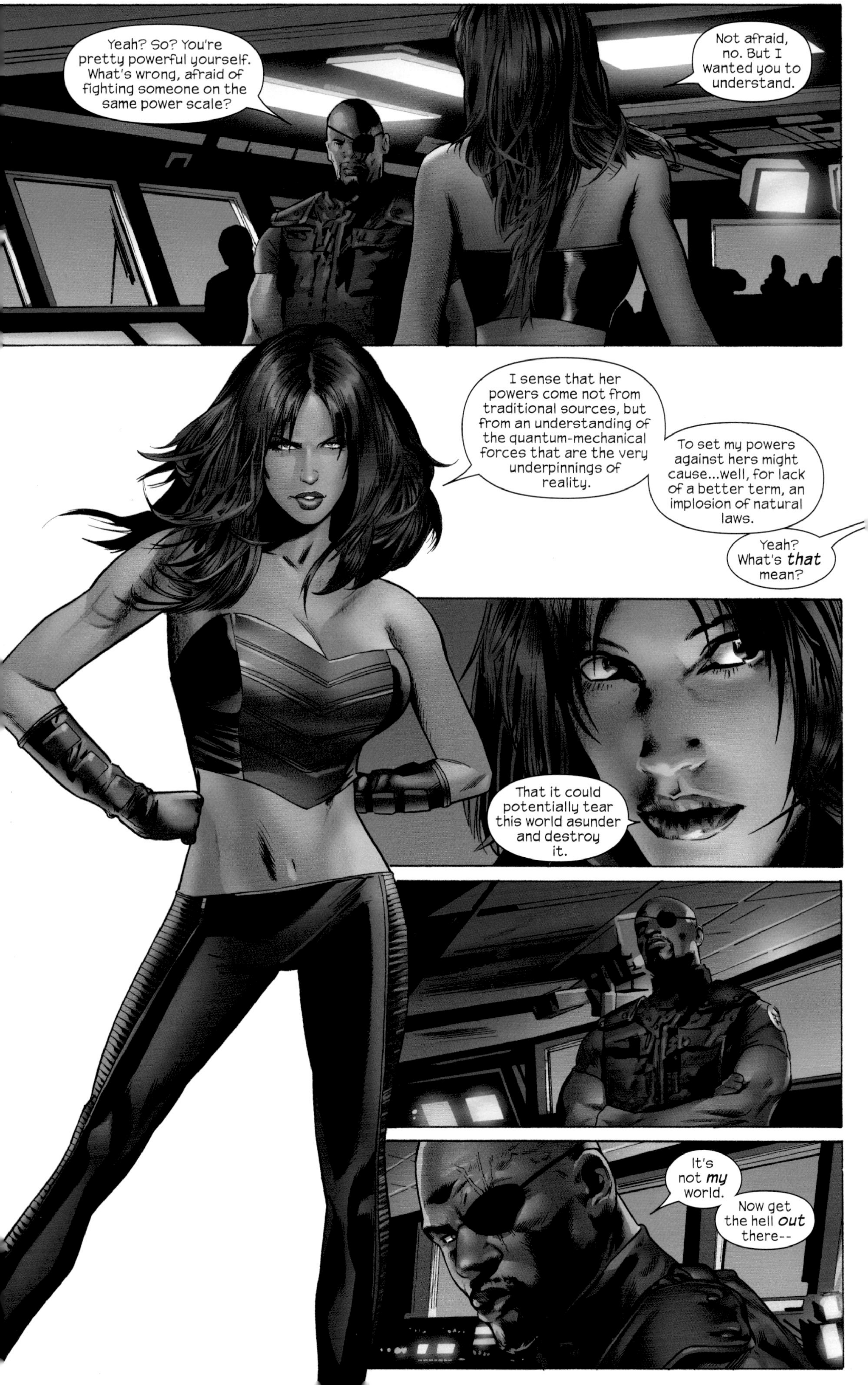
Yeah? So? You're pretty powerful yourself. What's wrong, afraid of fighting someone on the same power scale?
Not afraid, no. But I wanted you to understand.
I sense that her powers come not from traditional sources, but from an understanding of the quantum-mechanical forces that are the very underpinnings of reality.
To set my powers against hers might cause...well, for lack of a better term, an implosion of natural laws.
Yeah? What's *that* mean?
That it could potentially tear this world asunder and destroy it.
It's not *my* world.
Now get the hell *out* there--

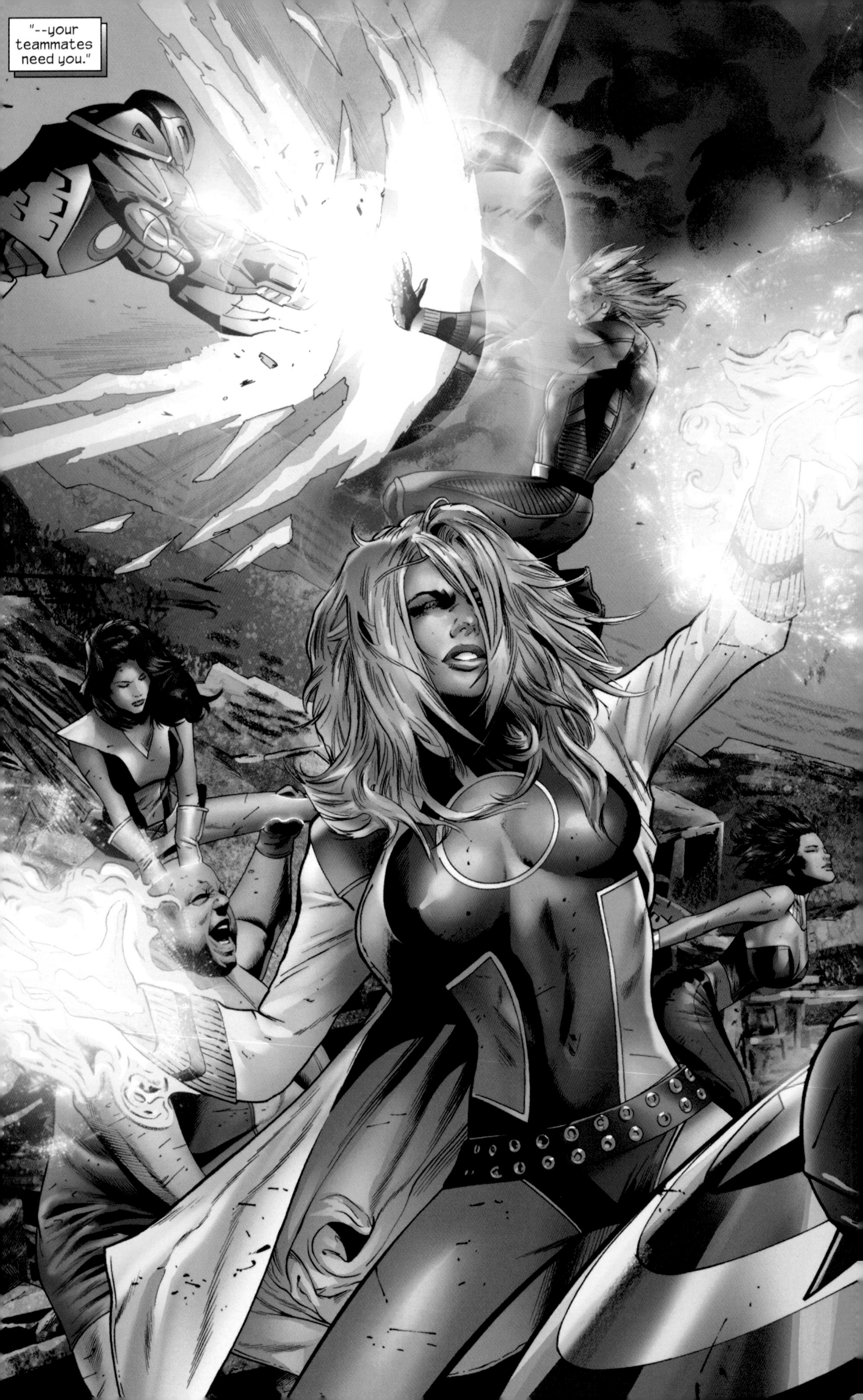
"--your teammates need you."

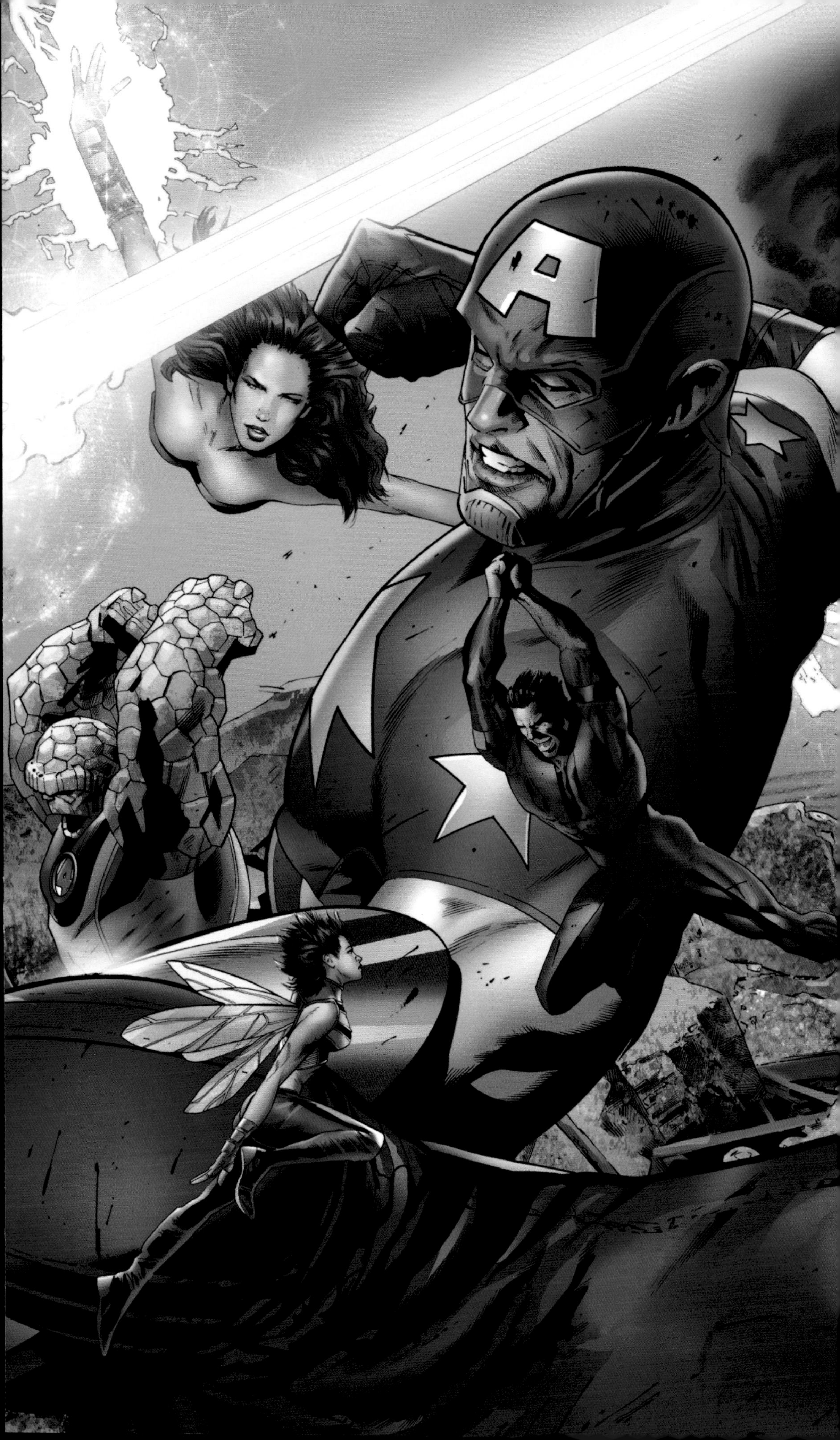

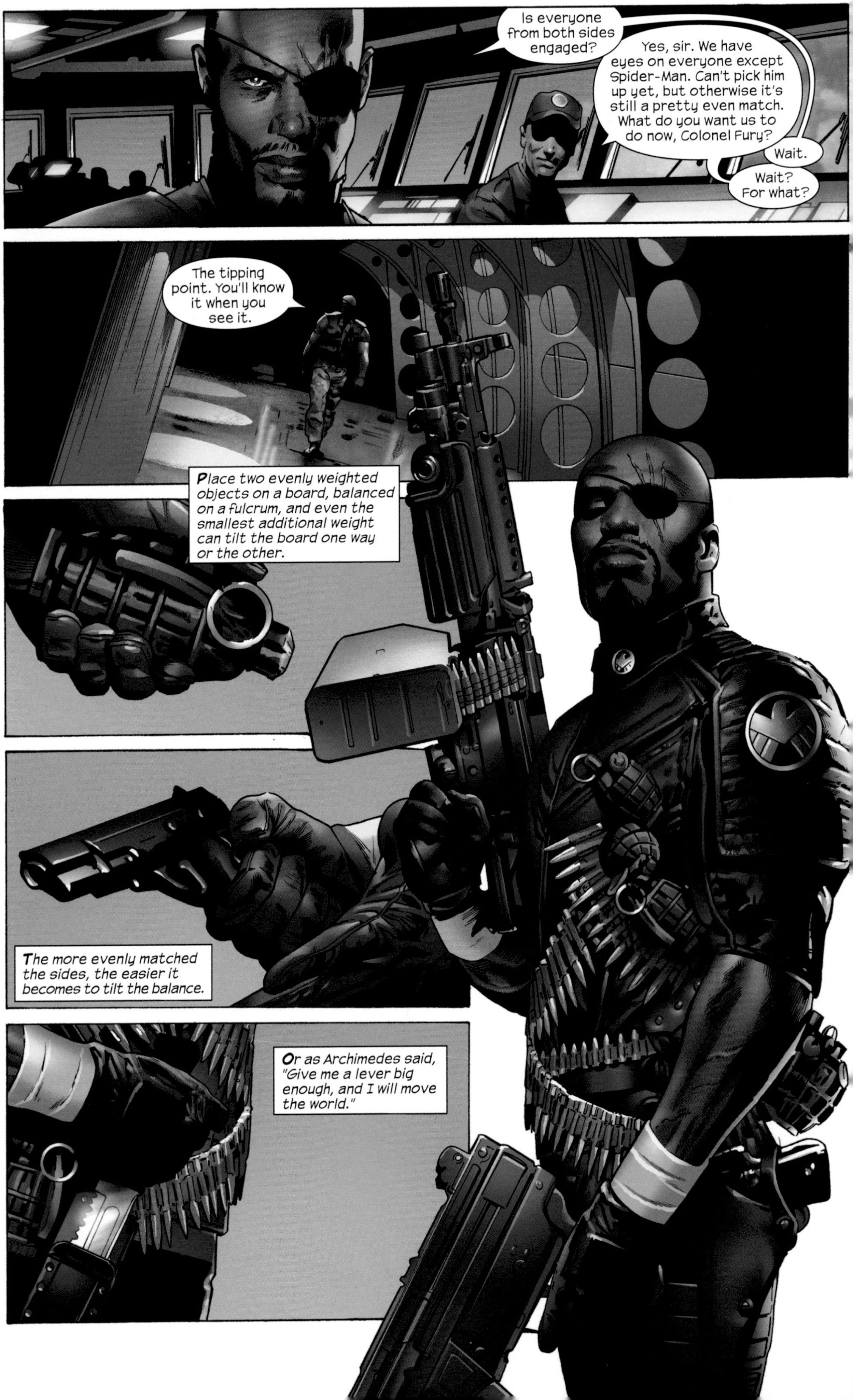

Is everyone from both sides engaged?
Yes, sir. We have eyes on everyone except Spider-Man. Can't pick him up yet, but otherwise it's still a pretty even match. What do you want us to do now, Colonel Fury?
Wait.
Wait? For what?
The tipping point. You'll know it when you see it.
Place two evenly weighted objects on a board, balanced on a fulcrum, and even the smallest additional weight can tilt the board one way or the other.
The more evenly matched the sides, the easier it becomes to tilt the balance.
Or as Archimedes said, "Give me a lever big enough, and I will move the world."

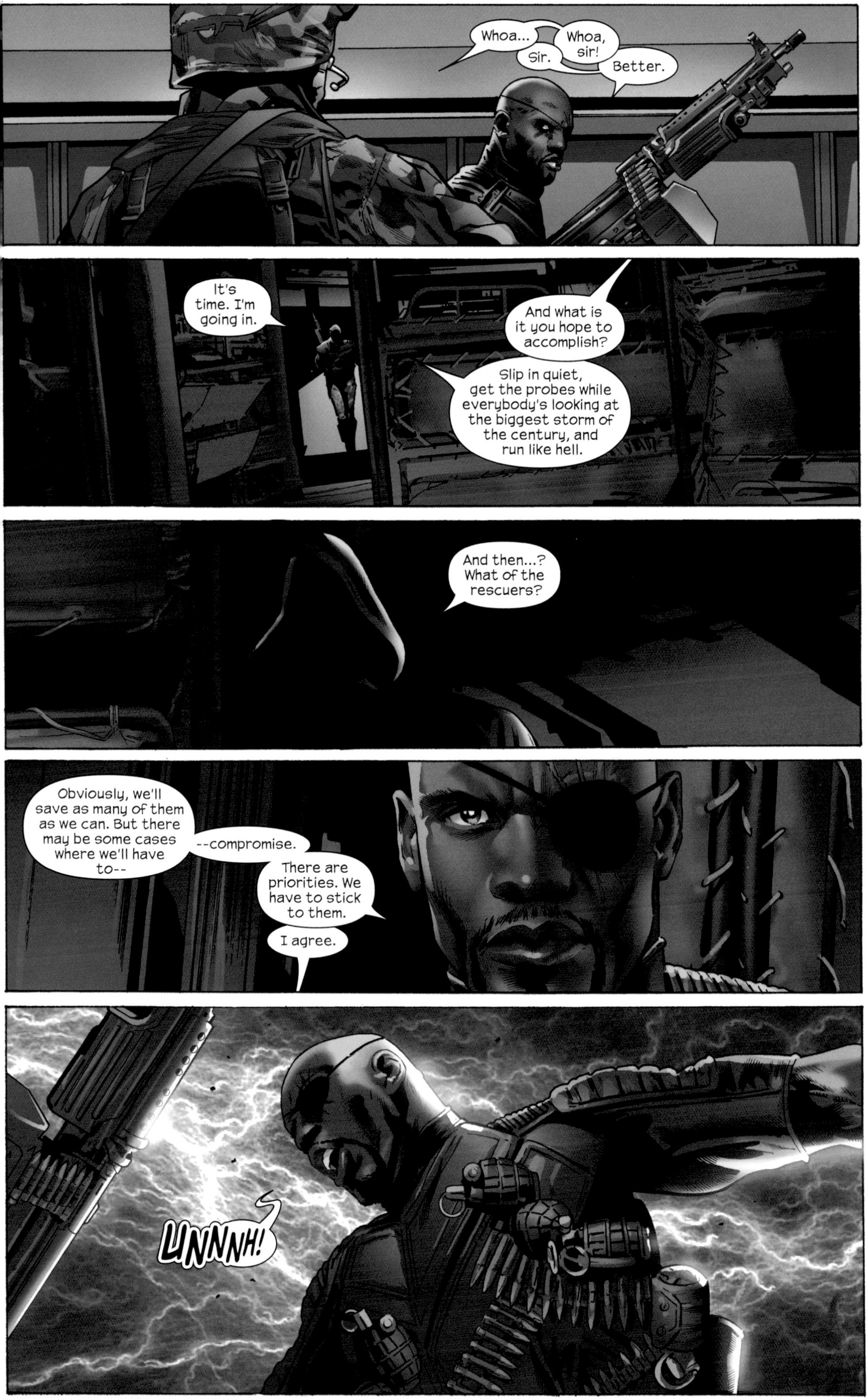
Whoa...
Whoa, sir!
Sir.
Better.
It's time. I'm going in.
And what is it you hope to accomplish?
Slip in quiet, get the probes while everybody's looking at the biggest storm of the century, and run like hell.
And then...? What of the rescuers?
Obviously, we'll save as many of them as we can. But there may be some cases where we'll have to--
--compromise.
There are priorities. We have to stick to them.
I agree.
UNNNH!

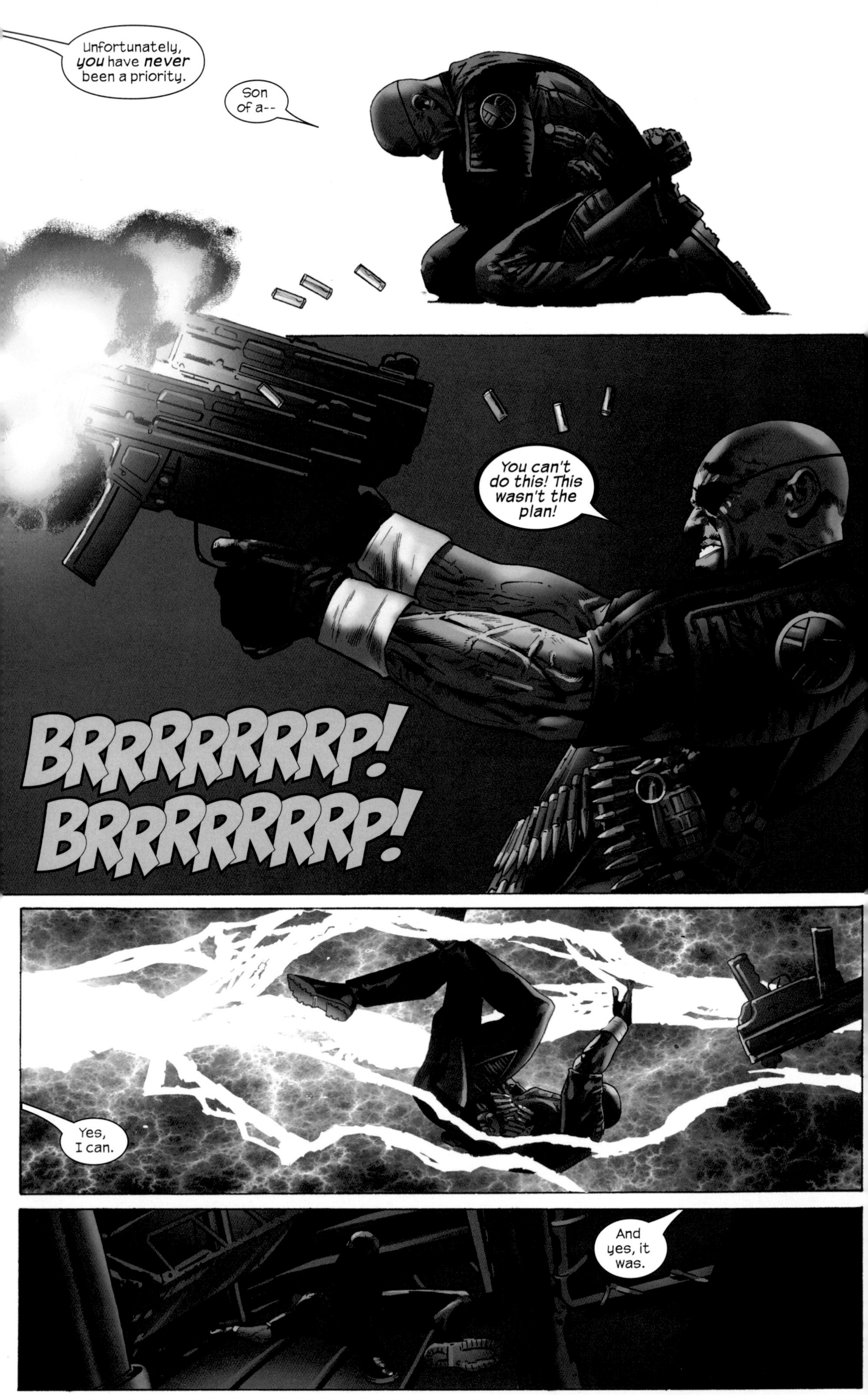

Unfortunately, *you* have ***never*** been a priority.
Son of a--
You can't do this! This wasn't the plan!
BRRRRRRRP! BRRRRRRRP!
Yes, I can.
And yes, it was.

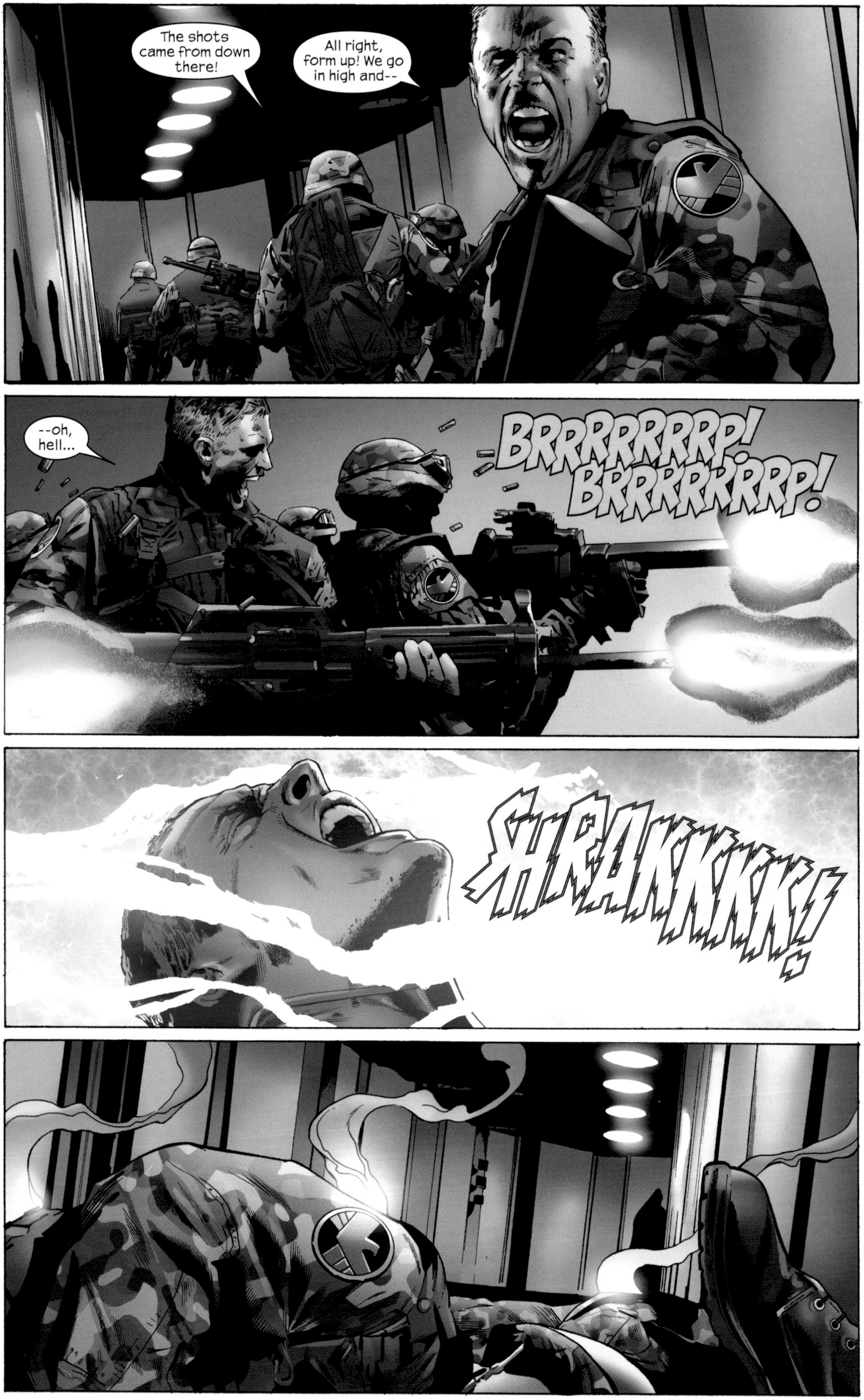
The shots came from down there!
All right, form up! We go in high and--
--oh, hell...
BRRRRRRRP! BRRRRRRRP!
SHRAKKKKK!

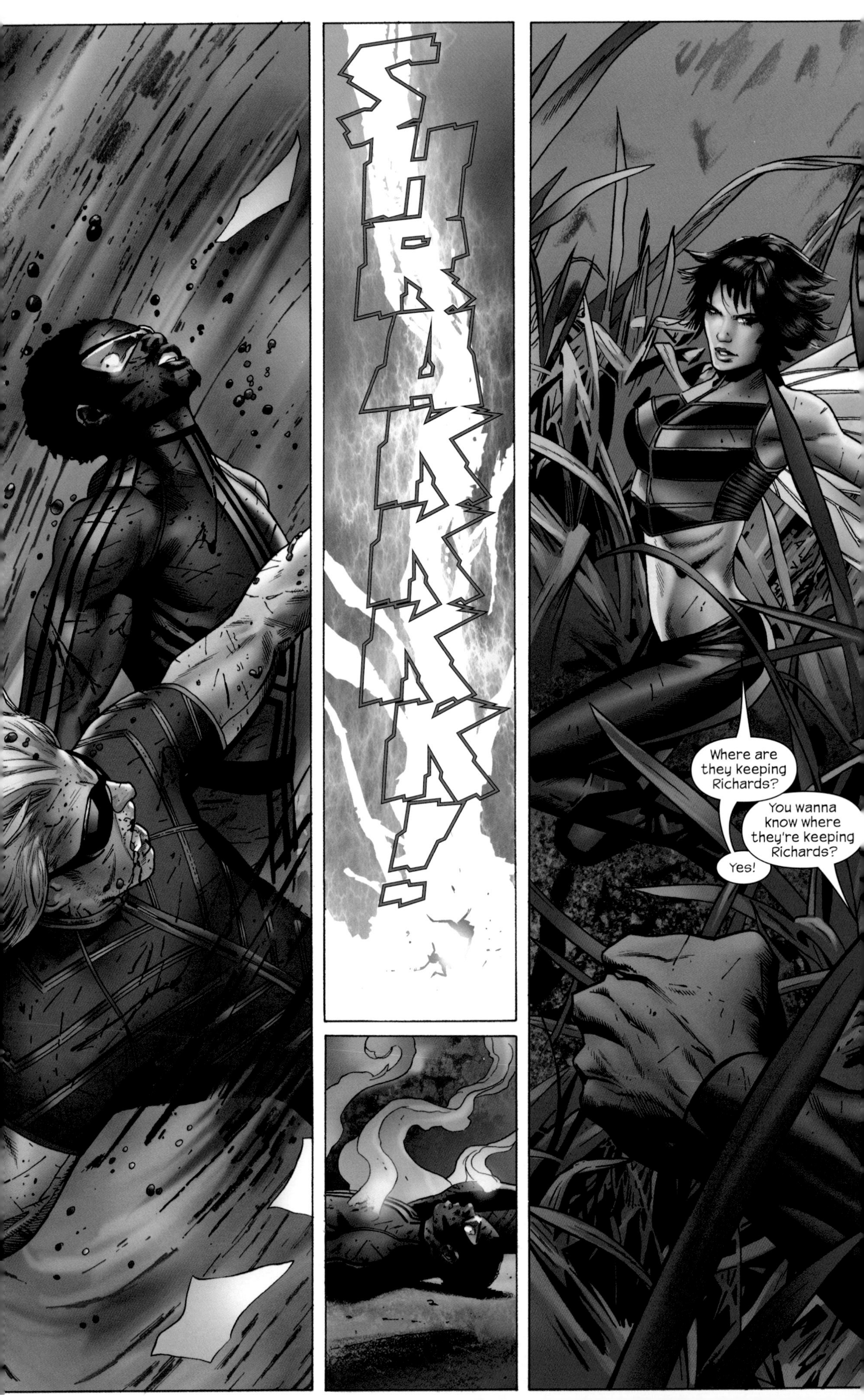
SHRAKK!
Where are they keeping Richards?
You wanna know where they're keeping Richards?
Yes!

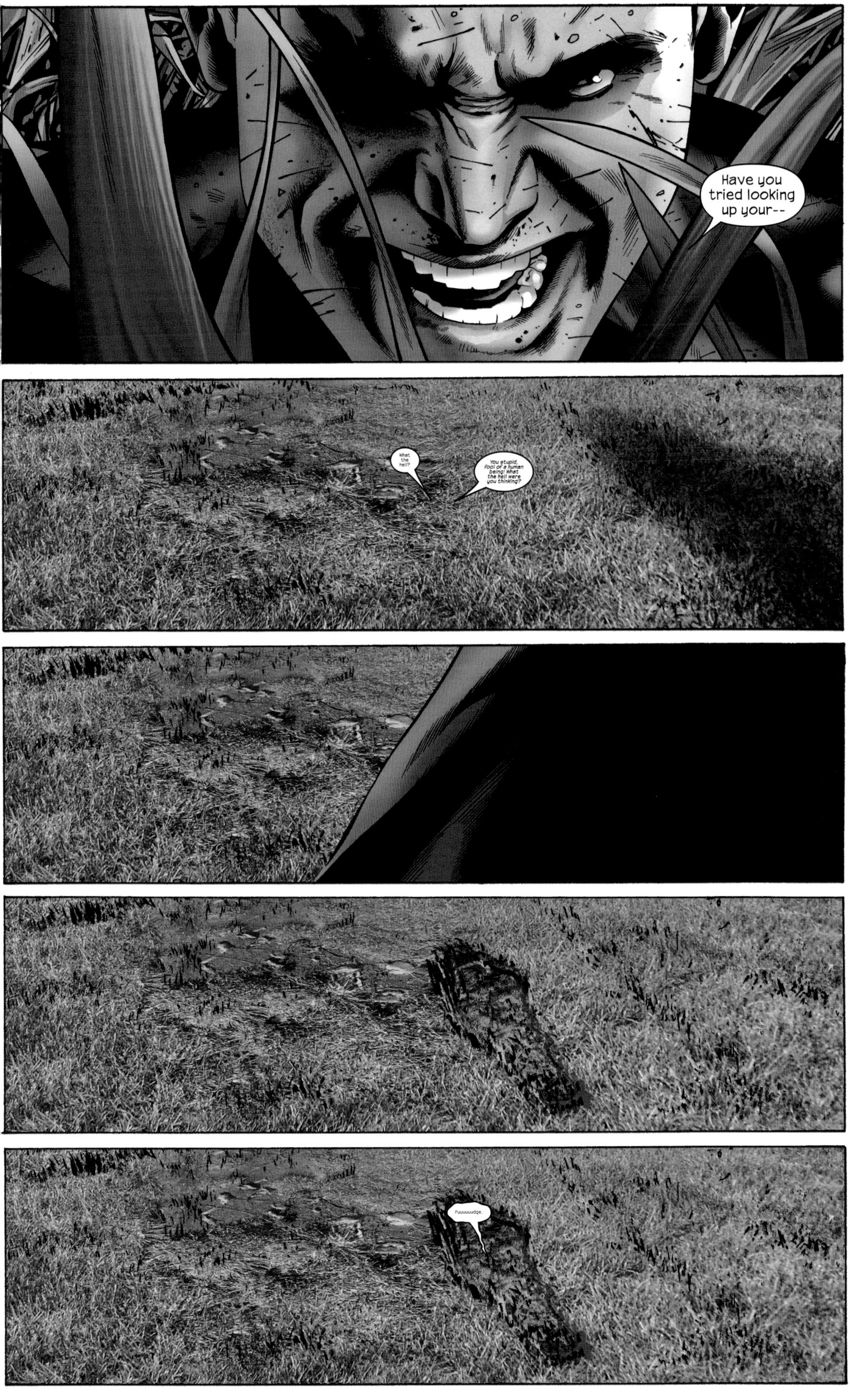
Have you tried looking up your--
What the hell?
You stupid, fool of a human being! What the hell were you thinking?
Fuuuuuudge.

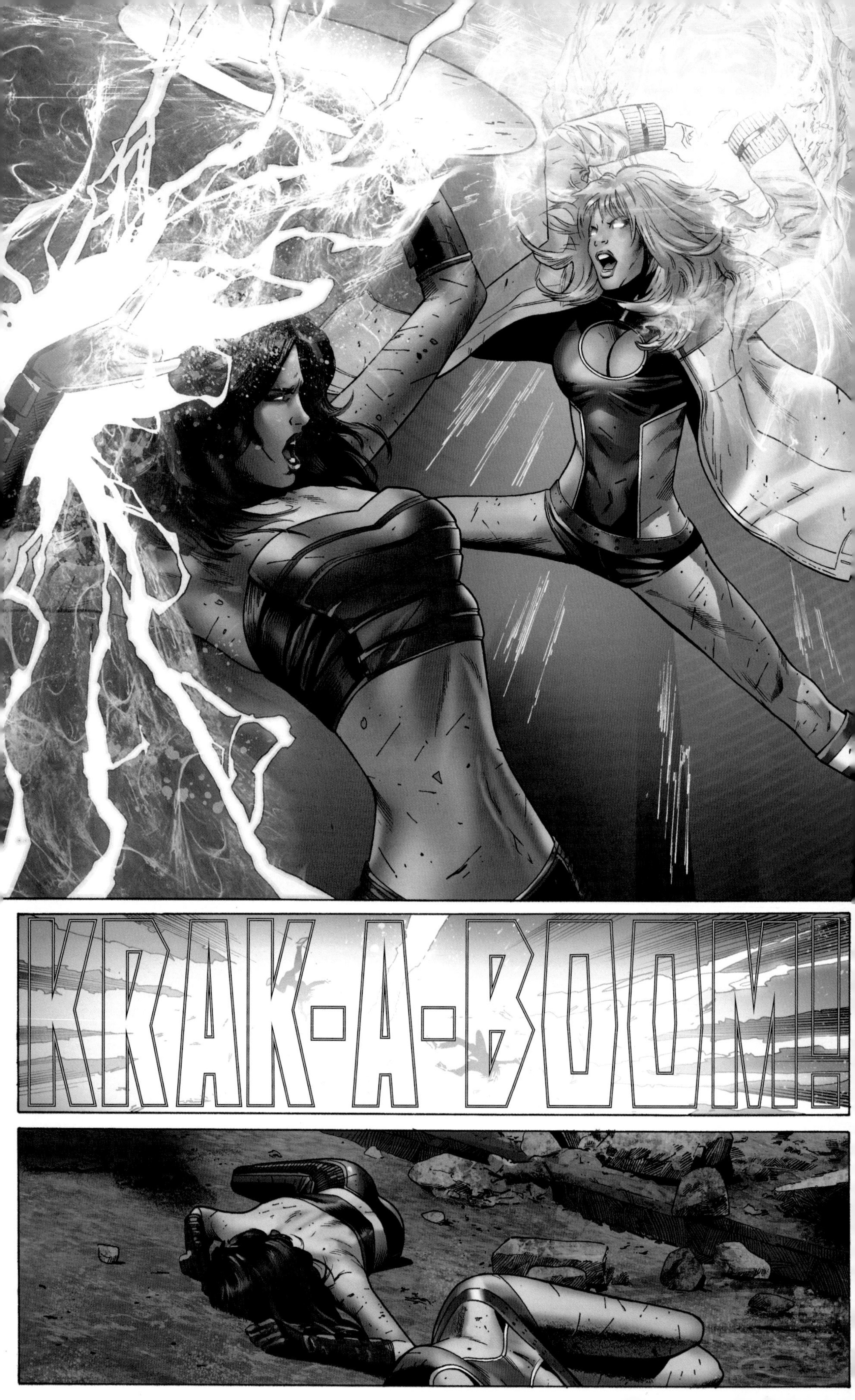
KRAK-A-BOOM!

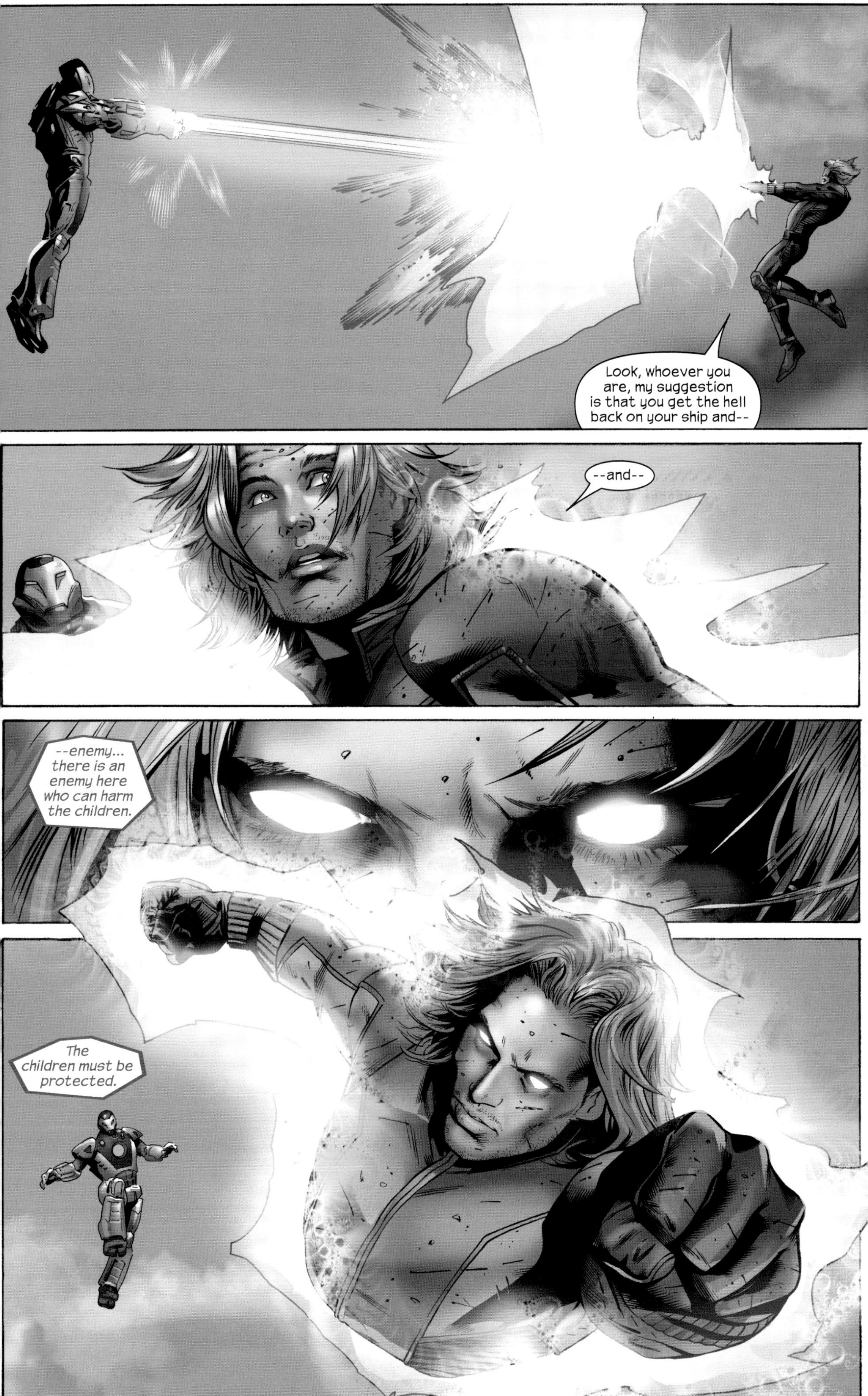
Look, whoever you are, my suggestion is that you get the hell back on your ship and--
--and--
--enemy... there is an enemy here who can harm the children.
The children must be protected.

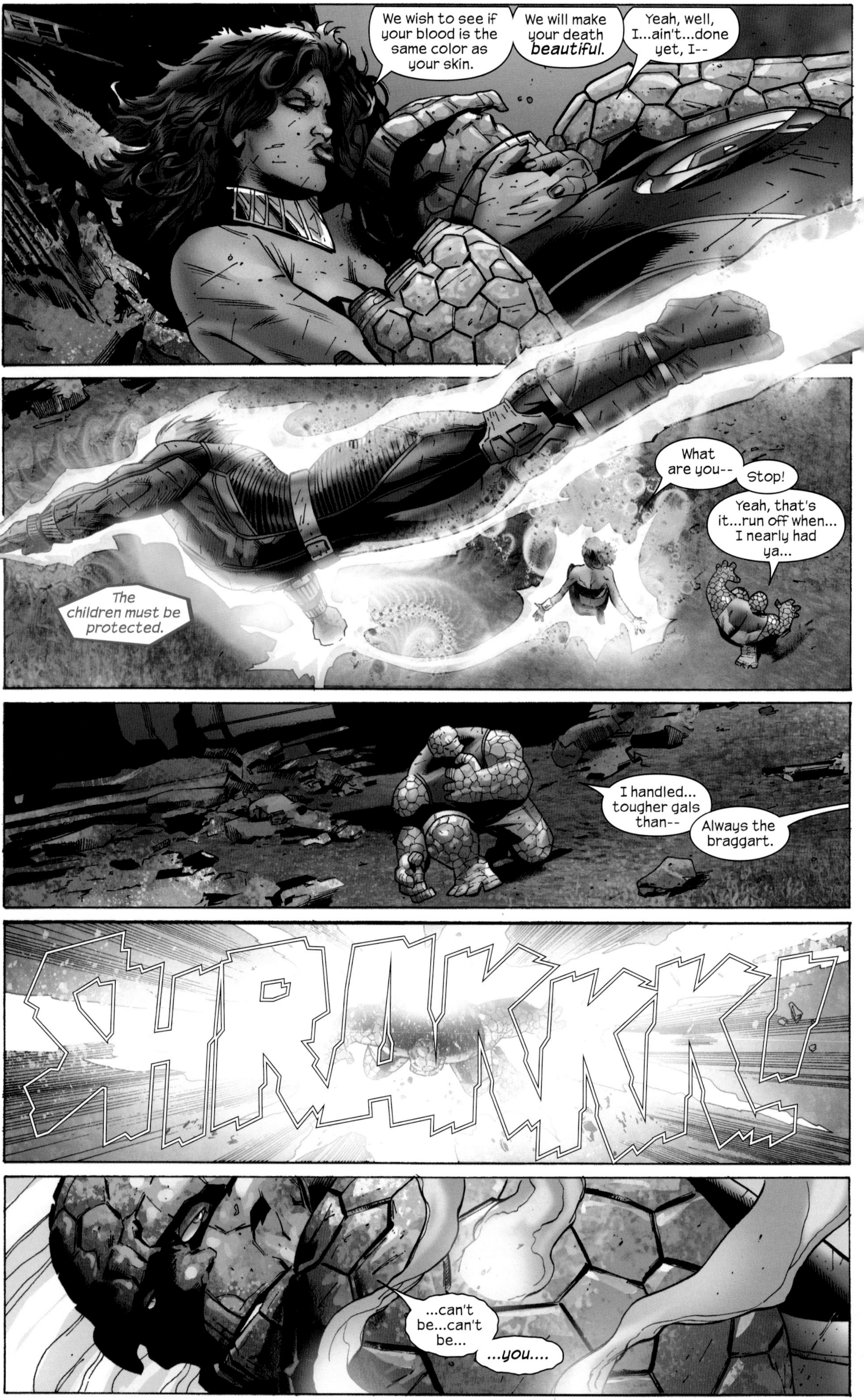
We wish to see if your blood is the same color as your skin.
We will make your death **beautiful**.
Yeah, well, I...ain't...done yet, I--
What are you--
Stop!
Yeah, that's it...run off when... I nearly had ya...
The children must be protected.
I handled... tougher gals than--
Always the braggart.
HRUKK!
...can't be...can't be...
...you....

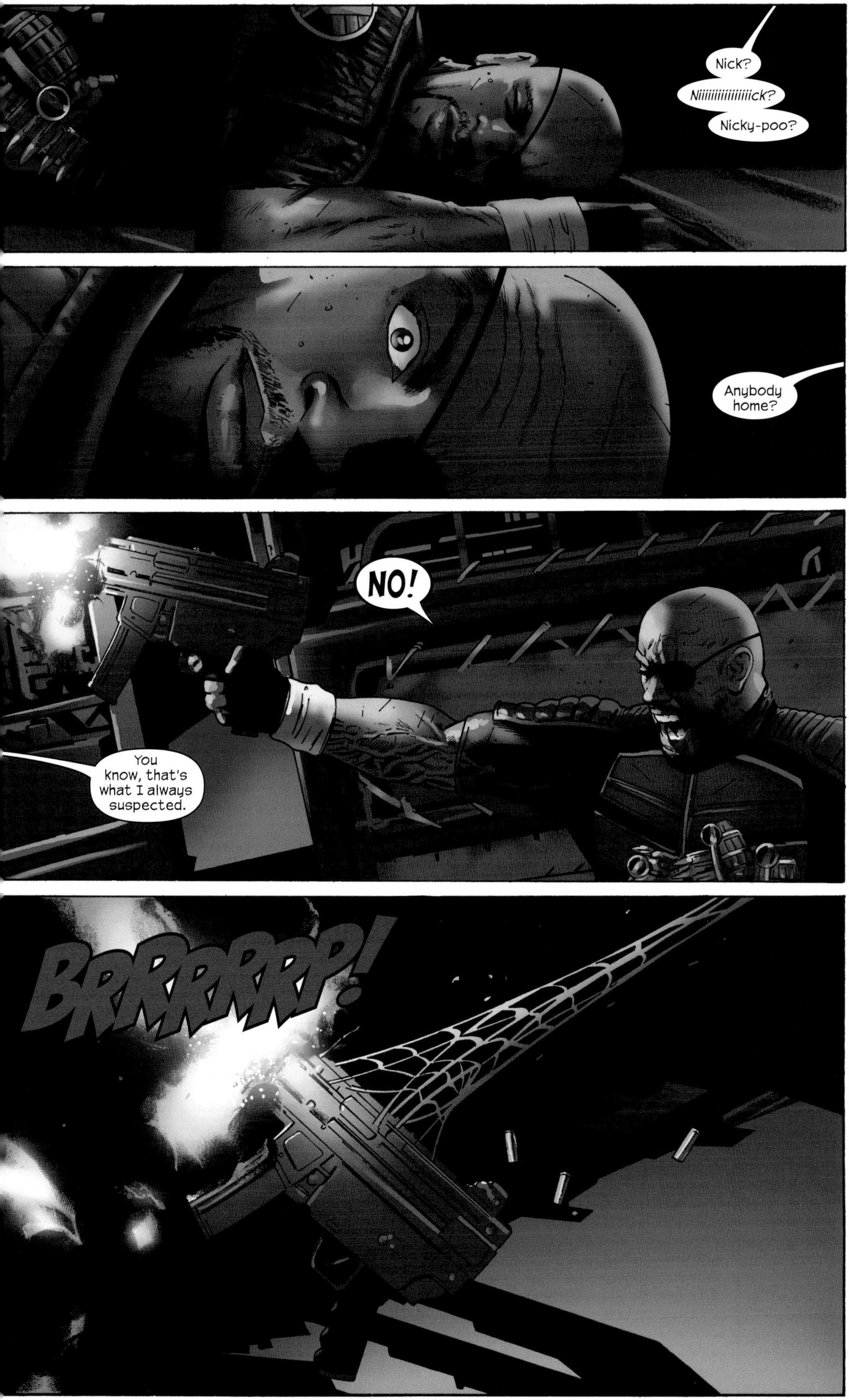

Nick?
Niiiiiiiiiiiiiiiick?
Nicky-poo?
Anybody home?
NO!
You know, that's what I always suspected.
BRRRRRRP!

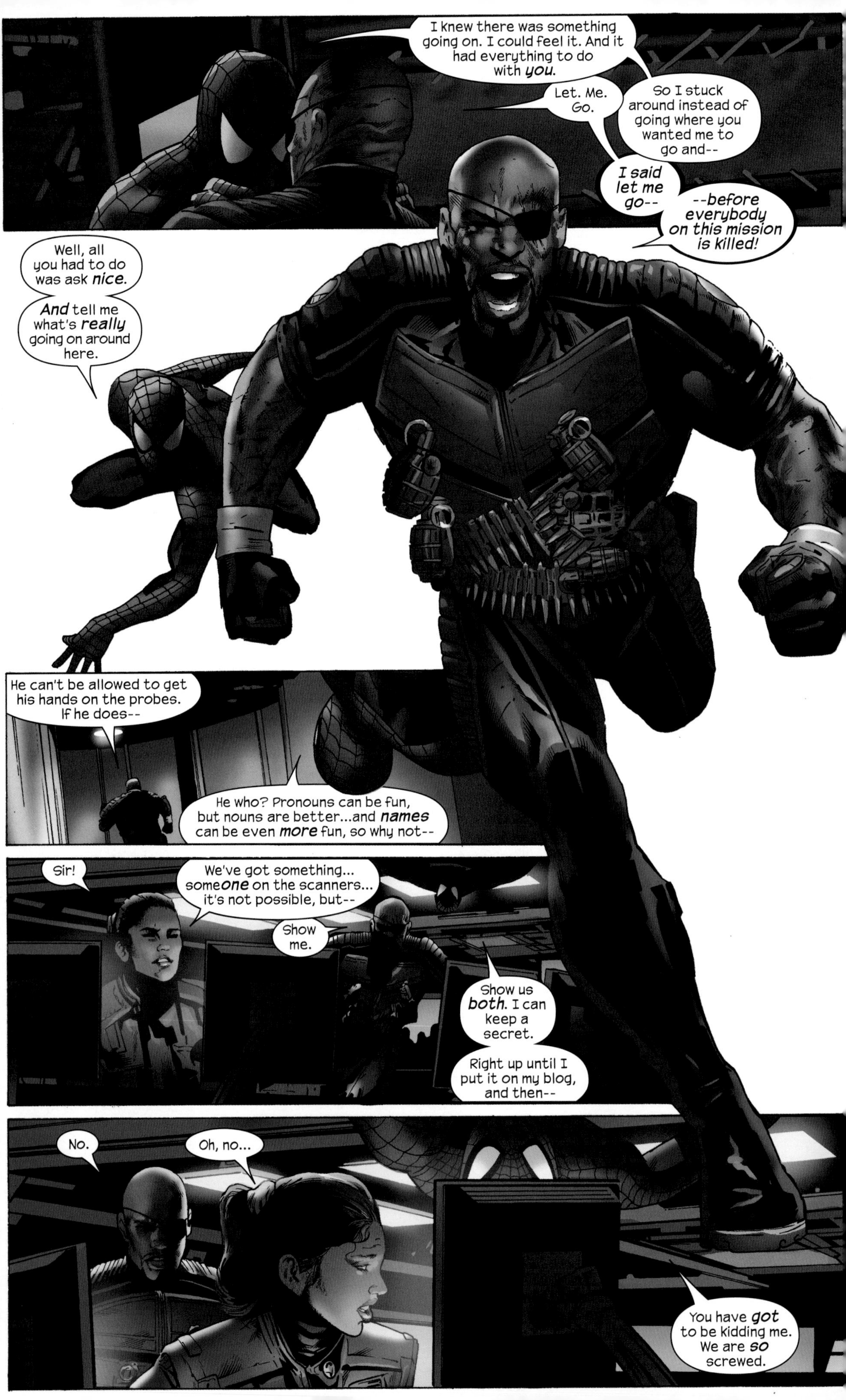
I knew there was something going on. I could feel it. And it had everything to do with you.
Let. Me. Go.
So I stuck around instead of going where you wanted me to go and--
I said let me go--
--before everybody on this mission is killed!
Well, all you had to do was ask nice.
And tell me what's really going on around here.
He can't be allowed to get his hands on the probes. If he does--
He who? Pronouns can be fun, but nouns are better...and names can be even more fun, so why not--
Sir!
We've got something... someone on the scanners... it's not possible, but--
Show me.
Show us both. I can keep a secret.
Right up until I put it on my blog, and then--
No.
Oh, no...
You have got to be kidding me. We are so screwed.

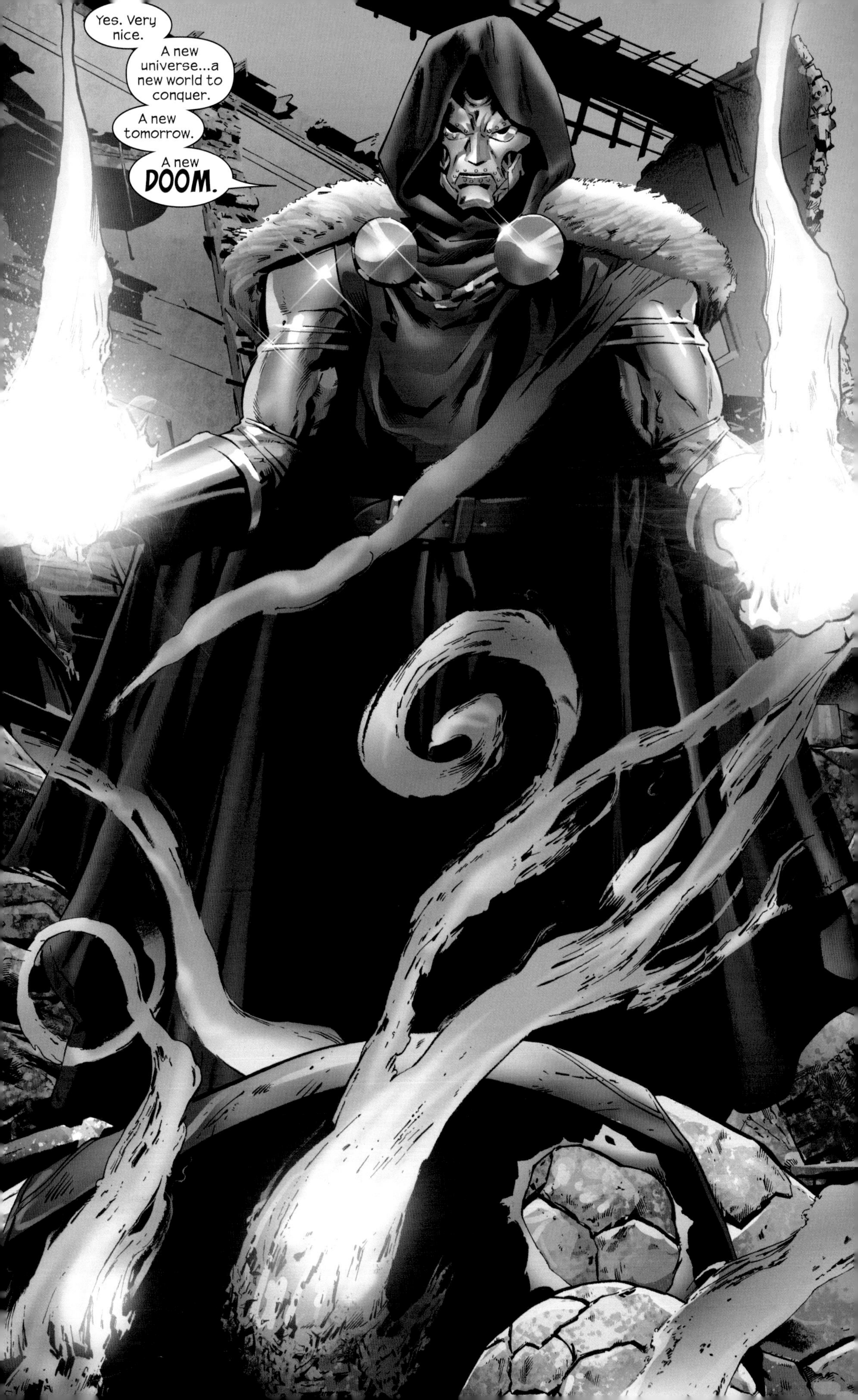

Yes. Very nice.
A new universe...a new world to conquer.
A new tomorrow.
A new DOOM.

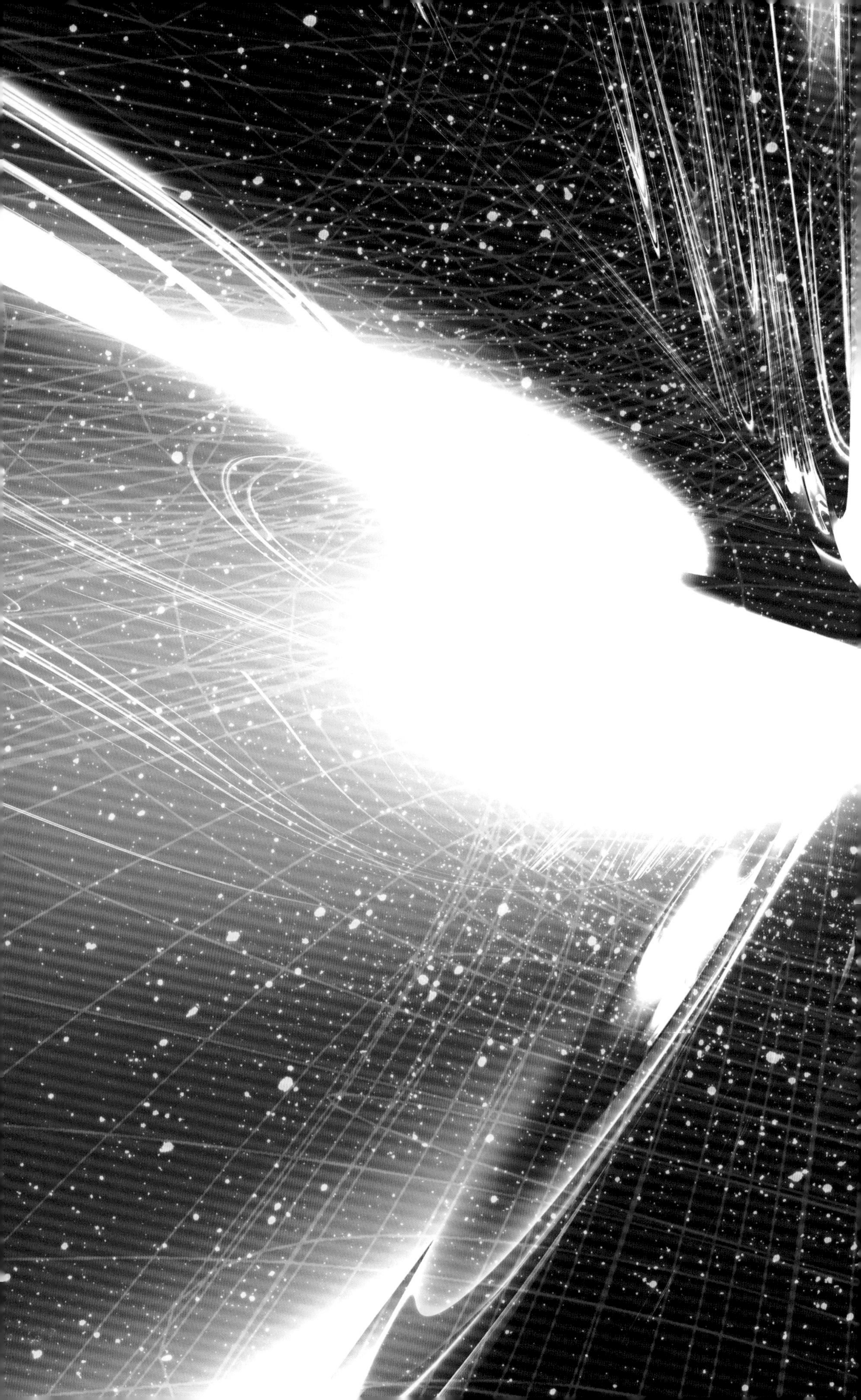

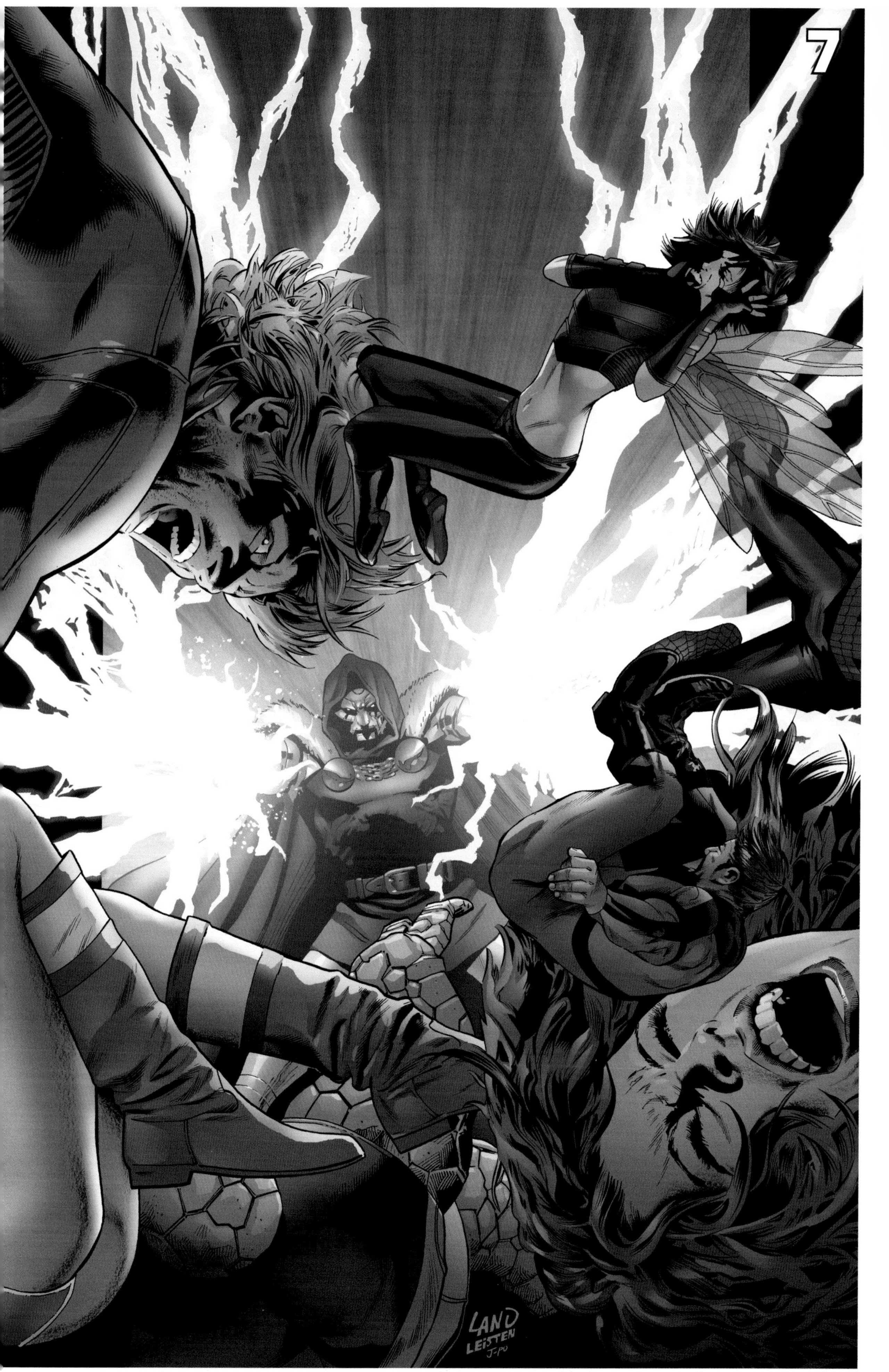
7
LAND
LEISTEN
J-PO

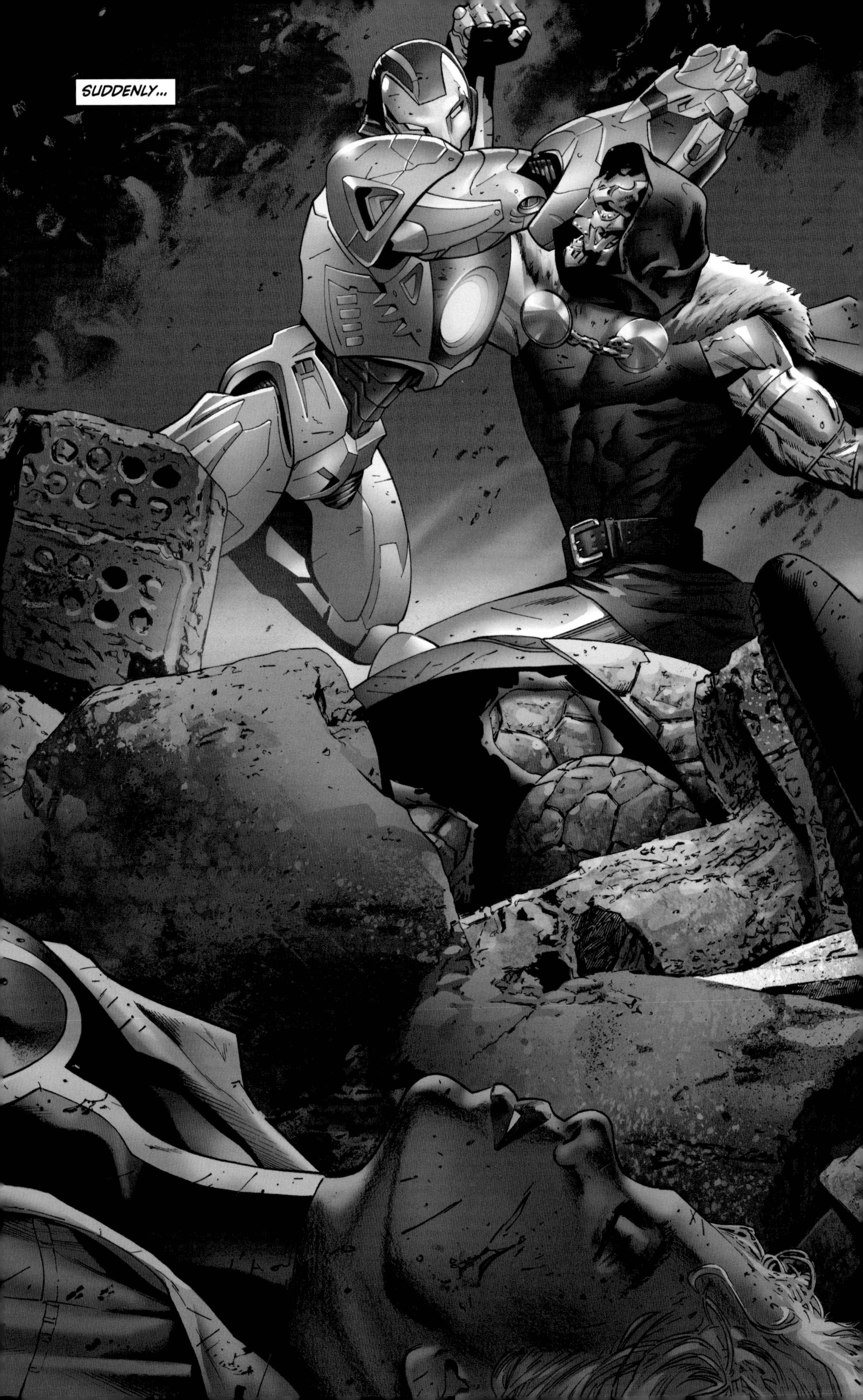
SUDDENLY...

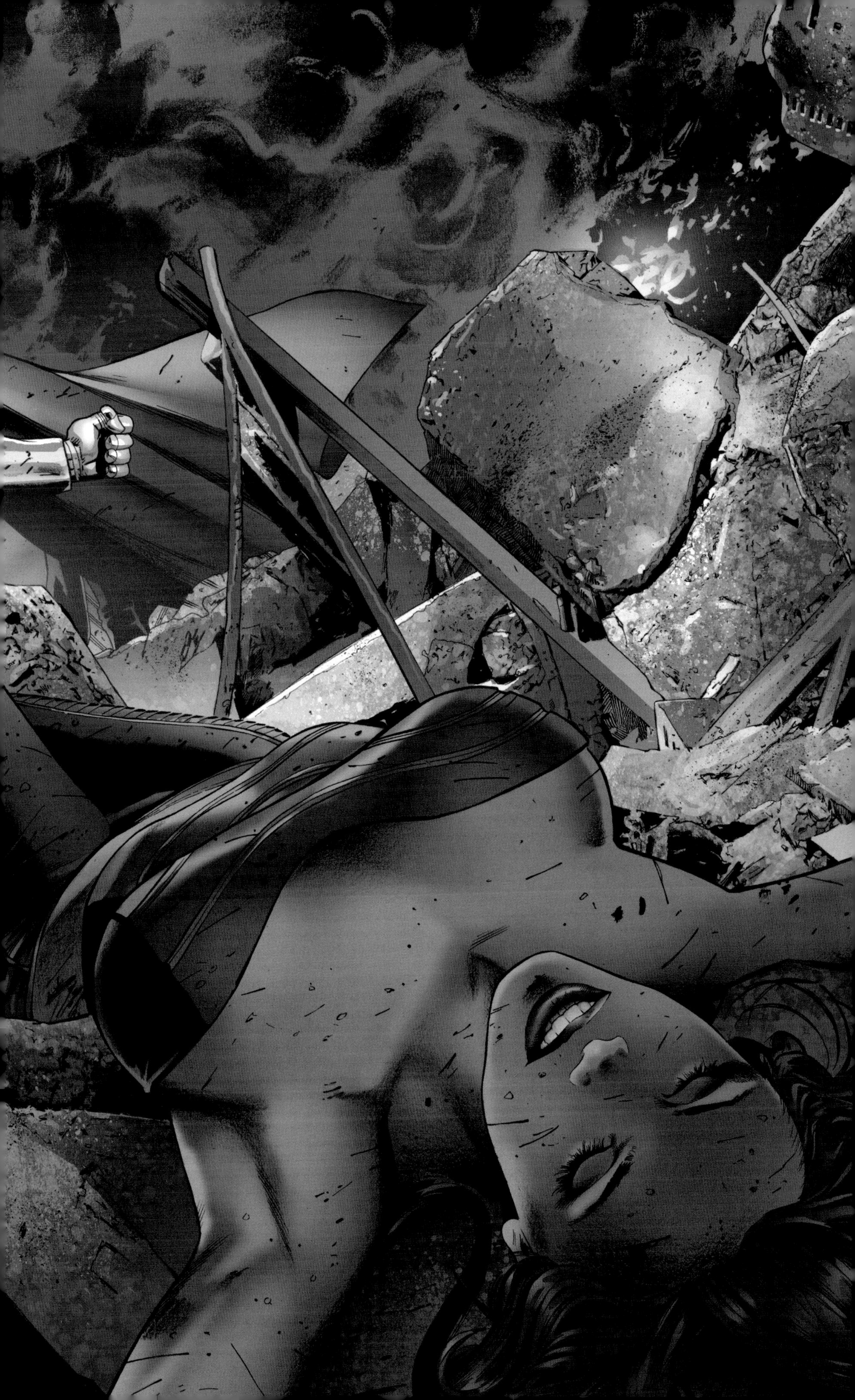

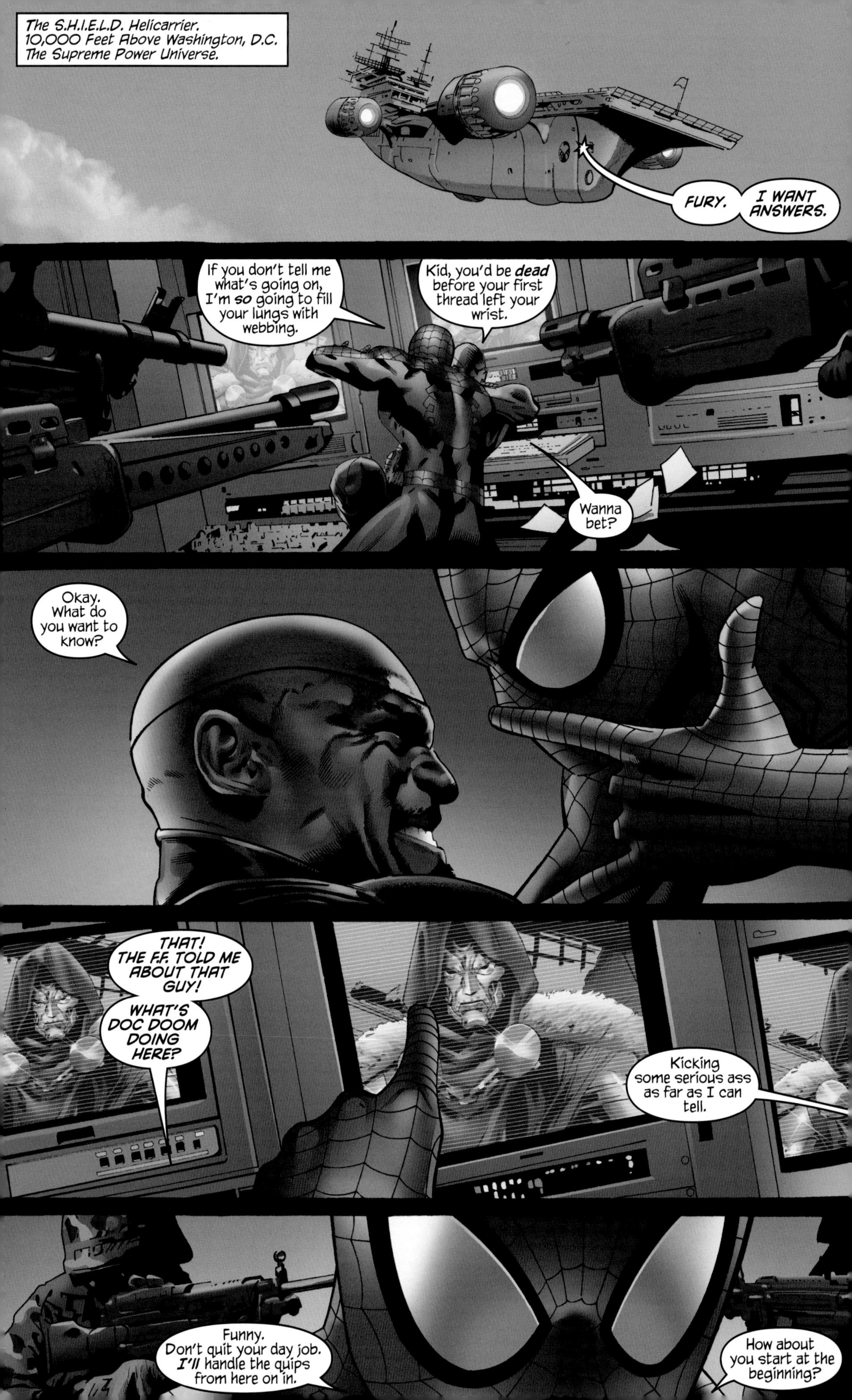

The S.H.I.E.L.D. Helicarrier.
10,000 Feet Above Washington, D.C.
The Supreme Power Universe.
FURY.
I WANT ANSWERS.
If you don't tell me what's going on, I'm so going to fill your lungs with webbing.
Kid, you'd be dead before your first thread left your wrist.
Wanna bet?
Okay. What do you want to know?
THAT! THE F.F. TOLD ME ABOUT THAT GUY!
WHAT'S DOC DOOM DOING HERE?
Kicking some serious ass as far as I can tell.
Funny. Don't quit your day job. I'll handle the quips from here on in.
How about you start at the beginning?

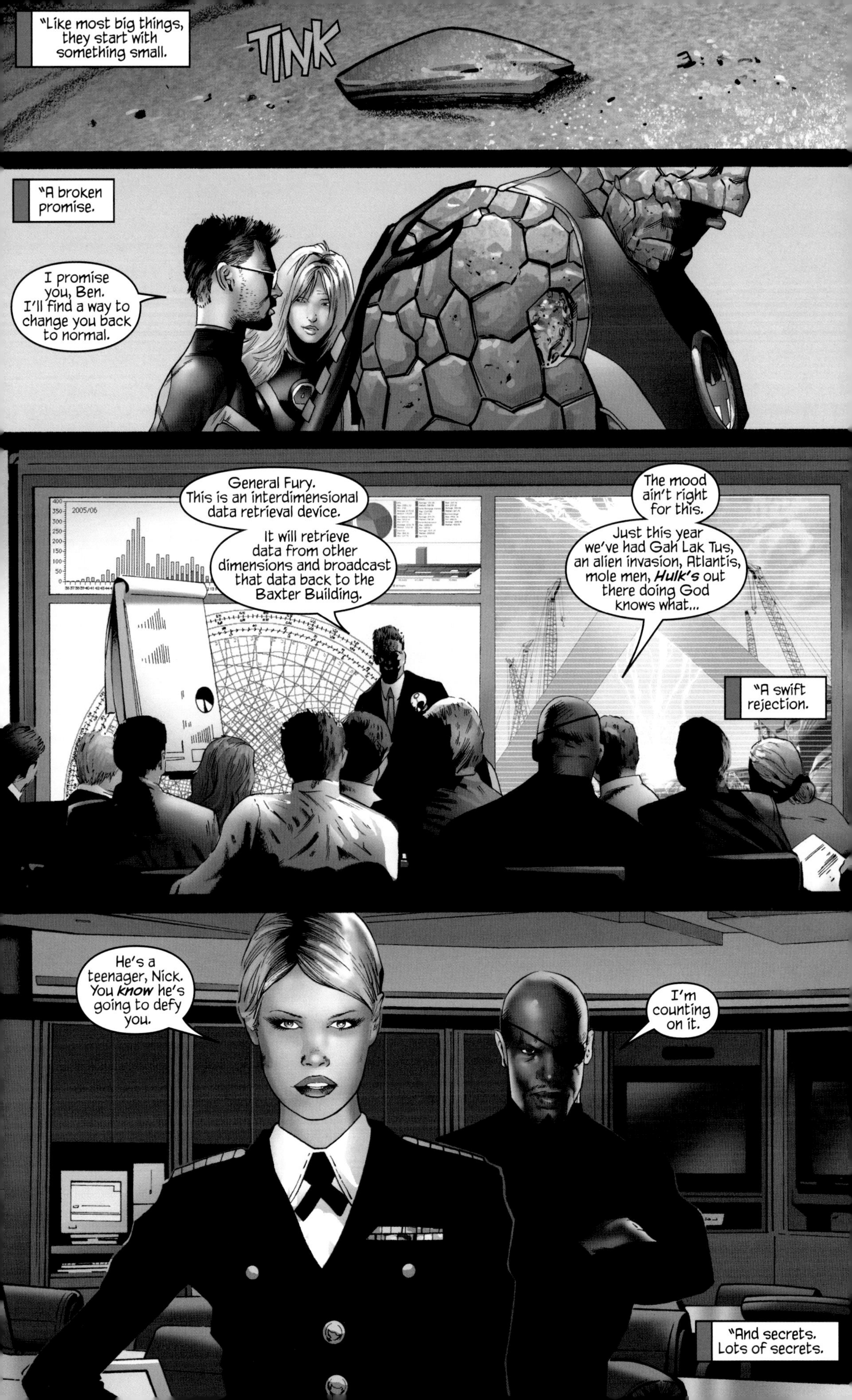
"Like most big things, they start with something small.
TINK
"A broken promise.
I promise you, Ben. I'll find a way to change you back to normal.
General Fury. This is an interdimensional data retrieval device.
It will retrieve data from other dimensions and broadcast that data back to the Baxter Building.
The mood ain't right for this.
Just this year we've had Gah Lak Tus, an alien invasion, Atlantis, mole men, *Hulk's* out there doing God knows what...
"A swift rejection.
He's a teenager, Nick. You *know* he's going to defy you.
I'm counting on it.
"And secrets. Lots of secrets.

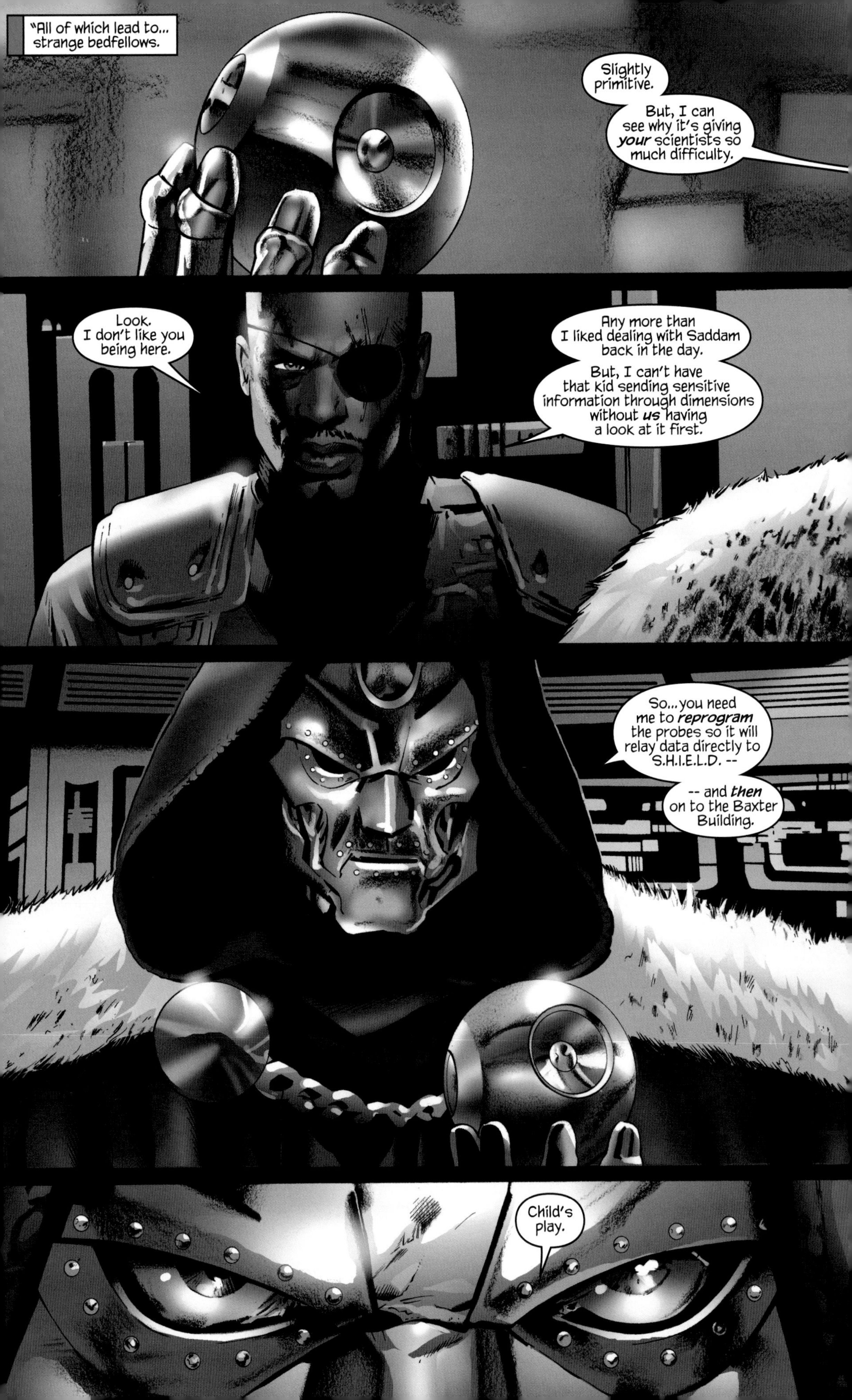
"All of which lead to... strange bedfellows.
Slightly primitive.
But, I can see why it's giving *your* scientists so much difficulty.
Look. I don't like you being here.
Any more than I liked dealing with Saddam back in the day.
But, I can't have that kid sending sensitive information through dimensions without *us* having a look at it first.
So... you need me to *reprogram* the probes so it will relay data directly to S.H.I.E.L.D. --
-- and *then* on to the Baxter Building.
Child's play.

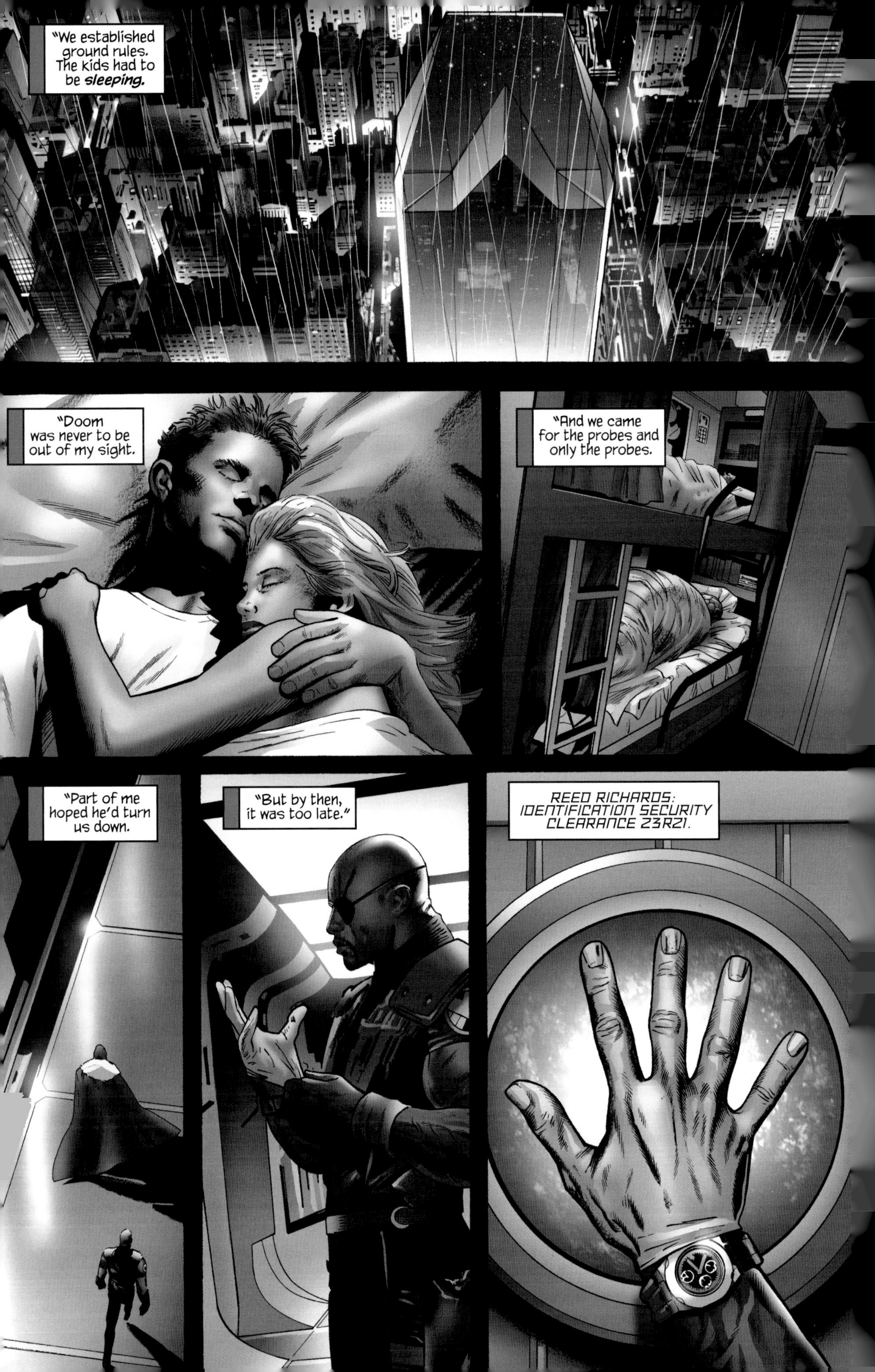
"We established ground rules. The kids had to be *sleeping.*
"Doom was never to be out of my sight.
"And we came for the probes and only the probes.
"Part of me hoped he'd turn us down.
"But by then, it was too late."
REED RICHARDS: IDENTIFICATION SECURITY CLEARANCE 23R21.

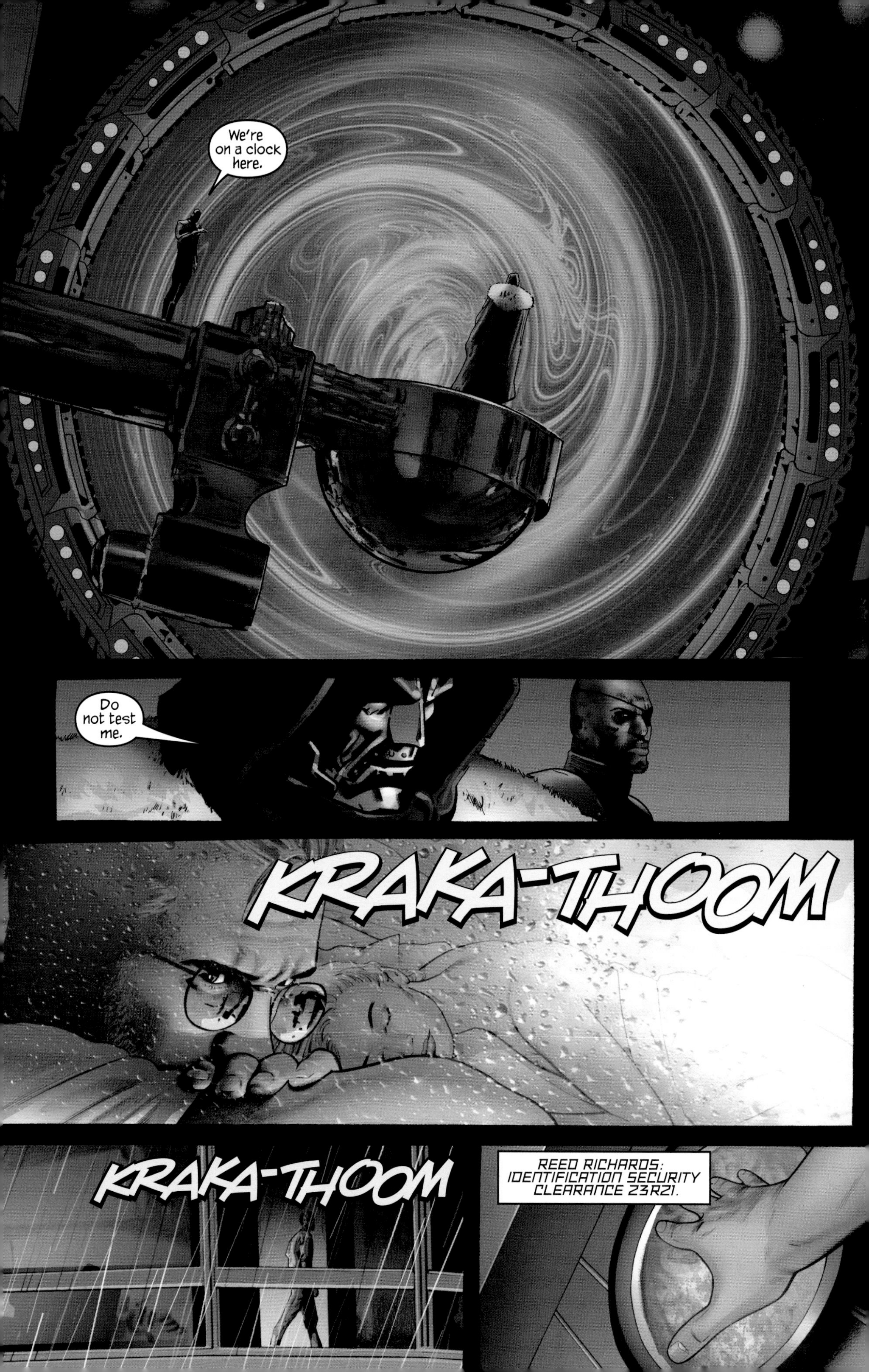
We're on a clock here.
Do not test me.
KRAKA-THOOM
KRAKA-THOOM
REED RICHARDS: IDENTIFICATION SECURITY CLEARANCE 23R21.

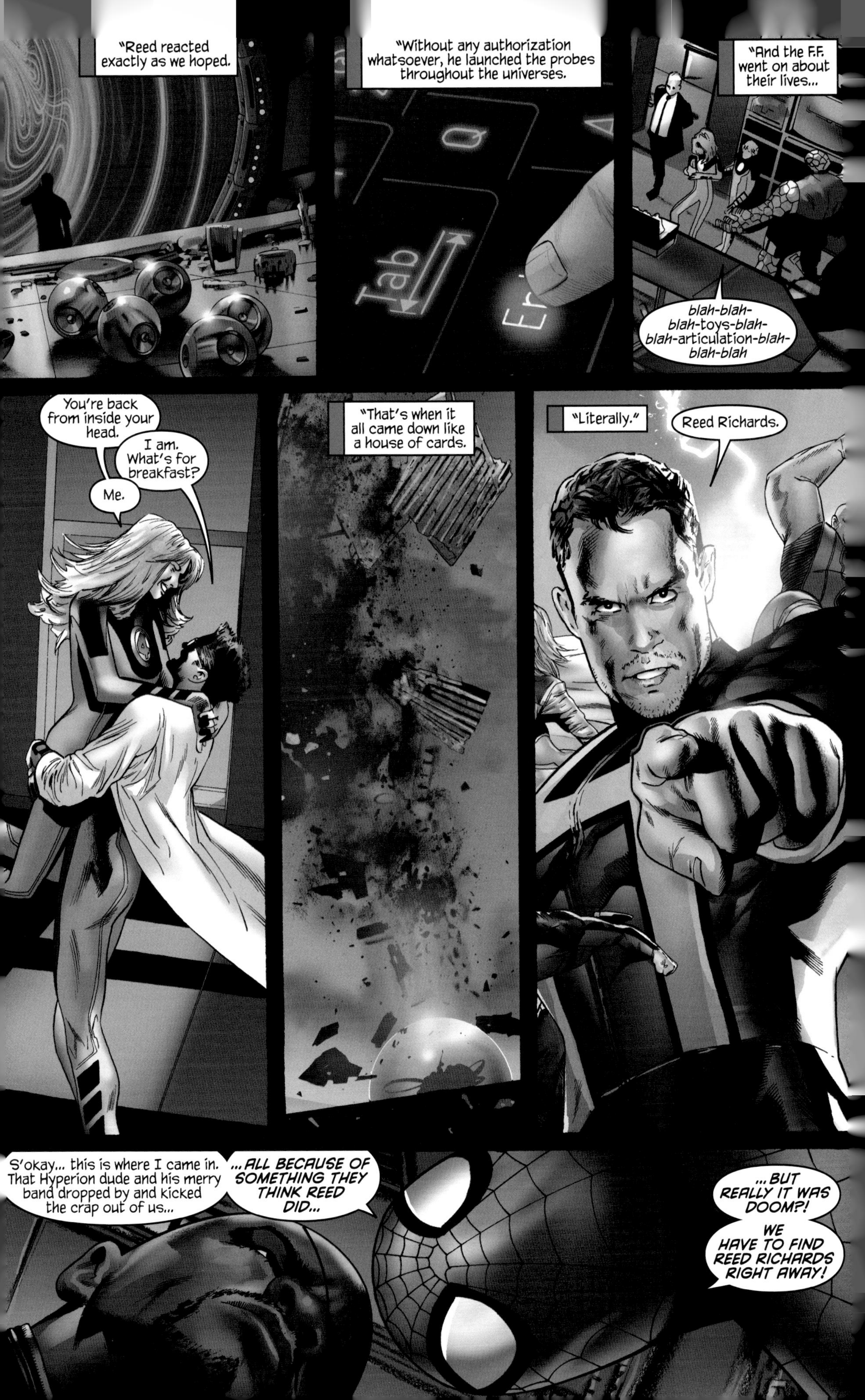
"Reed reacted exactly as we hoped.
"Without any authorization whatsoever, he launched the probes throughout the universes.
Tab
"And the F.F. went on about their lives...
blah-blah-blah-toys-blah-blah-articulation-blah-blah-blah
You're back from inside your head.
I am. What's for breakfast?
Me.
"That's when it all came down like a house of cards.
"Literally."
Reed Richards.
S'okay... this is where I came in. That Hyperion dude and his merry band dropped by and kicked the crap out of us...
...ALL BECAUSE OF SOMETHING THEY THINK REED DID...
...BUT REALLY IT WAS DOOM?!
WE HAVE TO FIND REED RICHARDS RIGHT AWAY!

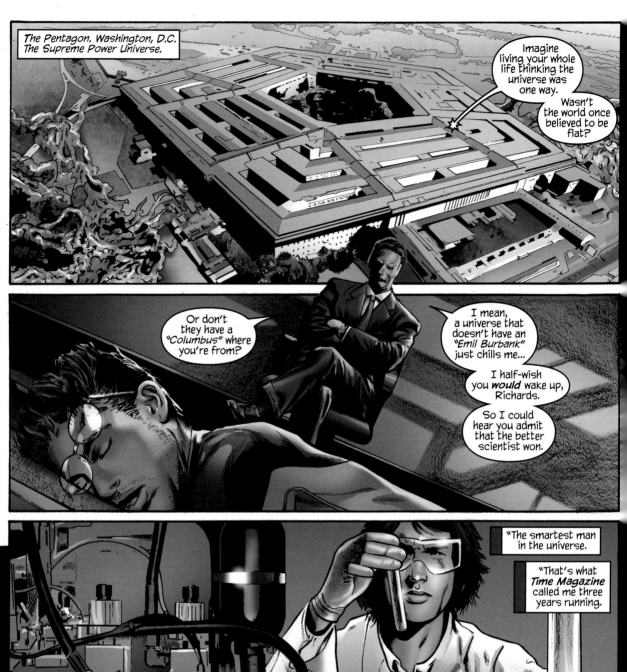

The Pentagon. Washington, D.C.
The Supreme Power Universe.

Imagine living your whole life thinking the universe was one way. Wasn't the world once believed to be flat?

Or don't they have a *"Columbus"* where you're from?

I mean, a universe that doesn't have an *"Emil Burbank"* just chills me...

I half-wish you *would* wake up, Richards.

So I could hear you admit that the better scientist won.

"The smartest man in the universe.

"That's what *Time Magazine* called me three years running.

"And for my admittedly *genius* contributions to various fields of science --

"-- I was awarded the Nobel Prize.

"Smartest man in the universe.

"Only *one* problem with that statement...

Lorem ipsum dolor sit amet, consectetuer adipiscing elit, sed diam nonummy nibh euismod tincidunt ut laoreet dolore magna aliquam erat volutpat. Ut wisi enim ad minim veniam, quis nostrud exerci tation ullamcorper suscipit lobortis nisl ut aliquip ex ea commodo consequat.

EMIL BURBANK

Duis autem vel eum iriure dolor in hendrerit in vulputate velit esse molestie consequat, vel illum dolore eu feugiat nulla facilisis at vero eros et accumsan et iusto odio dignissim qui blandit praesent luptatum zzril delenit augue duis dolore te feugait nulla facilisi. Lorem ipsum dolor sit amet, consectetuer adipiscing elit, sed diam nonummy nibh euismod tincidunt ut laoreet

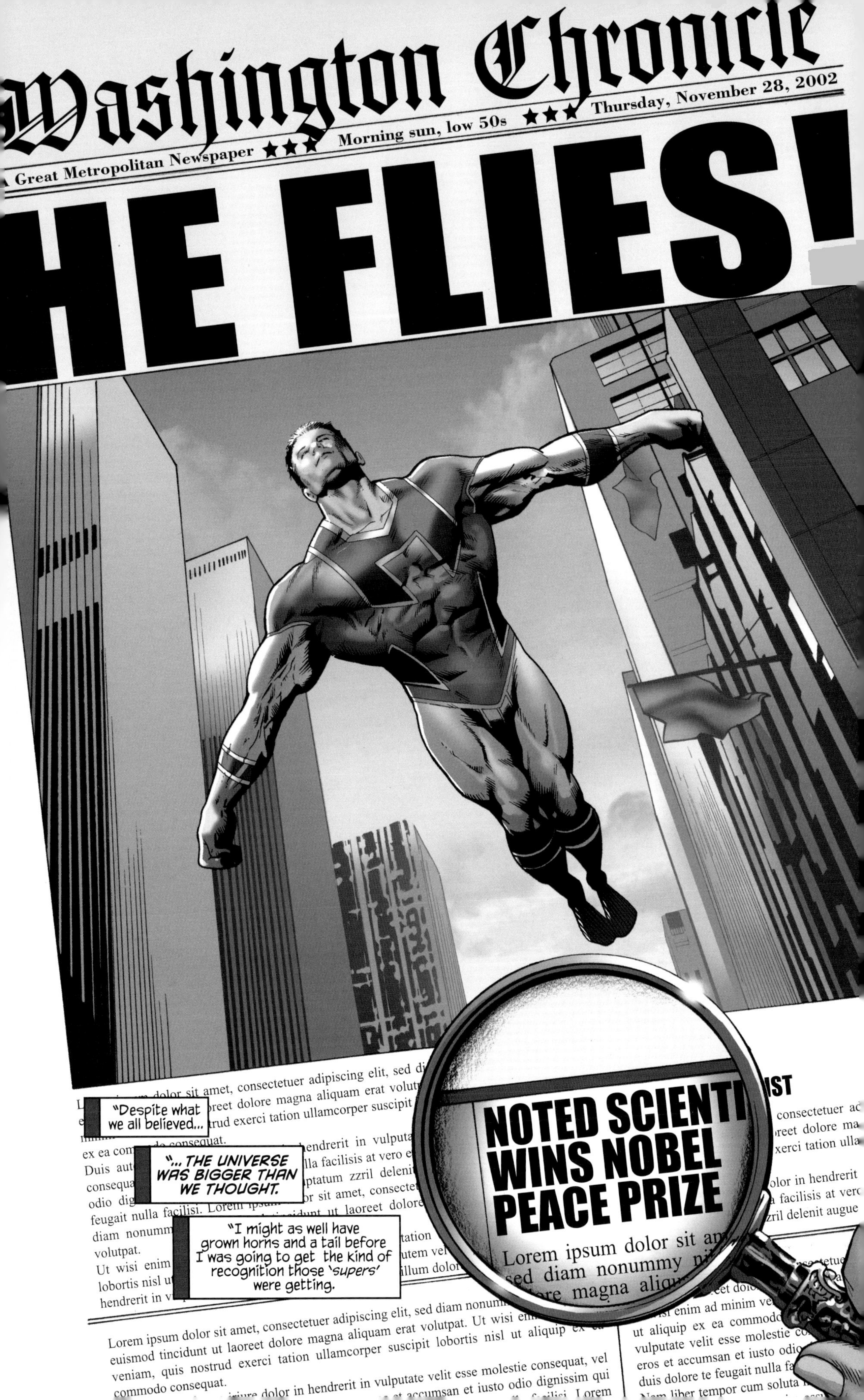

Washington Chronicle
A Great Metropolitan Newspaper ★★★ Morning sun, low 50s ★★★ Thursday, November 28, 2002
HE FLIES!
"Despite what we all believed...
"...THE UNIVERSE WAS BIGGER THAN WE THOUGHT.
"I might as well have grown horns and a tail before I was going to get the kind of recognition those 'supers' were getting.
NOTED SCIENTIST WINS NOBEL PEACE PRIZE

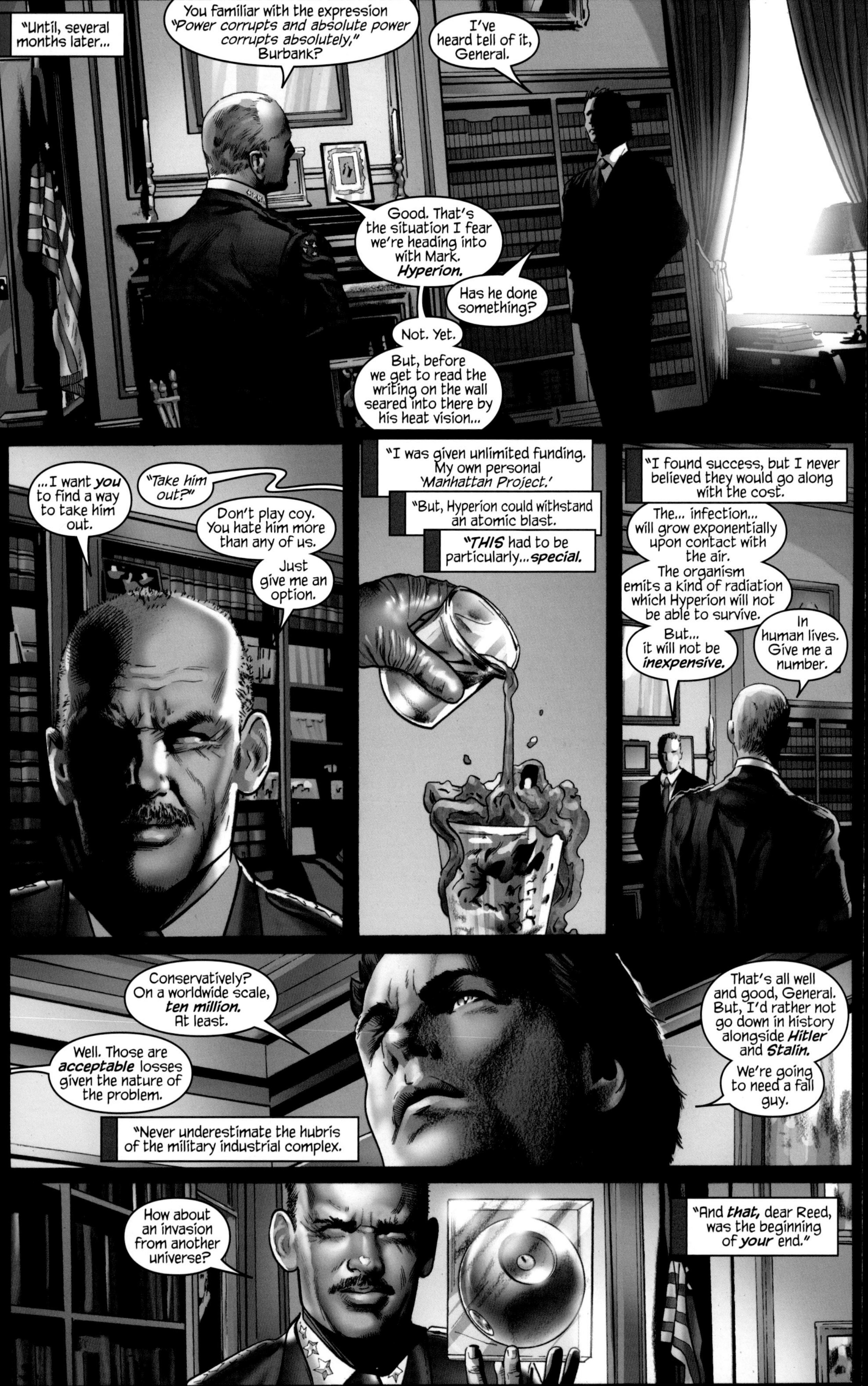
"Until, several months later...
You familiar with the expression "Power corrupts and absolute power corrupts absolutely," Burbank?
I've heard tell of it, General.
Good. That's the situation I fear we're heading into with Mark. Hyperion.
Has he done something?
Not. Yet.
But, before we get to read the writing on the wall seared into there by his heat vision...
...I want you to find a way to take him out.
"Take him out?"
Don't play coy. You hate him more than any of us.
Just give me an option.
"I was given unlimited funding. My own personal 'Manhattan Project.'
"But, Hyperion could withstand an atomic blast.
"THIS had to be particularly...special.
"I found success, but I never believed they would go along with the cost.
The... infection... will grow exponentially upon contact with the air.
The organism emits a kind of radiation which Hyperion will not be able to survive.
But... it will not be inexpensive.
In human lives. Give me a number.
Conservatively? On a worldwide scale, ten million. At least.
Well. Those are acceptable losses given the nature of the problem.
"Never underestimate the hubris of the military industrial complex.
That's all well and good, General. But, I'd rather not go down in history alongside Hitler and Stalin.
We're going to need a fall guy.
How about an invasion from another universe?
"And that, dear Reed, was the beginning of your end."

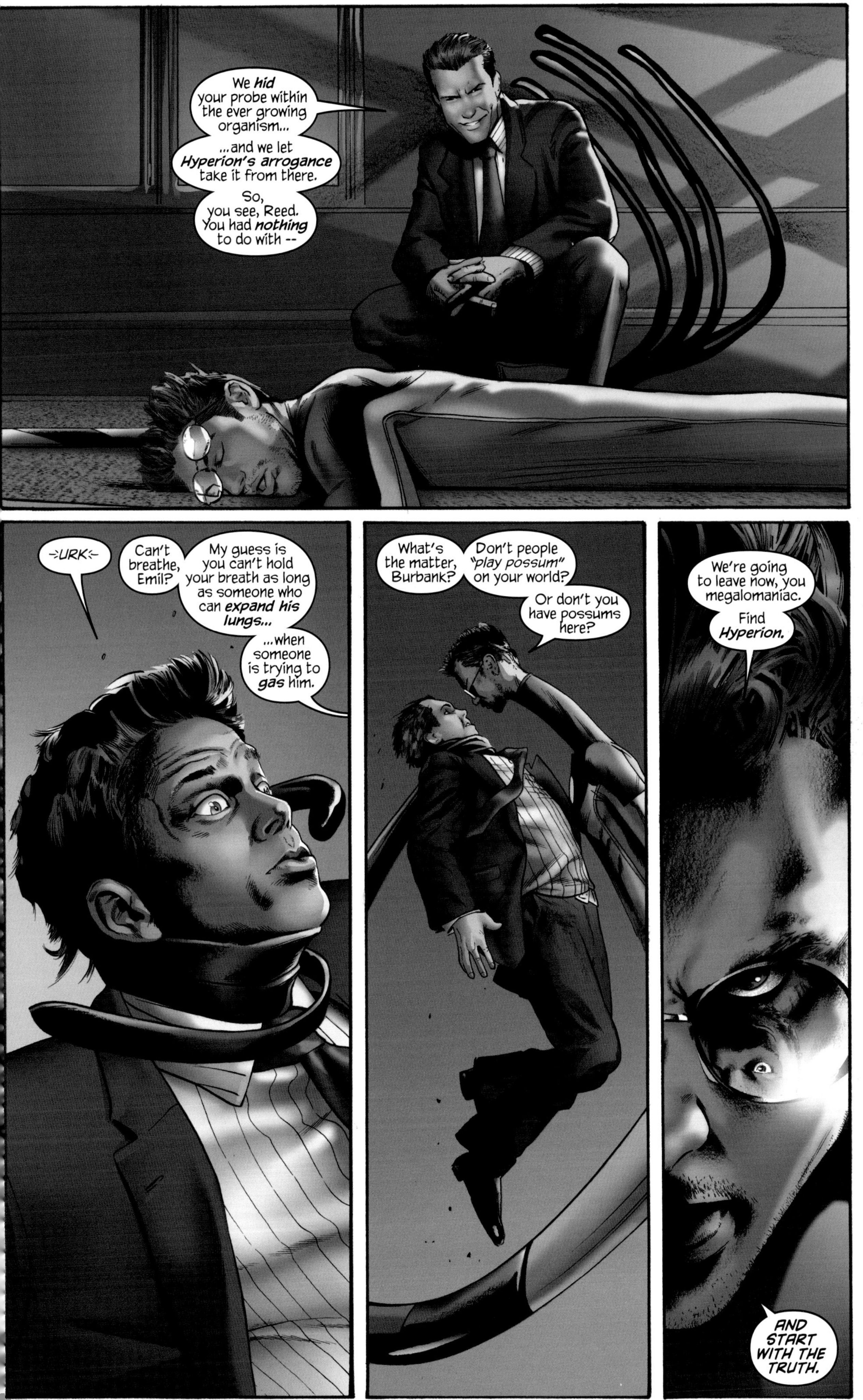
We hid your probe within the ever growing organism...
...and we let Hyperion's arrogance take it from there.
So, you see, Reed. You had nothing to do with --
-URK-
Can't breathe, Emil?
My guess is you can't hold your breath as long as someone who can expand his lungs...
...when someone is trying to gas him.
What's the matter, Burbank?
Don't people "play possum" on your world?
Or don't you have possums here?
We're going to leave now, you megalomaniac.
Find Hyperion.
AND START WITH THE TRUTH.

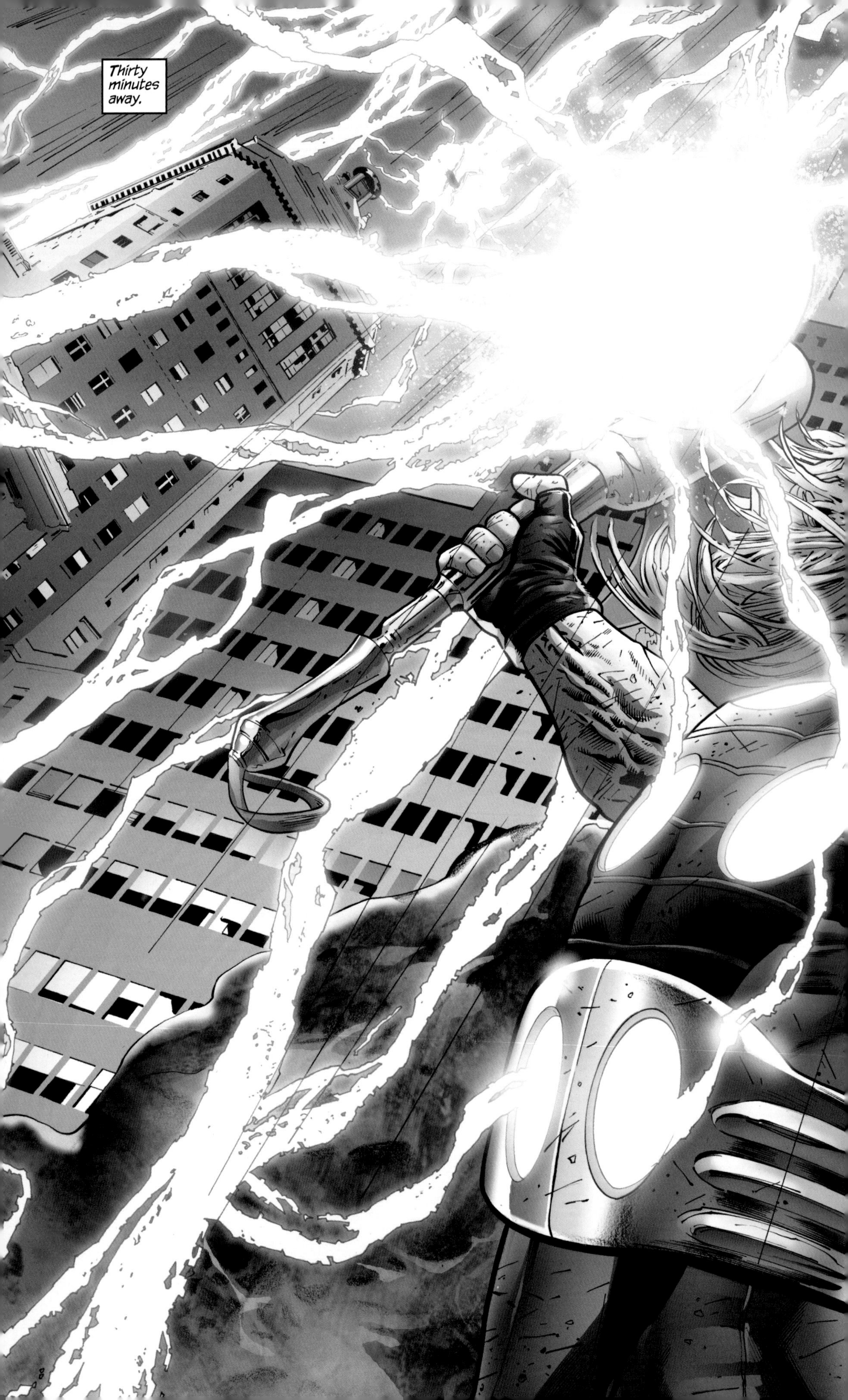
Thirty minutes away.

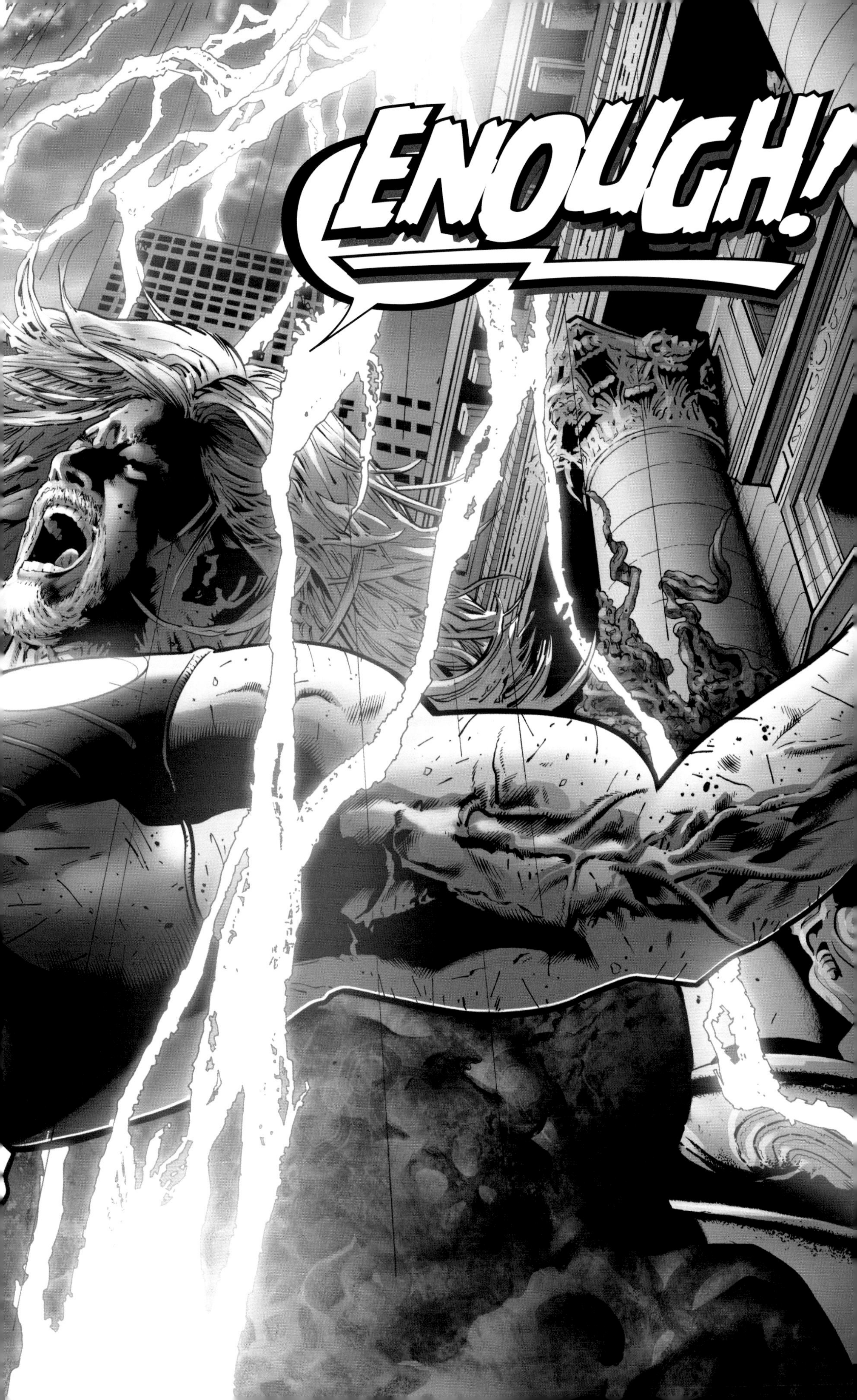
ENOUGH!

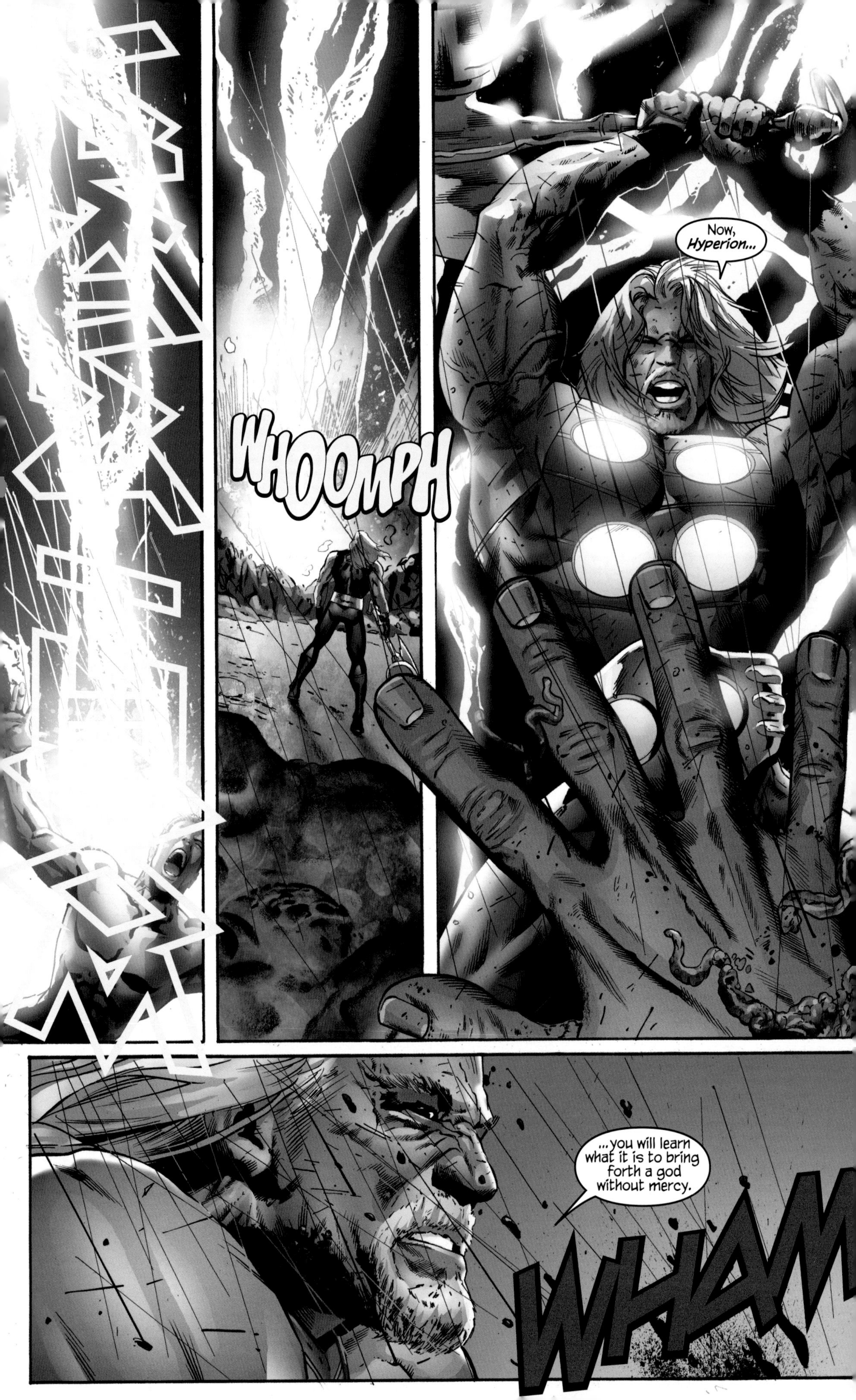
WHOOMPH
Now, Hyperion...
...you will learn what it is to bring forth a god without mercy.
WHAM

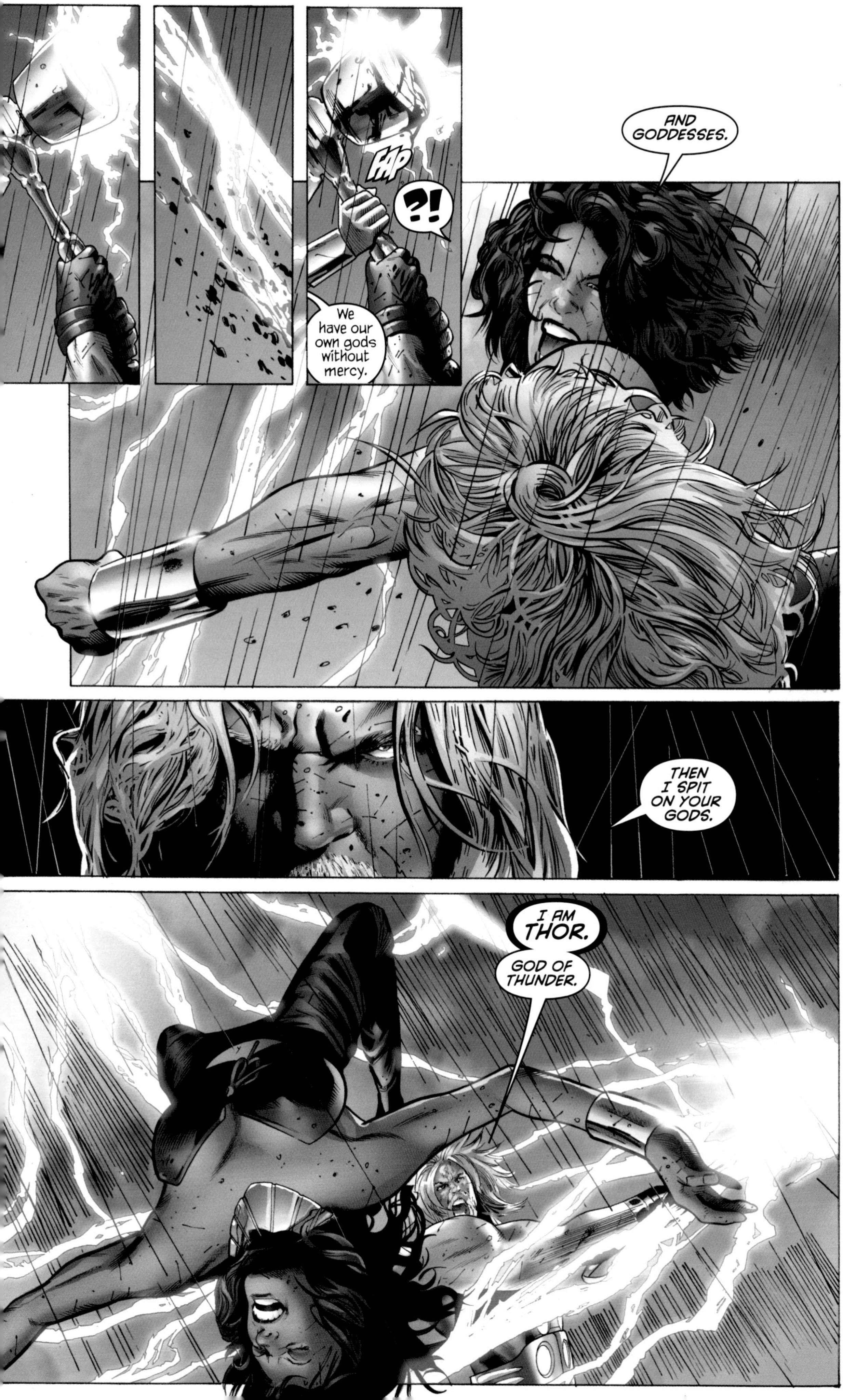
FAP
?!
We have our own gods without mercy.
AND GODDESSES.
THEN I SPIT ON YOUR GODS.
I AM THOR.
GOD OF THUNDER.

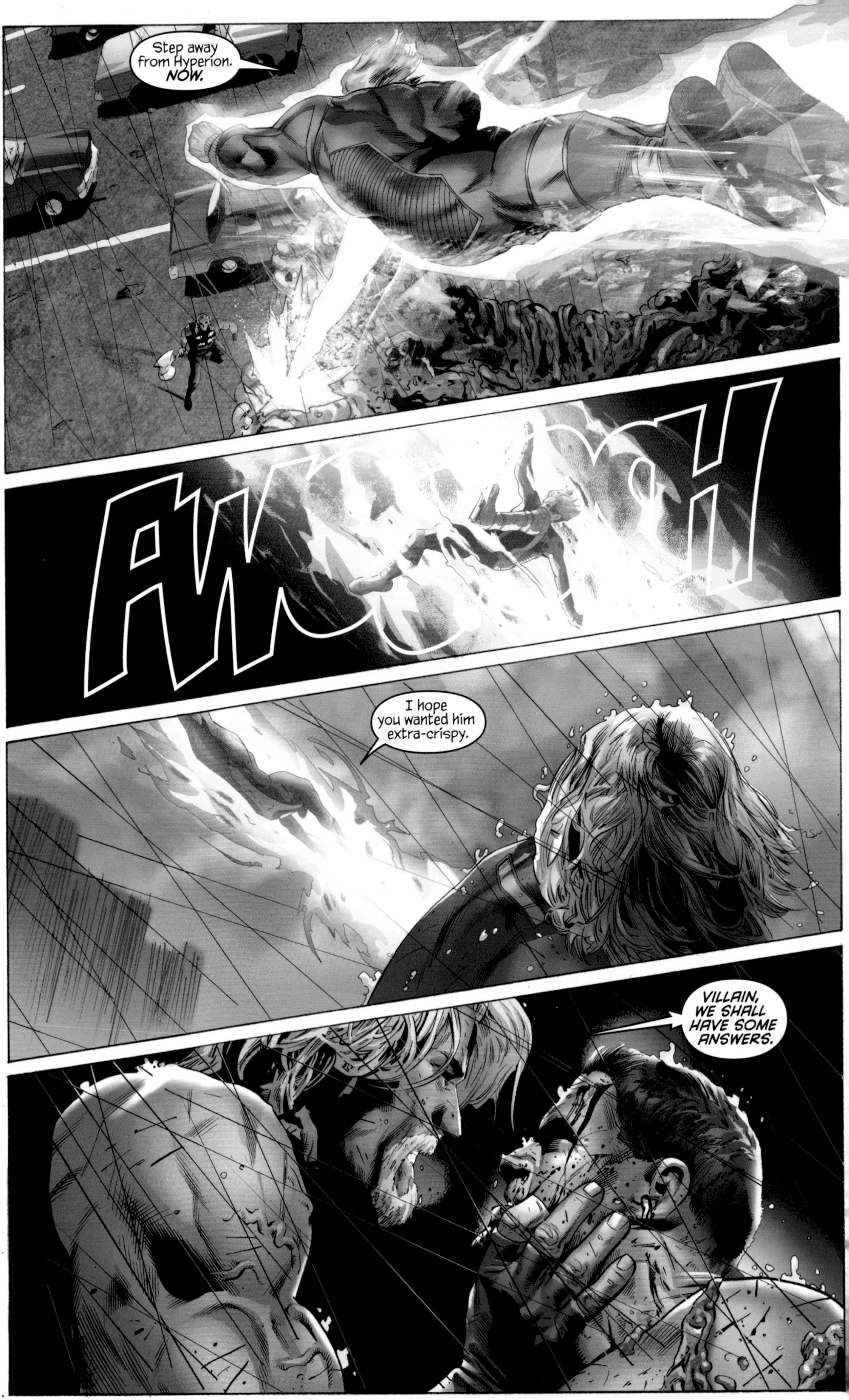

Step away from Hyperion. NOW.
AWOOOH
I hope you wanted him extra-crispy.
VILLAIN, WE SHALL HAVE SOME ANSWERS.

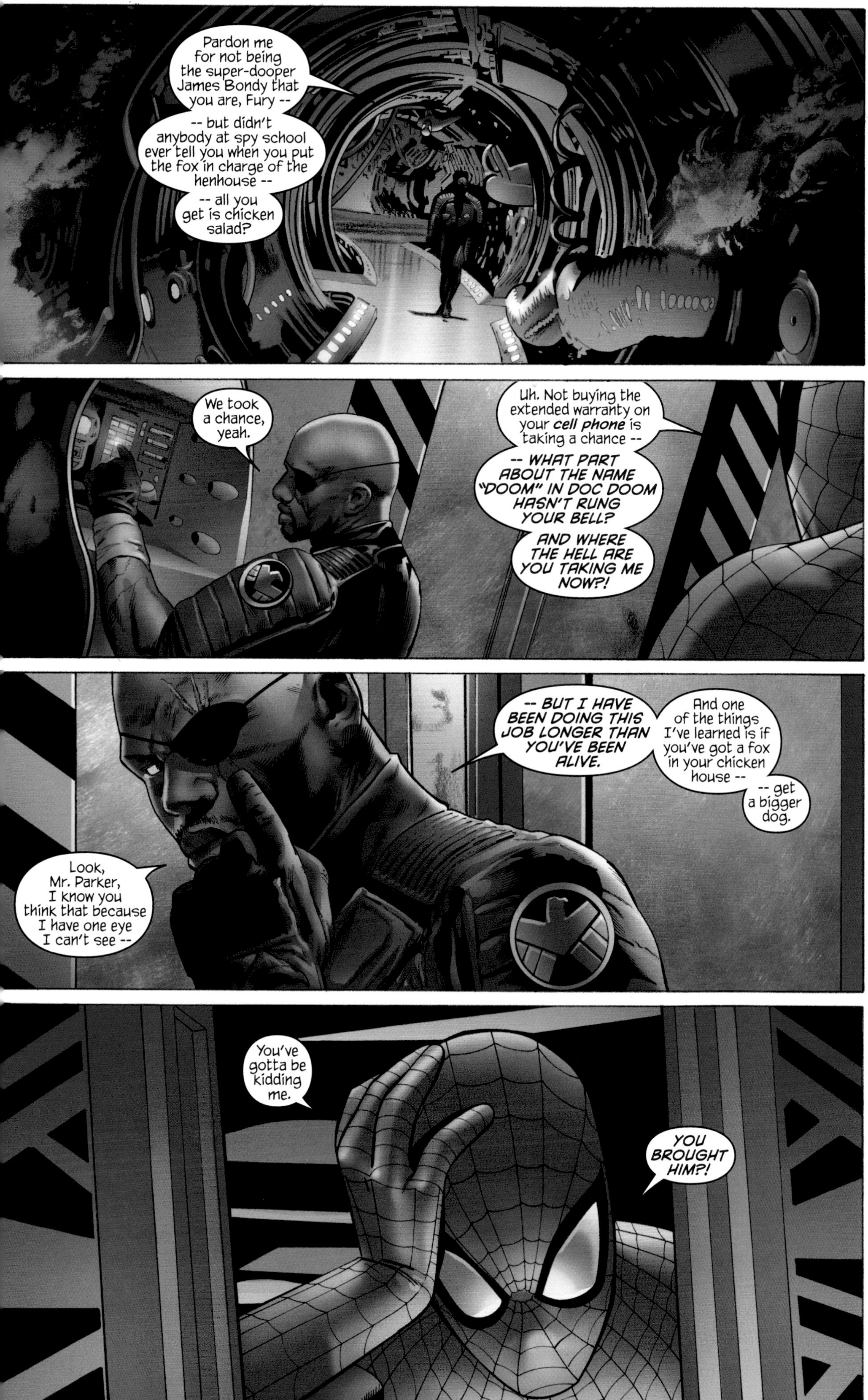
Pardon me for not being the super-dooper James Bondy that you are, Fury --
-- but didn't anybody at spy school ever tell you when you put the fox in charge of the henhouse --
-- all you get is chicken salad?
We took a chance, yeah.
Uh. Not buying the extended warranty on your *cell phone* is taking a chance --
-- WHAT PART ABOUT THE NAME "DOOM" IN DOC DOOM HASN'T RUNG YOUR BELL?
AND WHERE THE HELL ARE YOU TAKING ME NOW?!
Look, Mr. Parker, I know you think that because I have one eye I can't see --
-- BUT I HAVE BEEN DOING THIS JOB LONGER THAN YOU'VE BEEN ALIVE.
And one of the things I've learned is if you've got a fox in your chicken house --
-- get a bigger dog.
You've gotta be kidding me.
YOU BROUGHT HIM?!

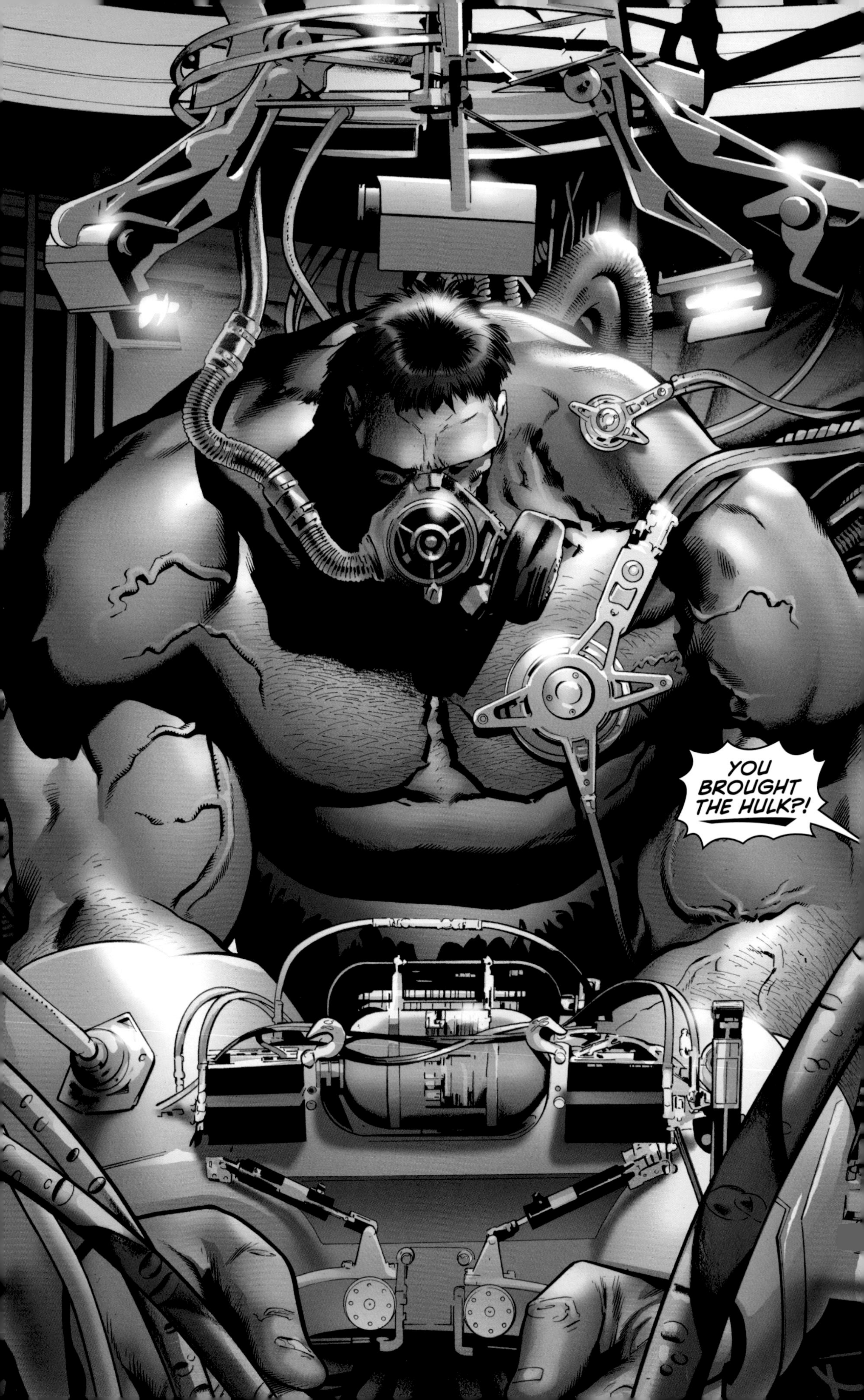
YOU BROUGHT THE HULK?!

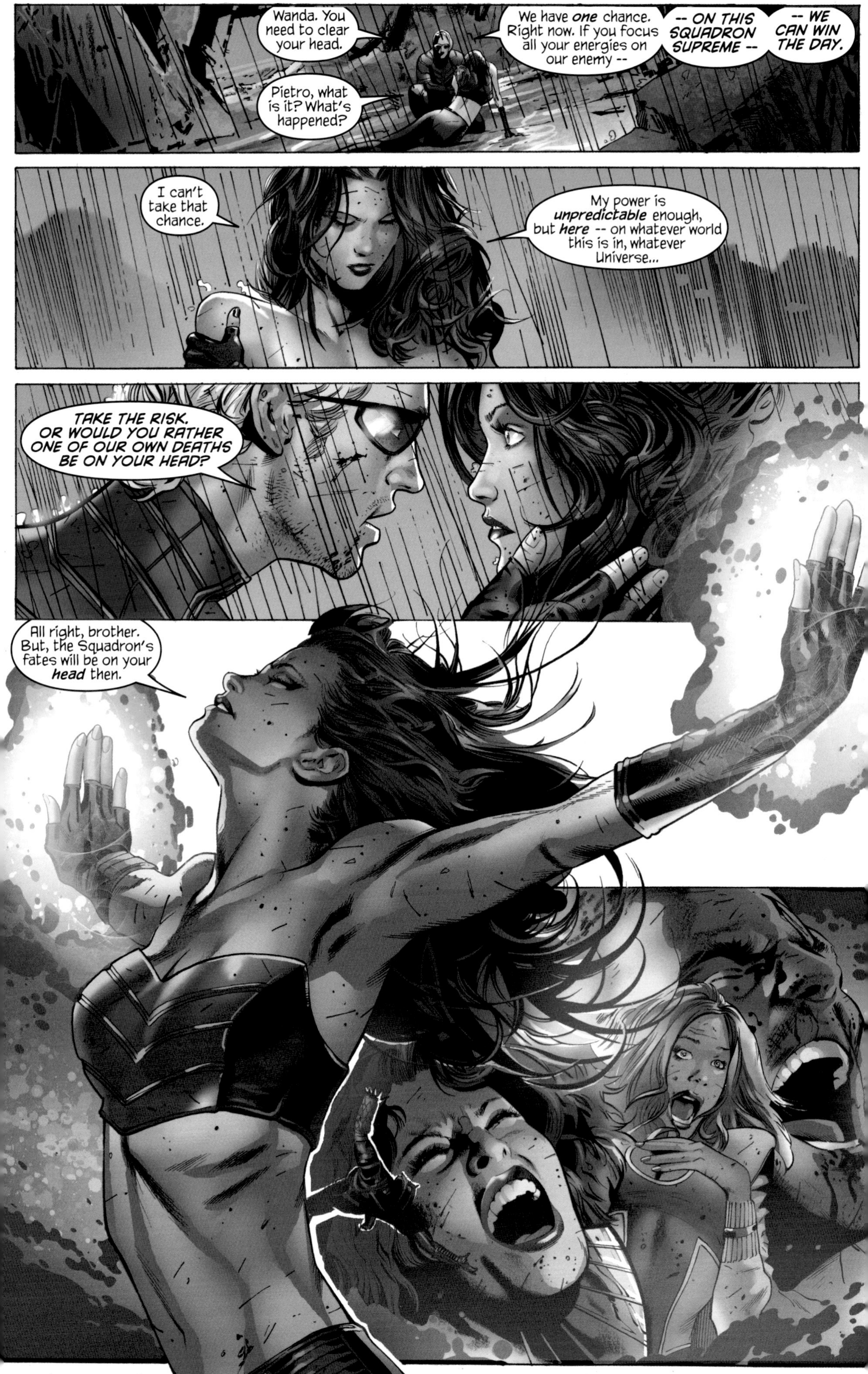
Wanda. You need to clear your head.
Pietro, what is it? What's happened?
We have one chance. Right now. If you focus all your energies on our enemy --
-- ON THIS SQUADRON SUPREME --
-- WE CAN WIN THE DAY.
I can't take that chance.
My power is unpredictable enough, but here -- on whatever world this is in, whatever Universe...
TAKE THE RISK. OR WOULD YOU RATHER ONE OF OUR OWN DEATHS BE ON YOUR HEAD?
All right, brother. But, the Squadron's fates will be on your head then.

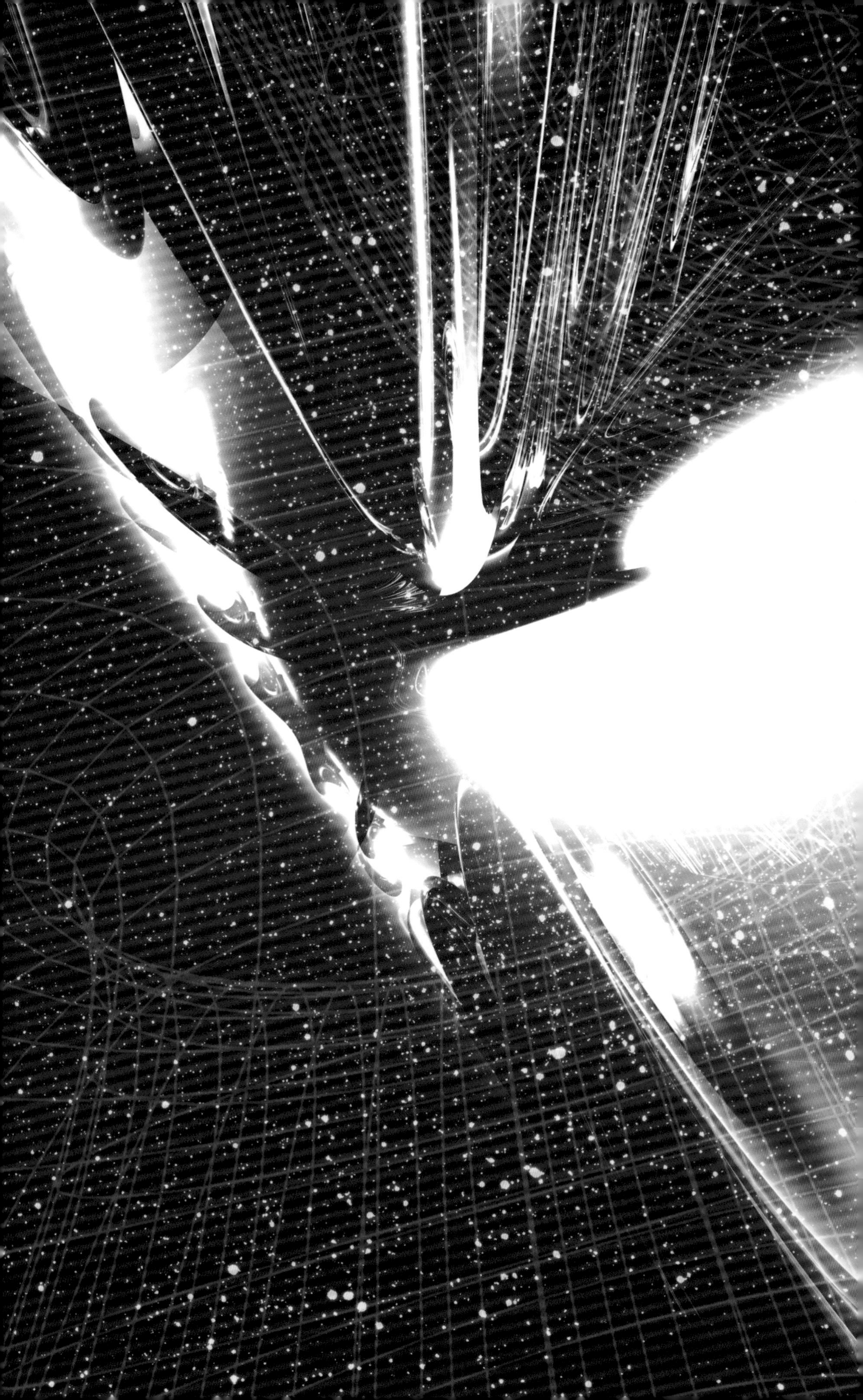

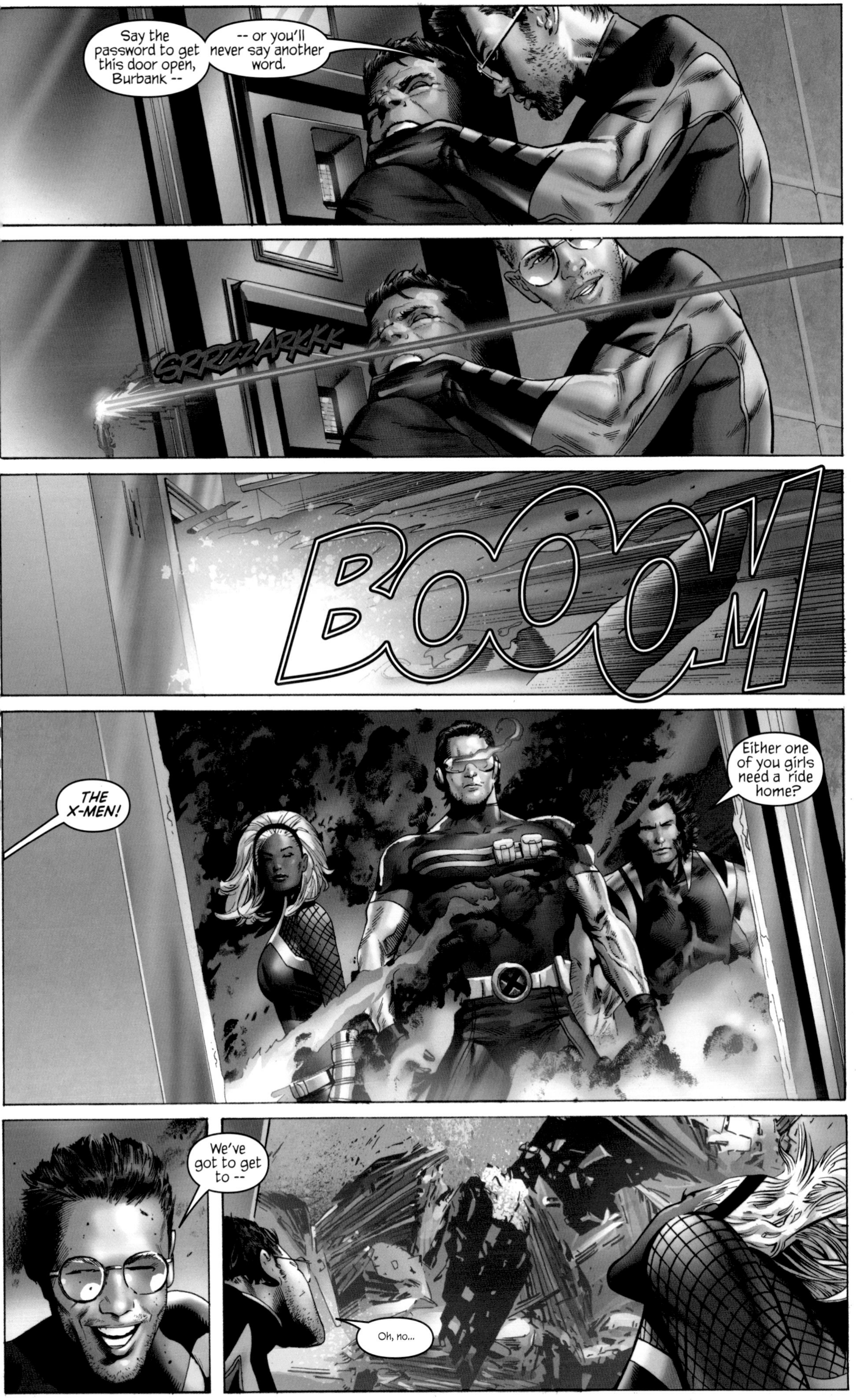

Say the password to get this door open, Burbank --
-- or you'll never say another word.
SRRIZZARKKK
BOOOM
THE X-MEN!
Either one of you girls need a ride home?
We've got to get to --
Oh, no...

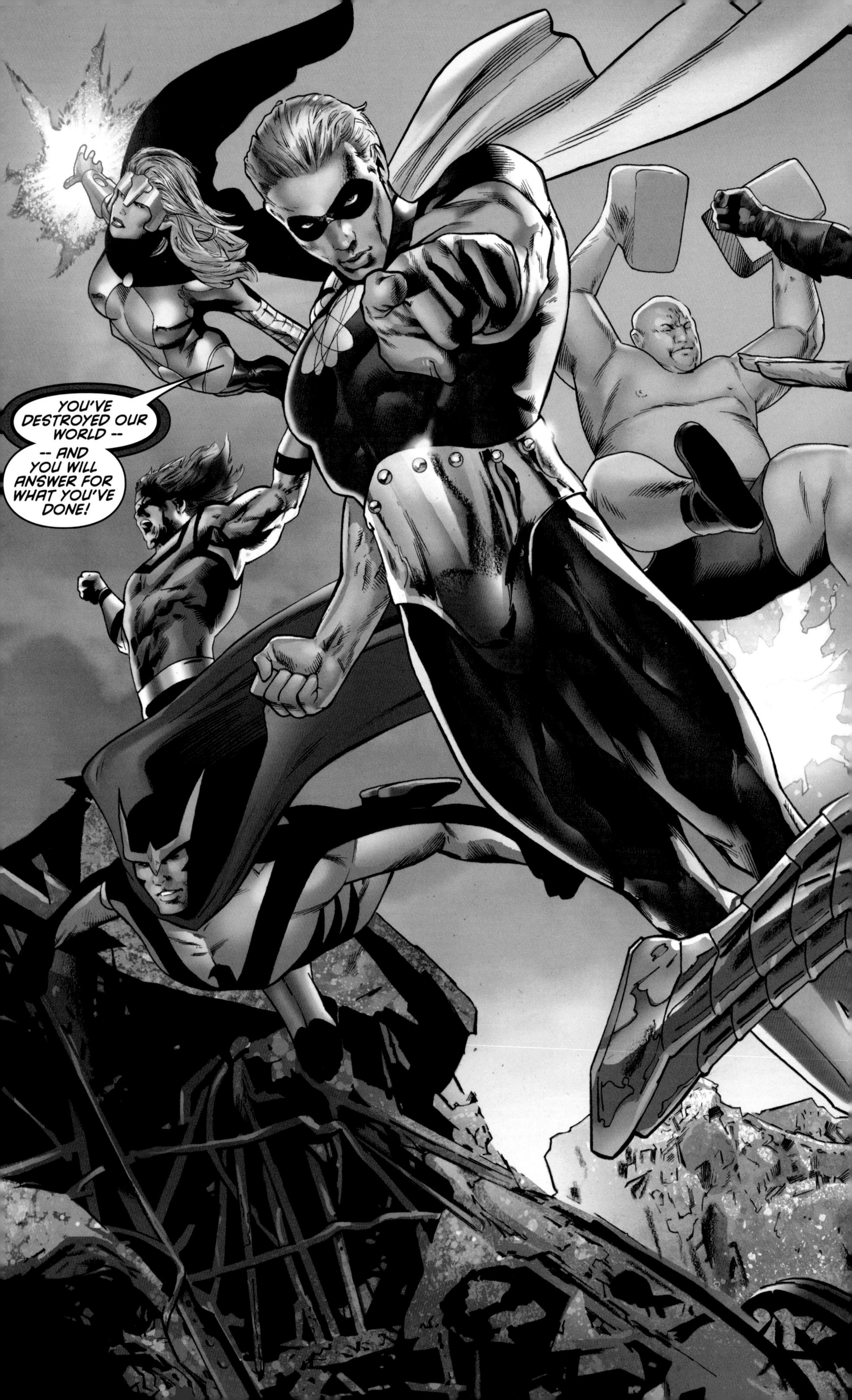
YOU'VE DESTROYED OUR WORLD --
-- AND YOU WILL ANSWER FOR WHAT YOU'VE DONE!

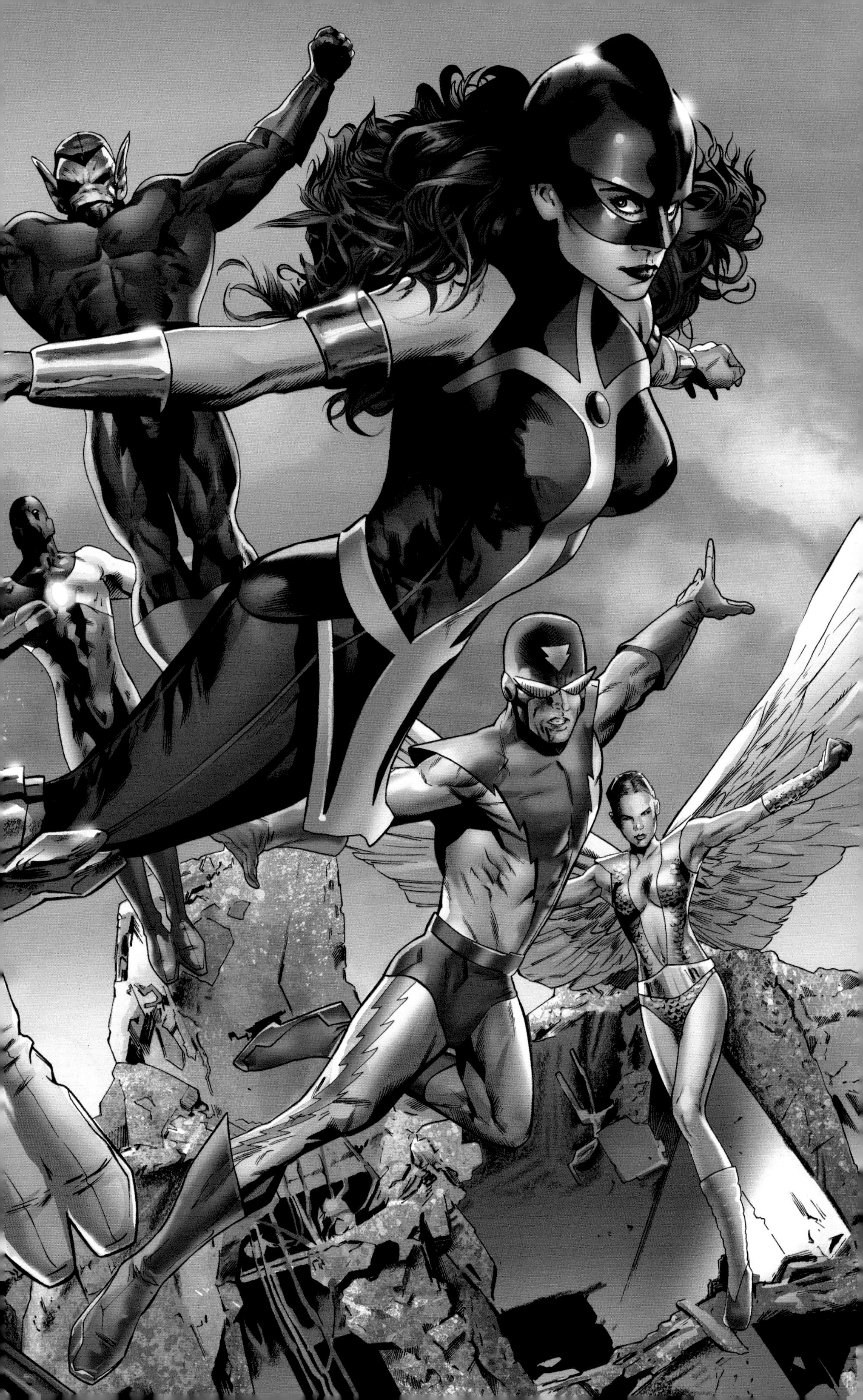

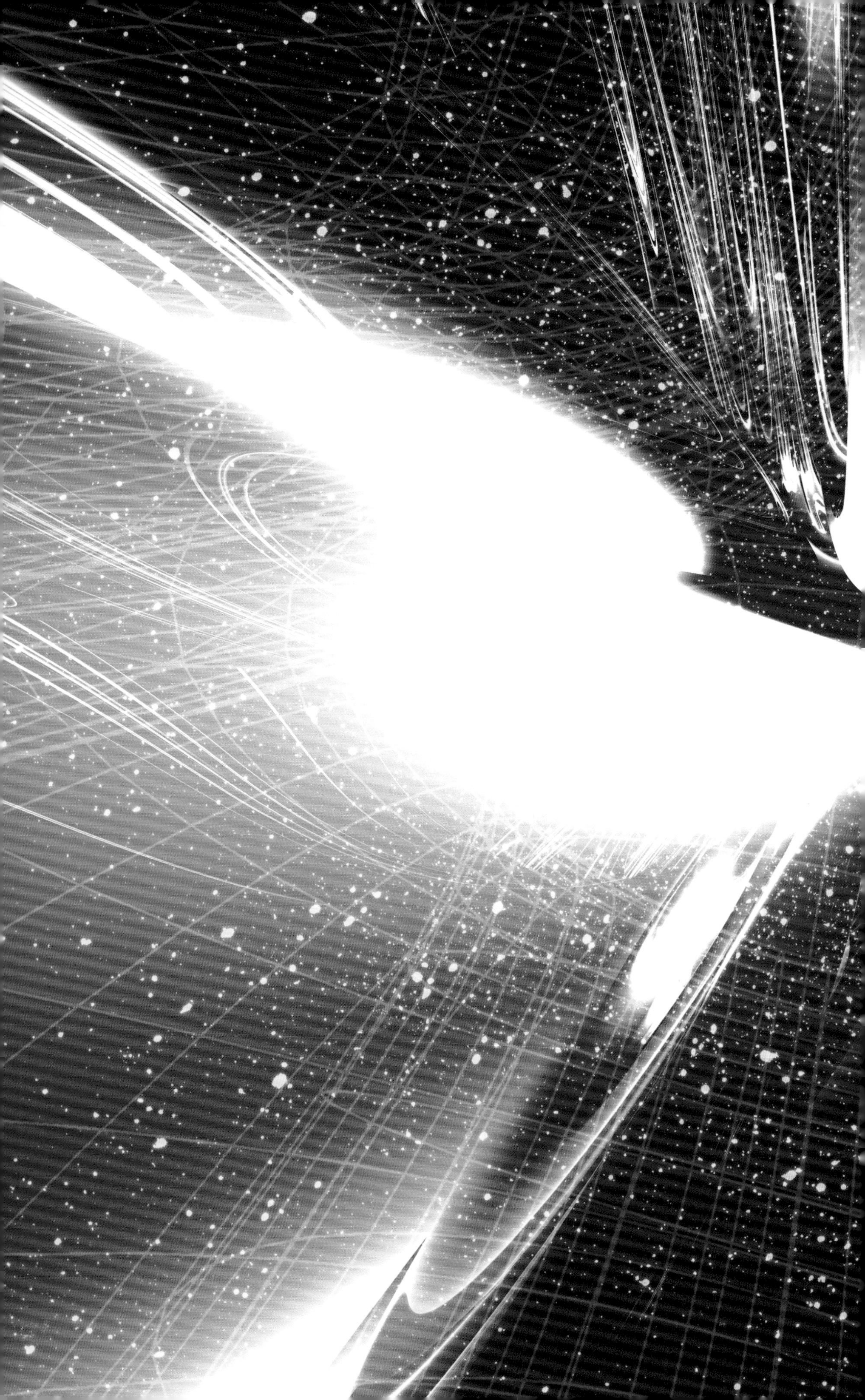

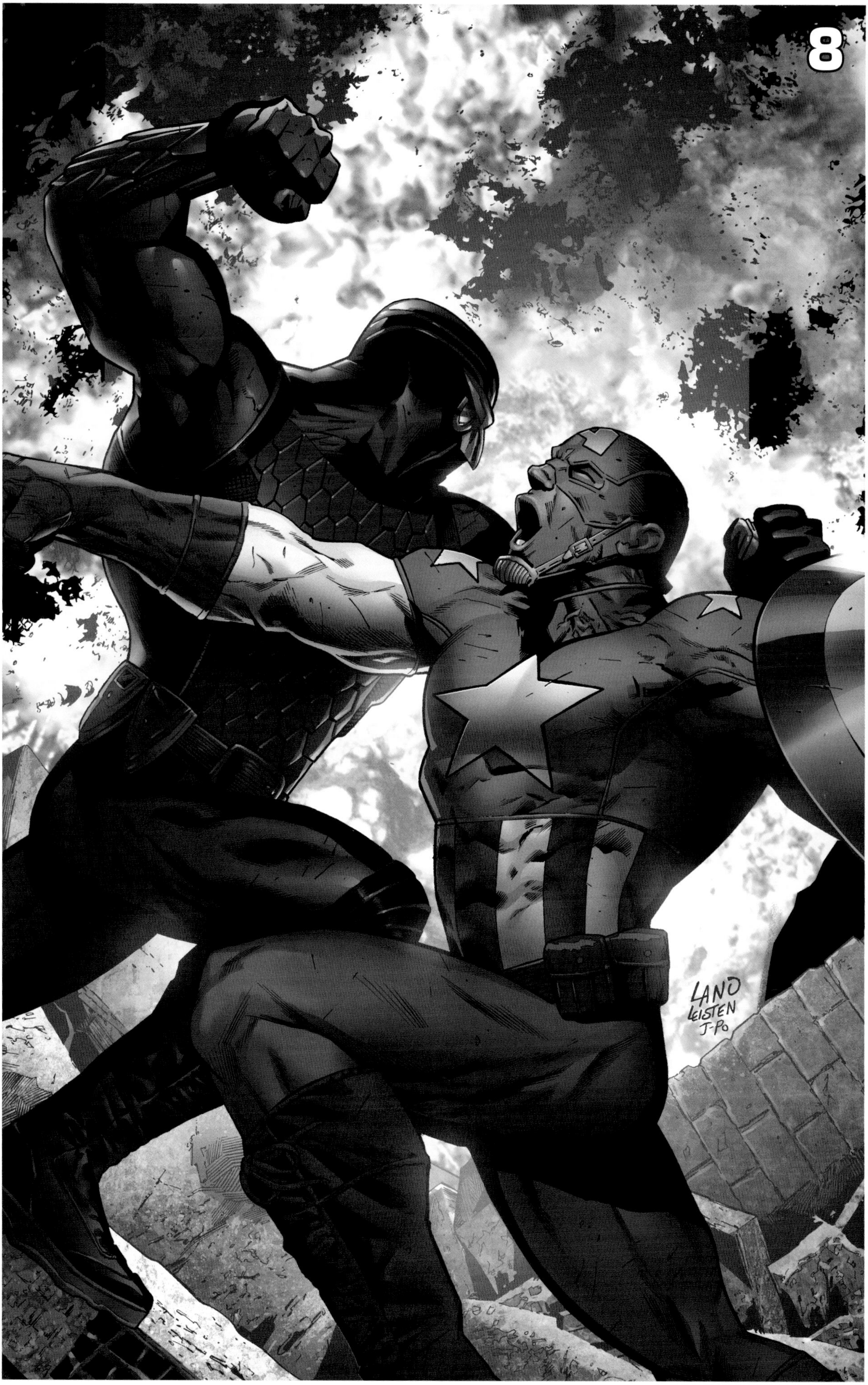
8
LAND
LEISTEN
J-Po

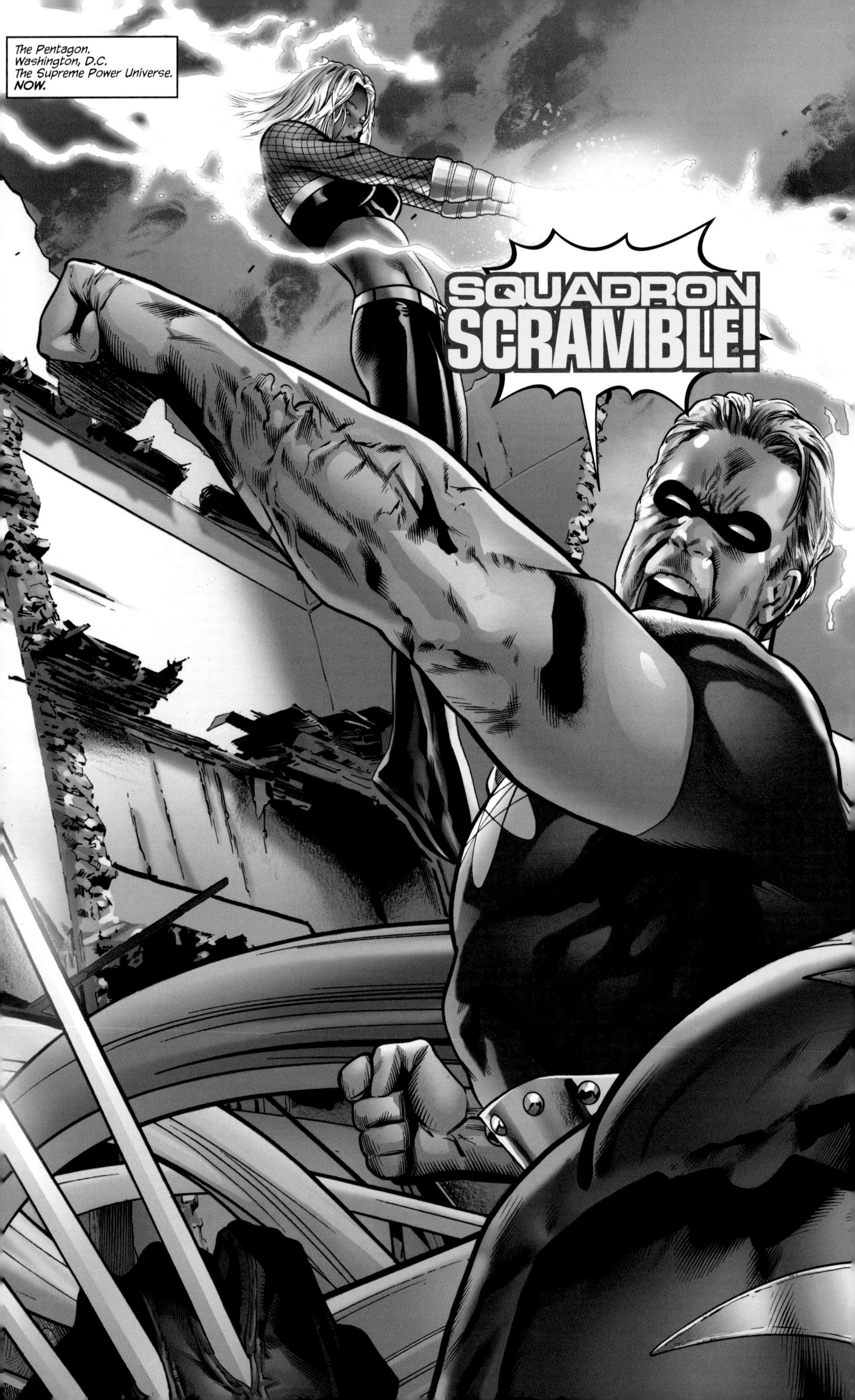
The Pentagon.
Washington, D.C.
The Supreme Power Universe.
NOW.
SQUADRON SCRAMBLE!

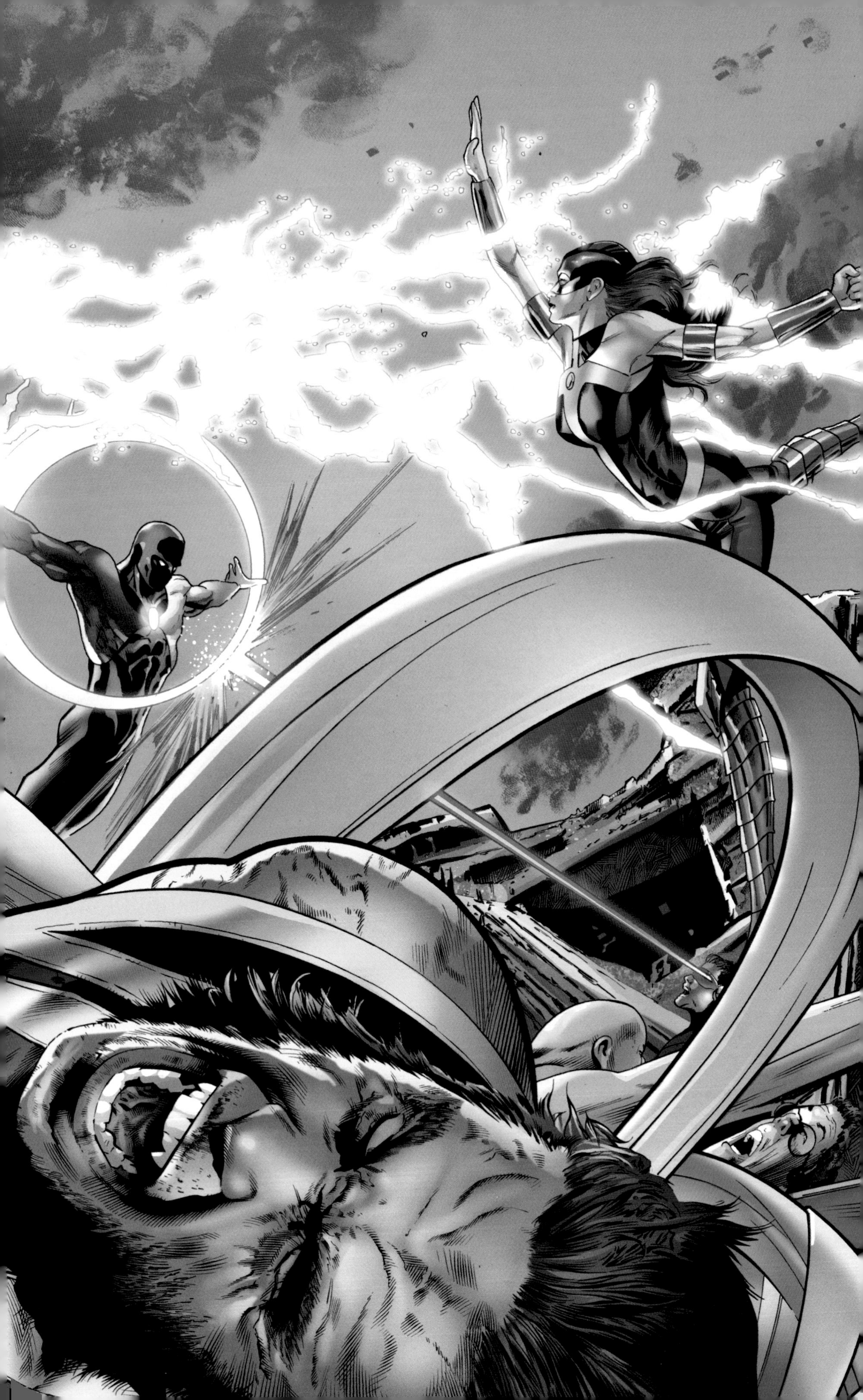

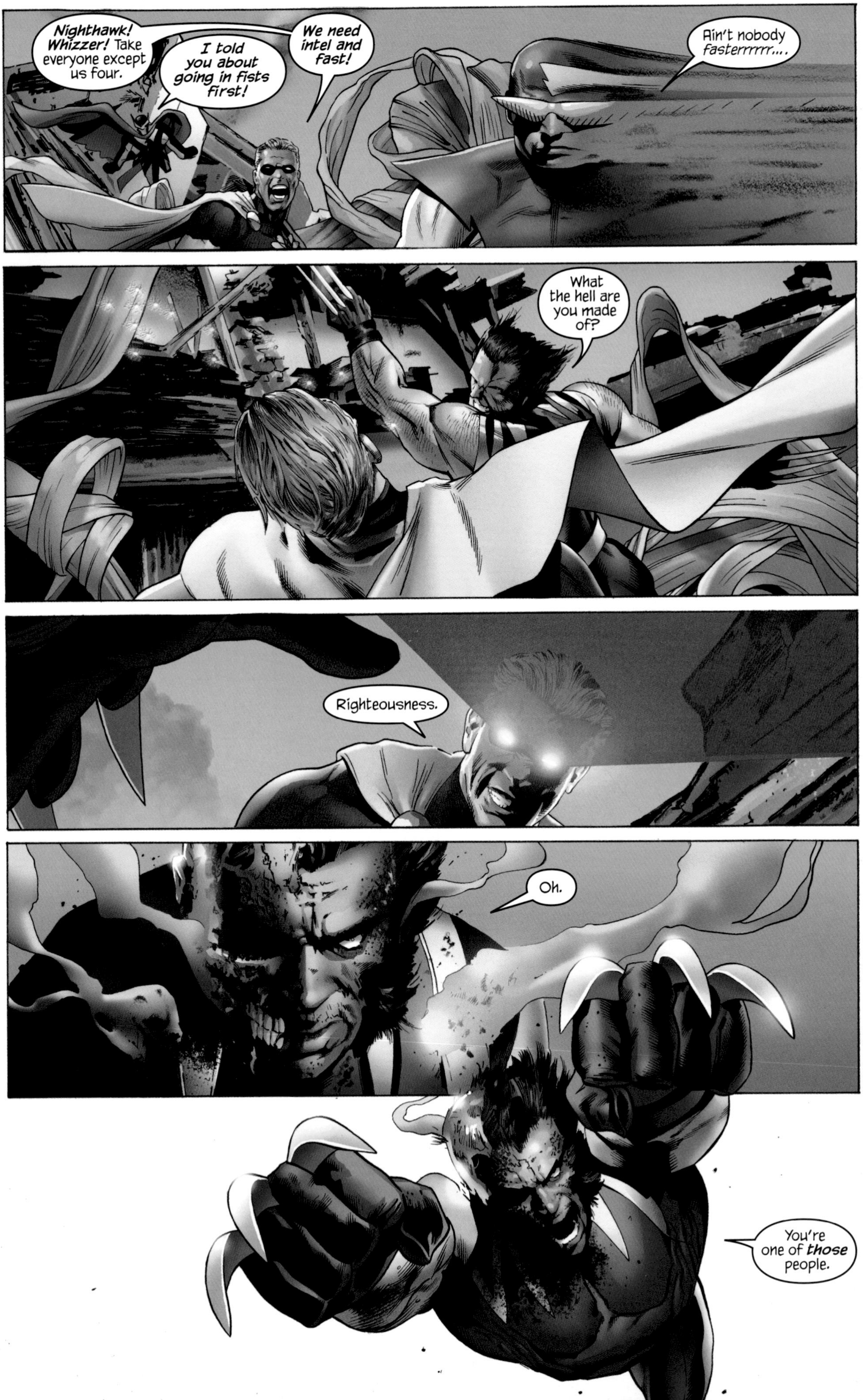

Nighthawk! Whizzer! Take everyone except us four.
We need intel and fast!
I told you about going in fists first!
Ain't nobody fasterrrrrr....
What the hell are you made of?
Righteousness.
Oh.
You're one of *those* people.

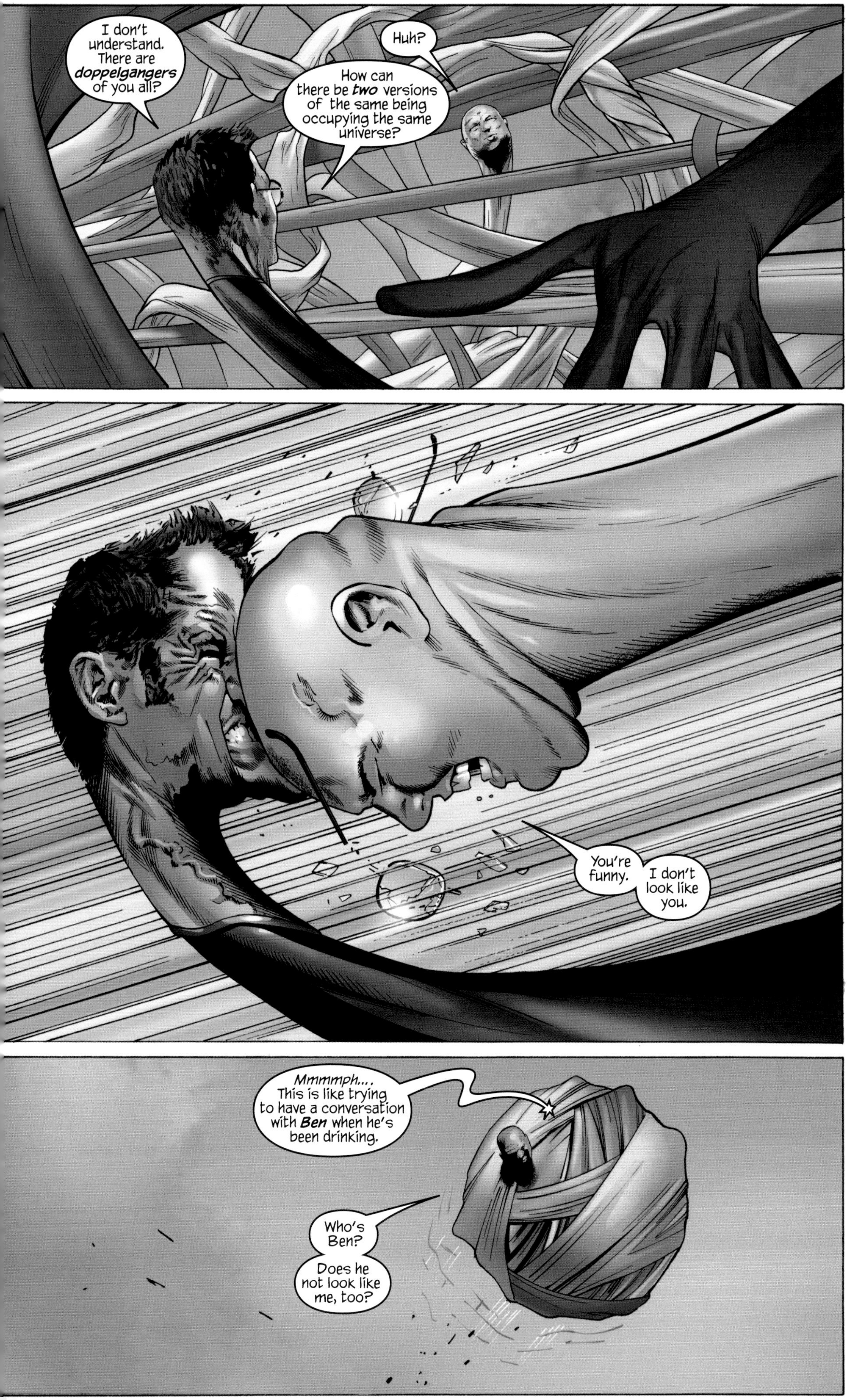
I don't understand. There are *doppelgangers* of you all?
Huh?
How can there be ***two*** versions of the same being occupying the same universe?
You're funny.
I don't look like you.
Mmmmph.... This is like trying to have a conversation with ***Ben*** when he's been drinking.
Who's Ben?
Does he not look like me, too?

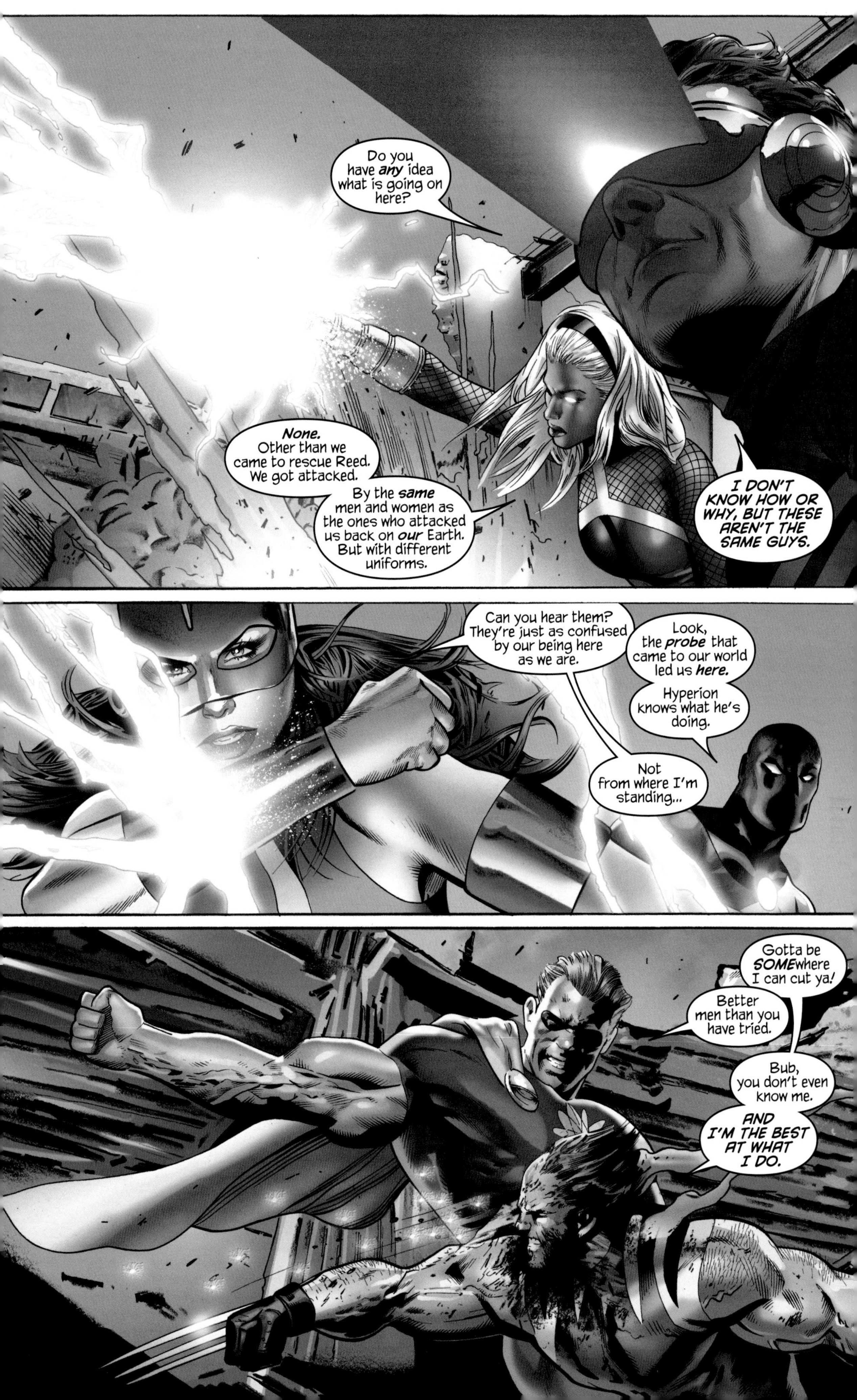
Do you have *any* idea what is going on here?
None. Other than we came to rescue Reed. We got attacked.
By the *same* men and women as the ones who attacked us back on *our* Earth. But with different uniforms.
I DON'T KNOW HOW OR WHY, BUT THESE AREN'T THE SAME GUYS.
Can you hear them? They're just as confused by our being here as we are.
Look, the *probe* that came to our world led us *here.*
Hyperion knows what he's doing.
Not from where I'm standing...
Gotta be *SOME*where I can cut ya!
Better men than you have tried.
Bub, you don't even know me.
AND I'M THE BEST AT WHAT I DO.

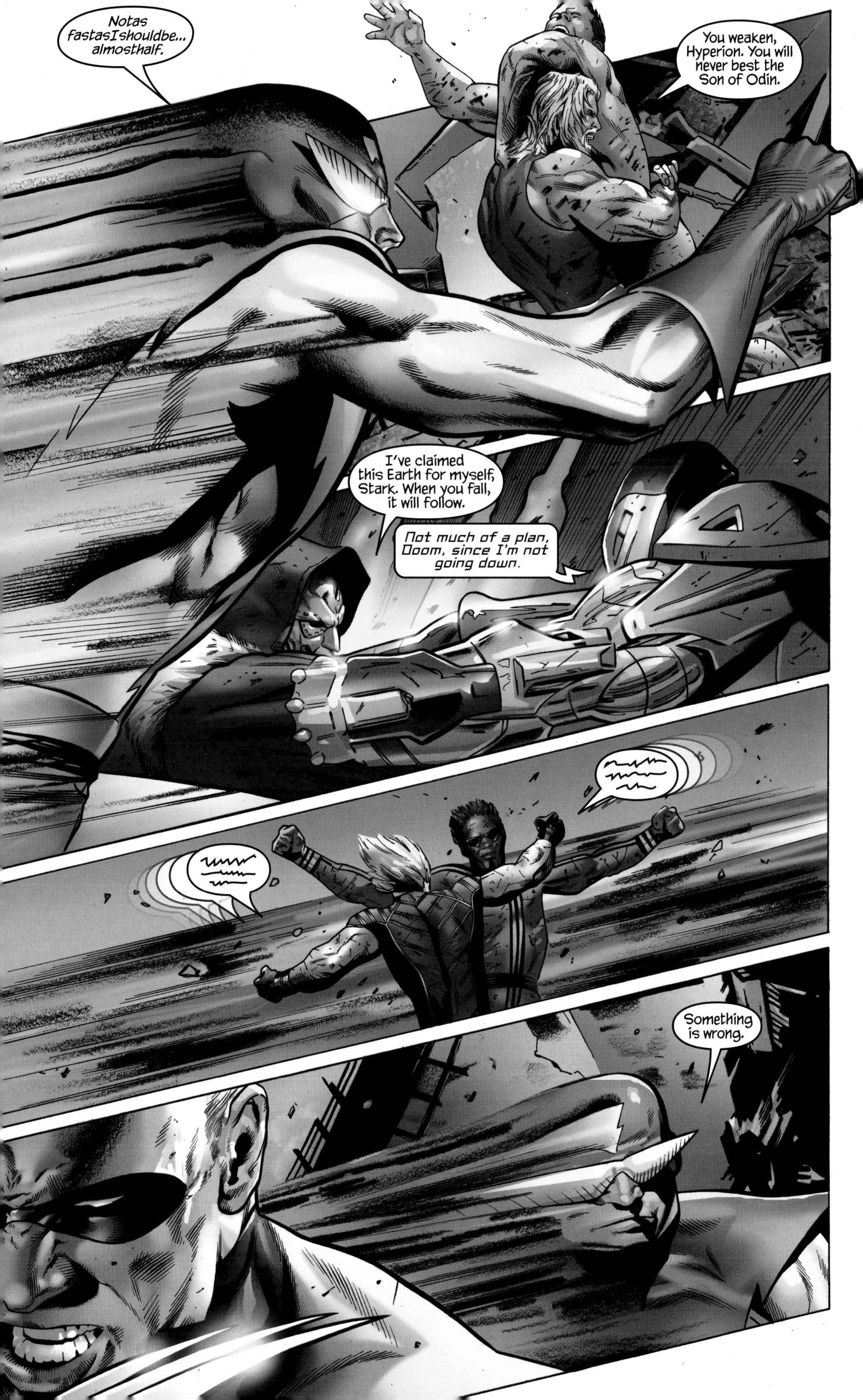
Notas fastasIshouldbe... almosthalf.
You weaken, Hyperion. You will never best the Son of Odin.
I've claimed this Earth for myself, Stark. When you fall, it will follow.
Not much of a plan, Doom, since I'm not going down.
Something is wrong.

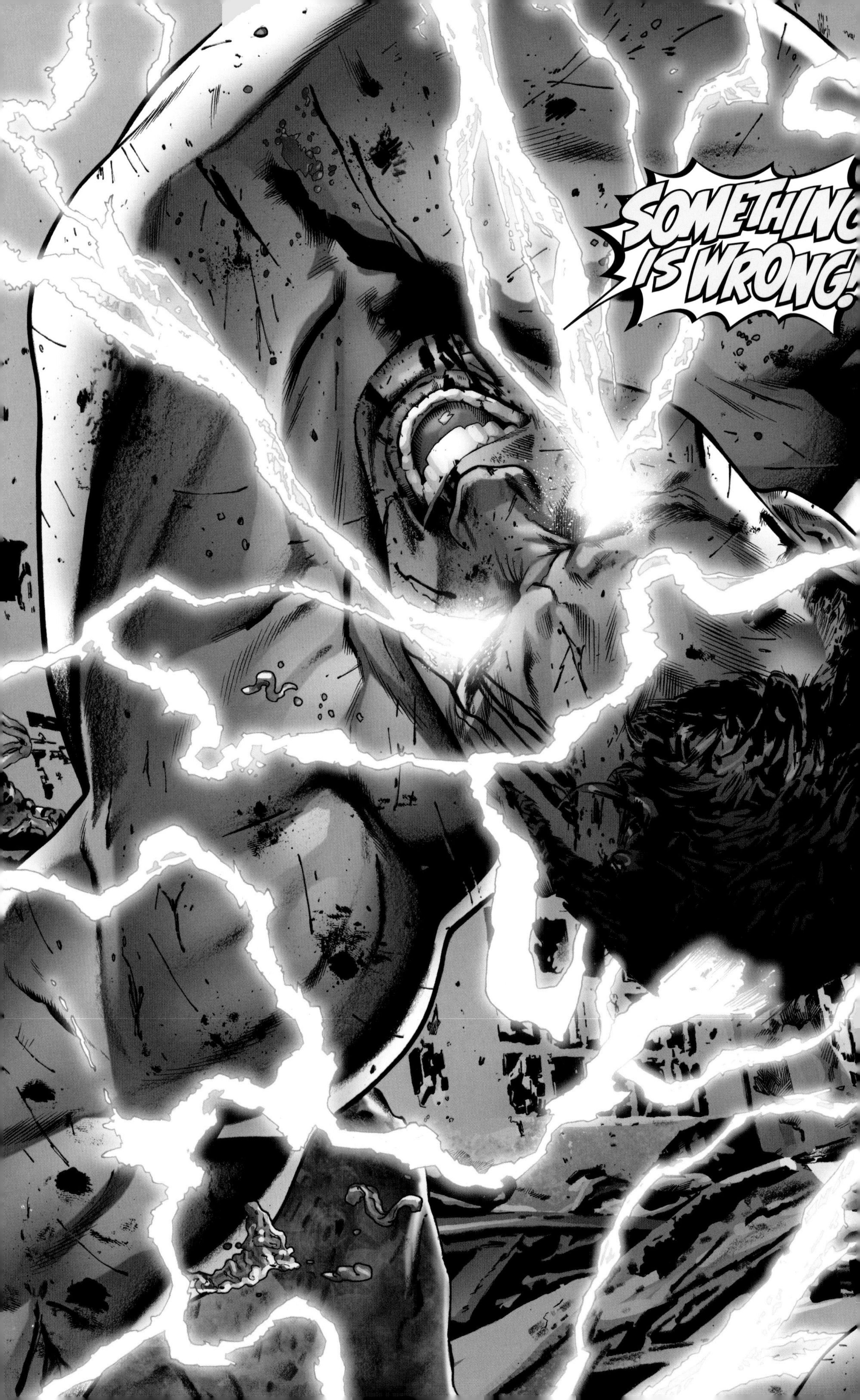
SOMETHING IS WRONG!

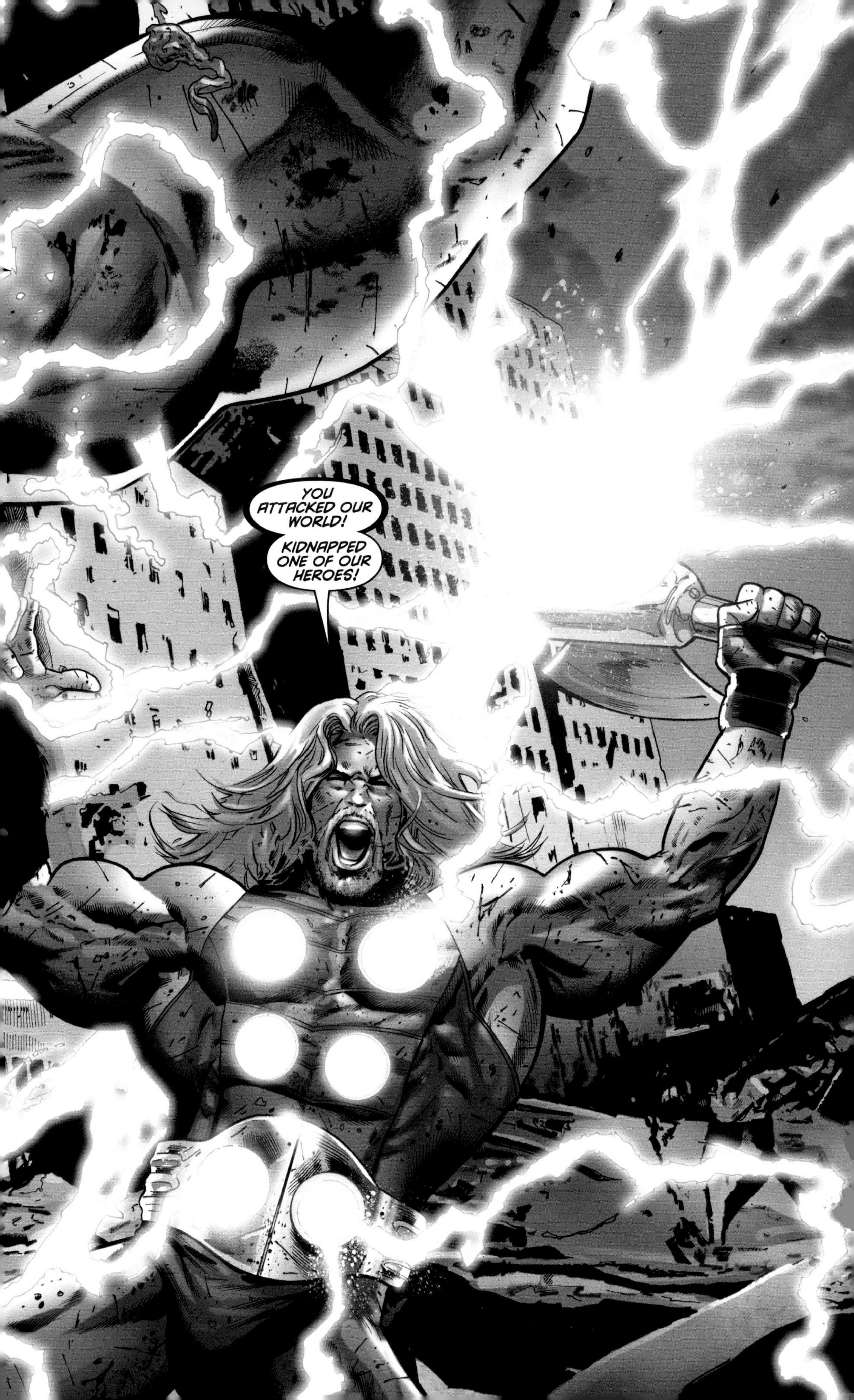
YOU ATTACKED OUR WORLD!
KIDNAPPED ONE OF OUR HEROES!

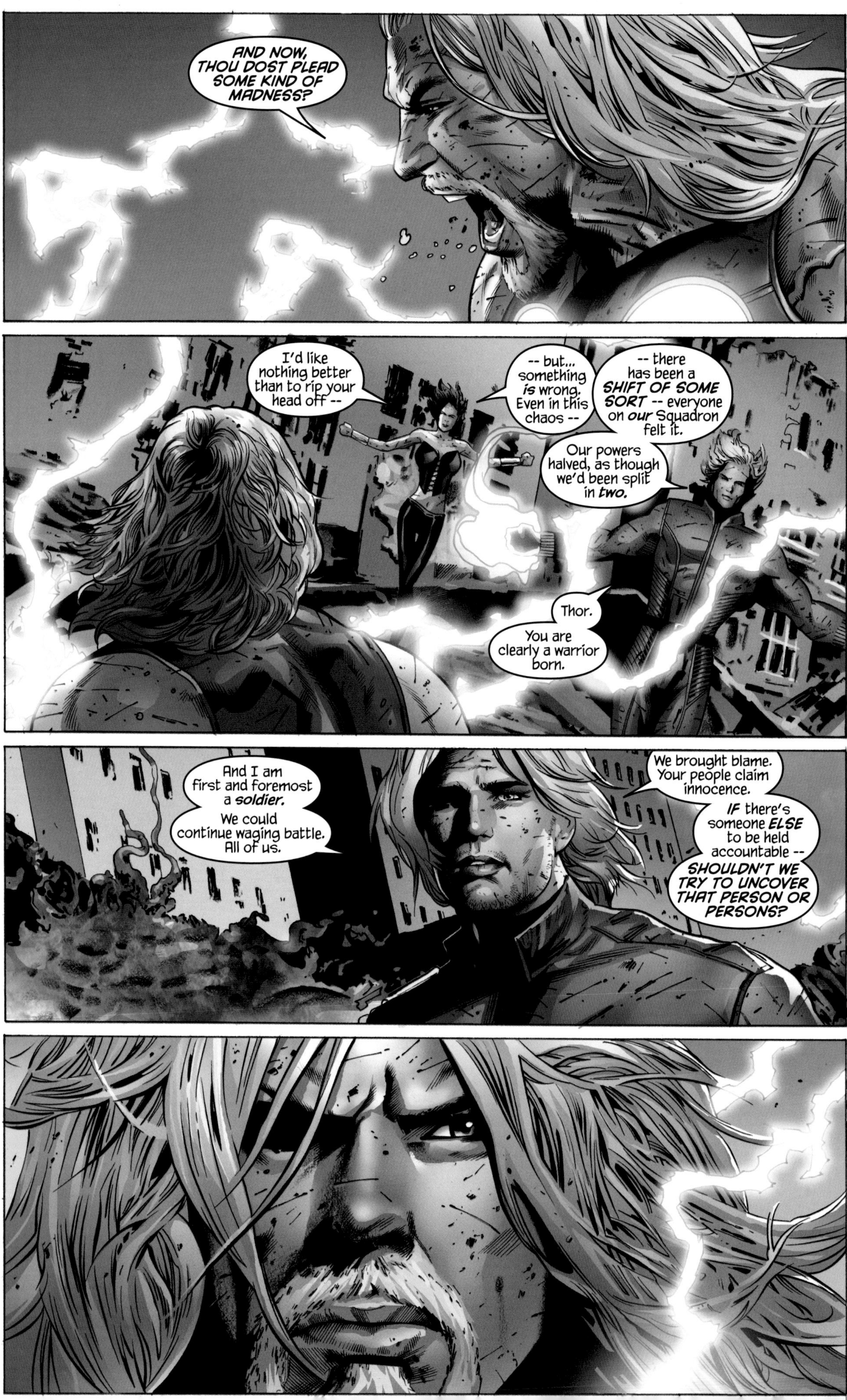
AND NOW, THOU DOST PLEAD SOME KIND OF MADNESS?
I'd like nothing better than to rip your head off --
-- but... something is wrong. Even in this chaos --
-- there has been a SHIFT OF SOME SORT -- everyone on our Squadron felt it.
Our powers halved, as though we'd been split in two.
Thor.
You are clearly a warrior born.
And I am first and foremost a soldier.
We could continue waging battle. All of us.
We brought blame. Your people claim innocence.
IF there's someone ELSE to be held accountable --
SHOULDN'T WE TRY TO UNCOVER THAT PERSON OR PERSONS?

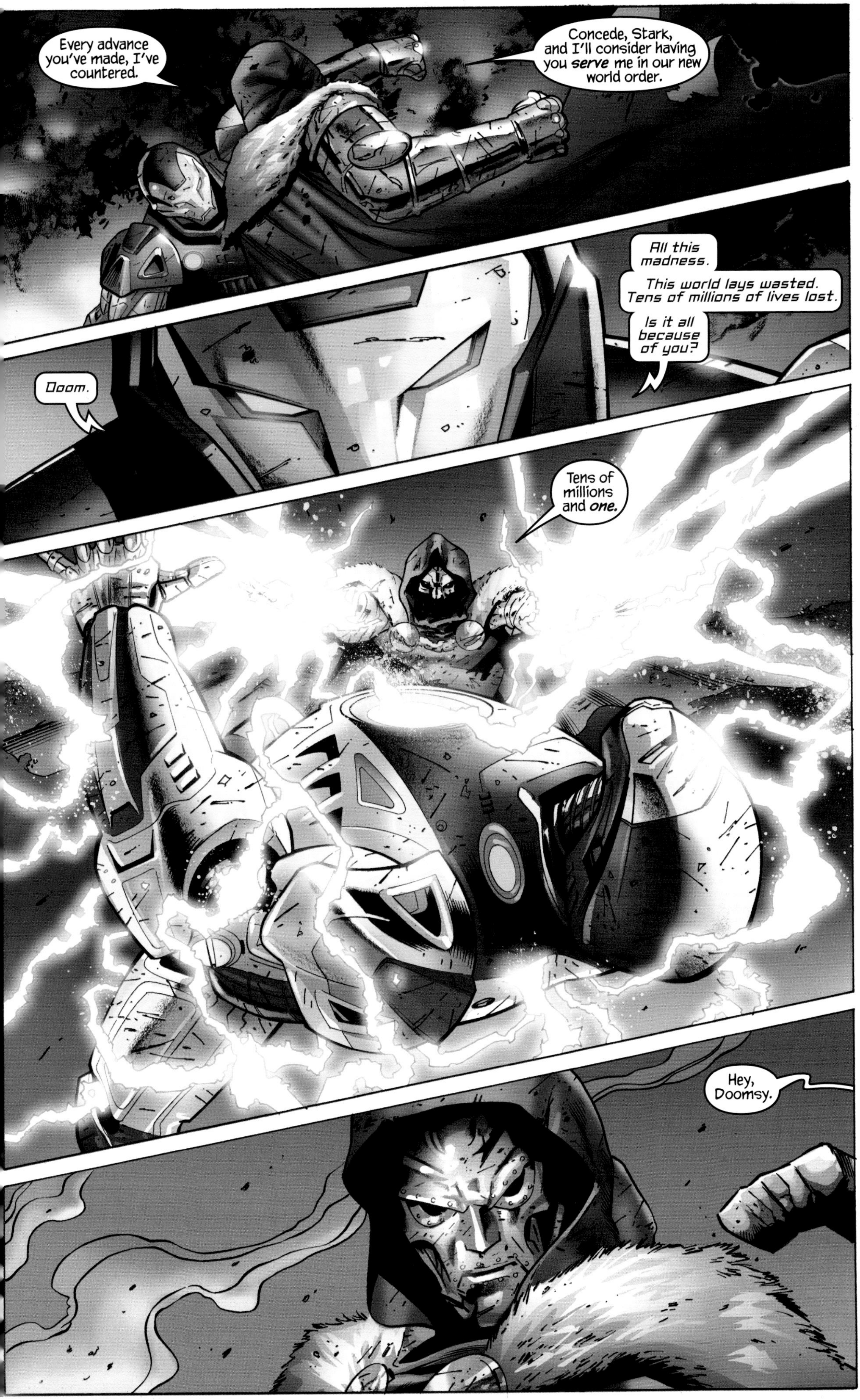
Every advance you've made, I've countered.
Concede, Stark, and I'll consider having you serve me in our new world order.
All this madness.
This world lays wasted. Tens of millions of lives lost.
Is it all because of you?
Doom.
Tens of millions and one.
Hey, Doomsy.

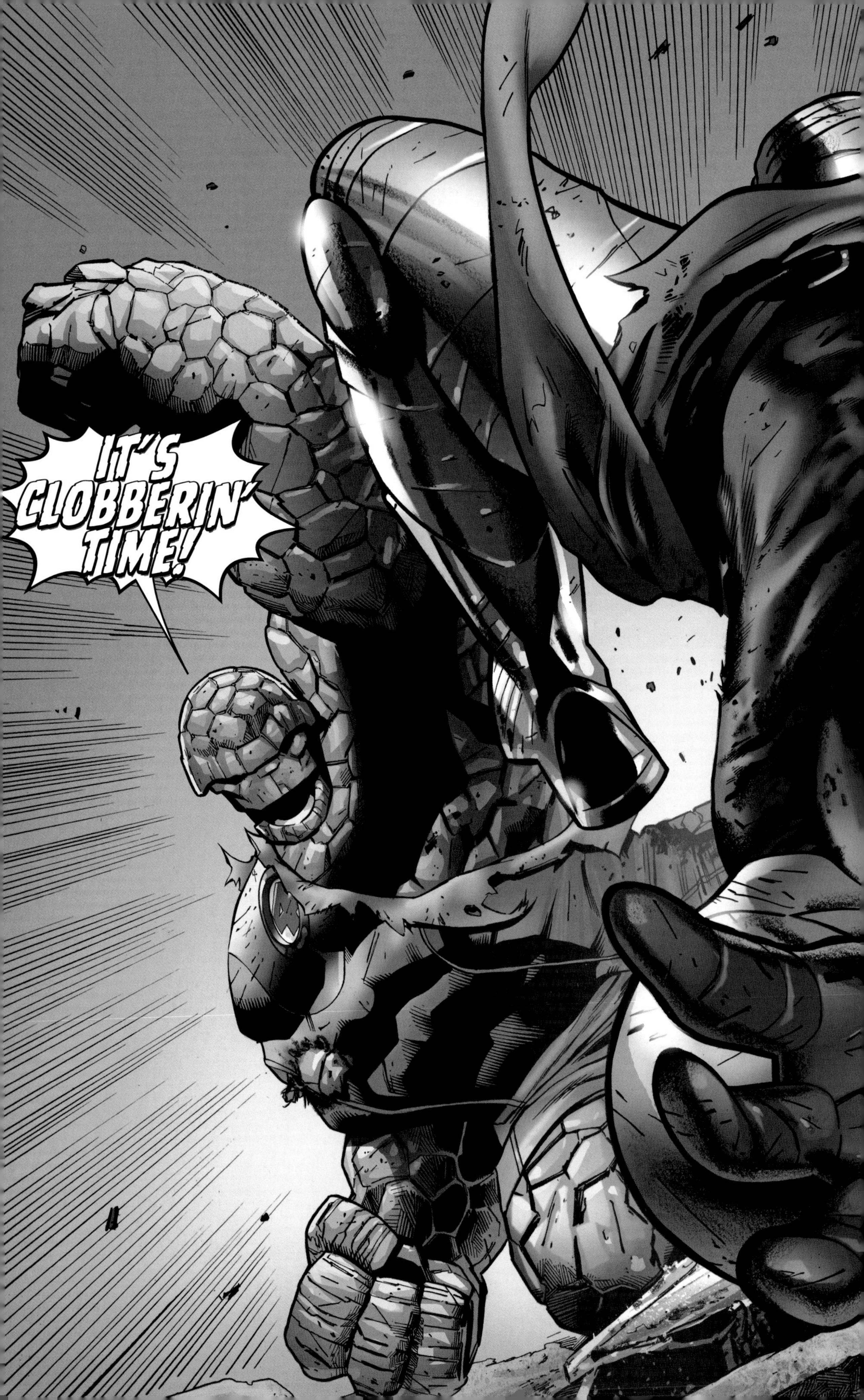
IT'S CLOBBERIN' TIME!

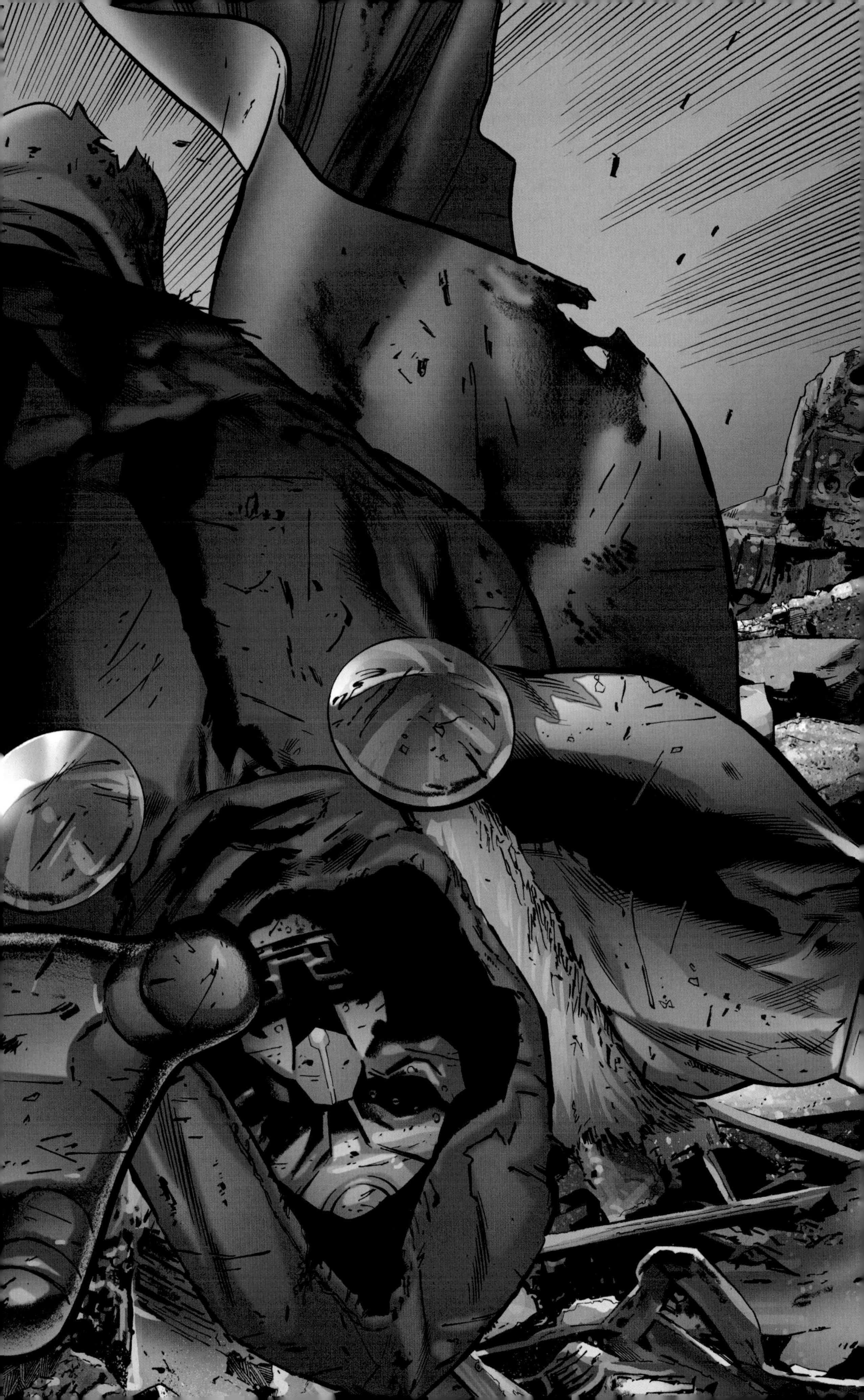

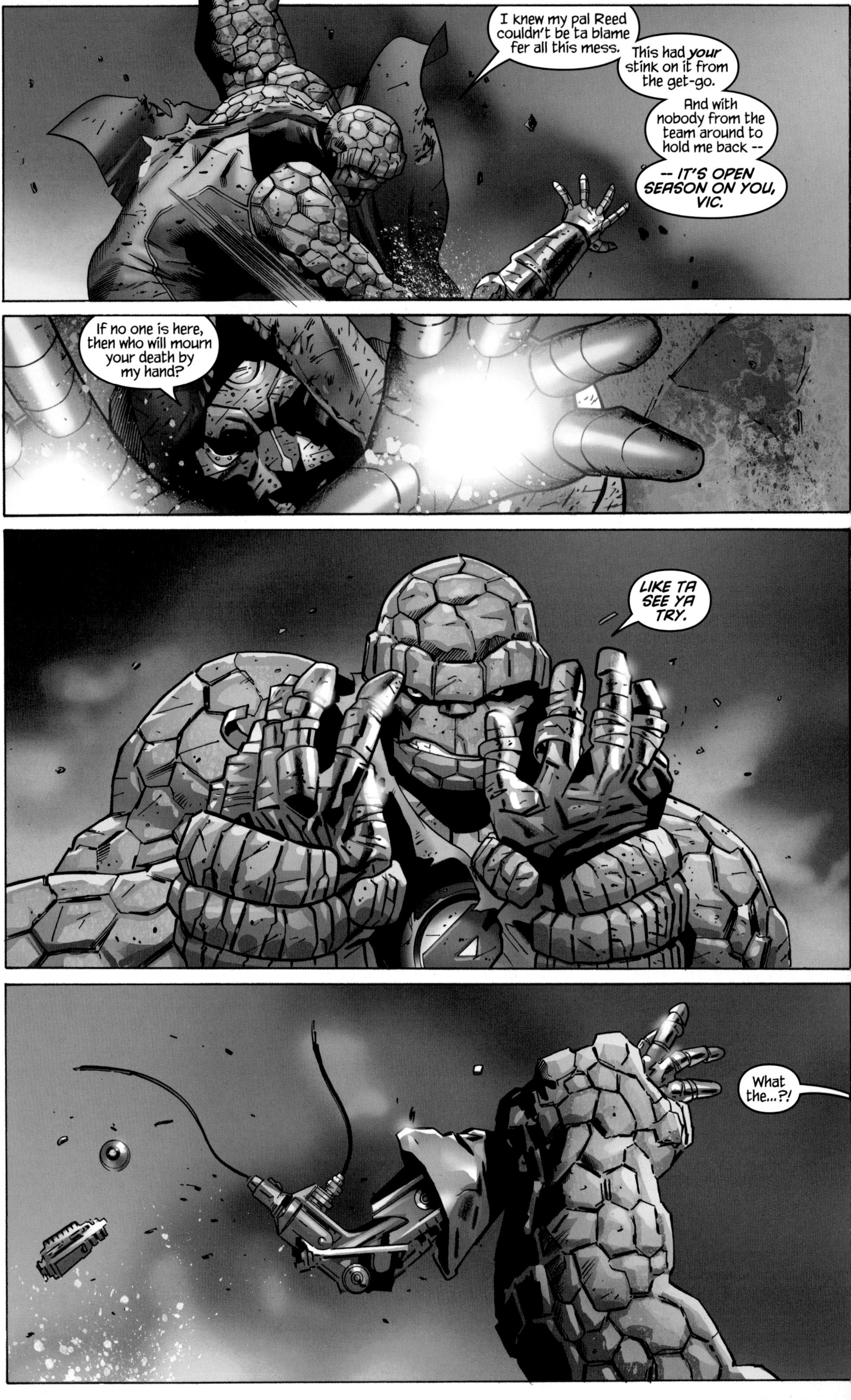
I knew my pal Reed couldn't be ta blame fer all this mess.
This had your stink on it from the get-go.
And with nobody from the team around to hold me back --
-- IT'S OPEN SEASON ON YOU, VIC.
If no one is here, then who will mourn your death by my hand?
LIKE TA SEE YA TRY.
What the...?!

I been fightin' --
-- A DANG-BLASTED ROBOT?!
I HATES ROBOTS!
WHAM WHAM WHAM
I WANT MY MONEY BACK!
I maybe ain't the smartest guy in the room --
-- But I got a feelin' Reed is gonna wanna have a look at this...
eew.

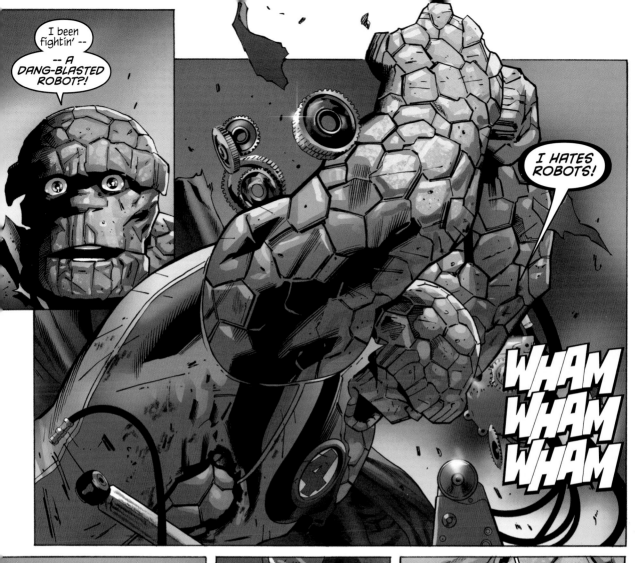

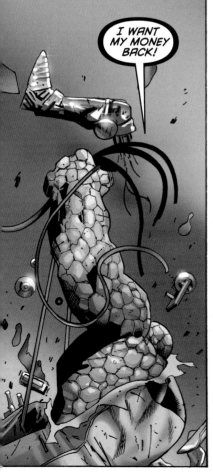

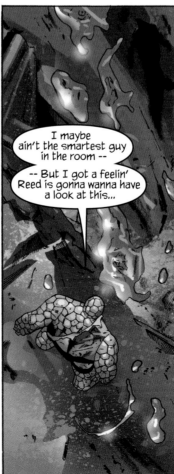

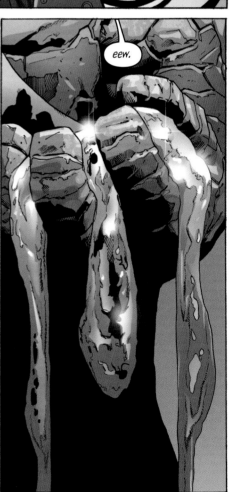

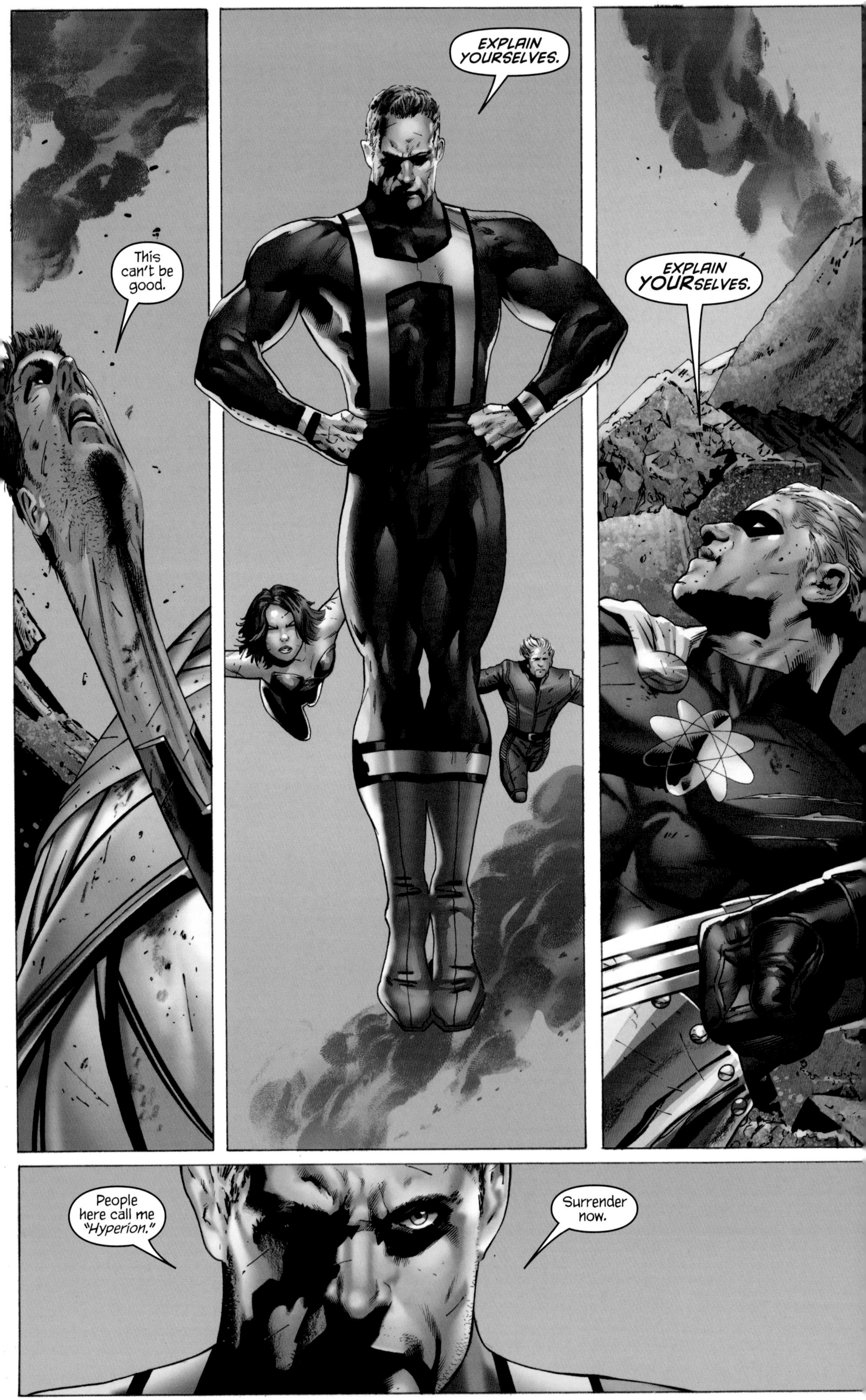
This can't be good.
EXPLAIN YOURSELVES.
EXPLAIN YOURSELVES.
People here call me "Hyperion."
Surrender now.

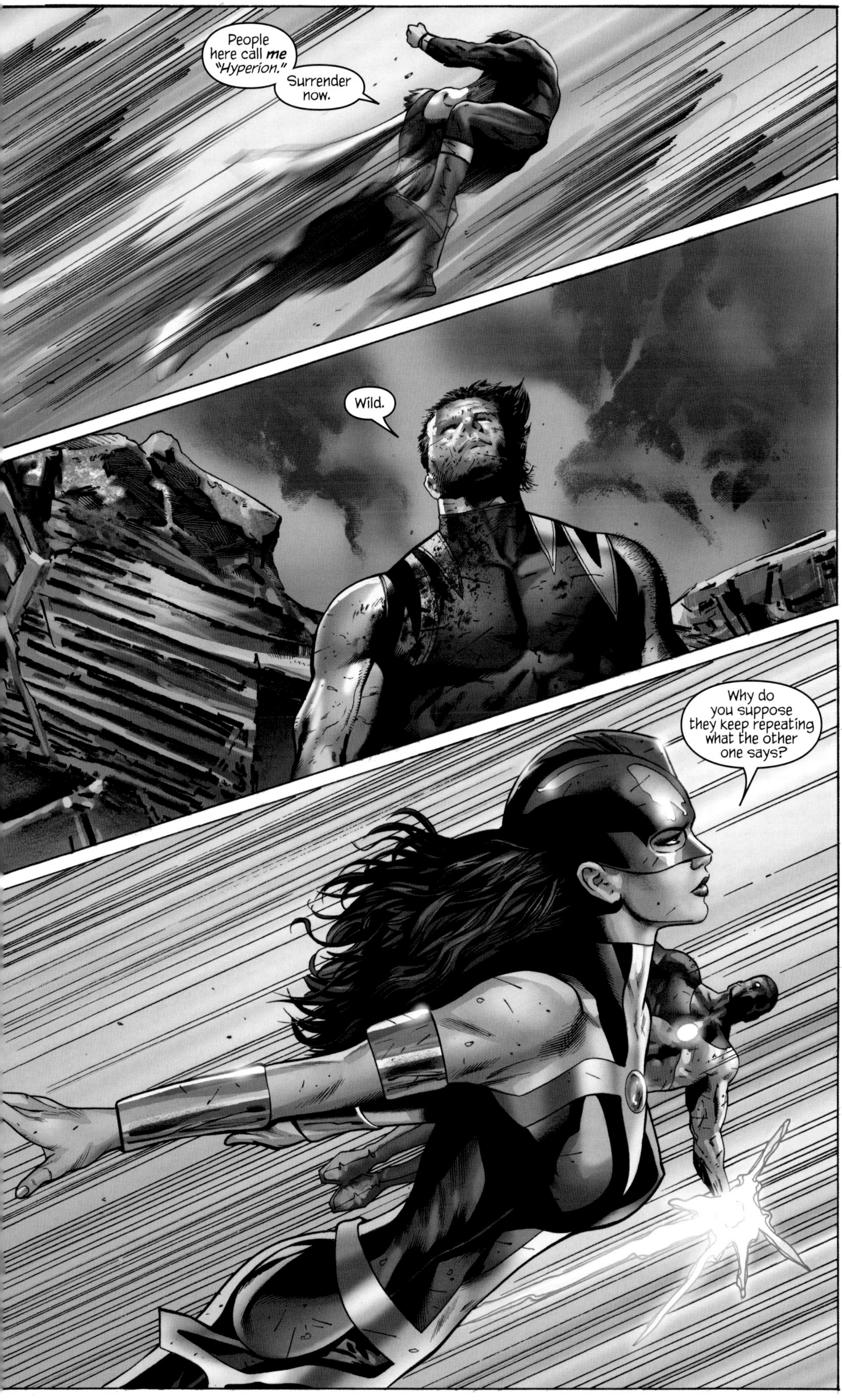
People here call ***me*** *"Hyperion."*
Surrender now.
Wild.
Why do you suppose they keep repeating what the other one says?

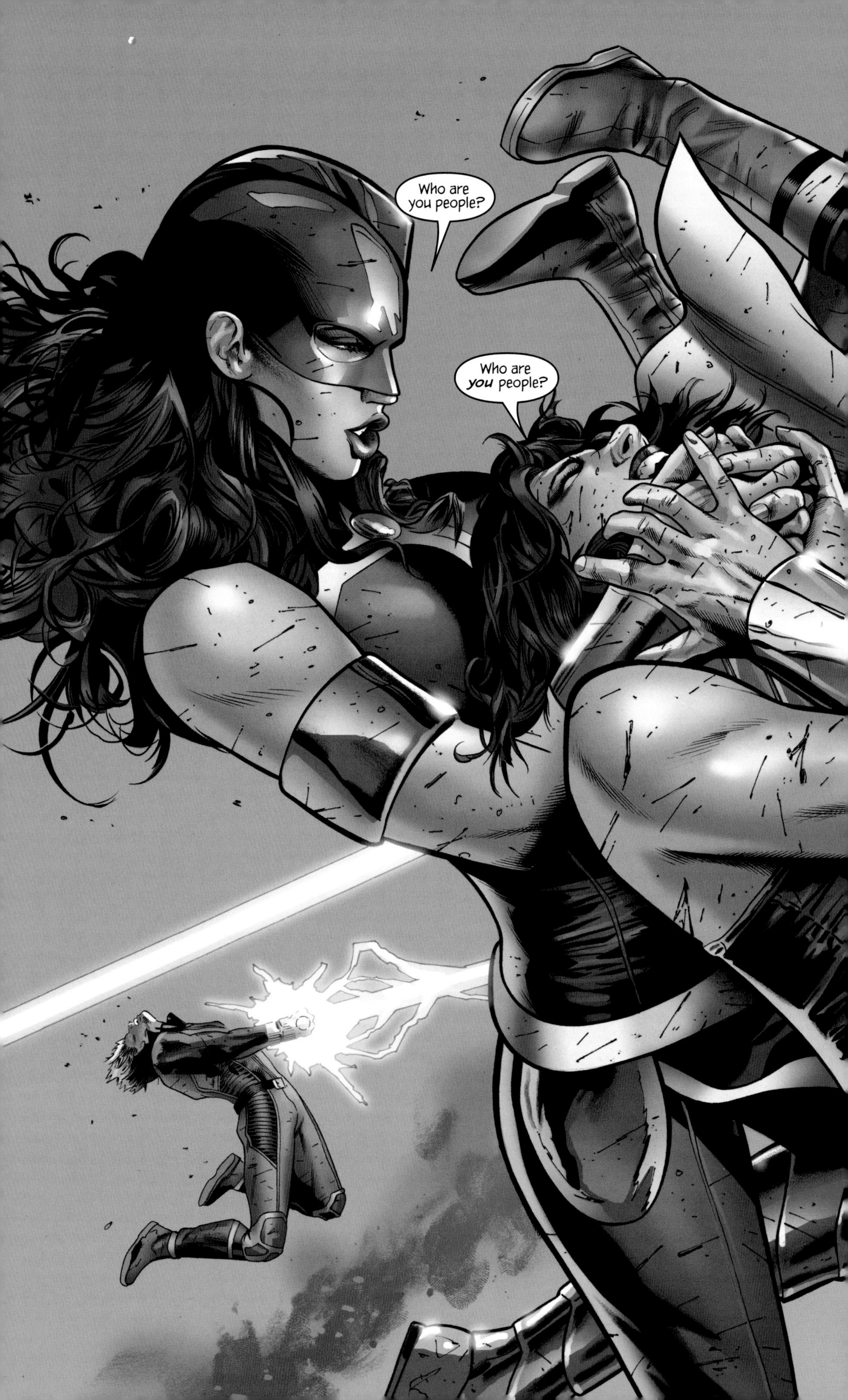
Who are you people?
Who are *you* people?

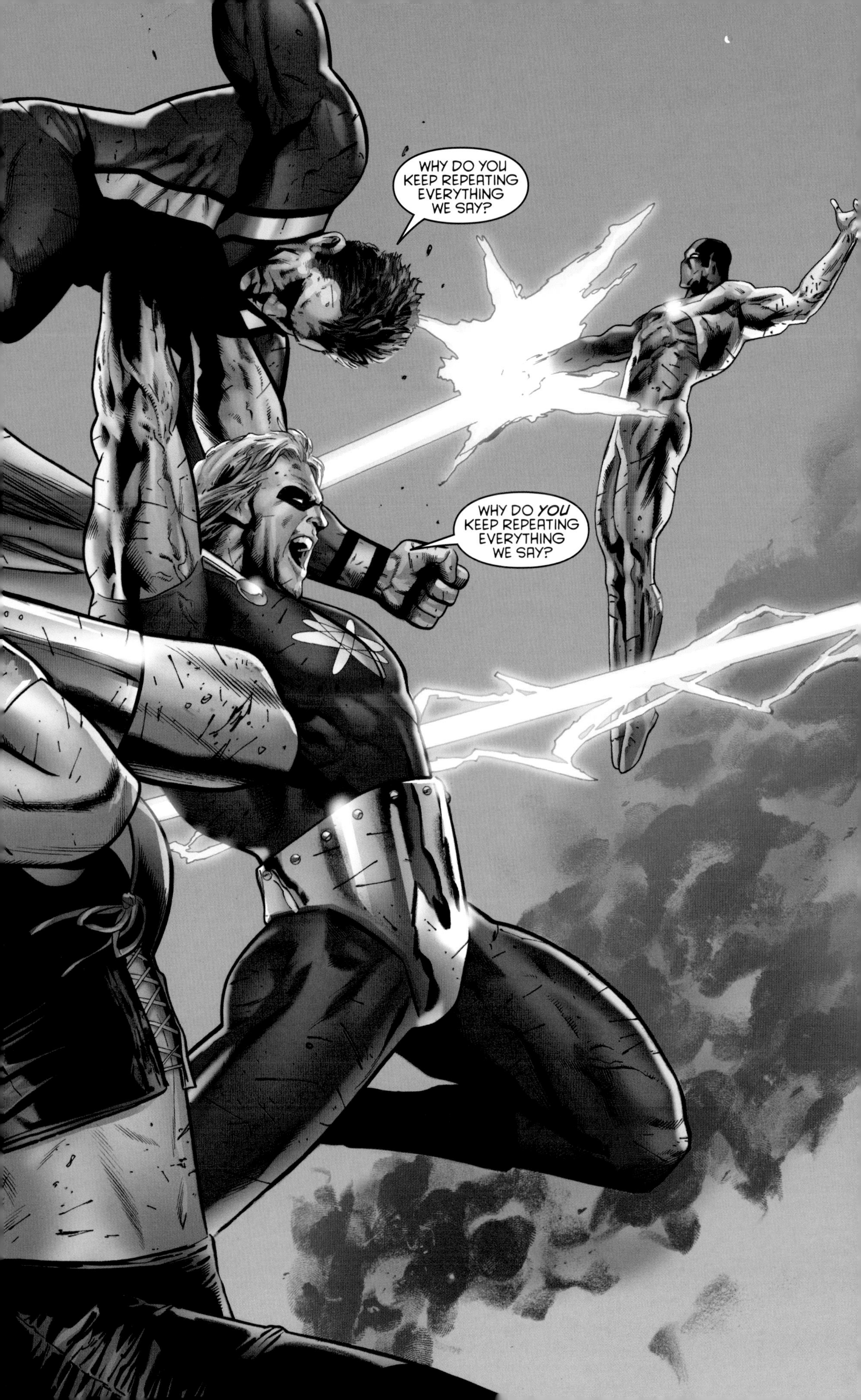
WHY DO YOU KEEP REPEATING EVERYTHING WE SAY?
WHY DO *YOU* KEEP REPEATING EVERYTHING WE SAY?

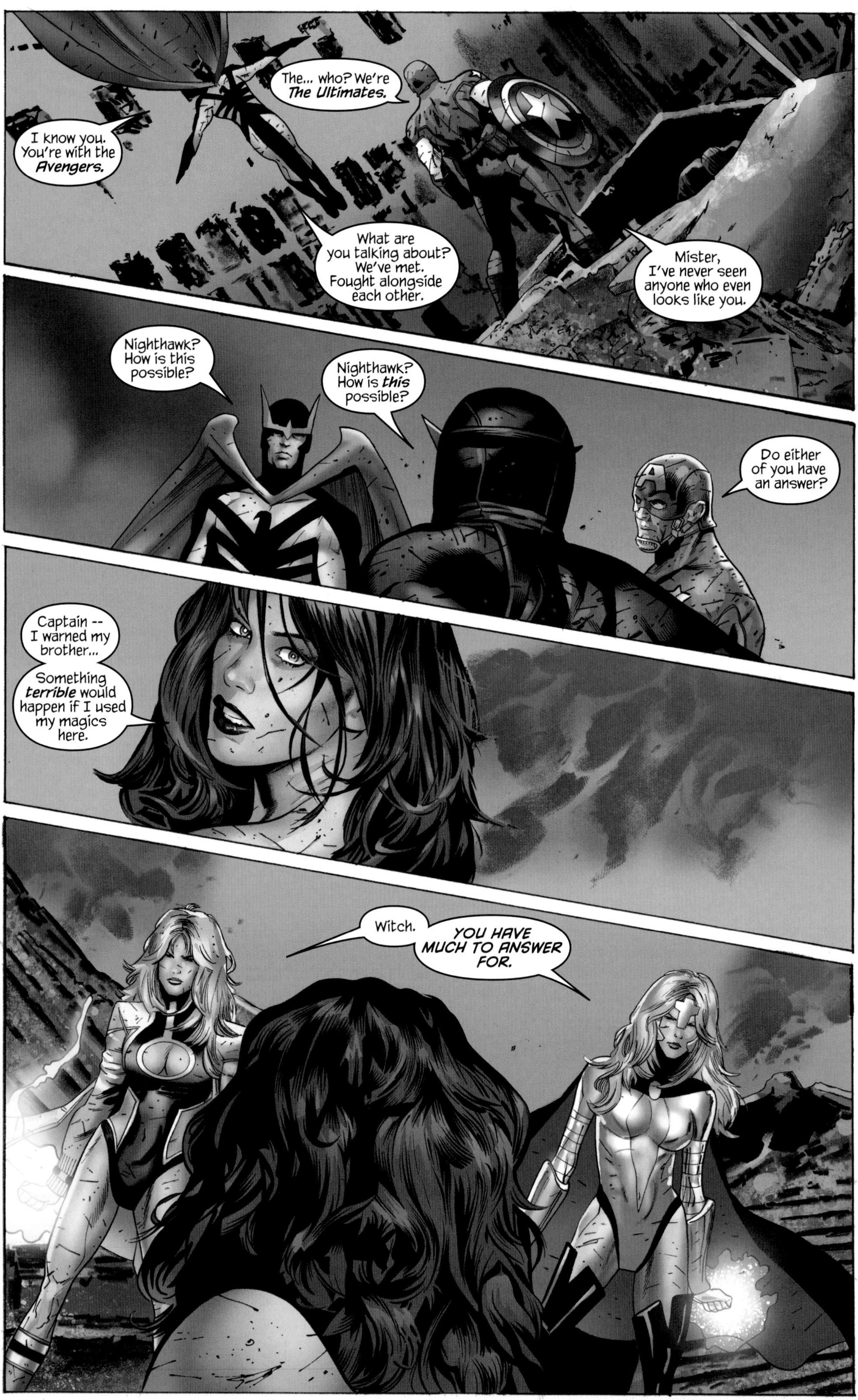
I know you. You're with the *Avengers.*
The... who? We're *The Ultimates.*
What are you talking about? We've met. Fought alongside each other.
Mister, I've never seen anyone who even looks like you.
Nighthawk? How is this possible?
Nighthawk? How is *this* possible?
Do either of you have an answer?
Captain -- I warned my brother...
Something *terrible* would happen if I used my magics here.
Witch.
YOU HAVE MUCH TO ANSWER FOR.

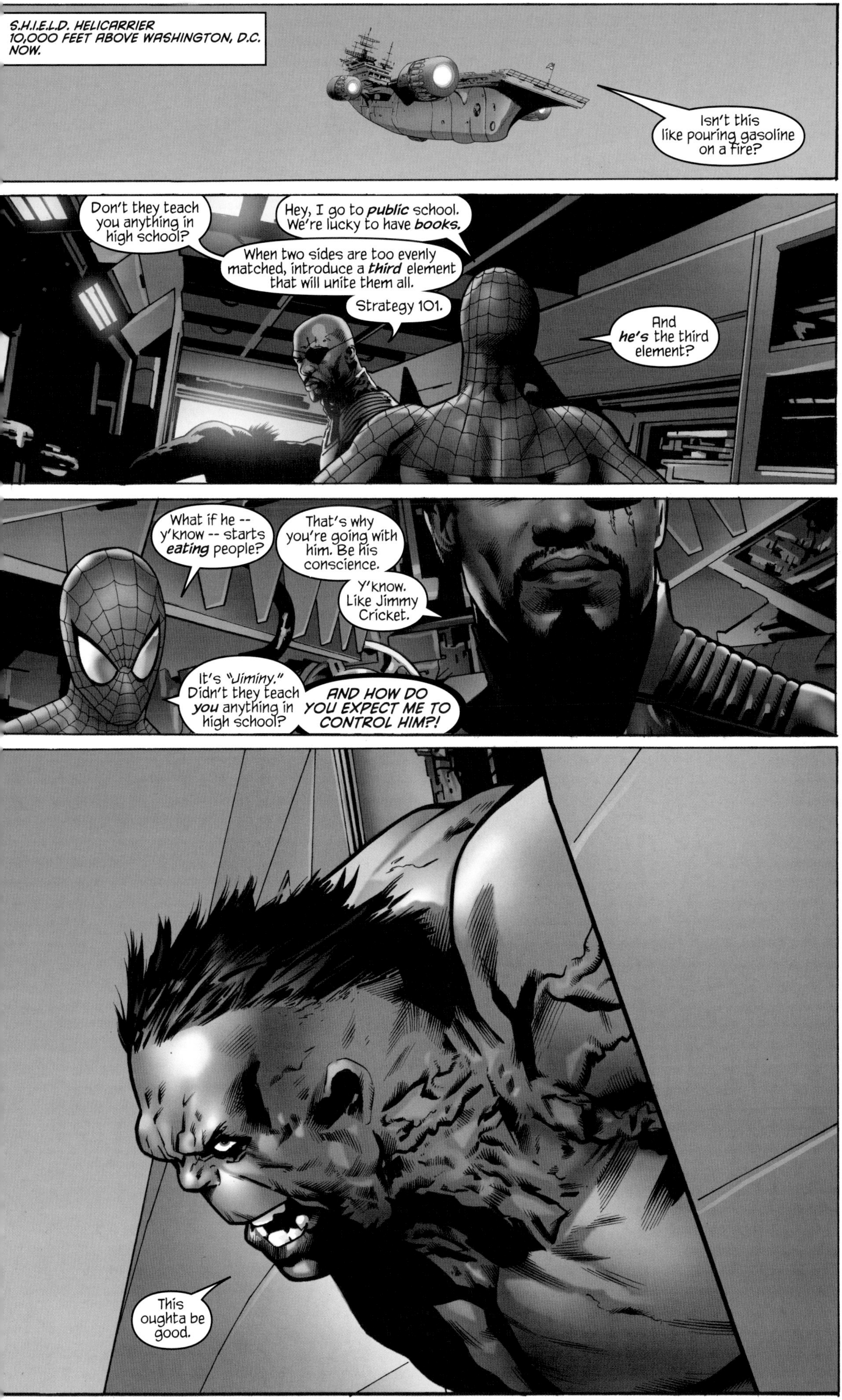

S.H.I.E.L.D. HELICARRIER 10,000 FEET ABOVE WASHINGTON, D.C. NOW.
Isn't this like pouring gasoline on a fire?
Don't they teach you anything in high school?
Hey, I go to *public* school. We're lucky to have *books.*
When two sides are too evenly matched, introduce a *third* element that will unite them all.
Strategy 101.
And *he's* the third element?
What if he -- y'know -- starts *eating* people?
That's why you're going with him. Be his conscience.
Y'know. Like Jimmy Cricket.
It's "Jiminy." Didn't they teach *you* anything in high school?
AND HOW DO YOU EXPECT ME TO CONTROL HIM?!
This oughta be good.

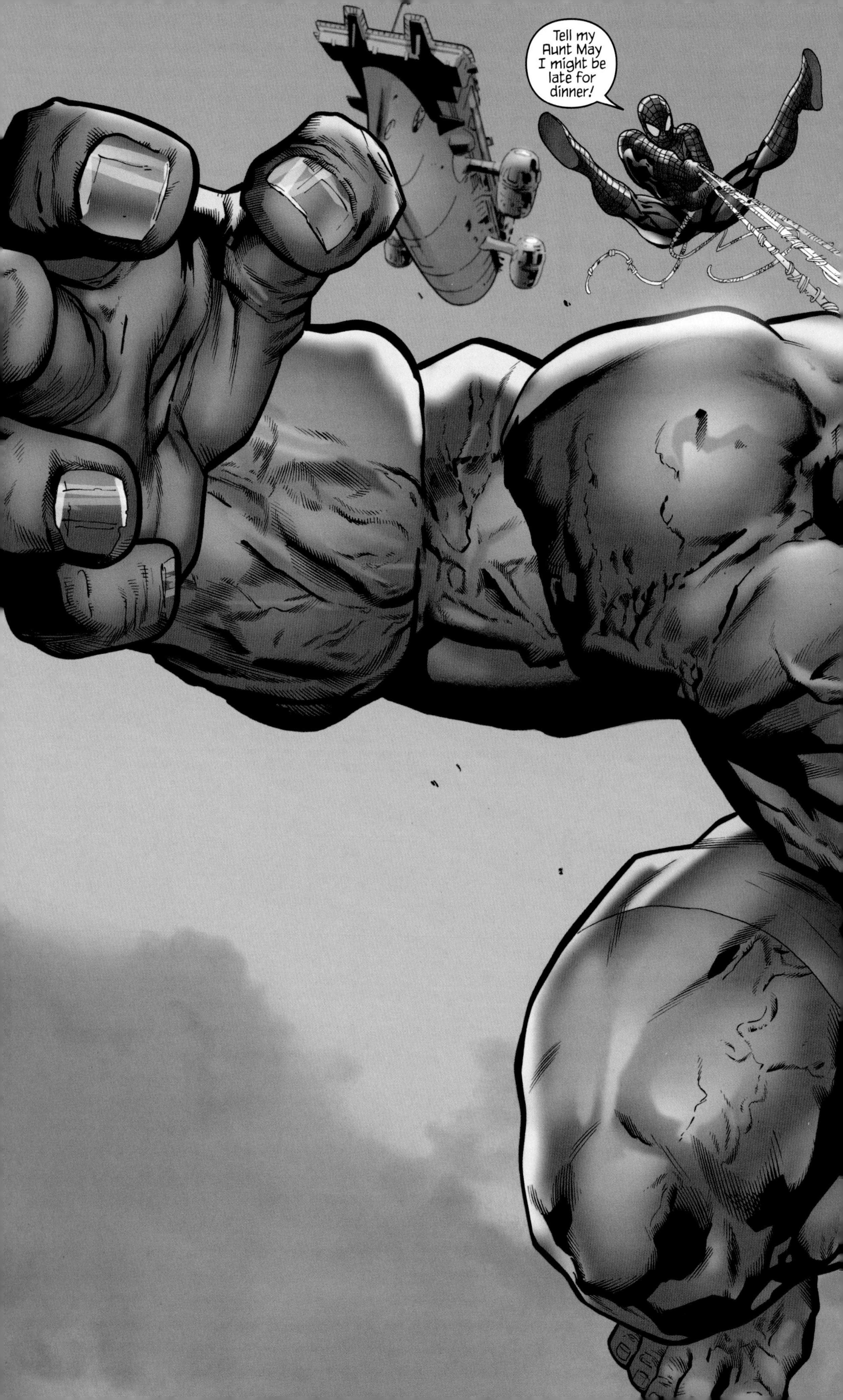
Tell my Aunt May I might be late for dinner!

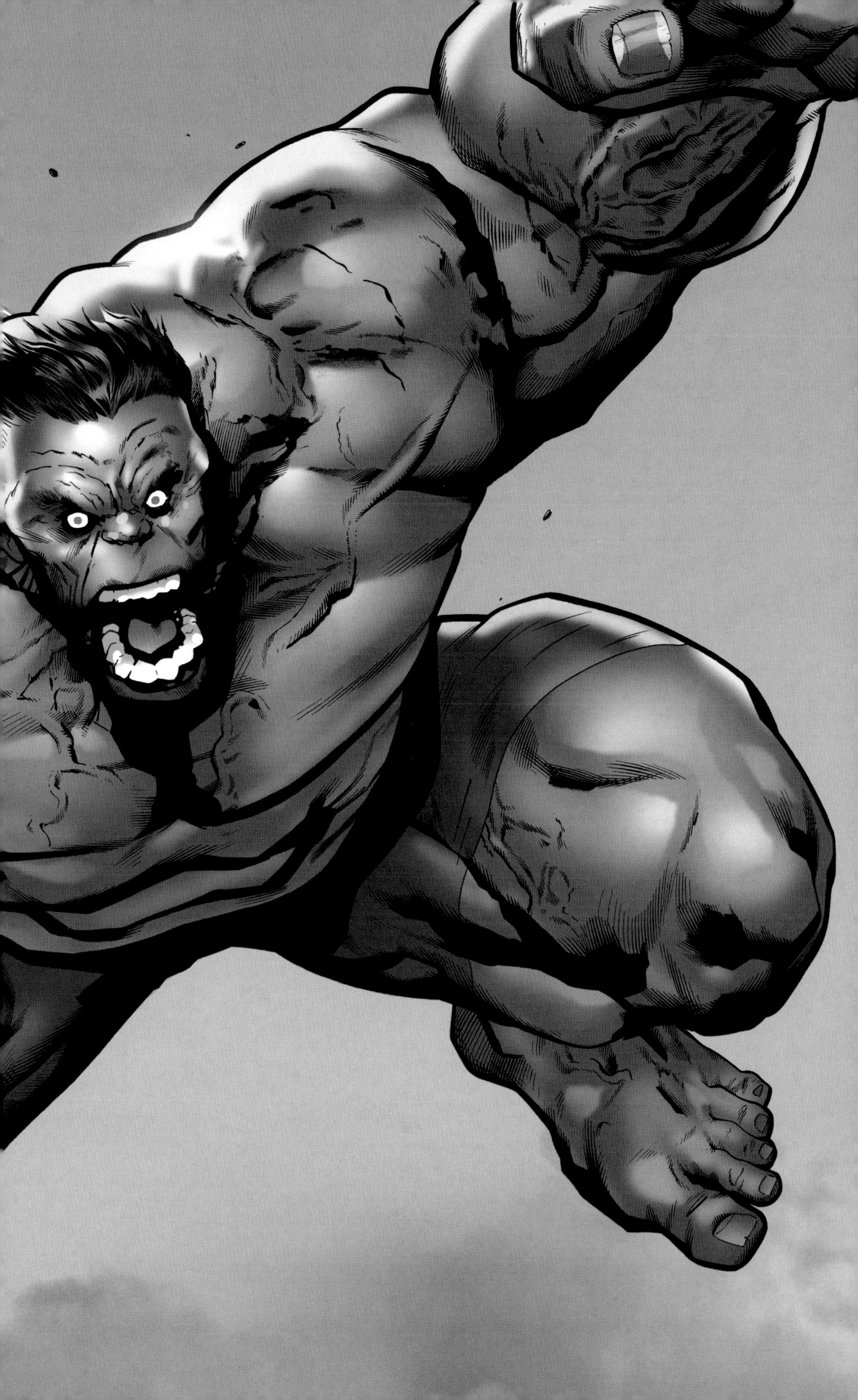

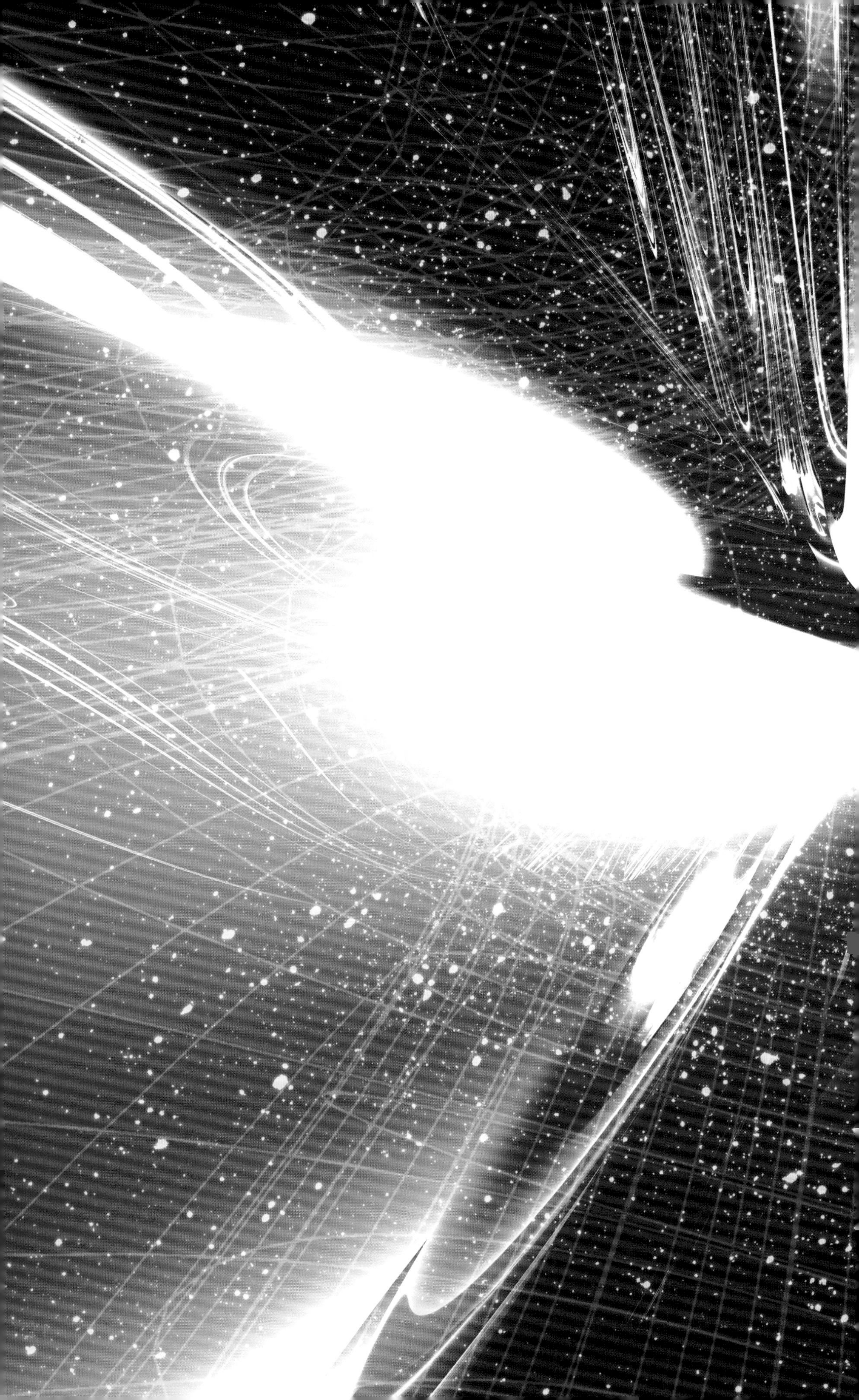

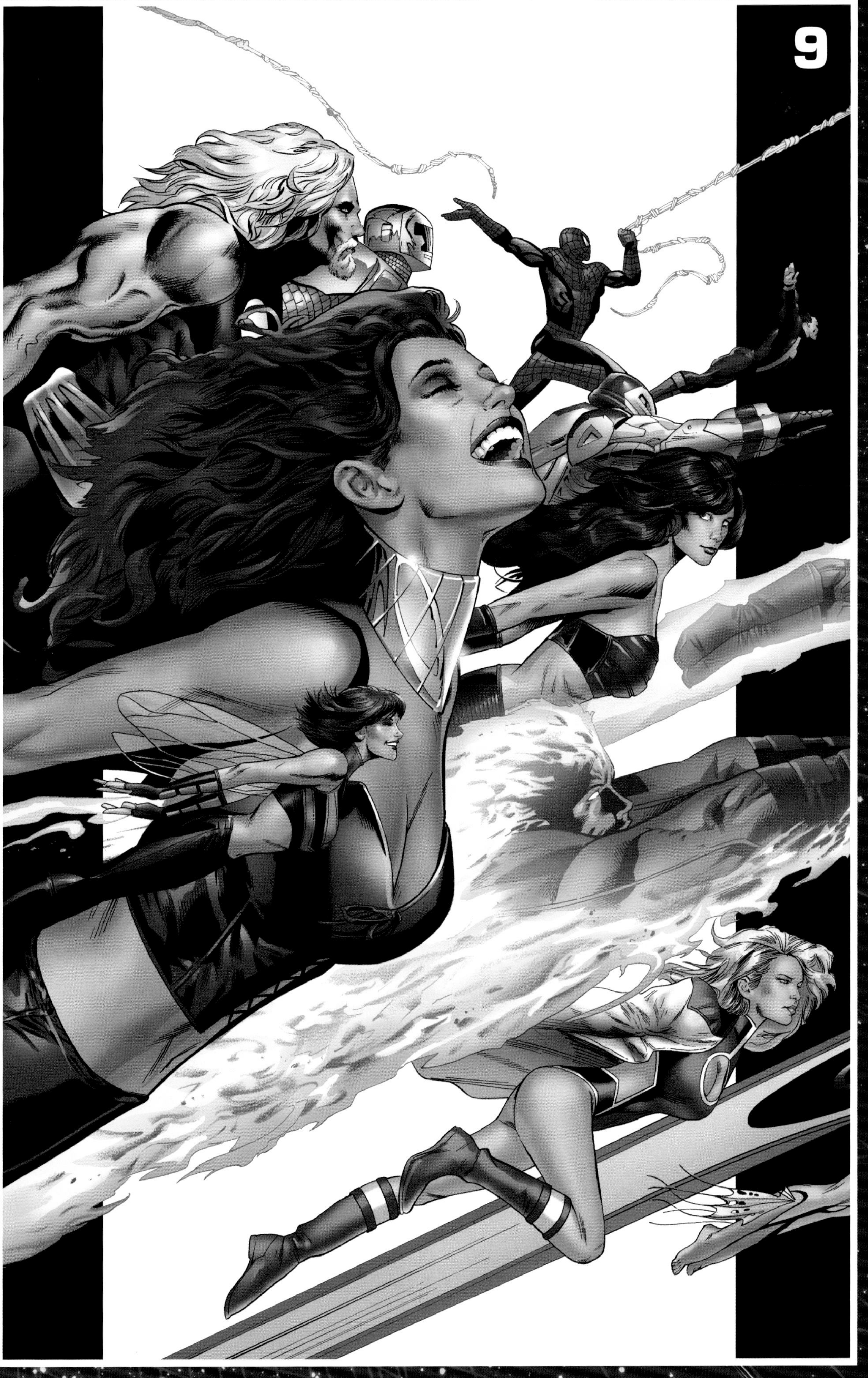

9

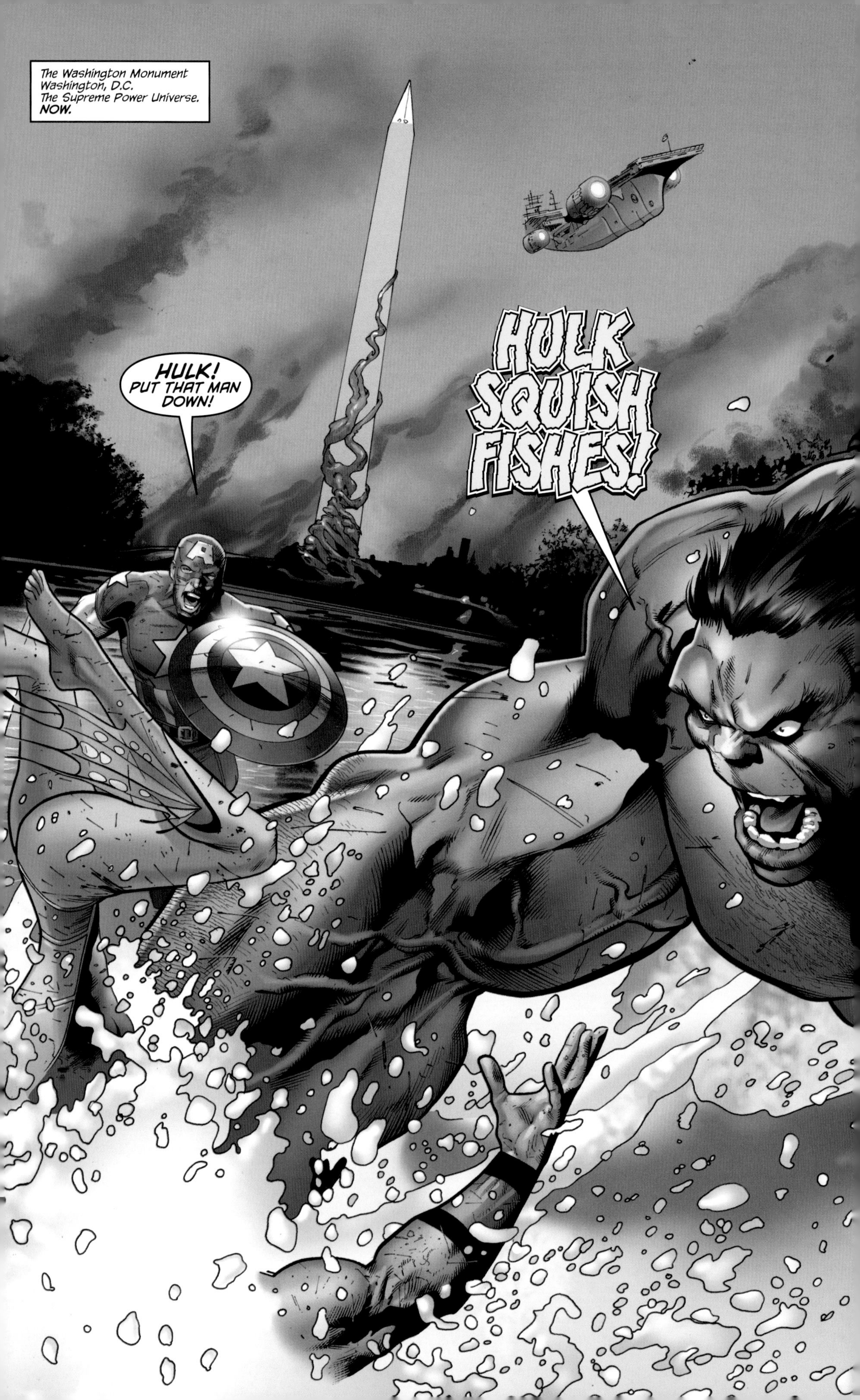
The Washington Monument
Washington, D.C.
The Supreme Power Universe.
NOW.
HULK! PUT THAT MAN DOWN!
HULK SQUISH FISHES!

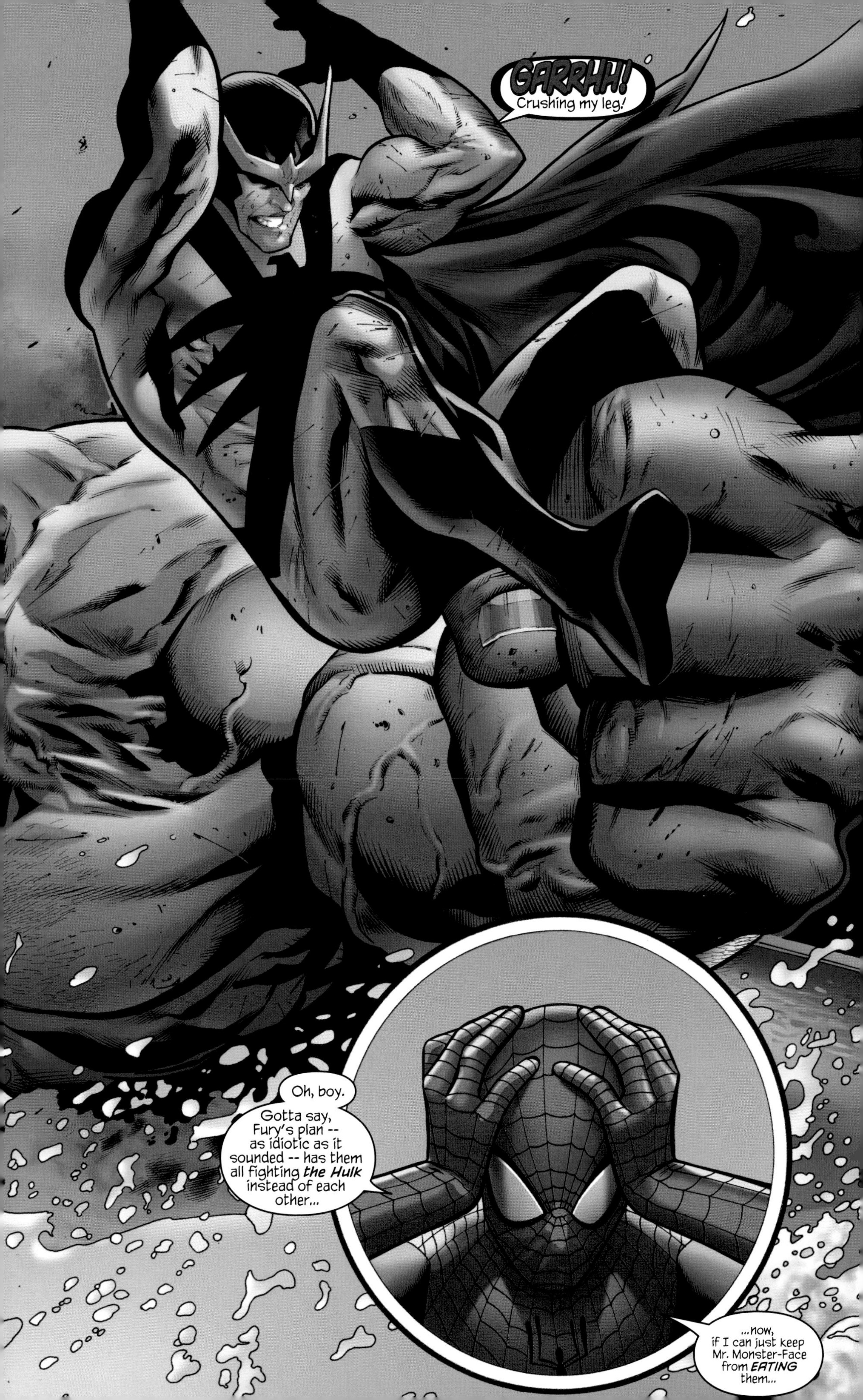
GARRHH!
Crushing my leg!
Oh, boy.
Gotta say, Fury's plan -- as idiotic as it sounded -- has them all fighting *the Hulk* instead of each other...
...now, if I can just keep Mr. Monster-Face from *EATING* them...

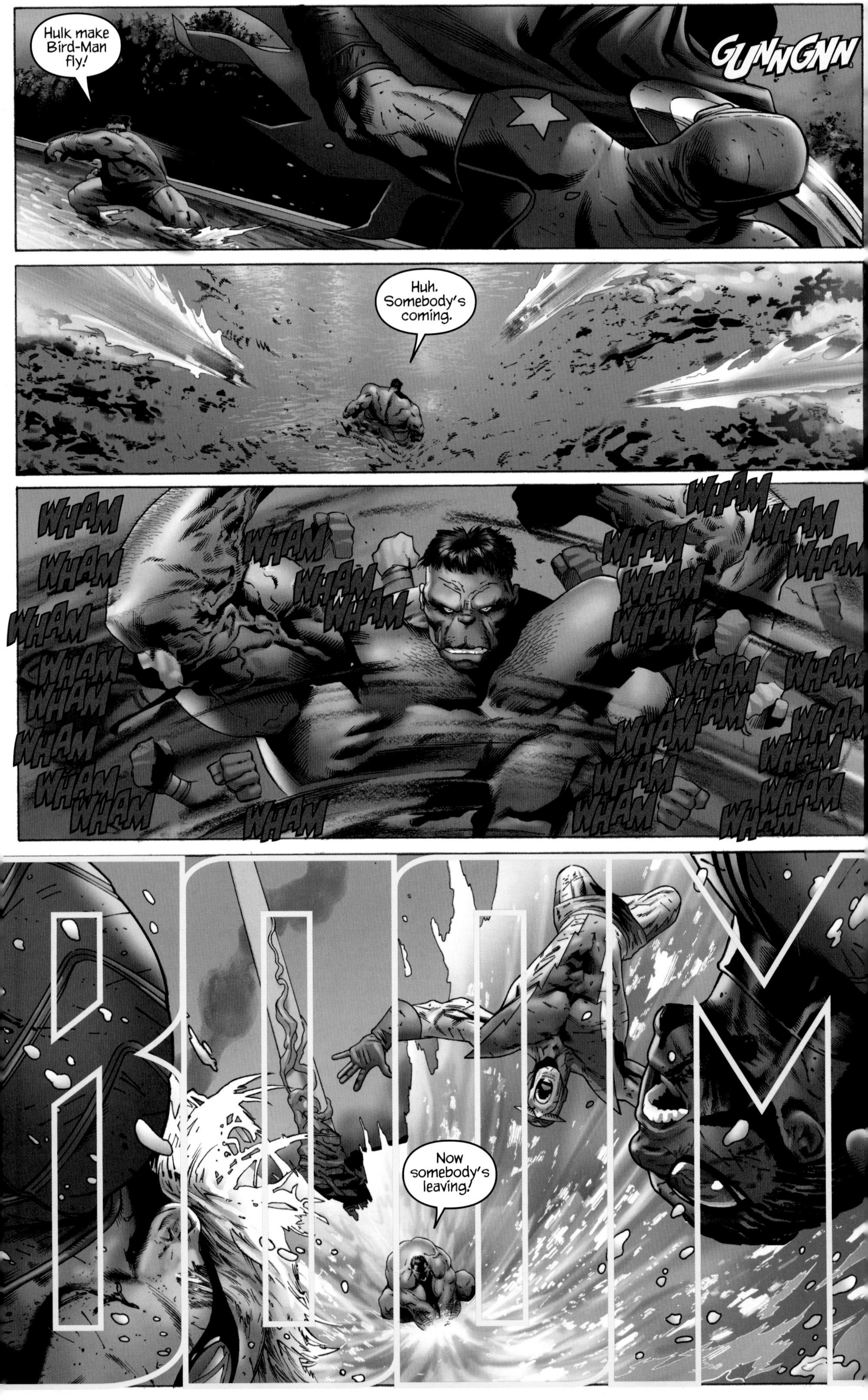
Hulk make Bird-Man fly!
GUNNGNN
Huh. Somebody's coming.
WHAM WHAM WHAM WHAM WHAM WHAM WHAM WHAM
WHAM WHAM WHAM WHAM
WHAM WHAM WHAM WHAM WHAM WHAM WHAM WHAM WHAM WHAM WHAM WHAM WHAM WHAM WHAM WHAM WHAM WHAM
BOOM
Now somebody's leaving!

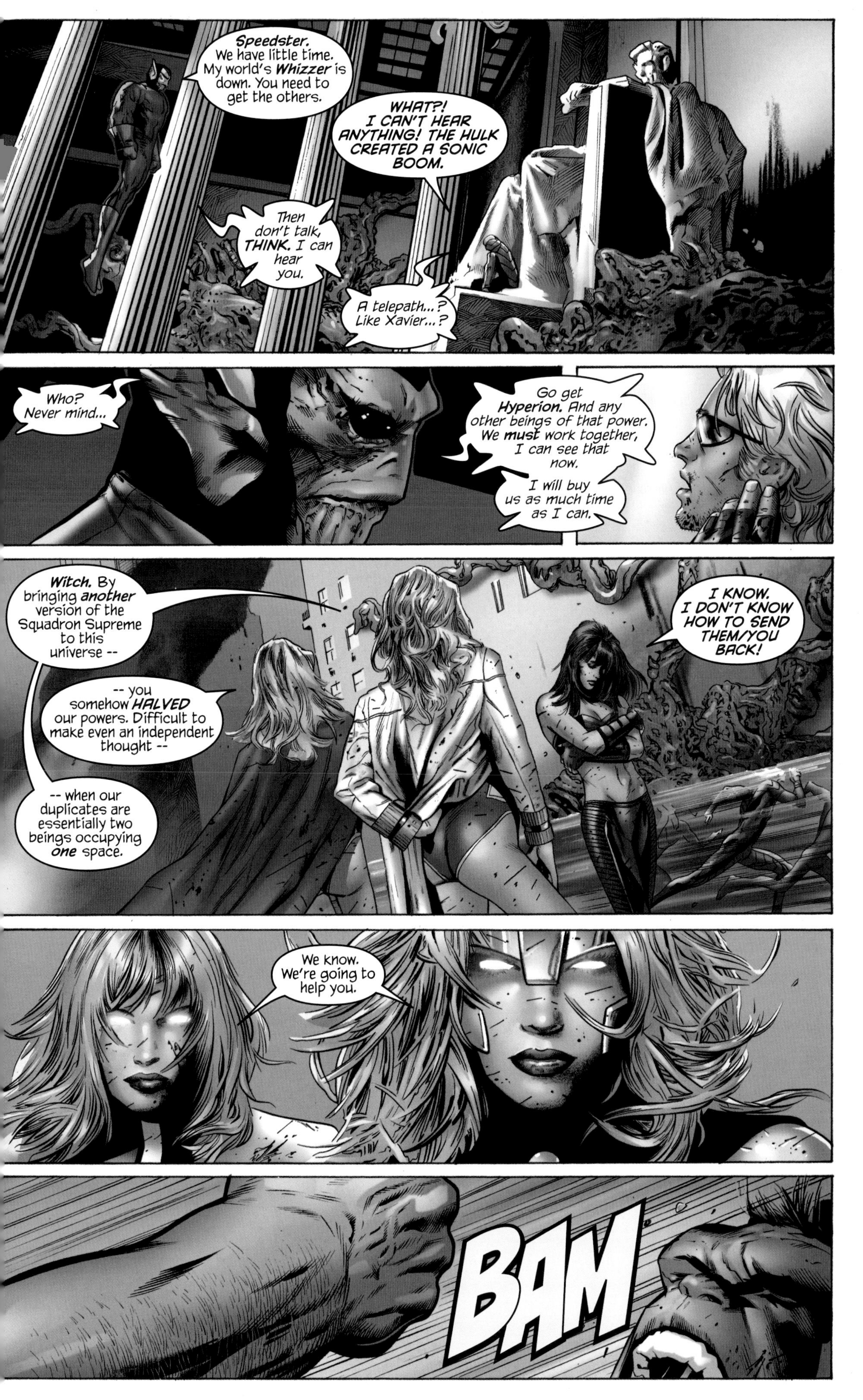

Speedster. We have little time. My world's Whizzer is down. You need to get the others.
WHAT?! I CAN'T HEAR ANYTHING! THE HULK CREATED A SONIC BOOM.
Then don't talk, THINK. I can hear you.
A telepath...? Like Xavier...?
Who? Never mind...
Go get Hyperion. And any other beings of that power. We must work together, I can see that now.
I will buy us as much time as I can.
Witch. By bringing another version of the Squadron Supreme to this universe --
-- you somehow HALVED our powers. Difficult to make even an independent thought --
-- when our duplicates are essentially two beings occupying one space.
I KNOW. I DON'T KNOW HOW TO SEND THEM/YOU BACK!
We know. We're going to help you.
BAM

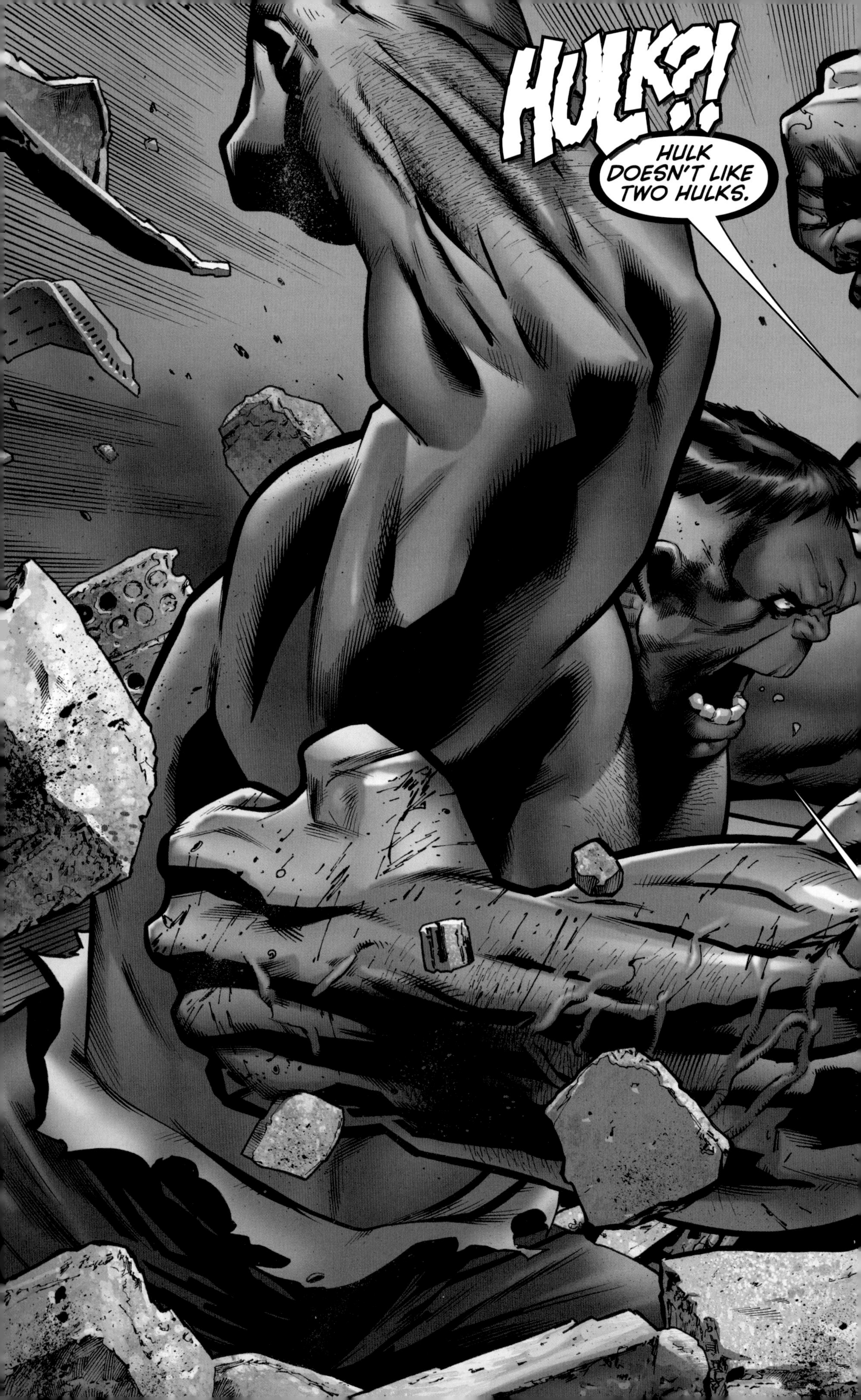
HULK?!
HULK DOESN'T LIKE TWO HULKS.

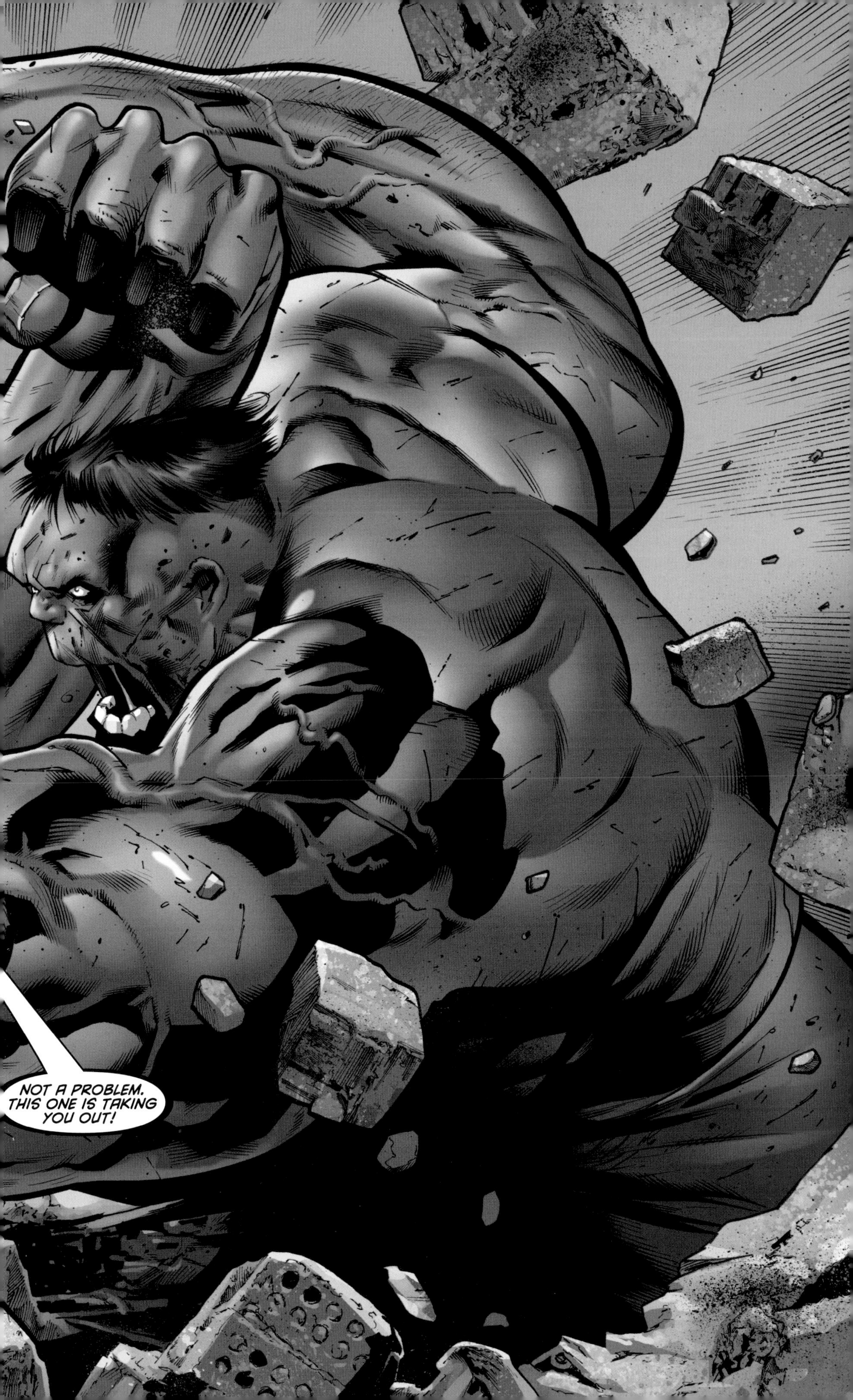
NOT A PROBLEM. THIS ONE IS TAKING YOU OUT!

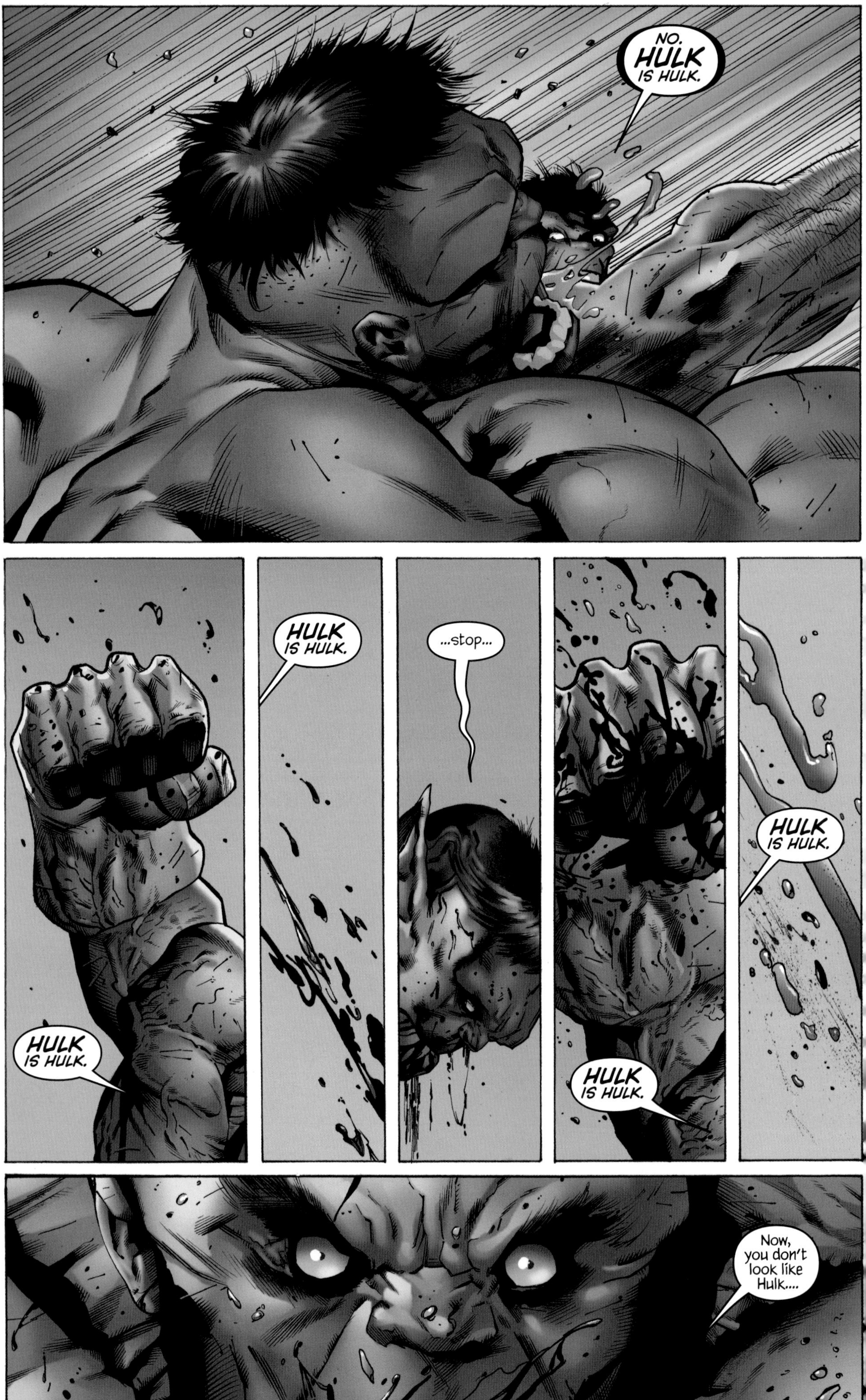
NO. HULK IS HULK.
HULK IS HULK.
HULK IS HULK.
...stop...
HULK IS HULK.
HULK IS HULK.
Now, you don't look like Hulk....

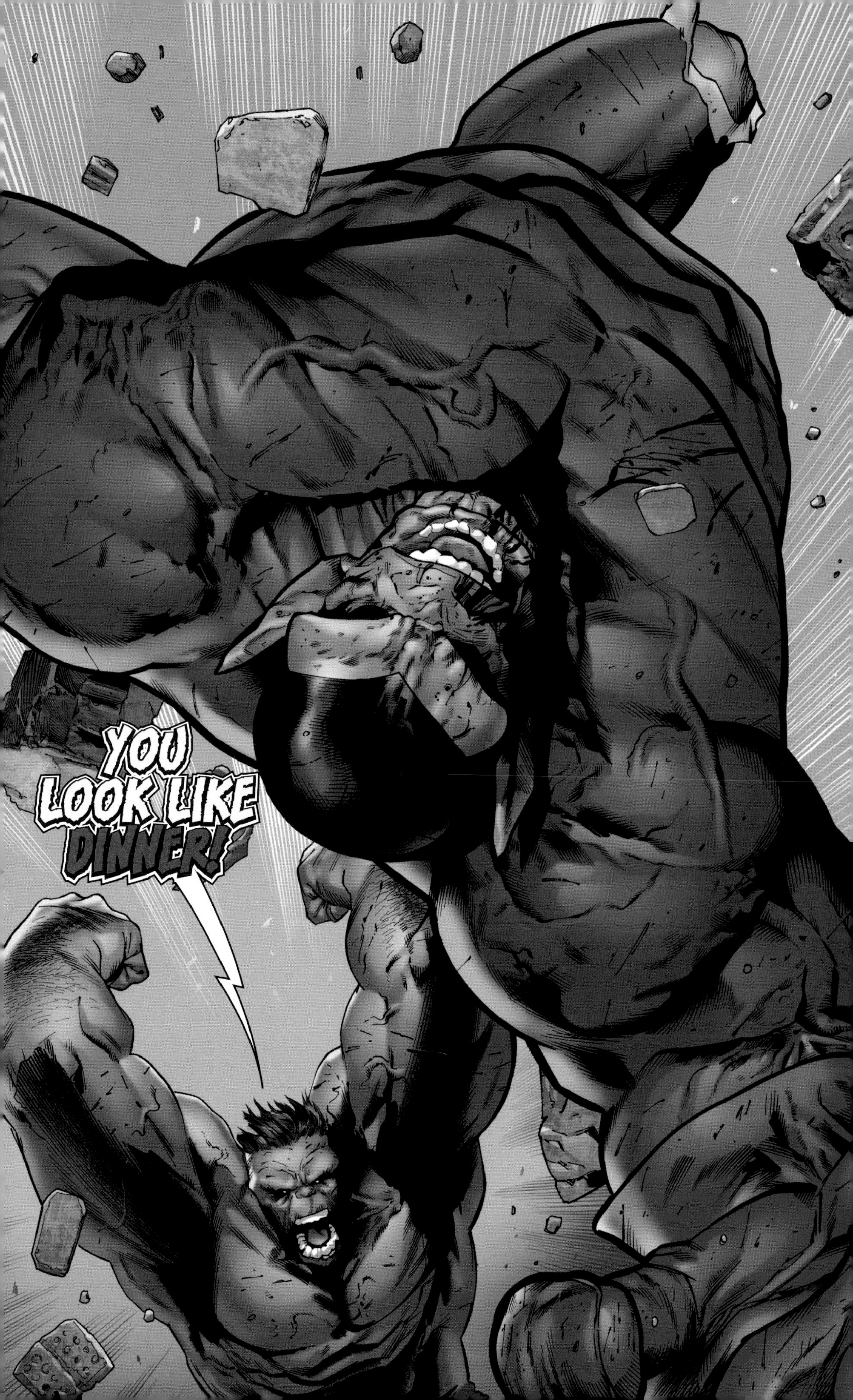
YOU LOOK LIKE DINNER!

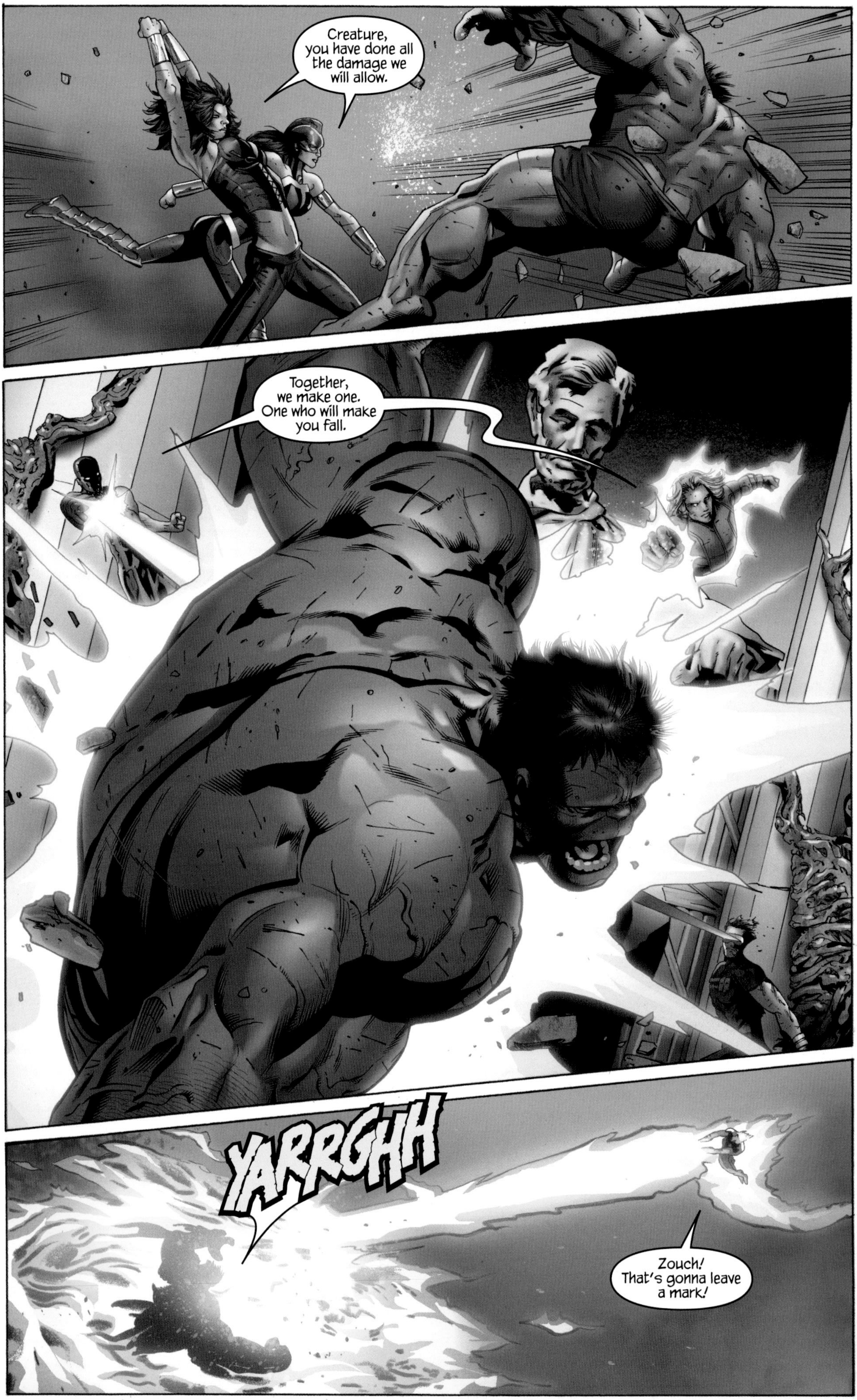
Creature, you have done all the damage we will allow.
Together, we make one. One who will make you fall.
YARRGHH
Zouch! That's gonna leave a mark!

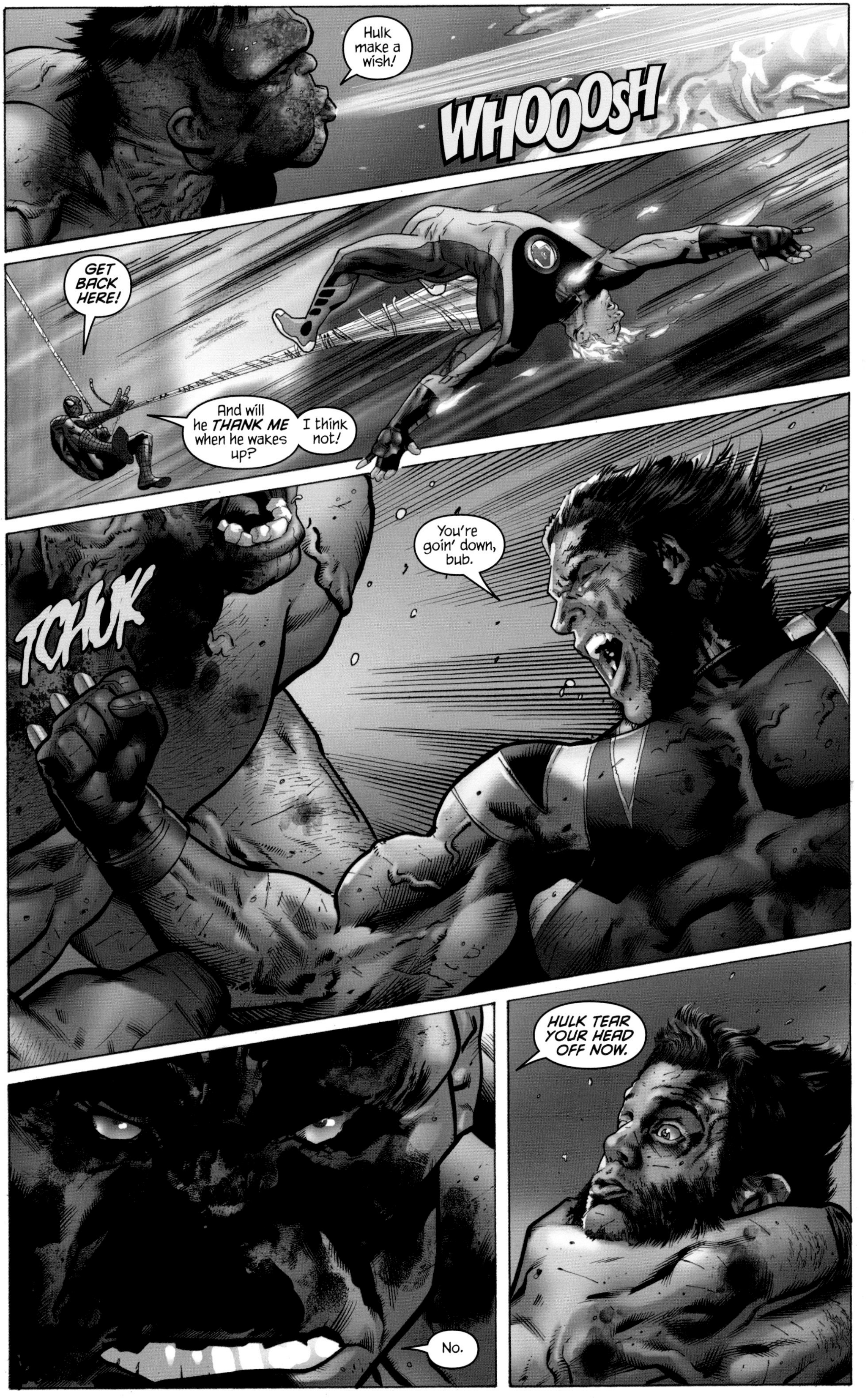

Hulk make a wish!
WHOOOSH
GET BACK HERE!
And will he THANK ME when he wakes up?
I think not!
TCHUK
You're goin' down, bub.
HULK TEAR YOUR HEAD OFF NOW.
No.

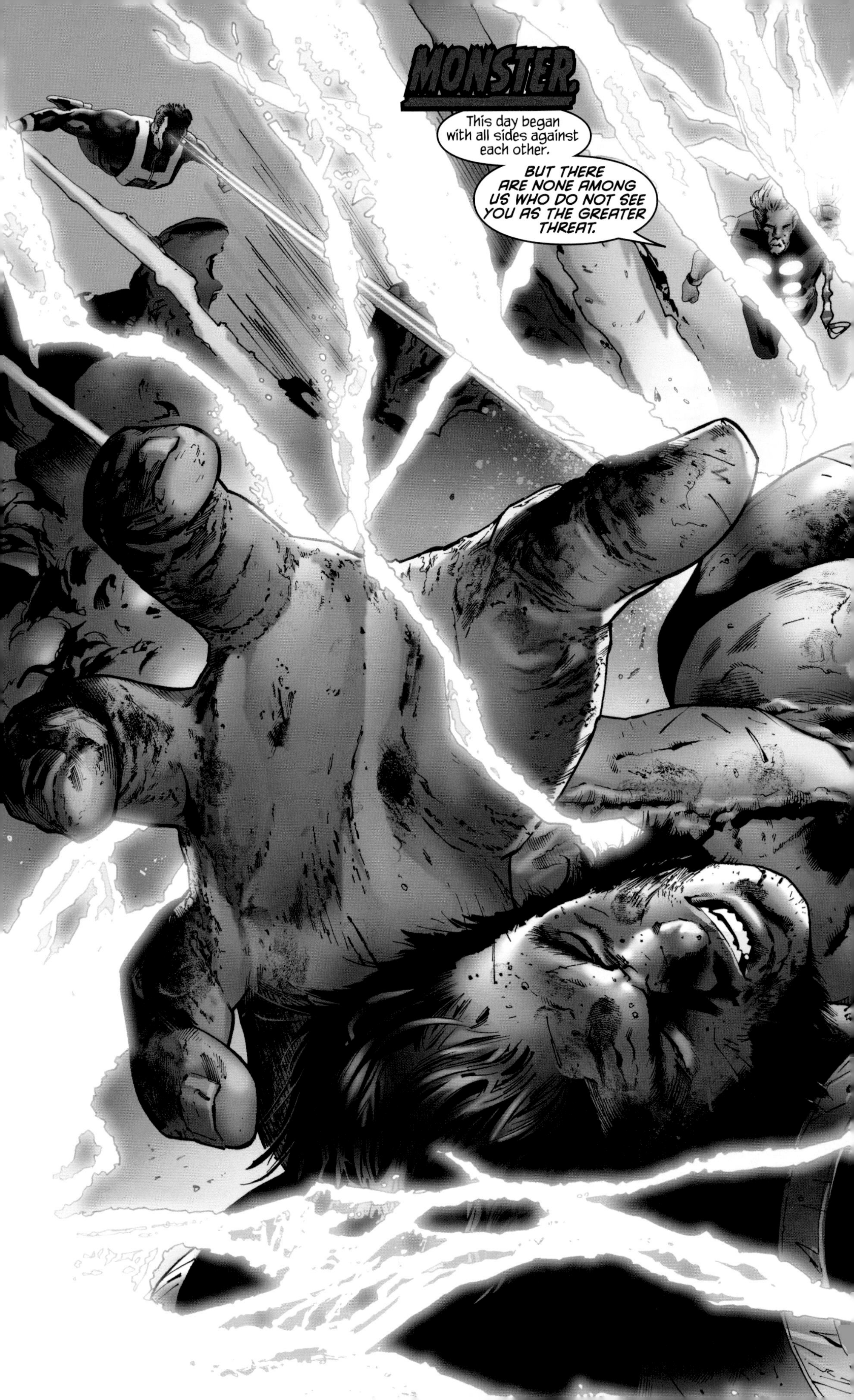
MONSTER.
This day began with all sides against each other.
BUT THERE ARE NONE AMONG US WHO DO NOT SEE YOU AS THE GREATER THREAT.

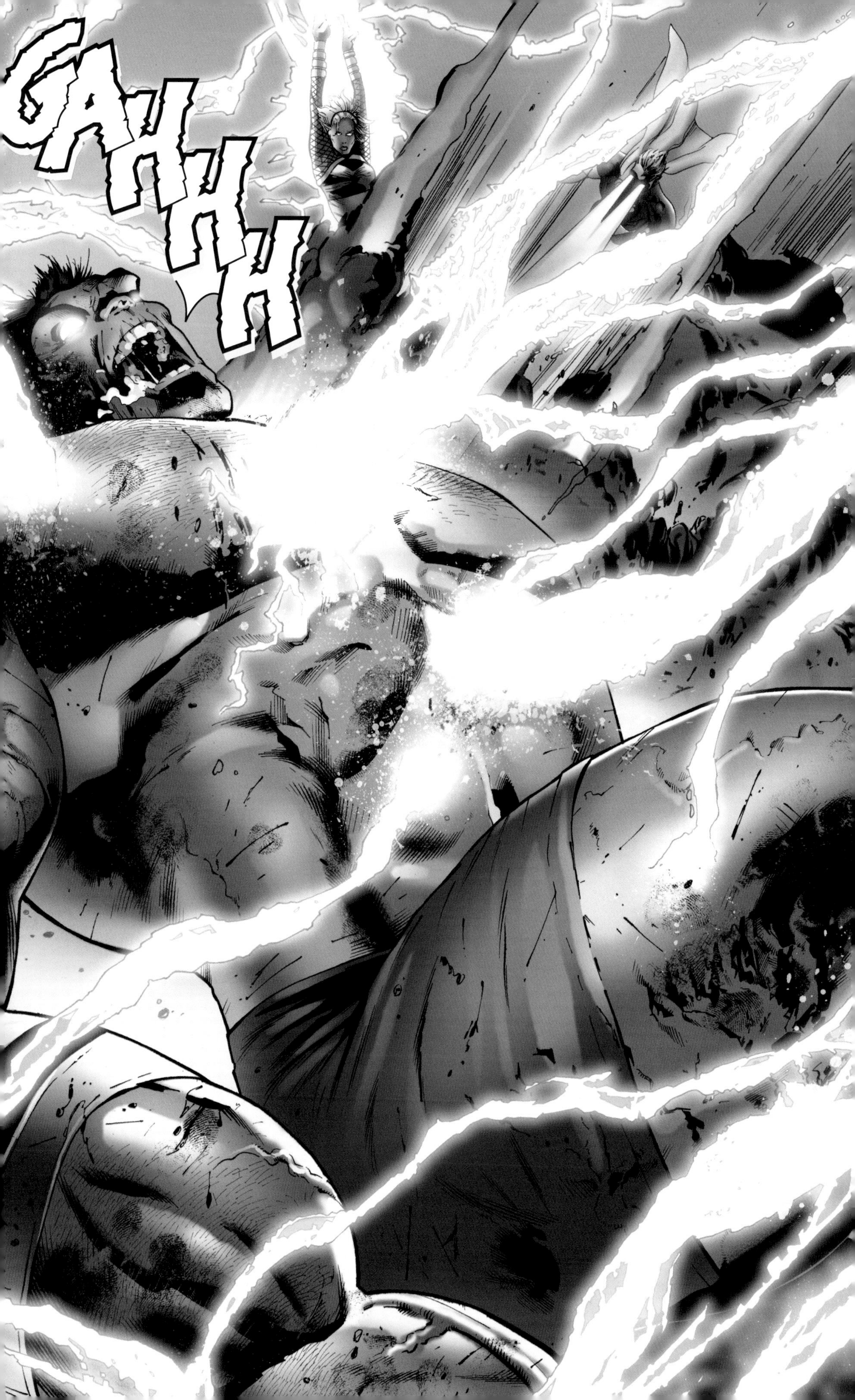
GAHHHH

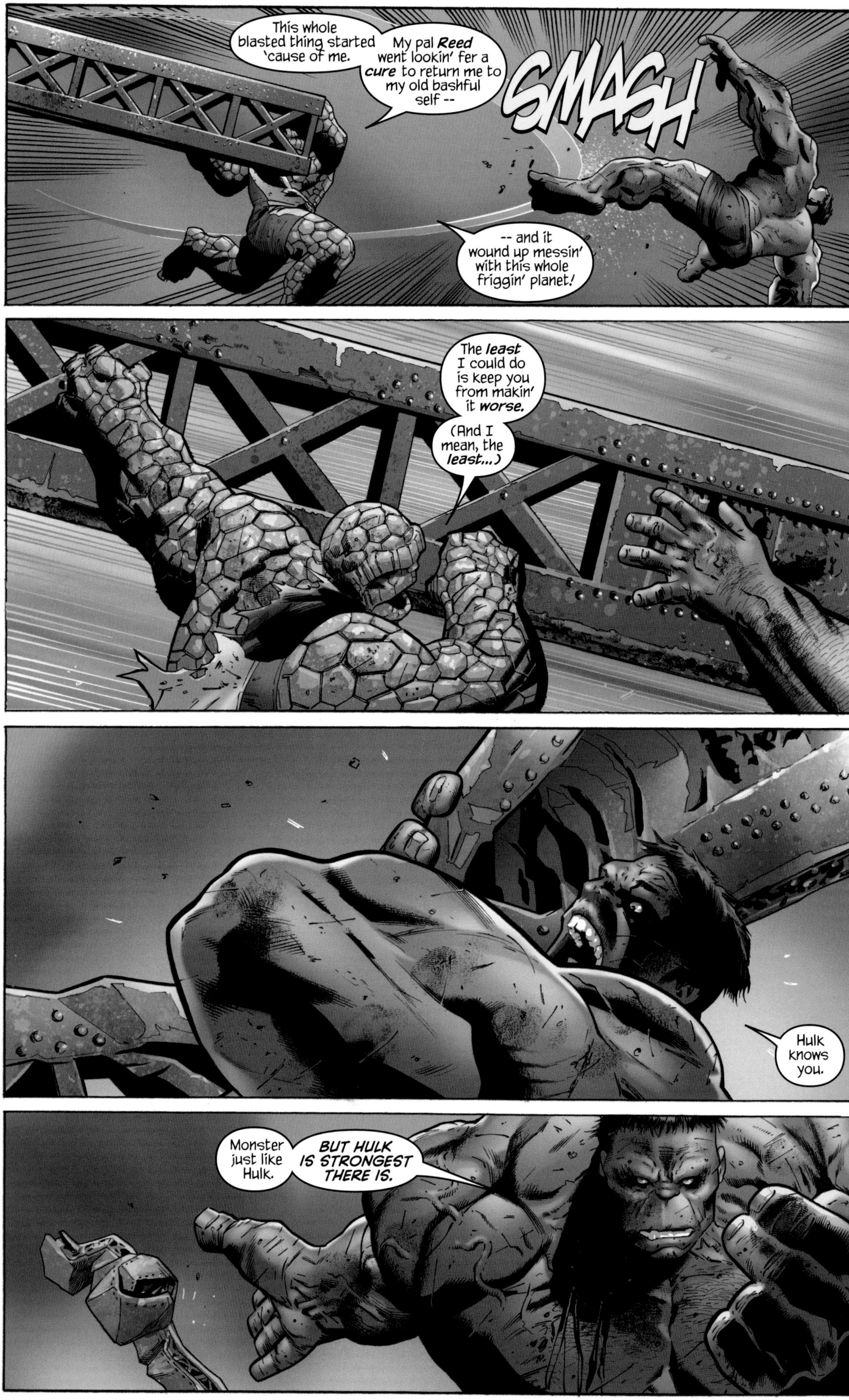
This whole blasted thing started 'cause of me.
My pal Reed went lookin' fer a cure to return me to my old bashful self --
SMASH
-- and it wound up messin' with this whole friggin' planet!
The least I could do is keep you from makin' it worse.
(And I mean, the least...)
Hulk knows you.
Monster just like Hulk.
BUT HULK IS STRONGEST THERE IS.

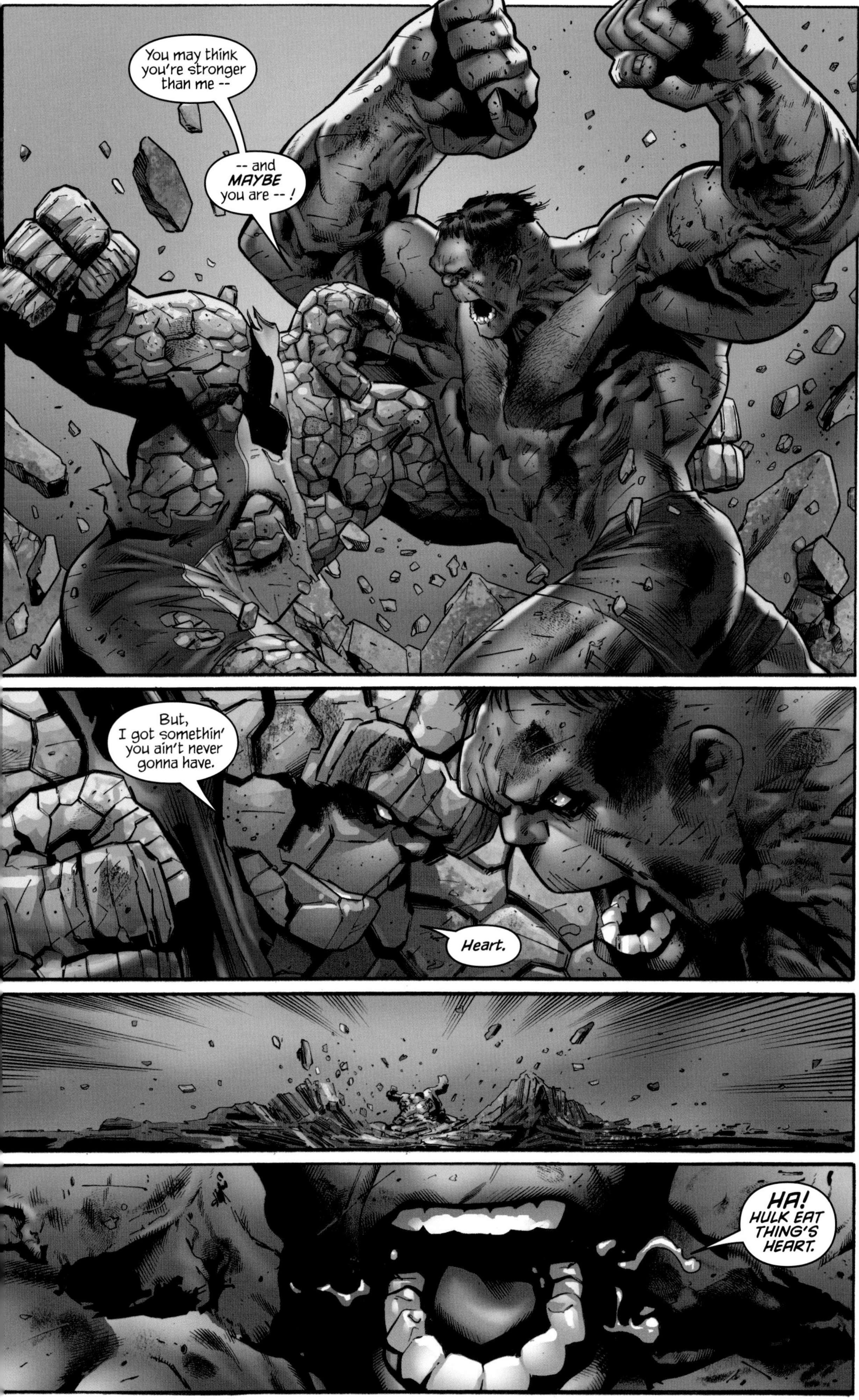
You may think you're stronger than me --
-- and MAYBE you are -- !
But, I got somethin' you ain't never gonna have.
Heart.
HA! HULK EAT THING'S HEART.

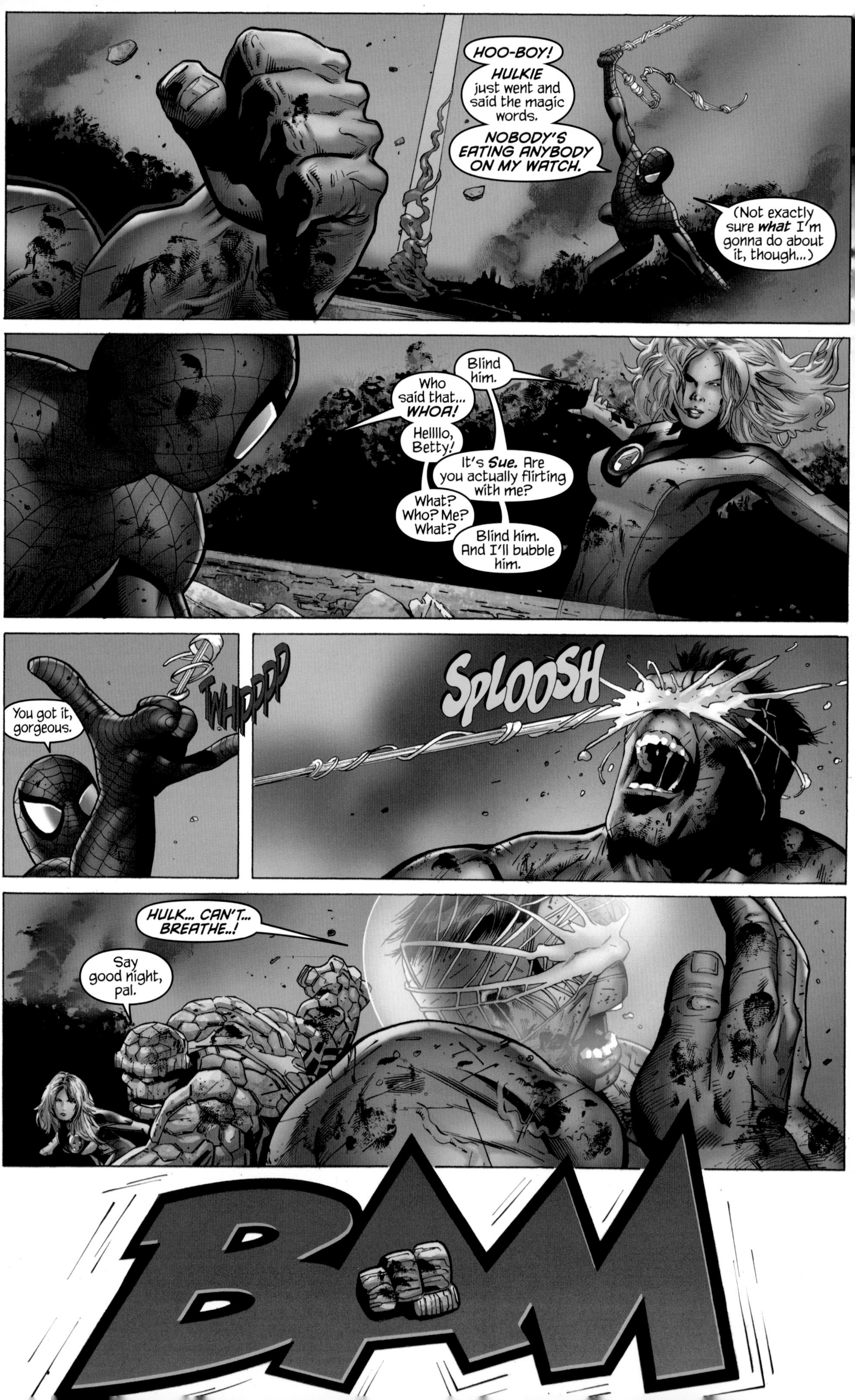
HOO-BOY!
HULKIE just went and said the magic words.
NOBODY'S EATING ANYBODY ON MY WATCH.
(Not exactly sure what I'm gonna do about it, though...)
Blind him.
Who said that... WHOA!
Hellllo, Betty!
It's Sue. Are you actually flirting with me?
What? Who? Me? What?
Blind him. And I'll bubble him.
You got it, gorgeous.
TWHPPP
SPLOOSH
HULK... CAN'T... BREATHE..!
Say good night, pal.
BAM

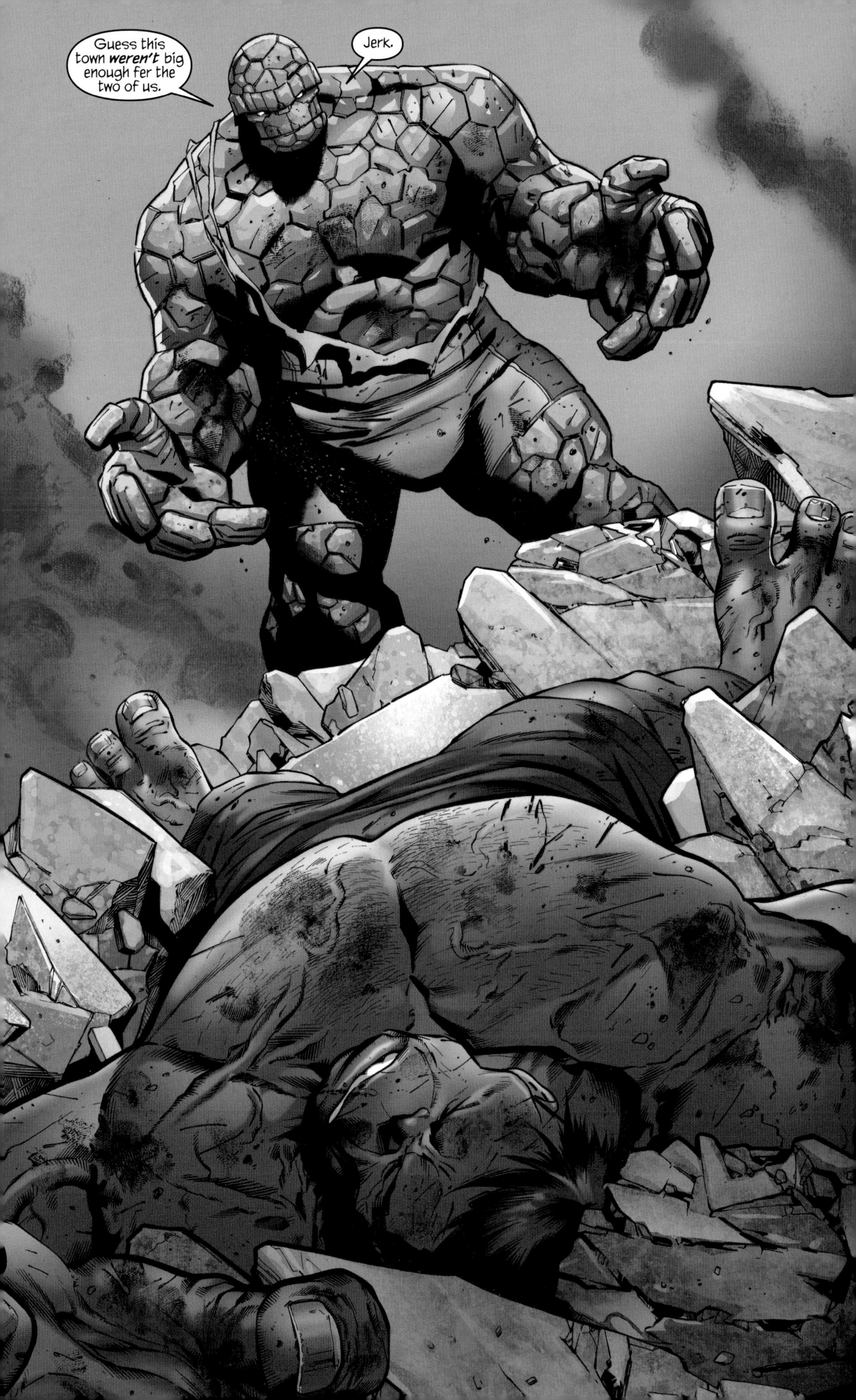
Guess this town *weren't* big enough fer the two of us.
Jerk.

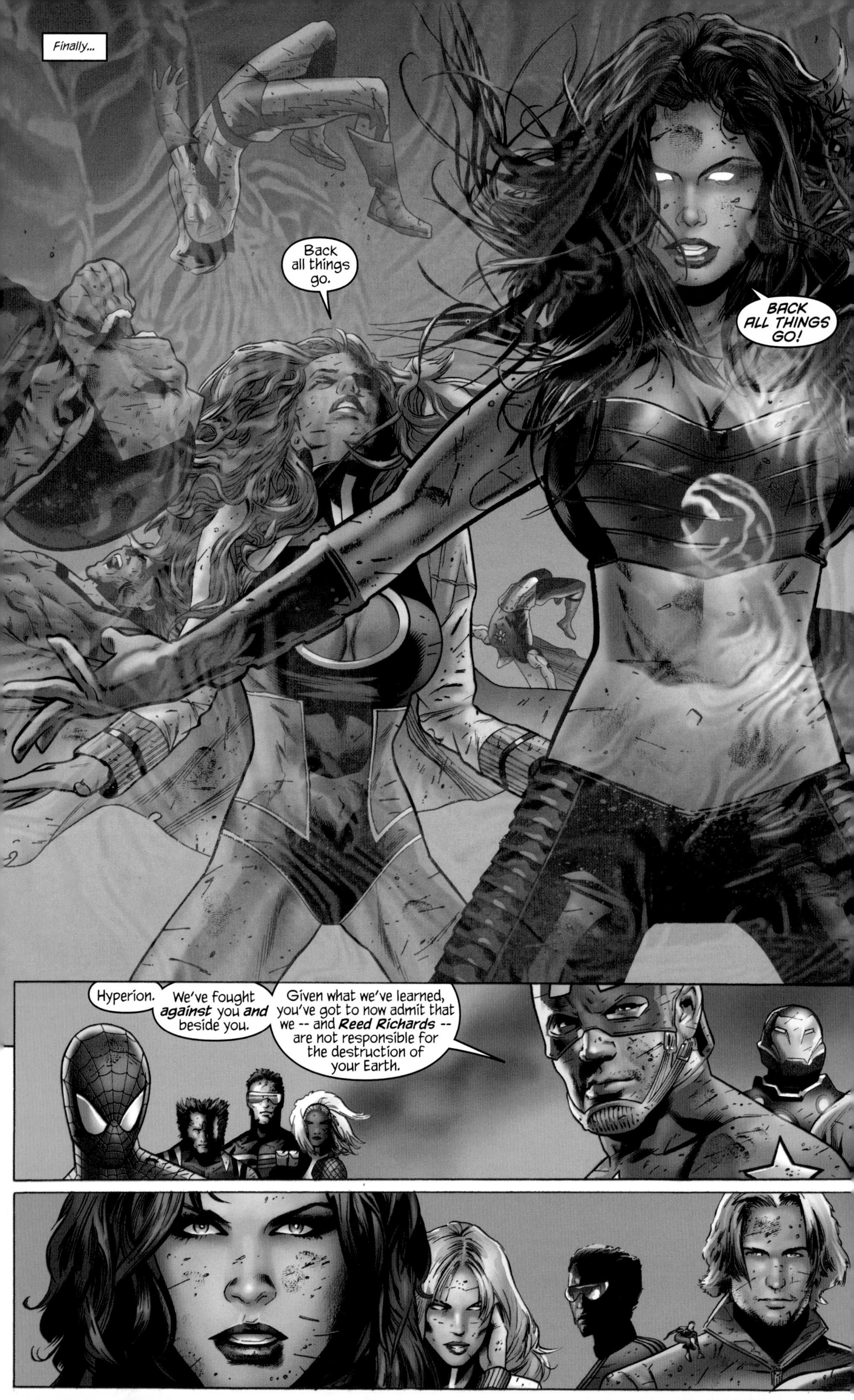
Finally...
Back all things go.
BACK ALL THINGS GO!
Hyperion.
We've fought *against* you *and* beside you.
Given what we've learned, you've got to now admit that we -- and *Reed Richards* -- are not responsible for the destruction of your Earth.

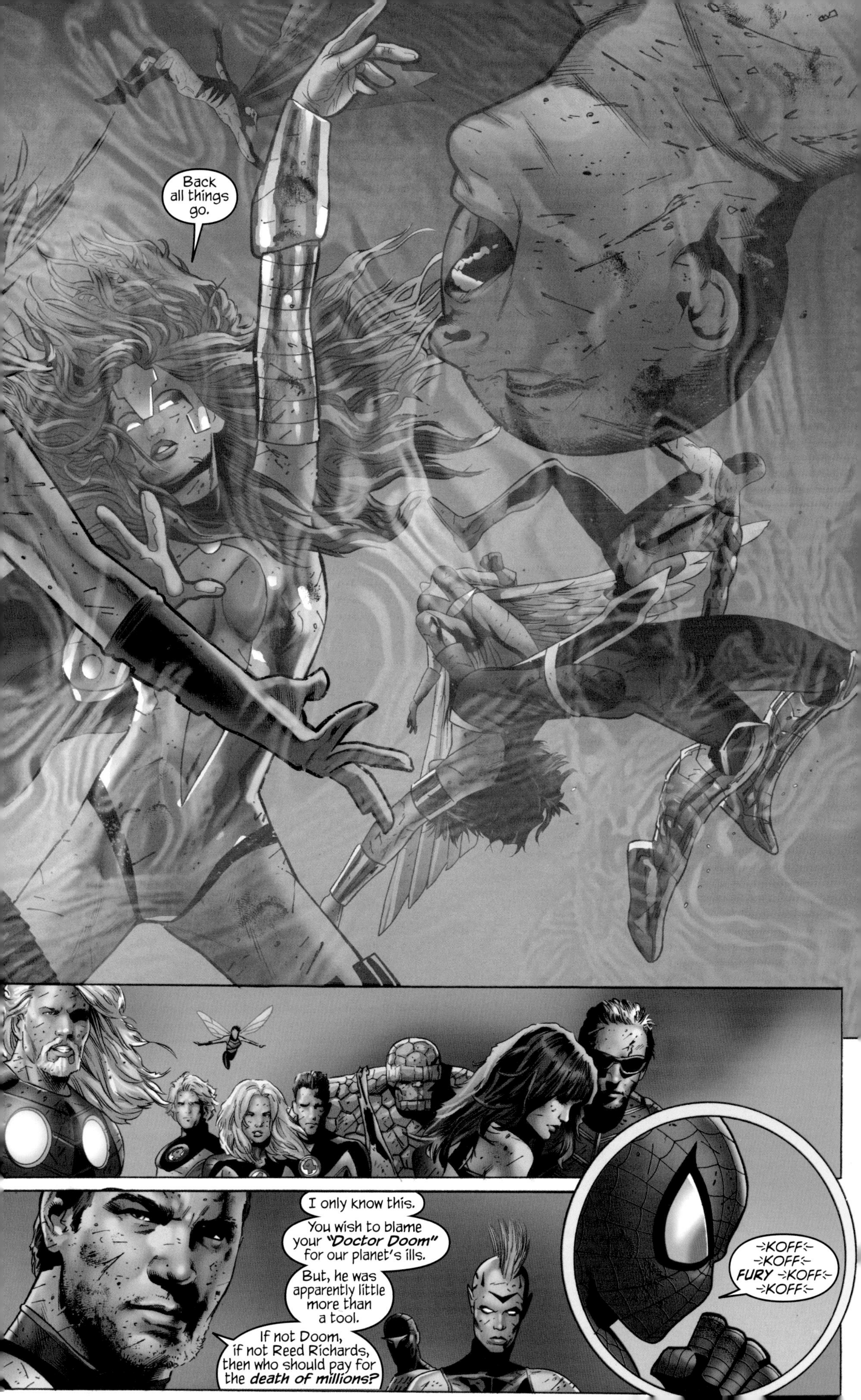
Back all things go.
I only know this.
You wish to blame your "Doctor Doom" for our planet's ills.
But, he was apparently little more than a tool.
If not Doom, if not Reed Richards, then who should pay for the death of millions?
-KOFF- -KOFF- FURY -KOFF- -KOFF-

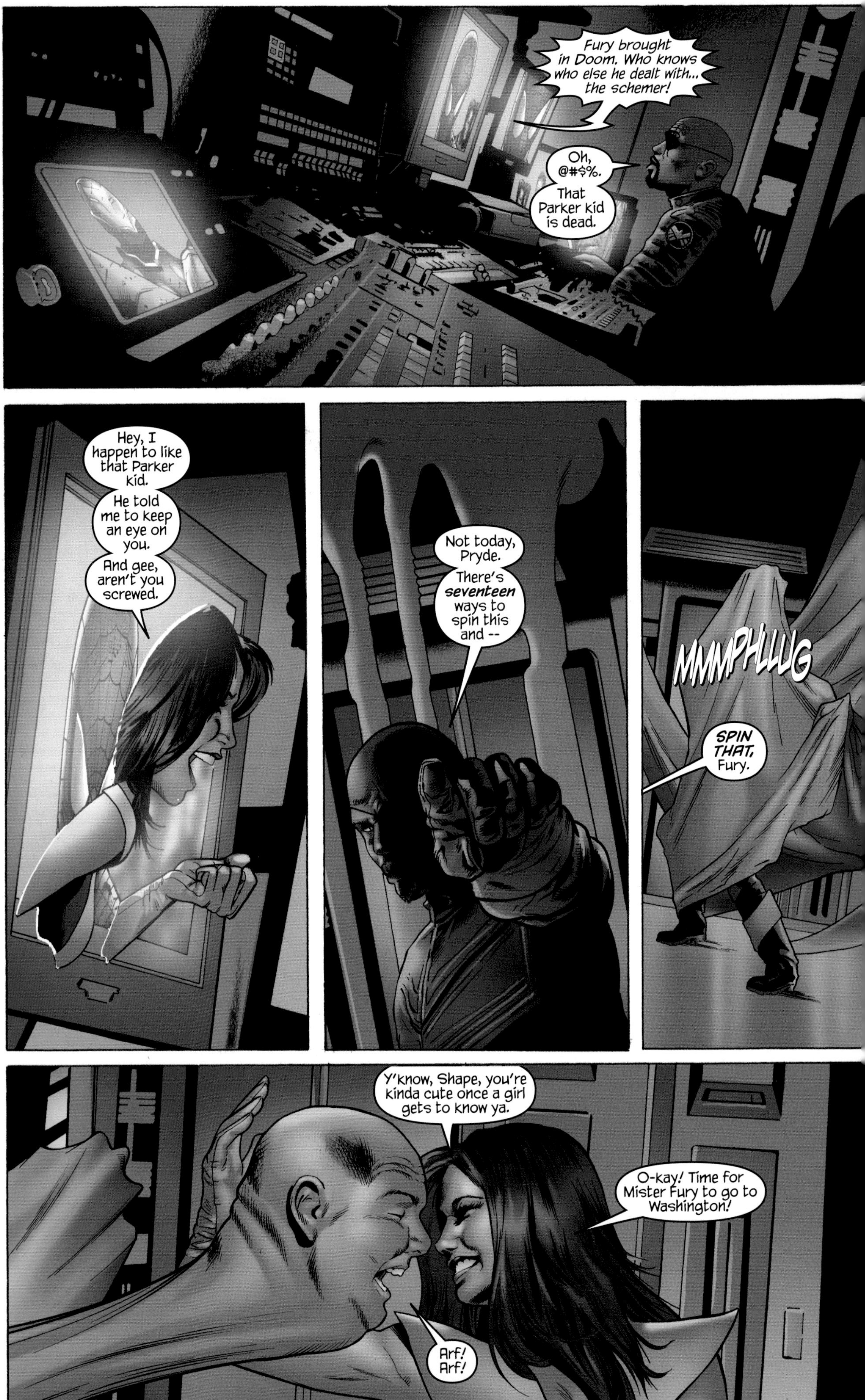

Fury brought in Doom. Who knows who else he dealt with... the schemer!
Oh, @#$%.
That Parker kid is dead.
Hey, I happen to like that Parker kid.
He told me to keep an eye on you.
And gee, aren't you screwed.
Not today, Pryde.
There's **seventeen** ways to spin this and --
MMMPHLLUG
SPIN THAT, Fury.
Y'know, Shape, you're kinda cute once a girl gets to know ya.
O-kay! Time for Mister Fury to go to Washington!
Arf! Arf!

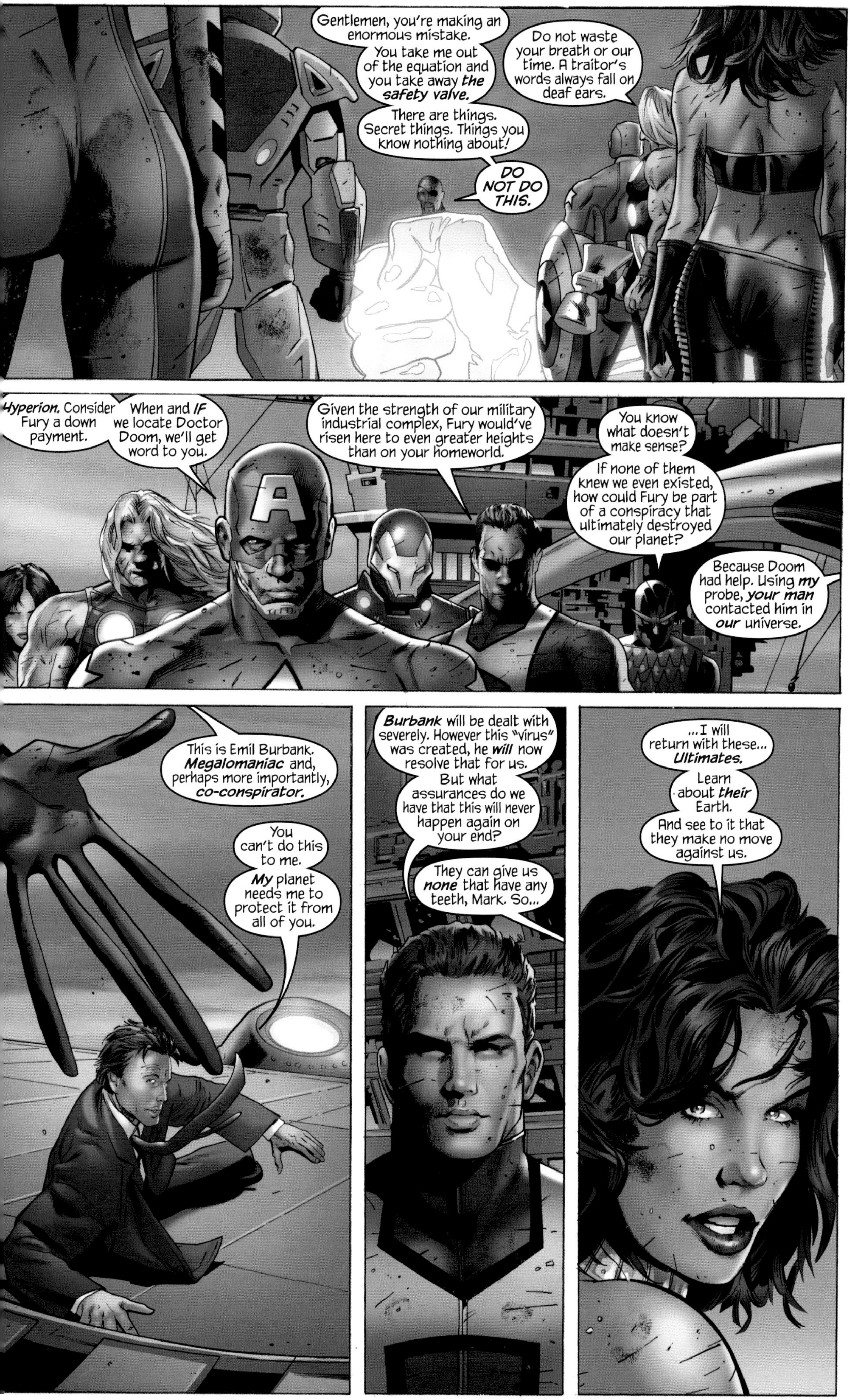
Gentlemen, you're making an enormous mistake.
You take me out of the equation and you take away *the safety valve.*
There are things. Secret things. Things you know nothing about!
Do not waste your breath or our time. A traitor's words always fall on deaf ears.
DO NOT DO THIS.
Hyperion. Consider Fury a down payment.
When and *IF* we locate Doctor Doom, we'll get word to you.
Given the strength of our military industrial complex, Fury would've risen here to even greater heights than on your homeworld.
You know what doesn't make sense?
If none of them knew we even existed, how could Fury be part of a conspiracy that ultimately destroyed our planet?
Because Doom had help. Using *my* probe, *your man* contacted him in *our* universe.
This is Emil Burbank. *Megalomaniac* and, perhaps more importantly, *co-conspirator.*
You can't do this to me.
My planet needs me to protect it from all of you.
Burbank will be dealt with severely. However this "virus" was created, he *will* now resolve that for us.
But what assurances do we have that this will never happen again on your end?
They can give us *none* that have any teeth, Mark. So...
...I will return with these... *Ultimates.*
Learn about *their* Earth.
And see to it that they make no move against us.

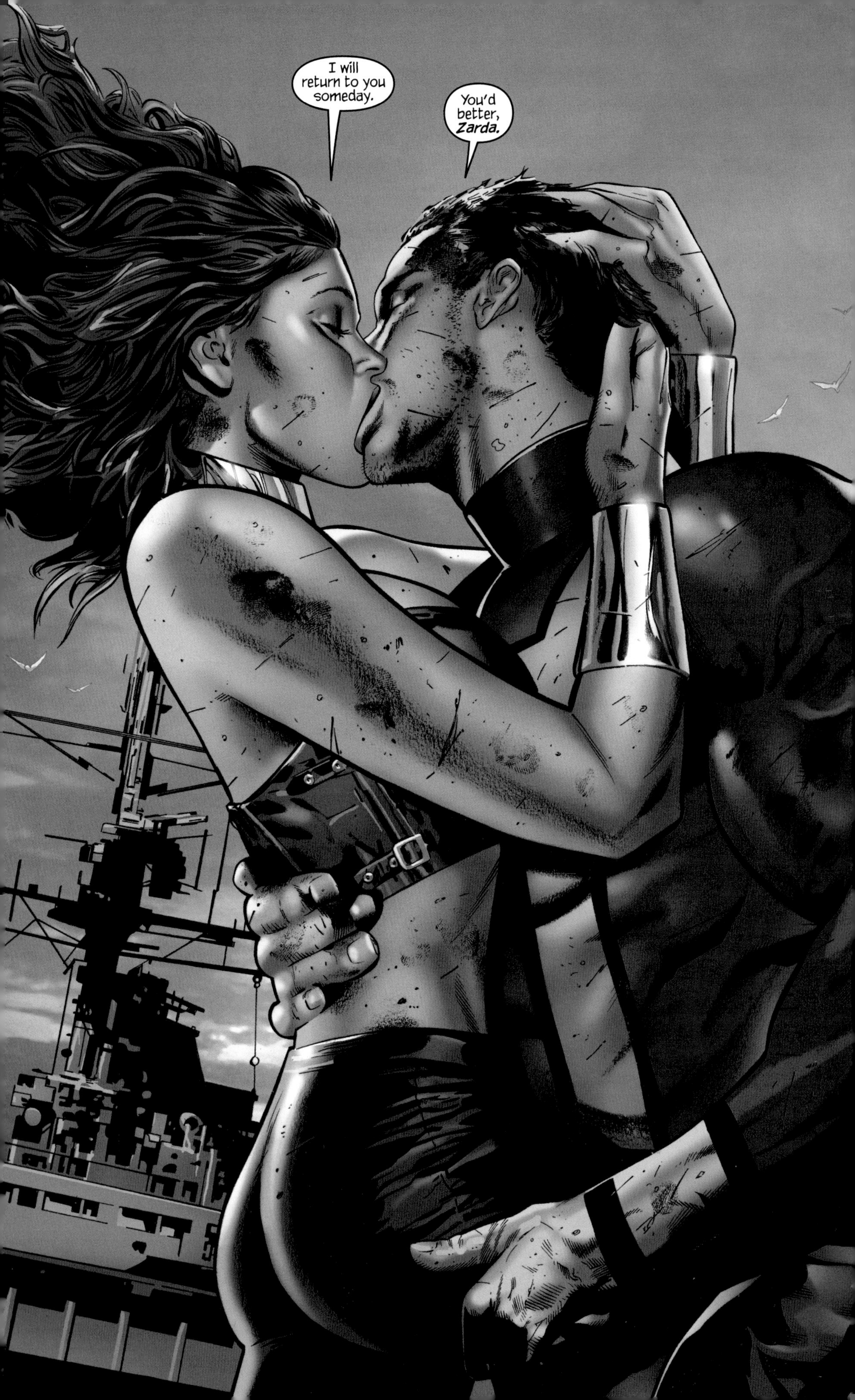
I will return to you someday.
You'd better, Zarda.

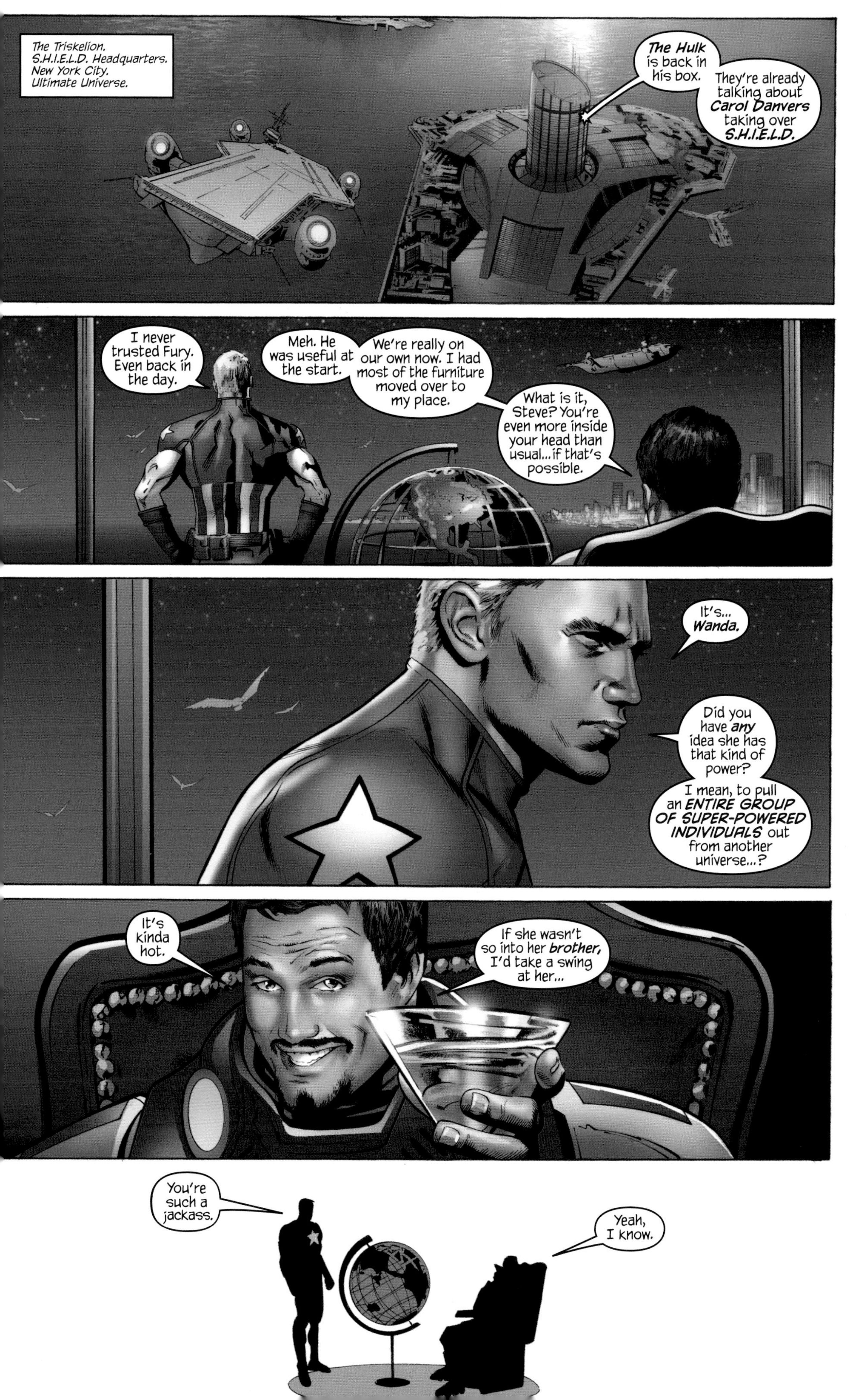
The Triskelion. S.H.I.E.L.D. Headquarters. New York City. Ultimate Universe.
The Hulk is back in his box.
They're already talking about Carol Danvers taking over S.H.I.E.L.D.
I never trusted Fury. Even back in the day.
Meh. He was useful at the start.
We're really on our own now. I had most of the furniture moved over to my place.
What is it, Steve? You're even more inside your head than usual... if that's possible.
It's... Wanda.
Did you have any idea she has that kind of power?
I mean, to pull an ENTIRE GROUP OF SUPER-POWERED INDIVIDUALS out from another universe...?
It's kinda hot.
If she wasn't so into her brother, I'd take a swing at her...
You're such a jackass.
Yeah, I know.

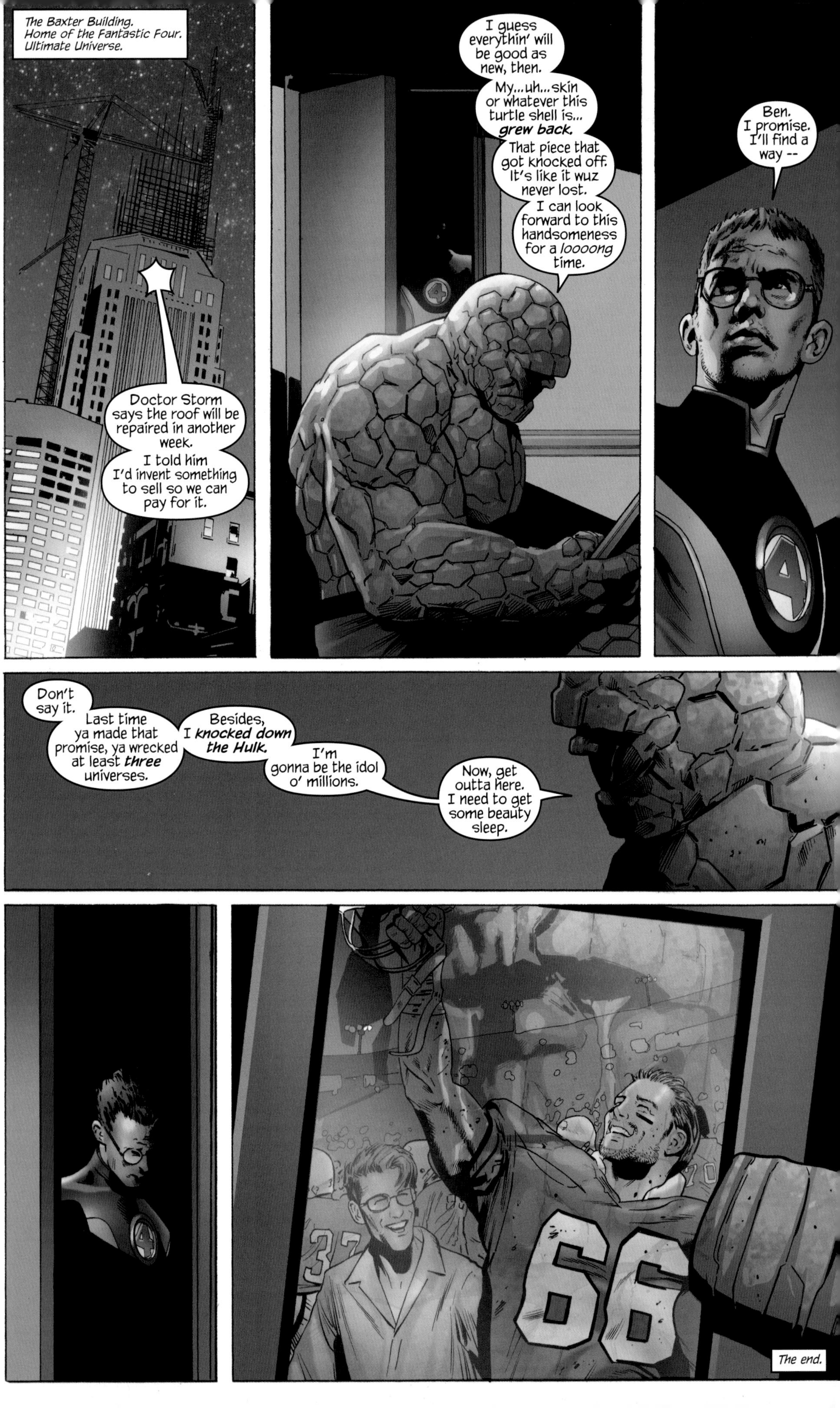
The Baxter Building. Home of the Fantastic Four. Ultimate Universe.
Doctor Storm says the roof will be repaired in another week.
I told him I'd invent something to sell so we can pay for it.
I guess everythin' will be good as new, then.
My...uh...skin or whatever this turtle shell is... grew back.
That piece that got knocked off. It's like it wuz never lost.
I can look forward to this handsomeness for a loooong time.
Ben. I promise. I'll find a way --
Don't say it.
Last time ya made that promise, ya wrecked at least three universes.
Besides, I knocked down the Hulk.
I'm gonna be the idol o' millions.
Now, get outta here. I need to get some beauty sleep.
The end.

THE FANTASTIC FOUR

Current Members: Human Torch (Johnny Storm), Invisible Woman (Susan Storm), Mr. Fantastic (Reed Richards), Thing (Ben Grimm)
Base of Operations: Baxter Building, Manhattan

History: Over a decade ago, the U.S. government, under the auspices of the Director of Mainland Technology Development, began gathering international child prodigies at a Manhattan laboratory facility in the Baxter Building, giving them the best resources and teachers the project could afford. Headed by scientist William Storm and the U.S. military's General Ross, the project discovered the N-Zone, an otherdimensional space which paralleled our own. When 11-year-old Reed Richards independently accessed this zone and began sending small toys into it, the project recruited him to join their work. Over the following ten years, Reed Richards, Victor Van Damme, and other students and instructors worked on the project before the government ultimately constructed its N-Zone teleportational gate in the Nevada desert, intending to teleport an apple to a receptor in Guantanamo Bay, Cuba.

Unbeknownst to the others, Victor Van Damme altered the device's settings and, upon its activation, the five people on its steps vanished into Unbeknownst to the others, Victor Van Damme altered the device's settings and, upon its activation, the five people on its steps vanished into interdimensional space, returning altered. Reed Richards returned to the same spot, transformed into a mass of pliable cells. Ben Grimm, Reed's childhood friend, was transported to Mexico and transformed into the rockish Thing; Johnny Storm was transported to Paris, his skin converted to flame-emitting cells; Victor Van Damme was transported to an unrevealed location and acquired a mechanized skin; while Sue Storm was transported into the Nevada desert, acquiring invisibility powers.

Arthur Molekevic, a fired Baxter Building instructor who had covertly observed the experiment and its transformed subjects, sent his artificial ani-men after the five. Initially retrieving Susan while the government gathered Reed, Ben, and Johnny at the Baxter Building, Molekevic then sent what seemed to be an enormous monster after them. Defeating it, they followed it to Molekevic's underground laboratories and retrieved Susan, inadvertently destroying the underground chambers in the process and apparently burying Molekevic. The government relocated the remaining

Baxter Building students to a secondary facility in Oregon, and dedicated the Manhattan facility to the quiet study of the altered four. When Van Damme attacked the Baxter Building six months later, Reed tracked him to Copenhagen. Refused permission to go to Denmark by the government, the quartet went anyway in Reed's childhood "Fantasti-Car," knowing they needed Victor's knowledge to restore themselves. Battling Van Damme, they were unable to defeat him before the government arrived and were forced by international law to set him free.

The four used a reconstructed N-Zone transporter to pilot a decommissioned U.S. Space Shuttle, heavily modified by Reed Richards and awkwardly christened the "Awesome" by Johnny Storm, to explore the N-Zone itself. The quartet made contact there with the being known as Nihil, who tried to kill them and followed them back to Earth, where both ships crashed in Las Vegas. The Fantastic Four were officially "outed" as super-humans on the Sunset Strip while defeating Nihil and his alien crew. Returning to the Baxter Building, they were briefly attacked by a rejected Baxter thinker named Rhona Burchill who was jealous of Reed's status, and subsequently aided the Ultimates, with Ben and Johnny fighting beside Nick Fury, Carol Danvers, and the Ultimates' Thor and Black Widow against the Kree, while Reed and Sue went into space with Iron Man to investigate Gah Lak Tus. The quartet also investigated the mystery of a secret race known as the Inhumans, then pursued a group of Chrono-Bandits across time after they duplicated a time machine which Reed and Sue had co-created. Recently Reed made interdimensional contact with another universe's version of the Fantastic Four, bringing the team into conflict with an alien world afflicted with a zombie-creating virus.

After capturing their extradimensional zombie counterparts, the FF fought Namor, Dr. Doom, Arthur Molekevic, Thanos, the Squadron Supreme and Diablo, rescued the Earth's kidnapped population from Zenn-La, and battled Red Ghost alongside Crimson Dynamo in Russia.

Writer: Mark O'English

SPIDER-MAN

Real Name: Peter Parker
Known Aliases: Arthur Simek
Identity: Known to S.H.I.E.L.D.; otherwise secret
Occupation: Student, Daily Bugle intern and website maintainer; former wrestler
Citizenship: USA
Place of Birth: Unrevealed
Known Relatives: Richard Parker (father, deceased), Mary Parker (mother, deceased),
Ben Parker (uncle, deceased), May Parker (aunt)
Group Affiliation: Formerly Knights, Osborn's "Six," member of UCW (Unlimited Class Wrestling)
Education: High school (not yet graduated)
First Appearance: (as Parker) Ultimate Spider-Man #1 (2000); (as Spider-Man) Ultimate Spider-Man #3 (2001)

History: Peter Parker is the son of scientist Richard Parker and his wife Mary. While Richard worked alongside Ed Brock on medical research, their two families grew close; though several years older, Eddie Brock, Jr. was close friends with Peter. Tragedy struck when both sets of parents were killed in a plane crash. Peter was taken in by his Uncle Ben and Aunt May, and lost touch with Eddie. Inheriting his father's intellect, Peter grew to be a quiet, bookish, boy. His best friends at Midtown High, his school in Queens, were Harry Osborn, son of industrialist Norman Osborn, and Mary Jane Watson, a fellow brain who lived across the street. Peter's relatively normal life changed abruptly during a school trip to Osborn Industries, Inc. The company had been working on a super soldier serum, the Oz Compound; a spider exposed to it escaped and bit Peter before it was destroyed.

Peter soon discovered that he had been mutated, gaining superhuman strength and agility and various spider-like powers. After Peter accidentally broke jock Flash Thompson's hand in a fight, the Parkers were hit with expensive medical bills; to help pay them, Peter secretly took up a wrestling challenge, wearing a mask to hide his youth and identity. The fight promoter gave him a more colorful costume and dubbed him Spider-Man, but his new career was cut short when he was accused of stealing money. Peter allowed a robber he encountered on the way home to escape because of his bad mood, an action that would later haunt him. He subsequently argued with his uncle over his slipping grades and recent poor attitude, and ran off to cool down; but when he returned home, he learned that a burglar had slain Uncle Ben in his absence. Overhearing some cops mention a cornered criminal who might be the burglar, Peter donned his costume and raced to capture him, only to find it was the same criminal he had allowed to escape earlier. Guilt-ridden, Peter finally accepted the great responsibility which came with his powers, becoming a crime fighter as Spider-Man.

Norman Osborn transformed into a monstrous, green goblin-like menace after mainlining the Oz Compound and attacked Peter's school, battling Spider-Man until he was shot down by police marksmen and presumed dead; Harry vanished into police custody for protection and questioning. Spider-Man encountered the criminal Shocker, the mutant Wolverine (on the run from Weapon X) and the rampaging Hulk. To help his aunt pay the bills, Peter tried to sell photos of Spider-Man to the Daily Bugle, and ended up hired to maintain the newspaper's website. Learning that Uncle Ben's killer worked for Wilson Fisk, the Kingpin of Crime, Peter set out to bring him down. After trying to get information from the Enforcers, he learned the Kingpin's whereabouts from ambitious underboss Mr. Big. Breaking into the Kingpin's office while Fisk hosted a party elsewhere in Fisk Tower, Spider-Man was spotted on the security cameras, defeated by Fisk's superpowered henchman Electro, unmasked, and thrown out a window. Kingpin, having figured out who had provided his intruder's information, personally murdered Mr. Big before having his body dumped in the river wearing Spider-Man's mask. Peter returned to Fisk's building, and after defeating Electro, the Enforcers and Fisk, sent the Daily Bugle security footage he had stolen showing the murder of Mr. Big; Fisk swiftly went into hiding.

Peter soon revealed his dual identity to Mary Jane, and they began dating. He fought alongside Iron Man at the U.N.; ran into Daredevil in Hell's Kitchen and helped apprehend the Punisher, a killer vigilante; encountered a lizard creature and a monster composed of swamp vegetation (both transformed scientists) in the sewers; and was mesmerized by Xandu into attacking the sorcerer Dr. Strange. He encountered the former Russian spy, the Black Widow, who stole his web-shooters; met the martial artist Shang-Chi; ran into a vampire and unidentified vampire slayer; and prevented a murder by the assassin Elektra. A new girl, Gwen Stacy, whose policeman father had investigated Uncle Ben's killing, joined Peter's school; soon after, Peter went to the mall with his friends where they bumped into the off-duty X-Men after Wolverine recognized Peter. Parker next faced the twin threats of Otto Octavius, alias Doctor Octopus, an Osborn scientist who had gained powers at the same time as Osborn himself; and Kraven, a reality TV show hunter who announced his intention to hunt and kill Spider-Man. After losing his first fight with Octopus, Spider-Man soundly defeated both him and Kraven outside an illegal genetic research lab in front of a horde of assembled press. The televised fight and a quick interview afterwards helped turn around negative public opinion about Spider-Man; minutes later, he fought one of the lab's rogue creations, the Sandman.

The next day at school, Harry returned — but Peter's joy evaporated when Norman resurfaced, too. The senior Osborn offered Peter a stark choice: work for him or see his loved ones killed by the Goblin. The following day, Peter learned from General Nick Fury that SHIELD was monitoring him and was aware of the Osborn situation, but could not intervene unless the Goblin made a public move. Spider-Man confronted Osborn to say he would not be intimidated, unaware that Harry had invited Mary Jane over; the Goblin seized her and carried her to the Queensboro Bridge, then dropped her off it; Spider-Man only narrowly managed to catch her. Facing both Spidey and SHIELD attack helicopters, Osborn fled back home and overdosed on the serum, mutating further. Peter pursued but was nearly killed before Harry walked in on the fight and saved him by driving a spike into the Goblin's back. The pursuing helicopters shot the Goblin, who turned back to Osborn and was taken into custody. In the aftermath, Nick Fury told Peter that when he turned 18 and was an adult, he would be forced to work for S.H.I.E.L.D.

Peter's friendship with Gwen Stacy grew as she began to confide in him regarding family troubles, though this meant he arrived minutes too late to help Iron Man capture the rampaging Rhino. When an imposter dressed as Spider-Man committed a string of robberies, the real Spider-Man was shot in the shoulder by police trying to apprehend him, and Fury sent the Wasp over to Peter's school to patch him up. While this was happening, the fake Spider-Man killed Captain John Stacy, Gwen's father. Enraged, Spider-Man foiled the imposter's latest bank robbery, beat him to a pulp and left him for the police, clearing his name. As her mother had run off with another man, Gwen moved in with the Parkers; Mary Jane, meanwhile, broke up with Peter, fearful he would one day be killed.

Finding boxes full of mementos of his parents in the basement prompted Peter to track down Eddie Brock. Now a university student, Eddie was trying to complete their parents' Venom Project, a protoplasmic medical dip nicknamed "the Suit" which could enhance its wearer's abilities while healing illness and injury — even curing cancer; however, some of Eddie's comments led Peter to wonder if their parents had been murdered by their corporate employers. As Spider-Man, he broke into Eddie's lab to examine the dip, but it enveloped his body, creating a new black costume. He briefly enjoyed this new look, easily stopping a kidnapping and beating an upgraded Shocker; but after the Suit took control of Peter and nearly killed a mugger, Peter had to electrocute himself to remove it. Seeing the danger of the dip, Peter went back to the lab to destroy the rest of it, confiding in Eddie that he was Spider-Man and apparently convincing Eddie to let him destroy the dip, unaware Eddie had more hidden away. Exposing himself to the Suit, Eddie became an insane, monstrous menace and attacked Peter. In the end, an accidental electrocution seemingly killed Eddie, though the subsequent disappearance of his belongings suggested Brock may have survived. After confronting Nick Fury to ask if his parents had been murdered, Peter returned to the lab where he found the rest of

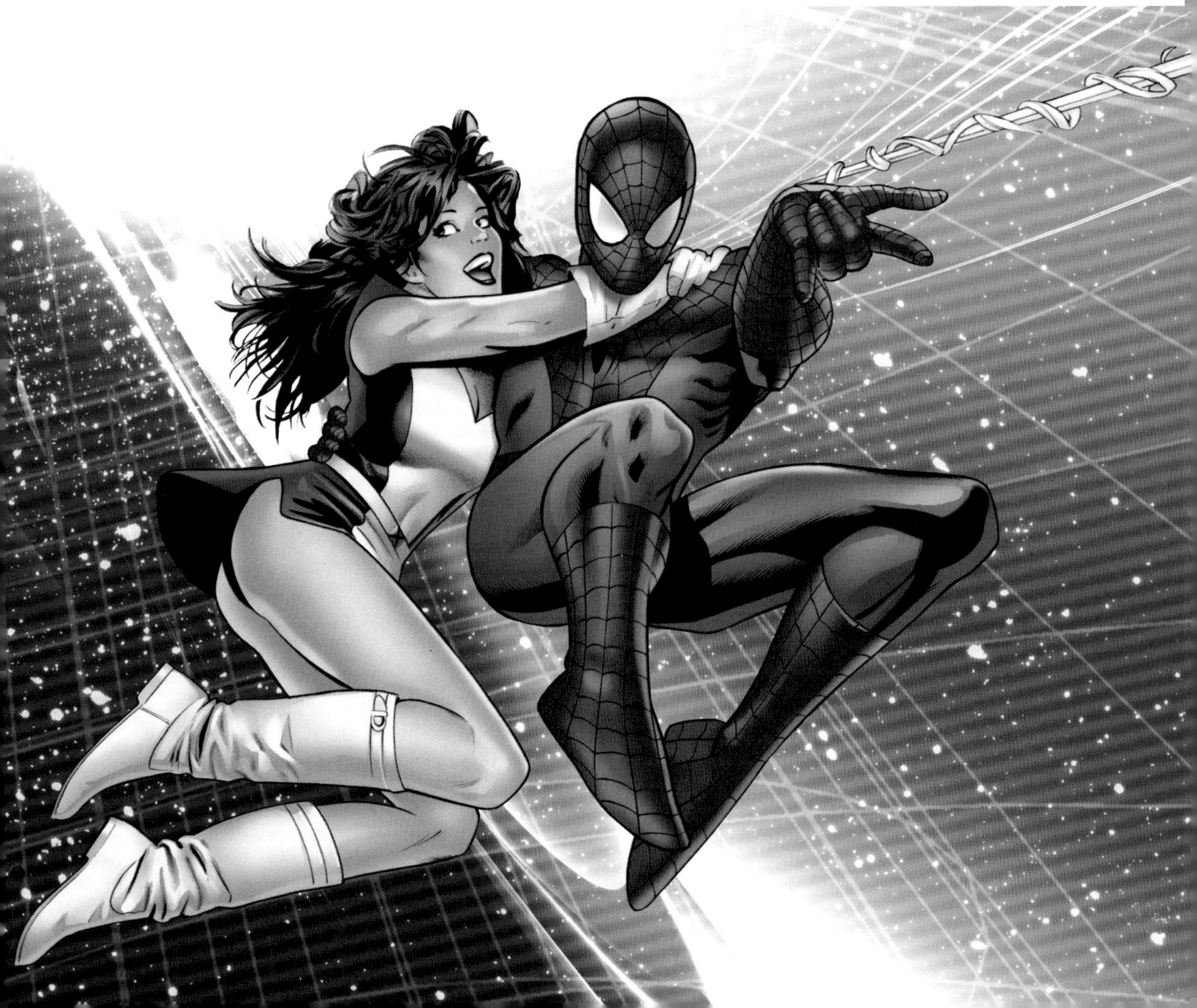

the dip gone and encountered Eddie's professor, Curt Conners, the former lizard-man, who deduced Peter was Spider-Man.

Shortly thereafter, Spider-Man got back together with Mary Jane as Peter; offered guidance to unstable Latverian mutant teen Geldoff alongside the X-Men, and stopped martial artist Danny Rand from using his "Iron Fist" on an aggressive man during a street fight. Wounded X-Man Wolverine later sought refuge in Peter's home while fleeing remnants of Weapon X. The Enforcers returned, as did their boss, the Kingpin, who had gone free after the murder evidence against him was ruled inadmissible. Sam Bullit ran for D.A. on an anti-Spider-Man platform, supported by Jameson and the Bugle, and when Peter spoke out against the Bugle's anti-Spidey stance, he was fired; however, reporter Ben Urich learned that Bullit was tied to the Kingpin and the Bugle withdrew its support. The Enforcers tried to intimidate Jameson into reversing this, but Spider-Man intervened. Soon after, Jameson admitted his mistake to Peter and reinstated him. Spider-Man next encountered the burglar known as the Black Cat, who became attracted to him. She had stolen a stone tablet sought by the Kingpin, and Elektra was hired to retrieve it. After a fruitless three-way skirmish between Black Cat, Elektra and Spider-Man, Peter and the Kingpin both figured out the Black Cat was secretly Felicia Hardy, who was soon trapped by Kingpin and Elektra. Spider-Man's arrival allowed her to free herself, and she threw the tablet into the river, only to be seemingly slain by Elektra.

Several of Spider-Man's foes, led by Norman Osborn, escaped SHIELD captivity. Fearing for Peter, Fury brought him to the Triskelion base used by the Ultimates and placed his loved ones under observation. The escapees attacked the Triskelion and captured Peter, blackmailing him into joining Osborn's "Six." This group attacked the White House but was opposed by the Ultimates, who informed Peter that Aunt May was safely in protective custody, prompting Spider-Man to turn on Osborn and help the Ultimates recapture the criminals. While Aunt May visited Florida, Peter heard a Spider-Man movie was being filmed and angrily confronted its film crew, but learned he had no legal recourse to stop the film. Equally put out by the news, Doctor Octopus attacked the movie set; when Spider-Man stepped in, Octopus defeated him and abducted him to Brazil, where Spider-Man bested Octopus in a rematch and hitched a ride back to the States in the cargo hold of a passenger jet. He narrowly beat his aunt home, only to be confronted by an angry Gwen, who had figured out his double identity and blamed him for her father's death. Peter managed to convince her otherwise, and she forgave him, joining his trusted circle of confidants. A short while later, the movie opened to great success.

Spider-Man stopped the maniac Gladiator, who had taken hostages in a museum, and met Captain Jeanne De Wolfe of the NYPD. Injured by Gladiator's blades, he sought medical assistance from Dr. Conners, who later experimented with Peter's blood in search of cures for disease, having obtained Peter's reluctant permission to do so. A few months later, a creature Conners had created by mixing Peter's DNA with his own reptile-infected DNA escaped, killing a number of people, including Gwen Stacy, as it followed echoes of Peter's memories back to his home. Peter accused Conners of being behind Gwen's death, and Conners revealed what he had done, just as the creature came out of hiding. Peter attacked it, eventually tricking

it into leaping into a fiery factory smokestack. Later, an angry Peter convinced Conners to turn himself in. Deciding that Spider-Man had caused enough death, Peter told Mary Jane he was dropping his dual identity, but he could not avoid his sense of responsibility, stopping a mugging while wearing a makeshift mask; he soon realized he could not quit.

When the X-Men's Jean Grey used her telepathy to punish Wolverine for an indiscretion, she unwittingly swapped the minds of Spider-Man and Wolverine, trapping each in the other's body. After a series of misadventures, the duo foiled another robbery attempt by the Shocker before Grey restored them to their rightful bodies. Later, Peter enjoyed a trip to the beach with Mary Jane, Kong, Liz and a new kid in school that Liz liked, Johnny Storm. After the secretly superhuman Storm was unexpectedly ignited by their campfire and flew off, he came back the next day to apologize to Liz; as Spider-Man, Peter offered Storm advice and they formed what might prove to be an enduring friendship. Together, they rescued people from a tenement fire.

After helping the Ultimates capture a rogue cyborg, Peter accompanied Ben Urich to interview the now-celebrity sorcerer Dr. Strange. Turned away by the Doctor's manservant Wong, Peter sensed something was wrong and returned as Spider-Man to investigate. Witnessing what he thought was Wong attacking the unconscious Doctor, he broke in through the window, unwittingly shattering the mansion's mystic defenses. The nightmare being who had been attacking Strange pulled Peter into a horrifying dream world until Strange managed to wake him, and Peter fled in terror. When Harry Osborn returned, Peter learned that he had dated Mary Jane prior to Peter, and that he too had been mutated in the same explosion that empowered Doctor Octopus and his father. Now mentally unstable and hallucinating, Harry transformed into the monstrous Hobgoblin. He went on a rampage, trying to get Peter to kill him, but Peter refused; when Fury and SHIELD arrived, they took Harry down hard, and an enraged Peter struck the government man. Afterwards, Peter broke up with Mary Jane, fearful for her safety and feeling he could no longer trust her. Meanwhile, unknown to Peter, Dr Octopus used a sample of Peter's blood to grow clones of Peter with slight DNA variations (Scorpion, "Kaine," Tarantula, Spider-Woman and an aged one brainwashed to believe he was Peter's dead father Richard), as well as a new Carnage mixed with DNA from Peter's dead friend Gwen Stacy.

When the ambitious criminal Hammerhead began a gang war to steal away the Kingpin's territory, his activities brought him into conflict with several vigilantes, Spider-Man included, as well as Black Cat, a somewhat ethical 20-something thief harboring an attraction to Spider-Man. The gang war climaxed in a melee between Hammerhead's gang, the vigilantes, and Kingpin's assassin Elektra, which ended with Elektra, the vigilante Moon Knight (Steven Grant), and Hammerhead all critical in hospital. Shortly after this, Peter was asked out by the X-Man Shadowcat (Kitty Pryde), who had grown attracted to him during prior encounters; as she possessed her own super powers, Peter believed she was less vulnerable to attack than MJ, and they began dating. After Spider-Man stopped Omega Red's rampage against Roxxon Oil, the latest in series of assaults against the company where Peter had intervened by chance, businessman Donald Roxxon became convinced Spider-Man must have known about the attacks in advance. He hired Silver Sable's mercenary Wild Pack to capture Spider-Man; after initially kidnapping Peter's fellow student Fred "Flash" Thompson by mistake, the Wild Pack snared Spider-Man, but while questioning him, Roxxon was attacked by the Vulture, who killed one of the Pack, before Spider-Man, with Sable's assistance, apprehended him.

Deadpool's cyborg Reavers invaded the X-Men's mansion to abduct the X-Men, and finding Spider-Man there, they captured him too. They released their victims on the island of Krakoa, to be hunted and killed live on international television. Though Spider-Man and the X-Men soon defeated the Reavers, the world learned that Spider-Man was dating Shadowcat; as Kitty did not wear a mask, this made it difficult for Peter to safely date Kitty while out of costume. Over the next few weeks Peter battled vampires alongside the undead Morbius, and joined other heroes in repelling a full-scale invasion of the US led by the super-powered Liberators. Having grown increasingly friendly with sympathetic police detective Jeanne DeWolfe, unaware she was the Kingpin's lover and corrupt, Spider-Man followed a lead she gave to the new Kingpin rival, the Kangaroo; to Peter's horror, moments after he and Daredevil apprehended Kangaroo, Jeanne was shot dead in front of him by the killer vigilante, the Punisher. Kitty began to suspect Peter still loved MJ, straining their relationship, shortly before Peter's clones escaped; while the mentally-disturbed Kaine kidnapped MJ, the others sought out Peter, including "Richard Parker," and the confused Carnage, who believed herself to be the real Gwen; both turned up at the Parker residence in Queens. Trying to explain Gwen's "resurrection" to Aunt May, Peter admitted to her that he was Spider-Man; moments later SHIELD arrived in force, and the already stressed May suffered a heart attack. After May was rushed to the hospital, Peter and Spider-Woman tracked down Kaine and MJ, to find that he had injected her with Oz and turned her into a monster; managing to restore her to human form just ahead of SHIELD's arrival, they learned from a gloating Dr. Octopus his part in recent events. Kaine was shot dead by SHIELD, while Tarantula died fighting Octopus before Peter and Spider-Woman subdued him; afterwards she swiftly fled for parts unknown, while MJ was apparently cured, May recovered from her heart attack, Richard died of old age, and both Scorpion and Carnage ended up in SHIELD custody. Having nearly lost her, Peter and MJ got back together, unaware that Kitty was watching.

After assisting the Ultimates and Fantastic Four against the Squadron Supreme, Peter officially broke up with Kitty, but when Kitty subsequently quit the X-Men, her mother enrolled her at Midtown High, making her Peter's newest classmate. Daredevil recruited Peter into his Knights, a coalition of crimefighters dedicated to bringing down the Kingpin. Despite one of their number proving to be a traitor, and another, the unstable Moon Knight, attacking Peter at school and delivering him to the Kingpin, they indirectly succeeded in getting the Kingpin arrested. Soon after Spider-Man battled the Spot, several of Peter's old foes escaped custody; Peter soon recaptured Electro, but even working with Kitty, the Green Goblin proved a harder catch, until SHIELD used Harry as bait. To Peter's distress, Harry died fighting his father; Norman, horrified at his own actions, let SHIELD agent Carol Danvers shoot him dead.

Writers: Stuart Vandal & Sean McQuaid

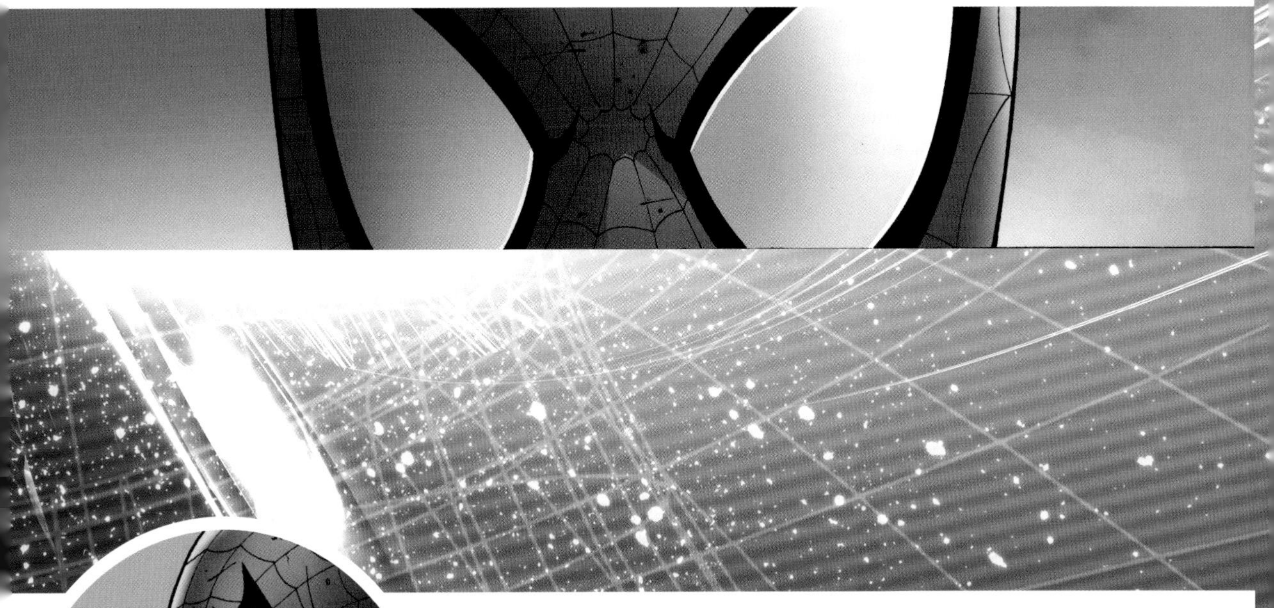

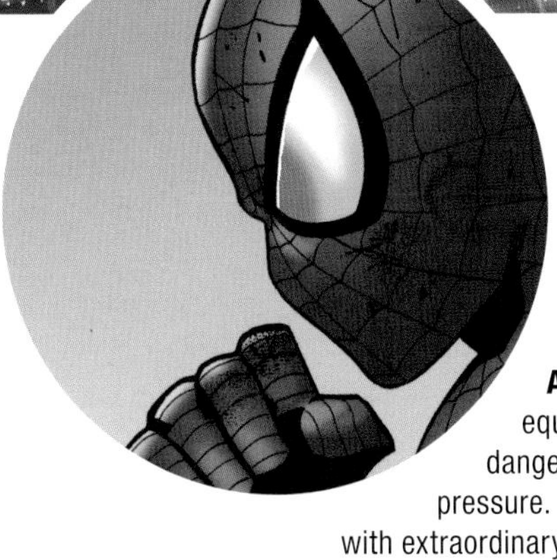

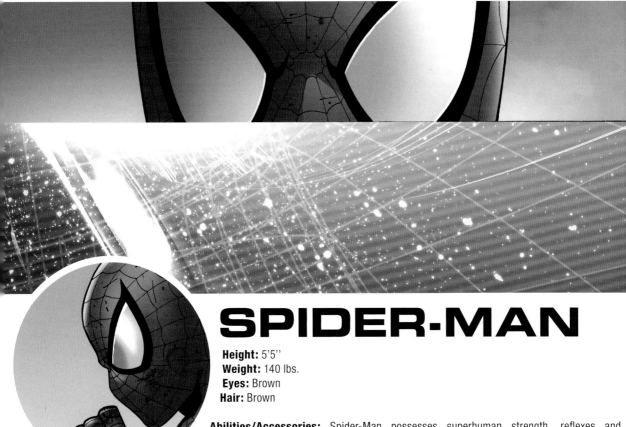

SPIDER-MAN

Height: 5'5"
Weight: 140 lbs.
Eyes: Brown
Hair: Brown

Abilities/Accessories: Spider-Man possesses superhuman strength, reflexes and equilibrium, the ability to cling to most surfaces, and a sixth sense that warns him of impending danger. Spider-Man's wrist-mounted web-shooters discharge thin strands of web-fluid at high pressure. On contact with air, the long-chain polymer knits and forms an extremely tough, flexible fiber with extraordinary adhesive qualities. In addition, Peter is an accomplished scientist for his age.

SUPREME POWER

Core Continuum Designation: Earth-31916
Significant Inhabitants: General Richard Alexander, Amphibian (Kingsley Rice), Atlanta Blur (Stanley Stewart), Emil Burbank, General Casey, Doctor Spectrum (Joe Ledger), Dr. Helen Fraser, Hyperion (Mark Milton), Inertia (Edith Freiberg), Arcanna Jones, Nighthawk (Kyle Richmond), Nuke (Al Gaines), Michael Redstone, Jason Scott, Shape (Raleigh Lund), Dr. William Adam Steadman, Tom Thumb, Zarda (alias Claire Debussy), Voice (John M'Butu), Whiteface (Steven Binst)
Significant Locations: Physically similar to the real-world Earth
First Appearance: Supreme Power #1 (2003)

History: In the late 1970s, a space pod crash-landed somewhere in middle America. The US government recovered the pod's passenger — a male infant, whom they named Mark Milton — and raised him in a secure environment to ensure an unquestioning devotion to America. As Mark grew up, he developed incredible powers — including super-strength, laser vision, and flight — which soon made his human captors very nervous.

The space pod that brought Mark to Earth, however, may have also brought more than just an infant. An extraterrestrial bacteria was emitted as it descended, which might have caused several mutations to newborn human children along its flight path. Among these were an amphibious newborn dumped into the sea by a horrified mother, and a boy in Georgia named Stanley Stewart who soon possessed superhuman speed.

Scientists studying Mark's vessel also discovered a crystal power source; to test it, the army brought in black ops agent Joe Ledger. The crystal bonded to him, leaving him comatose; all attempts to remove it proved fatal for those who tried. Unrelated to these incidents, teenager Kyle Richmond witnessed his parents murdered in a racial hate crime, driving him to become the vigilante Nighthawk.

In his late teens, Mark was covertly deployed; almost immediately, reporter Jason Scott spotted a story under news reports. Digging deeper, he learned of "Project Hyperion." Deciding the truth would inevitably come out, President Clinton ordered a controlled information release through Scott, and Hyperion went public, passed off as a human mutation. Sent to investigate the urban myth of the "Atlanta Blur," Mark encountered Stewart, who subsequently went public and established a friendship with Hyperion grounded in their mutual need for superhuman company. Hyperion also tracked down Nighthawk, but realized the vigilante was a normal man (Nighthawk viewed Hyperion as a bleeding heart liberal).

Ledger finally awoke and was sent out on covert ops. Hyperion soon learned of his existence and tracked him down. They fought until the crystal possessed the injured Ledger's body and carried him away to let him heal. He later awoke on the seabed alongside the now-grown aquatic child; they communed telepathically, forming a bond. Ledger named her Kingsley Rice; when later ordered to hunt her down, he decided to hide her instead. Hyperion, angry at being lied to, broke into the Project base to demand answers, but Project head General Casey detonated a bomb, hoping to kill him rather than let him go rogue. Hyperion survived, but was badly injured. Suddenly, from out of the earth, a beautiful woman named Zarda sensed Hyperion's need, emerged from her tomb, and flew to his side. She transferred some stolen life energy, healing him, and then told Mark that they were destined to rule the Earth together.

Project scientists used alien bacteria from the pod to experiment on convicts, creating more super agents. Thus empowered, serial killer Michael Redstone escaped, releasing the other test subjects at the same time. Nighthawk recruited the Blur and Hyperion to take him down, though there were extensive civilian casualties. Hyperion reluctantly allowed Ledger to take Redstone into custody. General Alexander, the new head of all superhuman projects, released Redstone into a country hostile to the U.S., hoping to destabilize the anti-U.S. regime; Alexander also began a smear campaign against Hyperion to bring him back under control, implicating him in Redstone's rampage and publicly revealing his alien origins.

Alexander sent super-agents Arcanna, Emil Burbank, Nuke and Shape to capture Hyperion, but during their battle they were accidentally transported two years forward in time, where they discovered a world ruled by Hyperion and his fellow superhumans (Earth-23373). Returning to their own time, despite his misgivings, Hyperion agreed to work with the US government again. Alongside other drafted superhumans, Hyperion and Blur joined the newly formed Squadron Supreme, and were sent to Africa to eliminate super-powered African dictator the Voice (John M'Butu); however, local superhumans apparently dealt with M'Butu first, and warned the Squadron that Africa was now off-limits to US interference. Refusing to join the Squadron, Nighthawk tracked down the serial killer Whiteface, then later, while temporarily superpowered, came to blows with Hyperion in Dafur. Redstone was recruited by the Chinese and returned to America, where he again battled Hyperion, Nighthawk and Blur. The Defense Department asked Burbank to develop a weapon capable of slaying Hyperion; however, it got loose, releasing a rapidly-growing organism that spread across most of the Eastern United States. Burbank used an extradimensional probe from Earth-1610 to divert attention from the true culprit, and the Squadron traveled to 1610 to capture the probe's creator, Mr. Fantastic (Reed Richards). After battling the heroes of that reality and a Squadron Supreme from another dimension (Earth-712), the Squadron learned the true culprits were Burbank and secret agent Nick Fury of Earth-1610, both of whom they took back to their own world for trial; with Hyperion still concerned about the potential threat Earth-1610 presented to their own world, Zarda elected to remain there for the moment and gather intelligence.

Writer: Stuart Vandal

THE ULTIMATES

ACTIVE MEMBERS: Black Panther, Captain America (Steve Rogers), Hawkeye (Clint Barton), Iron Man (Tony Stark), Quicksilver (Pietro Maximoff), Thor, Valkyrie, Wasp (Janet Pym)
FORMER MEMBERS: Black Widow (Natasha Romanov), Giant-Man (Hank Pym), Hulk (Bruce Banner), Lieberman (deceased reservist), Scarlet Witch (Wanda Maximoff)
Reserves: The Four Seasons, the Goliaths, Intangi-Girl, Owen, O'Donohue, Rocketman One (Dexter), Rocketman Two, Rocketman Three, Rusk, Son of Satan (Damien), Thunderbolt, unspecified others
Base of Operations: The Triskelion, Upper Bay, Manhattan

History: The world's foremost superhuman strike force, the Ultimates trace their origins back to World War II super-operative Captain America (Steve Rogers), whom the U.S. government empowered in part to oppose the Nazis' secret extraterrestrial Chitauri allies. Rogers appeared to die while helping destroy the Chitauri/Nazi war effort, and U.S. scientists tried for decades to duplicate his powers. In recent years, the super-soldier program's lead scientist was geneticist Bruce Banner, reporting to General Ross, head of the S.H.I.E.L.D. intelligence agency. Later, new S.H.I.E.L.D. director Nick Fury pushed through a multi-billion expansion of the super-soldier program, though Banner's temporary transformation into the monstrous Hulk resulted in his demotion to deputy under new head scientists Hank and Janet Pym, who did double duty as size-changing super-operatives Giant-Man and Wasp. Altruistic armored billionaire inventor Tony Stark soon joined as Iron Man. Enigmatic left-wing powerhouse Thor refused membership at first, but Captain America himself was found alive and revived from a state of suspended animation to join the team. Together, Rogers, Stark and the Pyms became the Ultimates, headquartered in the high-tech Triskelion complex and backed by a huge support staff, a large conventional military force and black ops agents. Banner's semi-estranged girlfriend Betty Ross (daughter of General Ross) was hired as Director of Communications and helped make the new team into celebrities while making Bruce's life miserable. The depressed Banner finally snapped and transformed into the Hulk again, embarking on a destructive rampage stopped by the Ultimates with the aid of Thor, who began working with the team thereafter.

The Hulk's true identity was concealed from the public, and the Ultimates became beloved national heroes. The group soon expanded: intelligence veterans Hawkeye and Black Widow and mutant ex-terrorists Quicksilver and Scarlet Witch were promoted from the black ops division to the core team. Meanwhile, Hank Pym nearly killed his wife during a violent domestic dispute and

was himself beaten into traction by Captain America, who later began dating the Wasp. Pym's former assistant Dr. Eamonn Brankin became the new scientific head of the program. Despite losing Giant-Man, the Ultimates saved the world from a Chitauri plot with the unwitting aid of the Hulk and became bigger icons than ever. They went on to apprehend Kraven, Electro, Luther Manning, the X-Men and Norman Osborn's "Six." Later allied with the European Super-Solider Initiative, the Ultimates became more controversial as they began operating in foreign territory, notably the Middle East. Thor quit, and a traitor within the group outed Banner as the Hulk. Seemingly executed for the Hulk's crimes, Banner secretly survived with the aid of Hank Pym, who was soon fired from the Ultimates altogether. Meanwhile, apparently exposed as a madman, Thor was brutally arrested by the team. The global community grew wary as the Ultimates developed many more superagents as their reserves, and anti-Ultimates sentiment accelerated when the team stripped a small "rogue" Middle Eastern nation of its nuclear capability. The traitor within the Ultimates – later revealed to be the Black Widow – responded by murdering Hawkeye's family, framing Captain America for the crime, and helping a foreign super-army invade America. Assisted by Hank Pym, this foreign force destroyed the Triskelion and occupied major American cities, slaughtering the reserves and capturing the remaining Ultimates in the process.

The Ultimates ended the Liberators' invasion with the aid of Thor – whose powers had been restored by his father, Odin – proving himself to be a true god of Asgard. They later broke away from government control, but still assisted SHIELD when Earth-31916's Squadron Supreme attacked. Their new recruits include Black Panther and Valkyrie.

Writer: Sean McQuaid

X-MEN

Current Members: Angel (Warren Worthington III), Beast (Hank McCoy), Bishop, Dazzler (Alison Blaire), Psylocke (Betsy Braddock), Pyro, Storm (Ororo Munroe), Wolverine (James Howlett)
Former Members: Colossus (Piotr Rasputin), Cyclops (Scott Summers), Iceman (Bobby Drake), Magician, Marvel Girl (Jean Grey), Nightcrawler (Kurt Wagner), Rogue (Marian), Shadowcat (Kitty Pryde), Syndicate, Professor Charles Xavier
Base of Operations: Xavier Institute for Gifted Children, Salem Center
First Appearance: Ultimate X-Men #1 (2001)

When the X-Men were called in to hunt down Xavier's murderous mutant son David, Iceman was badly injured and Colossus was forced to kill David. Iceman's parents removed him from the school and tried to sue Xavier, pressured by an anti-mutant senator; however, Iceman refused to co-operate, and dropped the suit. Shortly after Kitty Pryde joined the X-Men, Xavier sent Wolverine and Cyclops on a mission to the Savage Land; while there, Wolverine deliberately left Cyclops to die, jealous of his relationship with Marvel Girl. Meanwhile, the Hellfire Club revealed their true motivations when they tried to merge Marvel Girl with a hostile extra-dimensional entity, the Phoenix Force.

Magneto returned and the Brotherhood resumed its anti-human terrorism. Implicated as Magneto's allies since they had falsified reports of his death, the X-Men became fugitives, battling the Ultimates and escaping only due to the surprise return of Iceman. The X-Men located Magneto thanks to Cyclops, who had been found and healed by the Brotherhood. Defeating Magneto and saving Florida from nuclear destruction, the X-Men became national heroes; the White House pardoned them but placed them under the supervision of S.H.I.E.L.D. In the wake of this adventure, Nightcrawler and Rogue were recruited into the X-Men, and Cyclops fired Wolverine. Cyclops later relented, feeling Wolverine's best chance of redemption was with the X-Men.

The next few months saw a visit to the mansion from Spider-Man, an incursion by remnants of Weapon X, and the addition of Angel to the group. Beast left to join Emma Frost's rival mutant educational program, but was killed in a Sentinel attack; Dazzler, one of Frost's other recruits, joined the X-Men, though her rock chick ways irritated Xavier. The serial killer Sinister nearly slew Xavier and Iceman before Rogue defeated him. Believing a worldwide spate of horrendous nightmares might be a telepathic mutant's distress call, Xavier sent several X-Men to Siberia, where they encountered the Ultimates and learned of the coming of Gah Lak Tus; Xavier subsequently helped oppose the world destroyer.

After Rogue left the team to be with mutant thief Gambit, Xavier sent several X-Men to Genosha to find out if convicted murderer Longshot had been framed by the anti-mutant regime. They learned he was guilty, but not before an unauthorized mission led by Dazzler freed him. The X-Men subsequently tried to prevent some of Emma Frost's new students from breaking into S.H.I.E.L.D.'s Triskelion, bringing them into conflict with the Ultimates and Magneto once more.

The X-Men later helped repel the Liberator invasion. Magician joined the team, but left after they discovered he had manipulated them. Cable kidnapped Professor X, making the X-Men believe he was dead, and Cyclops disbanded them, but Bishop formed a new team.

History: Leaving the radical Brotherhood of Mutants and obtaining secret financial backing from the Hellfire Club, Charles Xavier established the Xavier Institute for Gifted Children in New York. He gathered Cyclops, Marvel Girl, Colossus, Storm and Beast as his X-Men, defending mutants while promoting peaceful co-existence with humanity. Iceman joined them after being saved from Sentinels, and Wolverine after the X-Men rescued him from Weapon X.

When the Brotherhood kidnapped the U.S. President's daughter, the X-Men freed her, gaining the President's favor and ending Sentinel attacks on innocent mutants. Cyclops briefly defected to the Brotherhood, unhappy Xavier was dealing with "the Evil Empire," but when Magneto attempted to destroy Washington with reprogrammed Sentinels, Cyclops returned to the fold. Weapon X soon abducted all the X-Men except Wolverine, coercing them to become operatives until the Brotherhood freed them.

Writer: Stuart Vandal

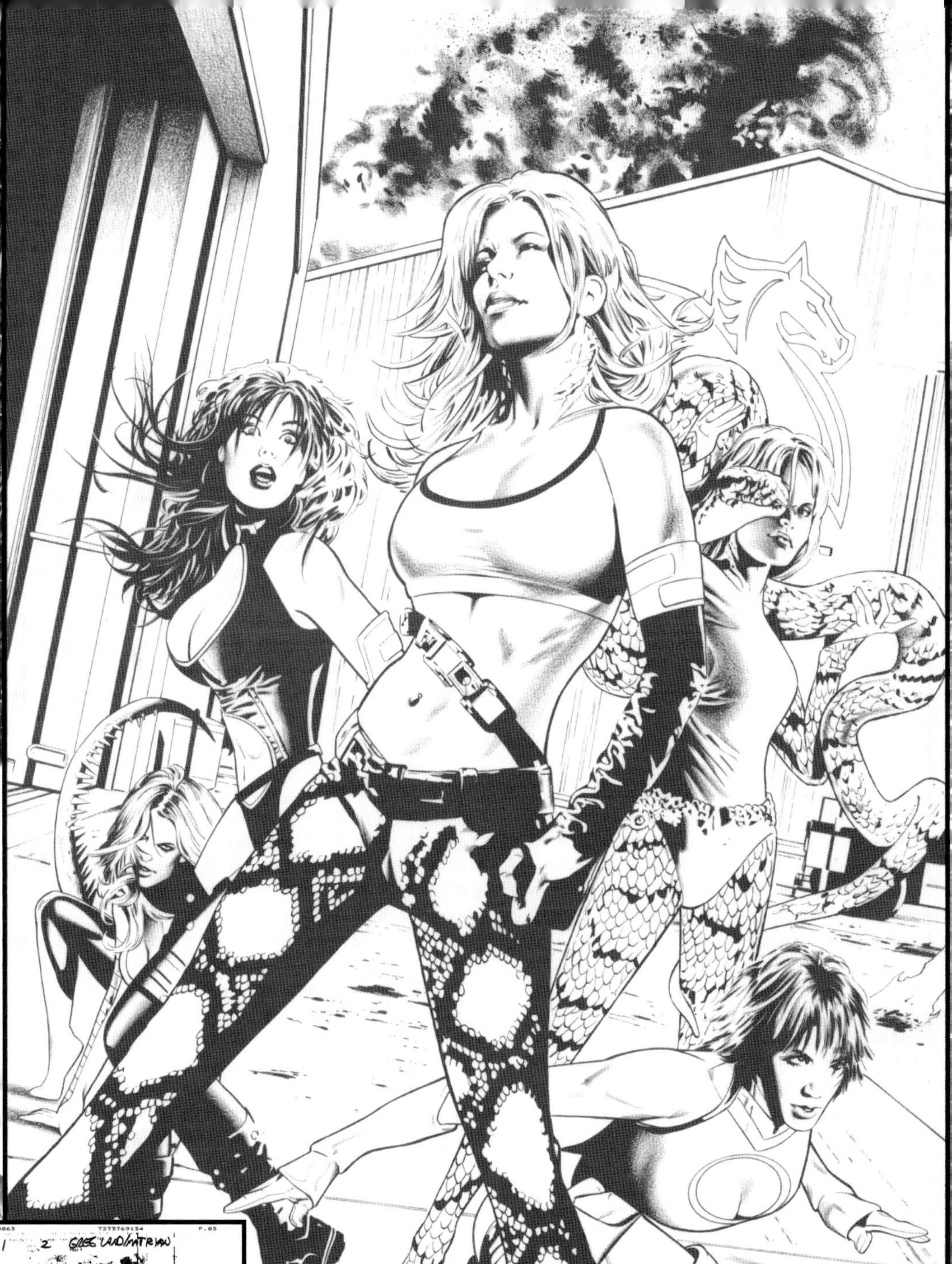

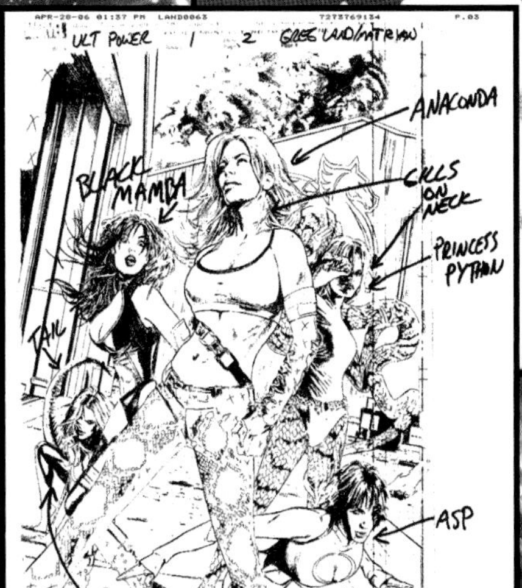

APR-28-06 01:37 PM LAND0063 7273769134 P.03
ULT POWER 1 2 GREG LAND/MATRYAN
ANACONDA
BLACK MAMBA
PRINCESS PYTHON
TAIL
ASP
DEATHADDER

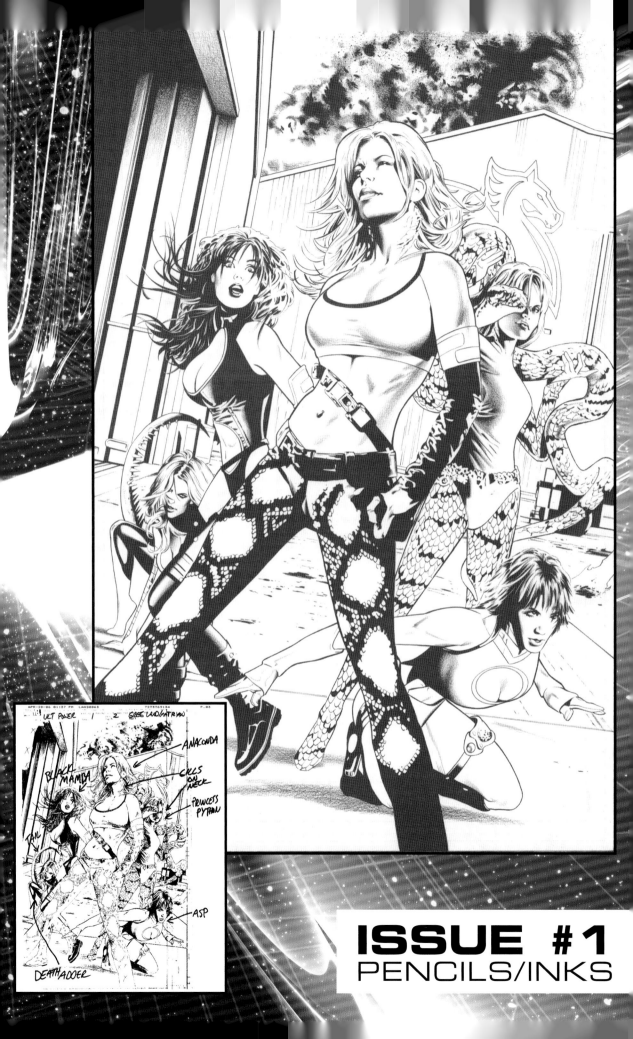

ISSUE #1
PENCILS/INKS

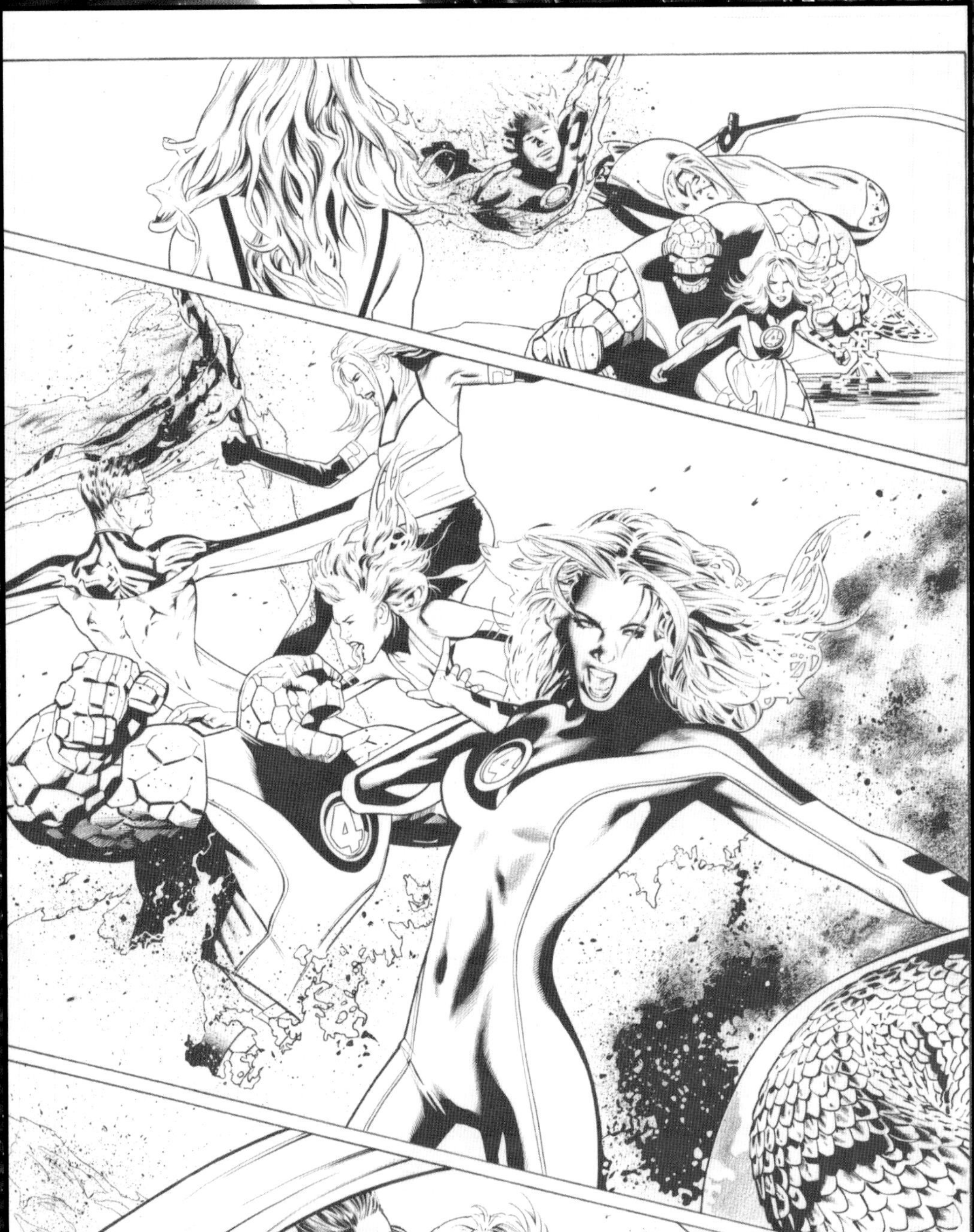

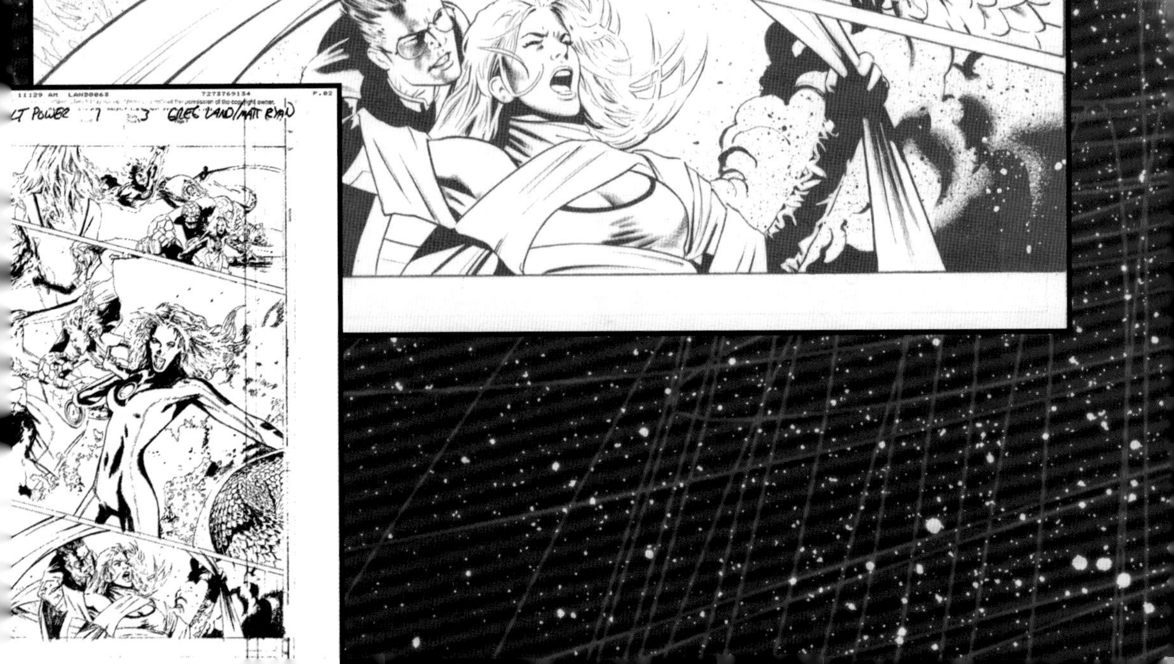
11:29 AM LAND0063 7275769134 P.02
permission of the copyright owner.
LT POWER 7 3 GREG LAND/MATT RYAN

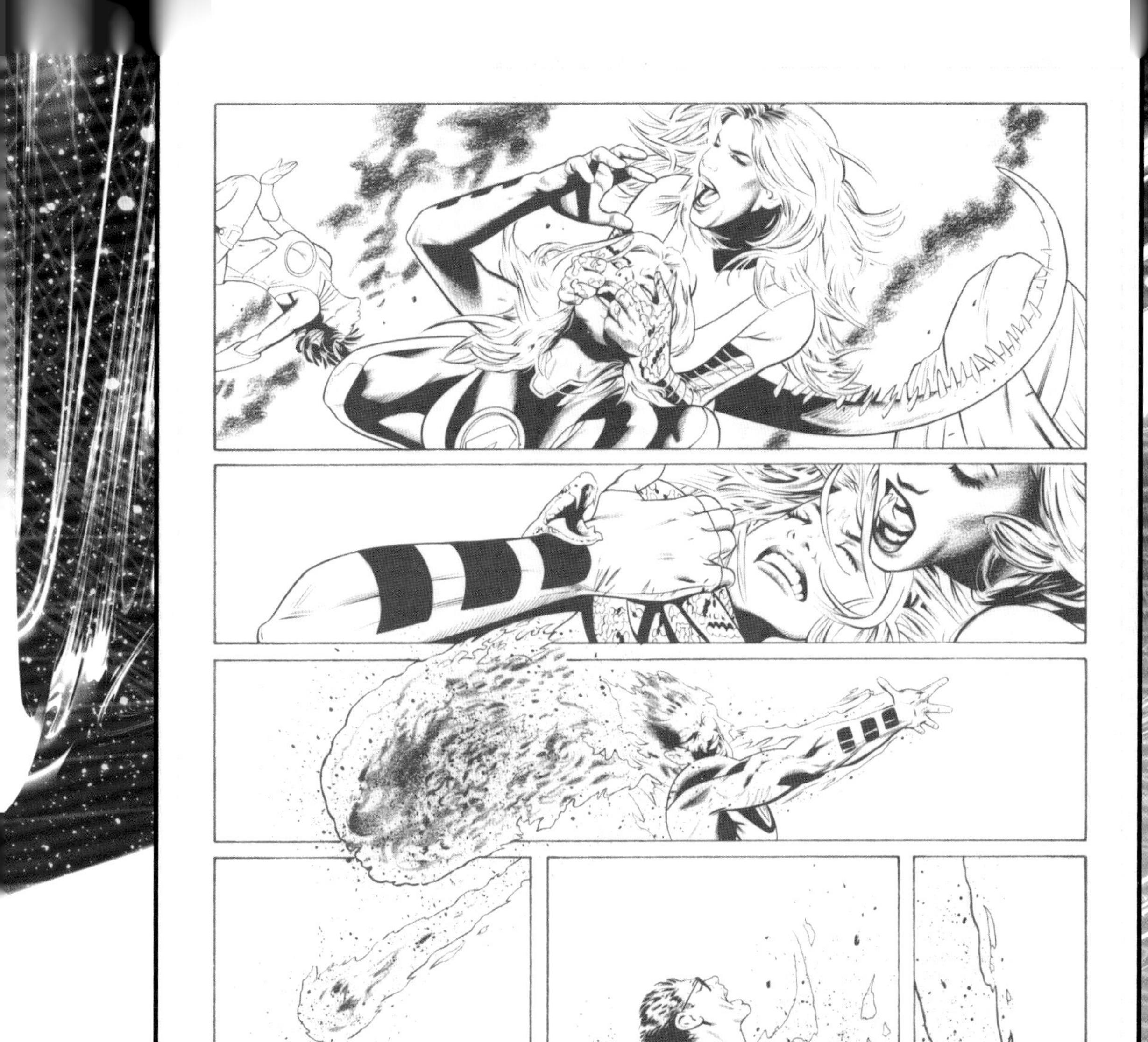

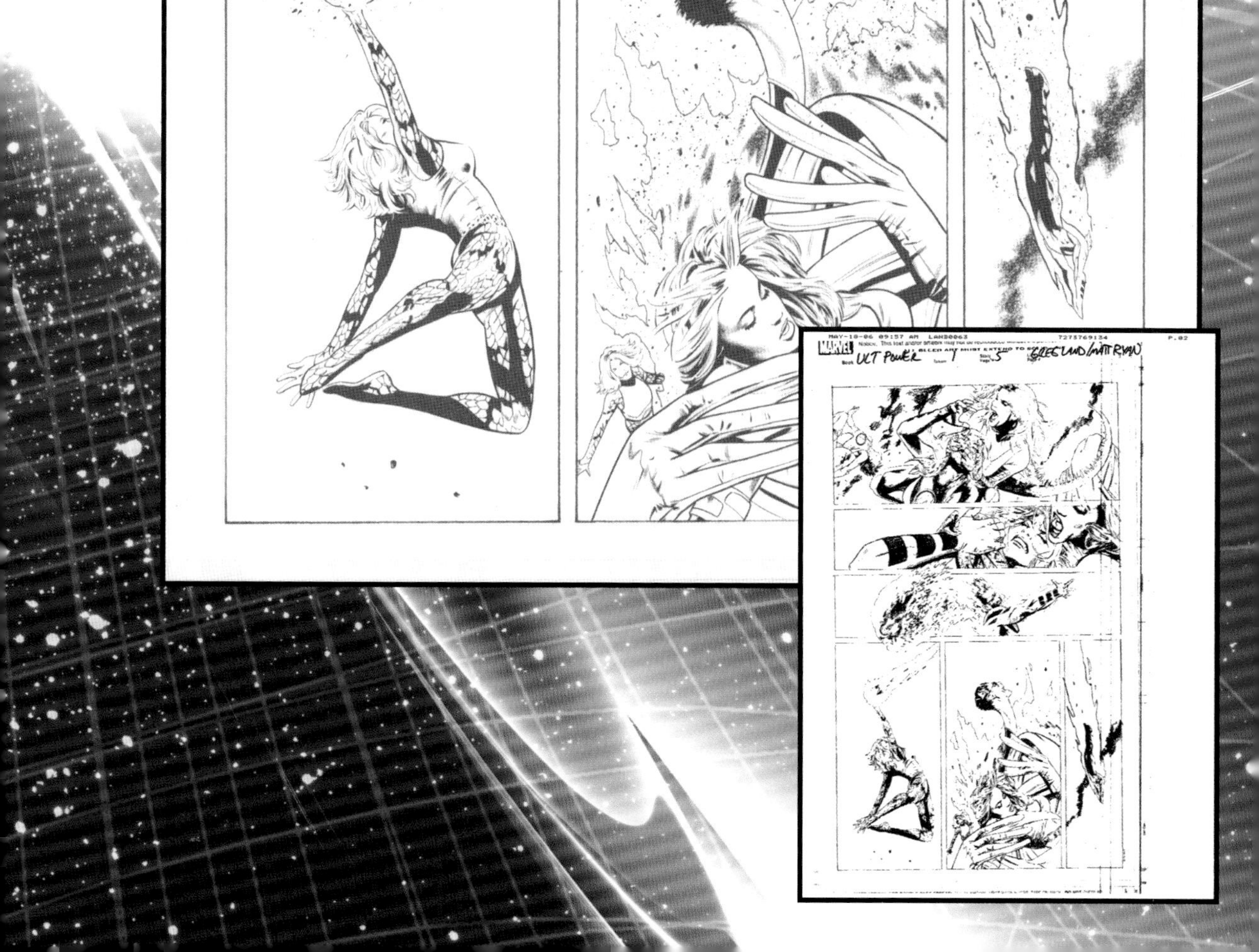
MAY-10-06 09:57 AM LAND0063
7275769134
P.02
MARVEL
ULT POWER
1
5
GREG LAND/MATT RYAN

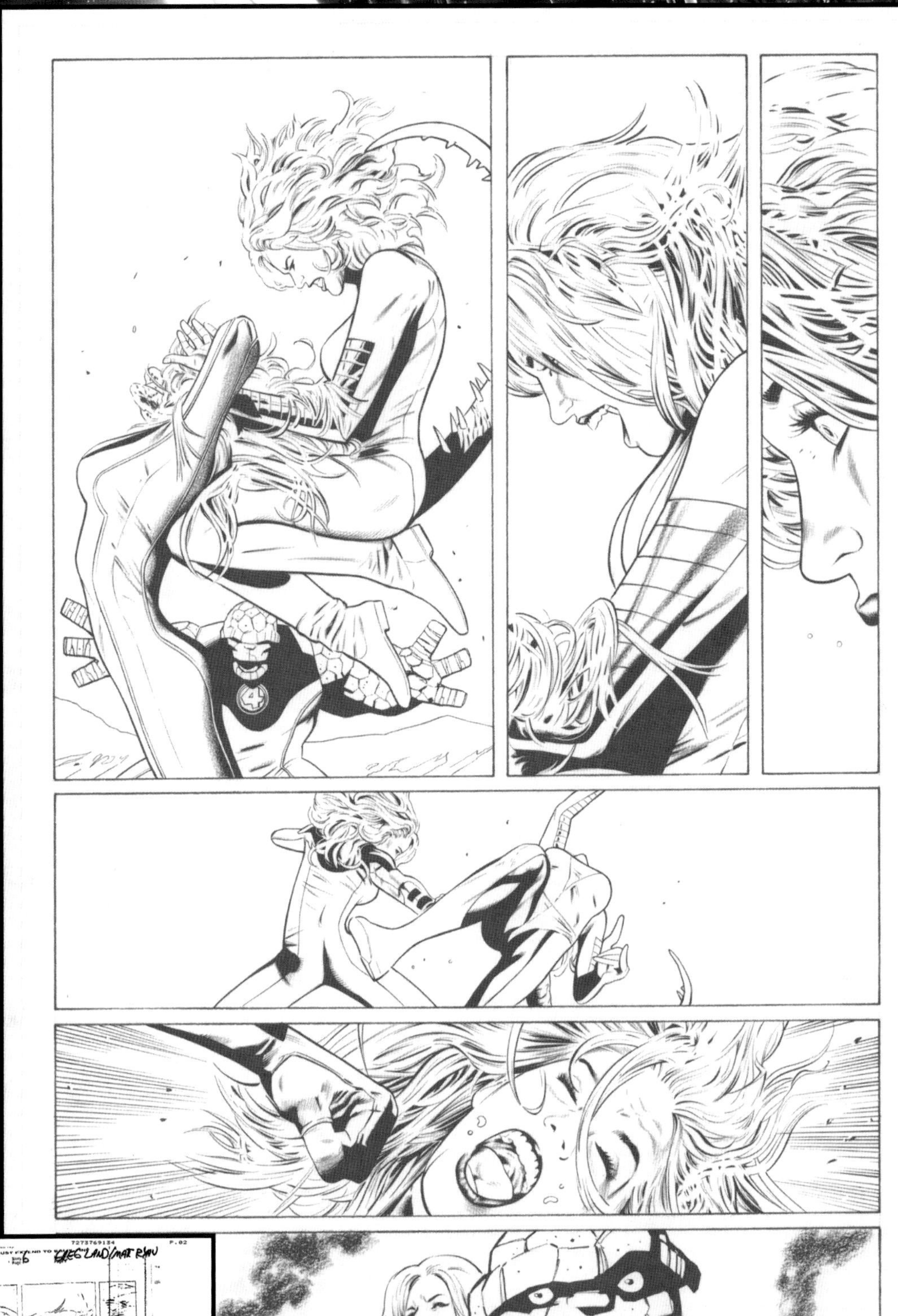

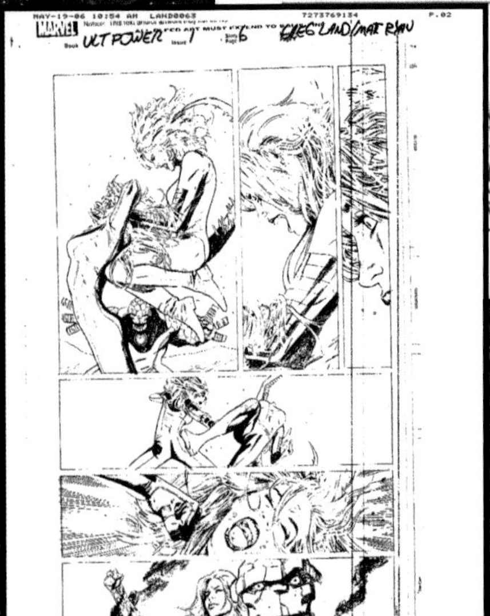
MAY-19-06 10:54 AM LAND0063
7273769134
P.02
MARVEL
Book ULT POWER
Issue 1
Page 6
GREG LAND/MAT RYAN

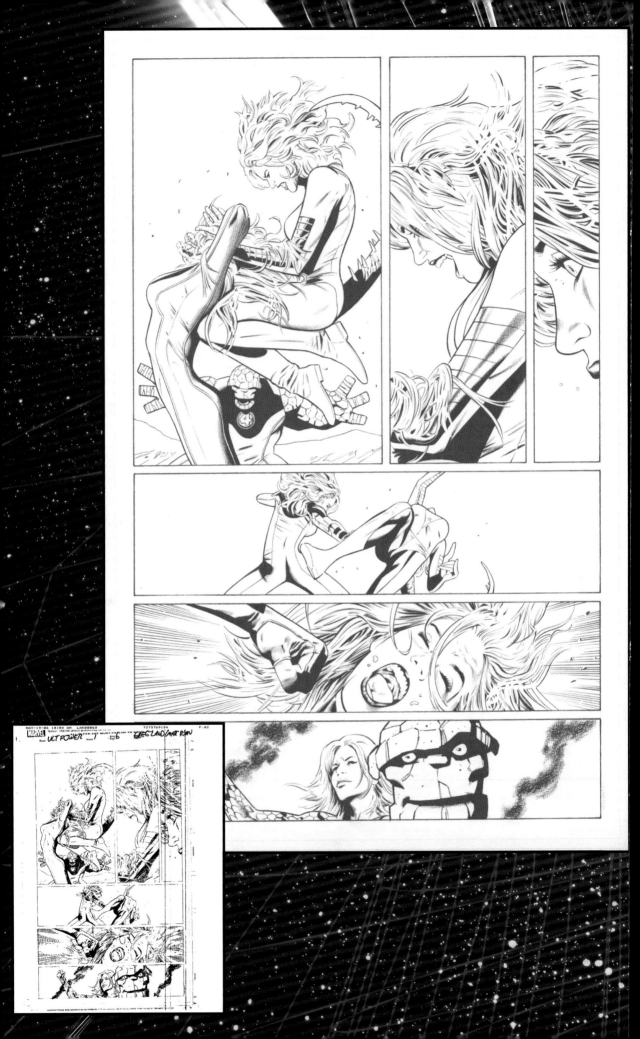

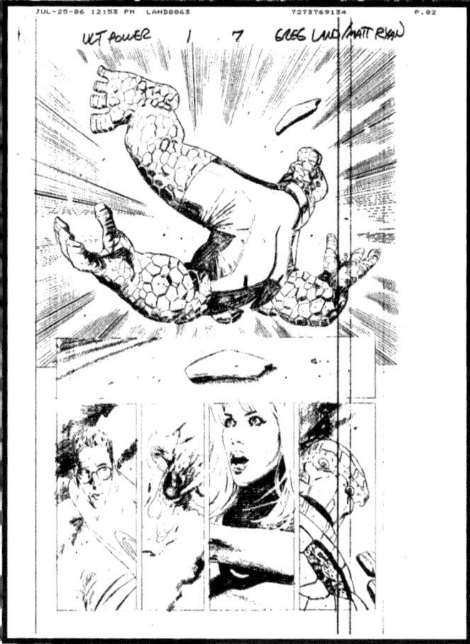
JUL-25-06 12:53 PM LAND0063 7273769134 P.02
ULT POWER 1 7 GREG LAND/MATT RYAN

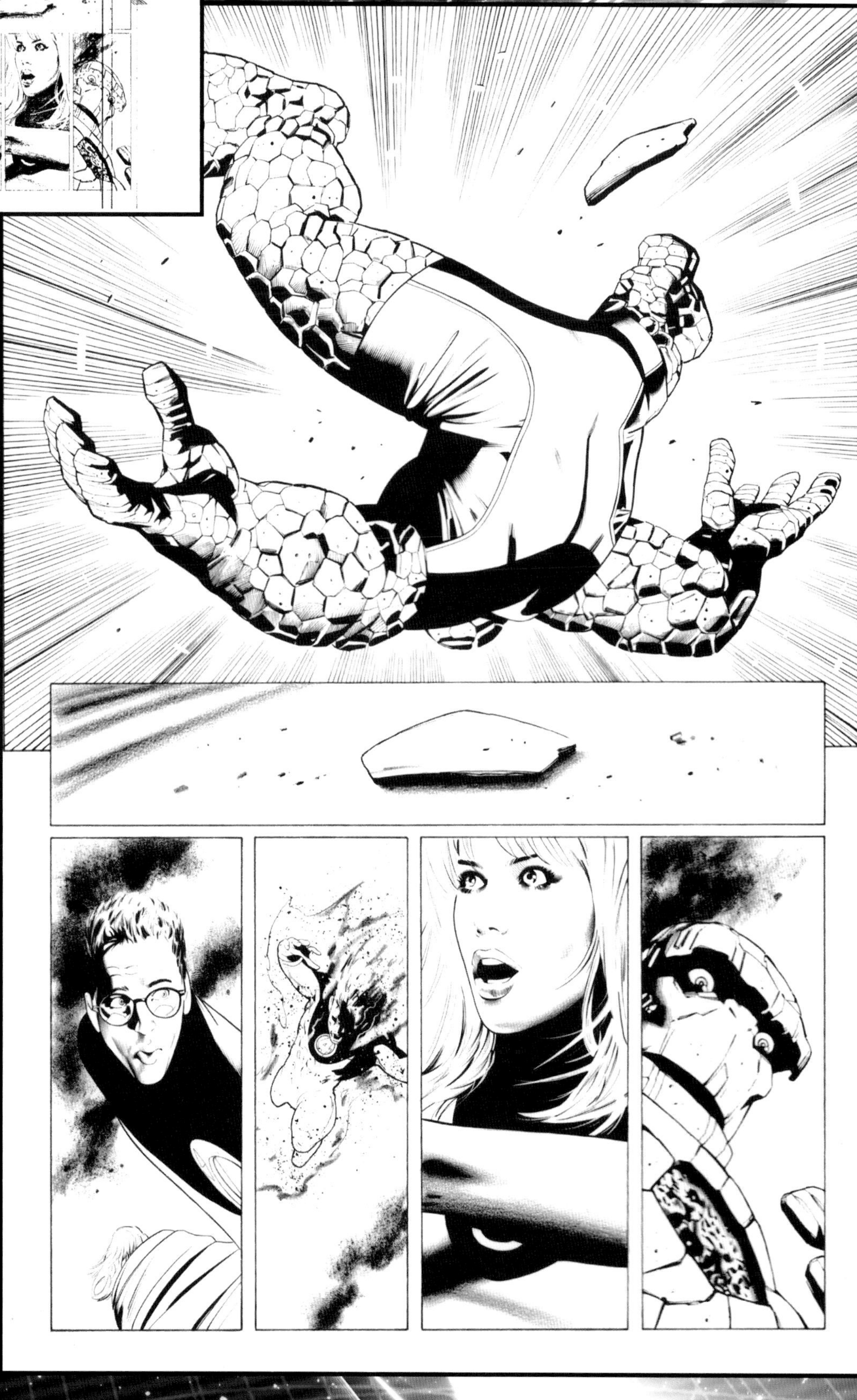

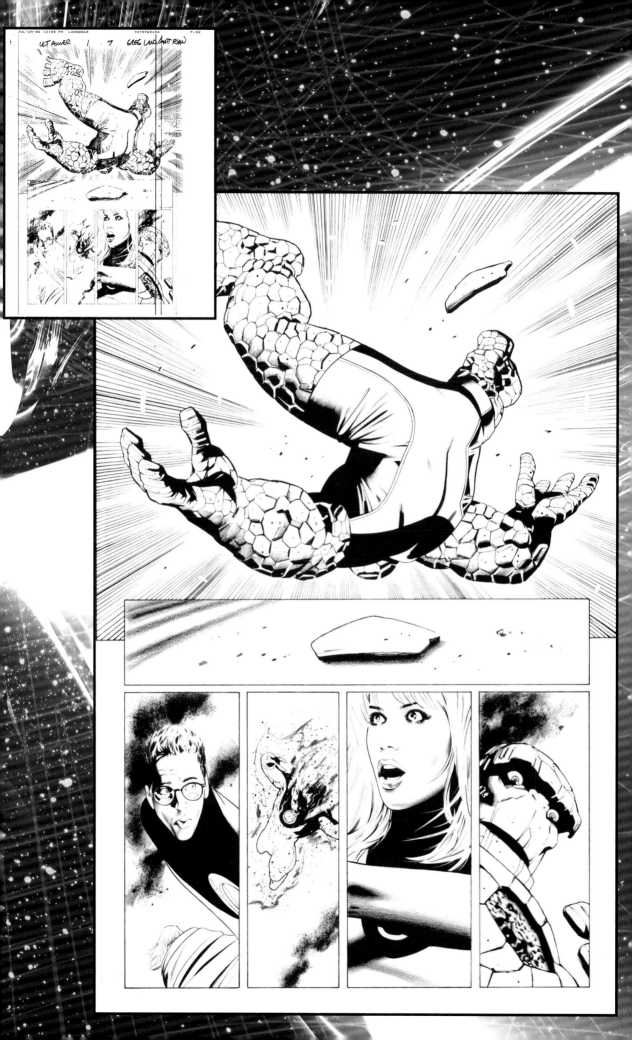

ISSUE #1 VARIANT COVER

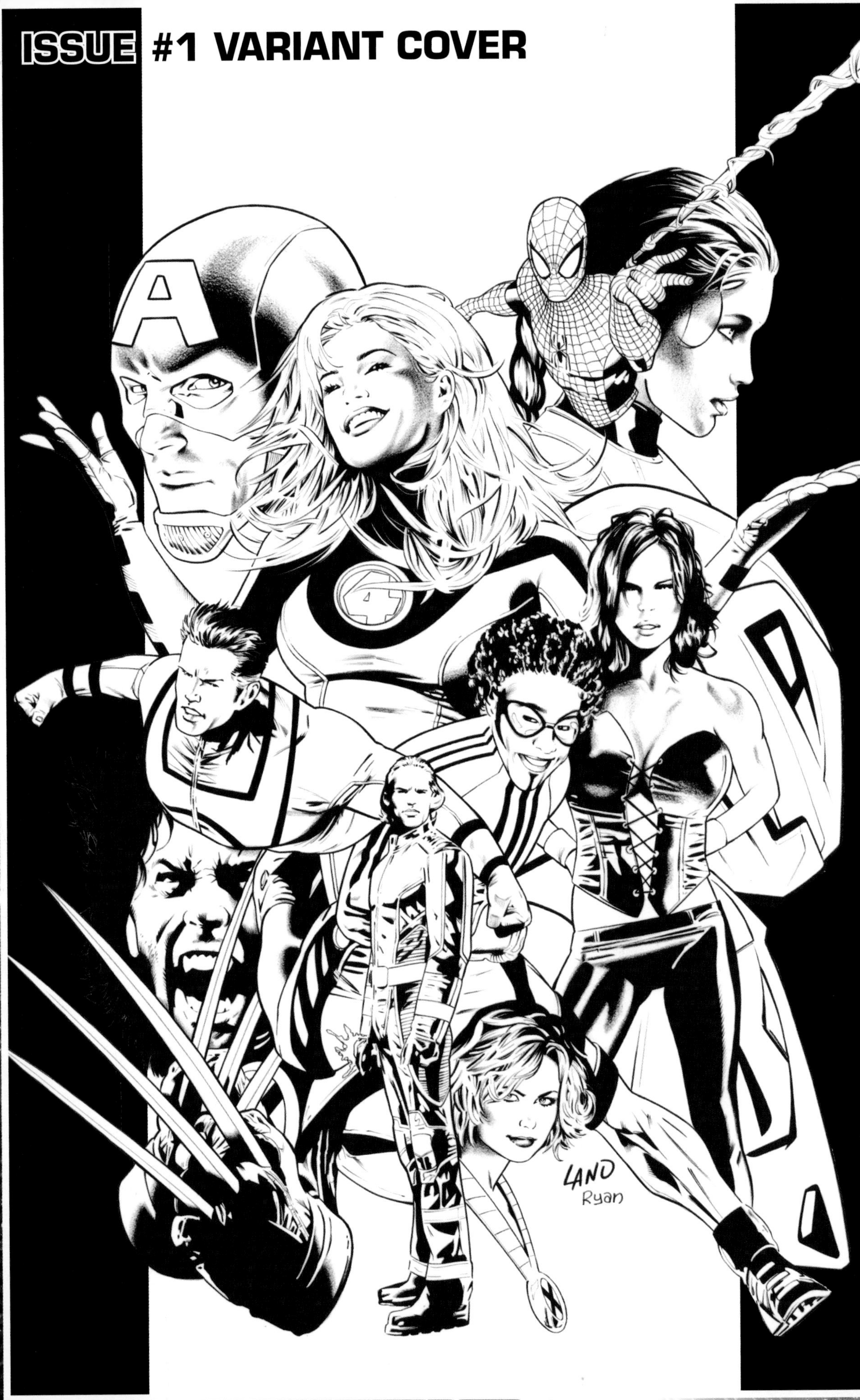
LAND
Ryan